46
MILES

To Colditz and Kelly; Emilia and Olivia

A beautiful family who I have
known for what seems most of my
life. Love you all to bits and thank
you for your support.

[signature]

27. June 2015.

46 MILES

A Journey of Repatriation and
Humbling Respect

JARRA BROWN

MENIN HOUSE

Menin House is an imprint of
Tommies Guides Military Book Specialists

Gemini House
136-140 Old Shoreham Road
Brighton
BN3 7BD

www.tommiesguides.co.uk

First published in Great Britain by
Menin House Publishers 2015

Limited Edition Hardback
ISBN 978-1-908336-81-1

Trade Paperback Edition
ISBN 978-1-908336-82-8

Cover design by Ryan Gearing
Typeset by Vivian Foster@Bookscribe

Printed and bound in Great Britain

FOREWORD

This book describes an extraordinary chapter in the history of an extraordinary Royal Air Force Station. I first arrived at RAF Lyneham as a young Hercules pilot in 1993. Over the following eighteen years I served four tours on the Station and grew to consider it my home; its community and its surrounding countryside became an integral part of my life.

But no one could have predicted the role this community, military and civilian, would play as our young men and women, fallen whilst serving combat operations, were repatriated to their families and to the country that had sent them to war. The initially spontaneous, then immaculately orchestrated reaction of Wiltshire folk to the painfully regular cortège, as it passed through (later Royal) Wootton Bassett was to come to symbolise the emotions of the Nation. Often seemingly mislaid values were re-awakened in the minds of British people: including those of patriotism and honour; this in recognition of the sacrifices that our young men and women were making on combat operations in Iraq and Afghanistan.

Of course it was the dignity of the families of these men and women, each in the midst of the most unimaginable pain that had the greatest effect on the Station. Indeed, nothing might have prepared me for that. But it is times like this that brings the very best out of people. At RAF Lyneham I was fortunate enough to succeed two outstanding Station Commanders, Group Captains Paul Atherton and Mike Neville (reflecting the tragic longevity this intensive period of repatriations spanned), each of whom had made the Station resilient to the demands of the Station's tragic role; helped of course by a superb team of Station personnel from Station Warrant Officer to Station Padre and many other Station support staff. But it was our own community policeman, Jarra Brown, who provided the bridge into the heart of the local community. Jarra was unstinting in his support to me and to the people of Wootton Bassett: those that were central to the role that this remarkable market town had taken on. Jarra was an old-fashioned bobby with a remarkable sense of duty and loyalty and with a heart that matched scale of the respect in which he was held.

I am grateful that Jarra has decided to document this important period of history; I commend his book to you.

Group Captain John Gladston CBE DFC RAF Retd
Former Station Commander
Royal Air Force Lyneham

To my beautiful wife Karen for the love and support, you gave me through the 30 years we have been together; my soul mate and my best friend. I look forward to sharing the new adventures in the years, which lay ahead.

My Daughters Lisa, and Kerry; grandchildren, Charlotte, Chloe, Mark, Lily-Mae and Harmony-Rose. I love you; three simple words that are easy to say; but when I say them they come from the bottom of my heart.

To my parents, me Mam and Dad for bringing me into this World and showing me the true old fashioned values that have been the foundation of my life. You will never be forgotten Dad.

To my brothers and sisters, Gillian, Melanie, Derek and Peter although we seldom see each other due to the lives we all live, you are always in my thoughts.

AUTHOR'S NOTES

Many have their own memories of the humbling scenes that evolved in RAF Lyneham, and Wootton Bassett; so our individual perceptions of the events that took place will differ. I write mine with honesty, integrity, compassion and sincerity in the hope to do justice to those who paid the ultimate sacrifice. It is my personal tribute in memory of the fallen and for their family and friends to understand that your loved one was shown the utmost respect, and was honoured by more than you may know.

Each and every one of the fallen are as valued as the next, but it would be impossible to write a passage about the day each of the 345 fallen heroes were repatriated home, through RAF Lyneham. I hope that this does not cause distress or offence, and you will see by the way I have written the book that your loss was recognised by so many who cared.

A total of 179 British Armed Forces personnel or MOD civilians have died serving in Iraq on Operation Telic since the start of the campaign in March 2003. In Afghanistan, 453 British forces personnel or MOD civilians have died whilst serving on Operation Herrick, since the start of operations in October 2001. All are recorded in the pages of remembrance in this book and are not forgotten.

ACKNOWLEDGEMENTS

Carol Miller; by chance or fate, you came into my life at the perfect time. With humour and skills from your distinguished career, you tweaked what I had written. There is one phrase you said that still makes me laugh, when you handed me the pages you had reviewed; referring to my efforts in comparison to Les Dawson in playing the piano, "all the right words, just a few not in the right order"; your message was received in the spirit it was delivered and with enthusiasm, working together, I was proud to forward the manuscript to the publisher, to polish.

Stephen McCourt, a photographer with the photographic section at RAF Lyneham during these humbling years and witness to so many scenes and more that I mention in this book. I was honoured when Stephen accepted my request to design the jacket of this book, as I know he was another that really did care. Stephen and his colleague Paul Couch created a DVD of images with music that provokes the emotions that so many felt on those solemn days. I hope, one day, we can encourage the MoD to allow this to be shared and raise funds for a military charity; it would be the perfect way to complement the words of this book.

Ryan Gearing the publisher for guidance and advice and believing in me to publish this book.

Vivian Foster for her skills in editing, proofreading and coating the words with a polish I could only have dreamed of. This was done with her sincerity, compassion and understanding in just how important this book is to many.

Ceri Pridding is a lady I first met when I walked the beat in Lyneham; always smiles on her face and part of the military family, she lived on the married quarter estate. A lovely Welsh lady with a sincere and unassuming nature; yet so much compassion for her community. She never forgot as you will clearly see the pain that was felt in the tragedy of January 2005.

Sandy Elliott, Cliff Warren, Jayne Taylor, Jenny Brown, Vicky Dunn and Andrea Johnson, we have communicated so many times. During our conversations, e-mails or chat on line, we have shed many tears; but amongst that was so much pride. I have learned so much about your special man and I feel I now know them from what you shared. The story I tell is very sensitive to say the least, yet each has encouraged me to publish this book. I seriously hope I have done your sons proud.

⊢⊷⊷○⊷⊣⊣

To an unknown soldier who served the Crown; the words in your poem are beautiful and had such a massive impact on me, thus the inspiration for the title of the book.

⊢⊷⊷○⊷⊣⊣

... And most importantly, those who died; may your names never be forgotten and be honoured by those who read the words written in this book. Whilst they do, may you look down on your loved ones and let them know that you are indeed – resting in peace.

Epigraph

The inspiration for the title of this book:

46 MILES
If I should fall in that far foreign land,
with my blood sweat and tears soaked up in the sand.
I shall not fear or fall with regret,
the 46 miles will never forget.
I won't lay to rest or just drift away,
46 miles will have something to say.
I have one last task, one more mission to be done,
46 miles before the going down of the sun.

As we step off, uncertain if it's our last,
I think of my friends that have already passed.
I remember the silence as Wootton Bassett stood still,
shoulder to shoulder the High St would fill.
Curiously as I stood, I felt so at ease,
surrounded by strangers outside the Cross Keys.
I have one last task, one more mission to be done,
46 miles before the going down of the sun.

From Tarmac to Motorway its 46 miles in all,
Police stand over me, keeping me safe standing tall.
They lead the way and watch over my kin,
for this I thank with all I have been.
The young and old fill 46 miles together,
flags and banners, salutes in all weather.
I have one last task, one more mission to be done,
46 miles before the going down of the sun.

This is how we go to these far foreign lands,
where our blood sweat and tears are soaked up in the sand.
Wootton Bassett did welcome us home,
standing side by side our families were shown.
We have done our best and given our all,
the nation remembers 46 miles stands tall.
I have one last task, one more mission to be done,
thank you Royal Wootton Bassett from a nation's grateful son.

Written by an unknown soldier

CHAPTER 1

C hurch bells are synonymous with middle England; of quiet market towns, leafy hamlets and sleepy villages. They have represented the start of new lives, new unions, calls to arms and national celebrations. When I hear church bells, I think of the fallen – the 345 people; 342 Men and 3 Women – who passed through beautiful rural Wiltshire into Oxfordshire; not hiking across its pastures or on the number 55 bus, but in a 2ft x 6ft box cloaked in the colours of our nation.

By the end of August 2011 the bells of St Bartholomew's Church in Wootton Bassett had tolled more times than I care to think about, each chime representing the moment the police convoy accompanying a hearse from RAF Lyneham entered the town's High Street. Heads bowed, the chatter of curious children was quietly hushed and gentlemen old enough to remember the conflict of 1939 to 1945 would remove their caps; those who could, pulling themselves out of their wheelchairs to pay their respects standing smartly to attention. It was a moment frozen in time, and the remarkable thing was that it wasn't orchestrated, it wasn't choreographed. There was no call to arms by the town crier. It was spontaneous, modest, unprompted respect; but let me rewind.

In September 2006, I came to serve the community of RAF Lyneham in a role that would be best described as an 'old fashioned village Bobby'; a position I thought I was more than comfortable to take on. My previous skills and courses completed over the last sixteen years, whilst serving a bigger community in Plymouth, had given me the knowledge and experience to take on most things I perceived I would encounter. Earlier in the year one of my Chief Inspectors, Dave Vaughan, was down visiting the station in Plymouth and pulled me to one side. Quite unexpectedly, he asked if I fancied a challenge, a new direction in my career; always open to new experiences I was keen to know what was on offer. Chief Inspector Vaughan explained that the RAF wanted to pay for a police officer to support their community whilst the station was involved in operational commitments across the globe.

I have to say the guvnor sold me a good package, which included working from my own initiatives and not directly supervised; pick my own hours to suit the job and full support of the division with resources. So I went home that night to consider the nuts and bolts of the job. Besides the actual work and commitment that was required, the biggest upheaval was to relocate and sell up. To be honest, the timing was right for a change in my career and suited my own plans which were retirement in six years' time. So for me, a traditional copper who believed in good old fashioned love thy neighbour policing and not target-led law enforcement, it was the dream; but without the support of Karen my wife, it was a non-runner. Moving away from Plymouth where my wife and our daughters, Kerry and Lisa, had been raised and where our one-year-old granddaughter Charlotte would grow up, needed a lot of consideration. We decided to do a bit of research of the area and logged onto the internet. I knew a little bit about RAF Lyneham, it was an RAF station where Hercules C130s flew from and was situated just off the M4. As a former soldier, a member of 59 Commando Squadron Royal Engineers for five years, we used to fly out from there on winter deployment to Norway.

Next, a visit to Wootton Bassett Police Station, where I met the local Inspector Mark Levitt and a couple of the officers in his team. They seemed keen to invite me to be part of their sector working closely together, so that was extremely encouraging. I viewed the crimes in the area and, as perceived, didn't expect too many dramas – maybe dealing with the odd missing cat, a misdemeanour or the odd domestic. Yeah, I think I could handle that. After a week or so of deliberating, the decision was made. Having scoped out the area for places to live, we'd settled on a mid-terrace, two bedroom house in a small market town called Wootton Bassett, just a few miles from the M4 for our regular trips to Devon to see the girls.

I raise a wry smile now when I think back to my last week in Plymouth and what my colleague Rich Bond said to me about the new job: 'Are you not going to get bored up there mate? Nothing happens.' My response couldn't have been further from the truth. 'Nah,' I replied. 'I really fancy a nice quiet number 'til I retire.'

What you are about to enter in opening this book is my true reflection of a chapter in time, written with thought, compassion, deep sadness and chest-swelling pride; of how history unfolded before my very eyes. This book is not about the politics of war, the whys and wherefores of the Iraq and Afghanistan conflict, hidden agendas or government strategies. It is about a town that captured the hearts of the nation; a town wanting to do the right thing at the right time for the right person; our Great British hero. It is dedicated to 345 people who passed through our little town having signed up to serve God and the Queen and who paid the ultimate price in the name of duty.

CHAPTER 2

Many months before my arrival in Wiltshire, this wonderful community was to experience tragedy on a scale that could not have possibly been imagined. Sunday 30 January 2005, was a peaceful winter's afternoon when the Iraq people were voting for the price of freedom, following the capture of the tyrant Saddam Hussein. News was rippling through the internet and newsfeeds that an RAF Lyneham C130 Hercules had crashed killing all on board, sending shock waves through the North Wiltshire community and throughout the country.

This tragic news was confirmed in the bland manner that only the Ministry of Defence can deliver: 'It is with very deep regret that the Ministry of Defence can confirm the deaths of ten UK service personnel, following the loss of an RAF C-130K XV179 Hercules aircraft over Iraq. An RAF C-130K Hercules crashed 30 kilometres north-west of Baghdad on Sunday 30 January 2005, at approximately 1635hrs local time. The aircraft was on a flight between Baghdad International Airport and Balad Airbase. Ten UK service personnel are missing believed killed; nine from Royal Air Force Lyneham and one from the Army.'

Ceri Pridding, the wife of a Royal Air Force Officer stationed at RAF Lyneham, living on the same military housing estate as some of those who perished, recalls her memories of that time:

'That day, Sunday the 30th, started like any other January day in weather, mood and activities but would end like no other. Being a Sunday we had been doing all the usual weekend tasks to prepare for the working week ahead and had popped out for the obligatory Sunday visit to the DIY superstore. On the way back to Lyneham, the car radio was on as a low murmur and we heard the news bulletin in the background with the familiarity of certain words catching our attention, "...Iraq...UK C130 aircraft...wreckage..." we raised the volume only to have missed the content.

As we headed straight back to Lyneham we speculated on what we had just heard. What could possibly have happened and who might have been impacted? My husband looked deeply disturbed and went immediately into work. The news repeated again on the kitchen radio and I called him and asked what he was allowed to share, he repeated the basic facts I had heard relayed moments before and confirmed that it was one of our own aircraft. Amongst the disbelief, I felt a guilty sense of relief as I was fortunate that my husband was here just several hundred yards up the road and safely at his desk. In the military, however, your family extends far beyond your "Quarter door" and on putting down the phone I put on my shoes and headed next door as I knew here my neighbour's husband was currently deployed to Iraq.

Not quite sure how I was going to broach the subject, I walked into my neighbour's kitchen, the door always open and the usual kiddie-driven chaos was in full swing. I asked had she heard from her husband lately and we made a bit of idle chit-chat; it soon became clear that she was oblivious to what I knew. I told her that I had something to tell her, took her by the hand and told her all I knew. The panic was evident as the colour drained from her face and I repeated what little details I had; we were both aware that with several crews "in Theatre" it could be anyone's family involved, no one currently knew who was safe or who was missing. She attempted several calls and finally made contact with her husband and, like me, her immediate relief sprang to fears for everyone else within our extended military family.

The rest of the day was a mixture of rumour, anguish and disbelief with speculation of which crew was affected. Official cars moved around the estate and the military police locked down the base adding to the fears and tension. Our beautiful leafy lined roads no longer seemed like the safe haven we once felt, they were as if the cold reality of war and terrorism had knocked on our doors right here in Wiltshire. Into the evening, the speculation continued, and as a driver arrived to take my husband to a brief at Whitehall, we waited for the further inevitable confirmation of the personnel involved. For those men not deployed they waited to hear of their "brothers" and families and gathered to support each other.

Finally, the official notification was released and each affected family was visited by both military personnel and a liaison officer. A direct neighbour, as a wife of a pilot, volunteered for the unenviable task of accompanying these visits to the wives who were like her sisters. This was no longer just a news headline but a living nightmare for the whole community. I recall the harrowing scenes and desperate cries of a wife with a young family within our street refusing to answer the door. Screaming at the officials "Fuck Off, Fuck Off", believing that if she didn't answer the door and they didn't deliver the news, that it would not be true. How could it be true? These young men with young families had left for a detachment as they had done countless times before to areas of equally extreme danger. How could it have happened to our men? The eldest was just forty-two years old.

Living in the era of rapid communications there seemed no way of avoiding the stark footage in the following days on the television, on the hour, every hour, images of wreckage flashed before us. With unprecedented, embedded journalism our thirst for news was turned in on us as our community was now the news. Fear spread with further rumours that terrorists, making claims of their involvement, were set to parade body parts as trophies of their twisted war. We braced ourselves for worse days to come.

Monday passed in a blur with more speculation and disbelief. As an act of solidarity and sympathy flowers were starting to gather at the gates of the base as both Military and members of local communities showed their support. The names of the nine RAF Air Crew and the Army lance corporal were finally officially released on Tuesday 1 February bringing to the fore the dreadful human cost.

The round of events that followed will be familiar only to those who have experienced and lived through tragedies of such scale with the ripple effect of grief, endless reviews, questions and analysis. The already strong community pulled together further, with letters home from the local school offering extended support with so many young families directly affected. A member of their own staff had also been widowed in this tragedy whilst on maternity leave. In all, eleven children had lost a father. A remembrance service held in a maintenance hangar had all the hallmarks of the military precision and dignity; but even here the strong bond with the local community was evident with the inclusion of the beautiful poem *Hercules* written by Mrs Sheila Webb.

Hercules of iron wing
Of your glory let anthem sing
Faced with foreign desert lands
Where evil thrives and terror spans
Strong and mighty men of peace
Your legacy will never cease
Pride and sadness interlace
47 squadron-Lyneham base
Show your spirit at full mast
And tip your wing at each flypast
Then cast away all earthly things
To fly back home on golden wings.

In the days that followed the focus turned to the repatriation of the crew. As was protocol at the time, service personnel lost in Iraq were retuned via Brize Norton and this triggered a rigorous debate that the crew should be repatriated to Lyneham; finally this was granted and a suitable homecoming was planned. On Tuesday 8 February, I recall standing in the garden as the giant C-17

Globemaster plane swept in for its final approach to the base. The engines of the huge plane roared overhead as the music of the Central Bands of the Royal Air Force and the RAF Regiment carried on the wind from the runway.

As each of those lost were carefully delivered home, for ninety minutes the sombre music echoed throughout the community. Slowly, methodically, and with what is known as military precision they were carried off that huge aircraft by their respective bearer parties and lowered into the waiting hearse. First carried off as senior service was the Army Soldier leading; then followed one by one the nine of the Royal Air Forces finest, each should be mentioned in order of March.

Acting Lance Corporal **Steven Jones**, Royal Signals, aged 25,
Squadron Leader **Patrick Marshall**, Headquarters Strike Command, aged 39
Flight Lieutenant **David Stead**, 47 Squadron, RAF Lyneham, aged 35
Flight Lieutenant **Andrew Smith**, 47 Squadron, RAF Lyneham, aged 25
Flight Lieutenant **Paul Pardoel**, 47 Squadron, RAF Lyneham, aged 35
Master Air Engineer **Gary Nicholson**, 47 Squadron, RAF Lyneham, aged 42
Chief Technician **Richard Brown**, RAF Lyneham, aged 40
Flight Sergeant **Mark Gibson**, 47 Squadron, RAF Lyneham, aged 34
Sergeant **Robert O'Connor**, RAF Lyneham, aged 38
Corporal **David Williams**, RAF Lyneham, aged 37

Like many others not at the ceremony, in order to pay my respects I headed to the end of the street. With my neighbours, we lined the pavements at the exit to the base as the coffins started their final journey to the Great Western Hospital in Swindon. The police outriders appeared and close behind them the first coffin and then the second, slowly followed by the third and then the fourth, fifth, sixth and seventh – the cortège seemed endless – then eighth, ninth and finally the tenth, all flanked in their nation's flags. For me, on the periphery, this was the moment of impact for the sheer volume of the loss, with the sight of so many flag-draped coffins and the sad finality of it all. On a crisp winter's day the grim situation seemed utterly hopeless and the shared grief almost overwhelming.

Those respects continued, with the support from their rural neighbours, as they also lined their High Street in Wootton Bassett. In the weeks that followed, the private funerals were held culminating in a memorial service at Salisbury cathedral. As with all resilient military communities life moved on; a sadder place as families of those affected slowly moved away but the memories of those lost would always remain with those of us who shared this as our home.'

CHAPTER 3

After accepting the job opportunity up in Lyneham we spent a long weekend in the area house hunting and getting a feel for the place. Wootton Bassett, put quite simply, is a small market town in Wiltshire, with a population of about 12,000. The town is situated in the north of the county, about three miles south of junction 16 on the M4 motorway and six miles to the southwest of Swindon. Wootton Bassett's Town Hall is probably the best known landmark as it stands proudly on fifteen concrete pillars on the High Street. We liked the place from the off and I looked forward to the next couple of weeks and starting, what I hoped, would be the final chapter of my policing career. The time flew by fast enough and suddenly our farewells to my colleagues in Plymouth were made.

A new exciting challenge in new surroundings was just what I fancied, however, on Saturday 2 September 2006, two days before I was to commence my duties at RAF Lyneham, that enjoyable feeling had been wiped away. I was sat at home when I saw the headlines on Sky News – an RAF aircraft had crashed in Afghanistan. At that time the full details were not clear, only that an RAF aircraft had come down. My initial reaction was shock, but as concern hit home that I was to start work at Lyneham on Monday morning, I hoped it was not them again. The details were very vague and remained so throughout the night. The following morning I heard no further updates as I set off on my way up the A303 to Wiltshire. Throughout the journey I was tuned into the radio, and then it was announced. The aircraft that crashed was a Nimrod MR 2, reconnaissance plane from RAF Kinloss. A feeling of relief, how selfish was I, then sorrow as further details were revealed. The MoD had released that those killed were twelve Royal Air Force personnel, one Royal Marine and one Army soldier.

The reporter continued to say that these deaths bring the total number of UK servicemen killed in Afghanistan since the US-led Coalition invasion in November 2001 to 36. He concluded by saying it was Britain's biggest single loss of life in either Afghanistan or Iraq since the War on Terror began five years ago. That news bulletin really sunk in maybe due to the new environment I was to work in, but it was even more engraved into my mind on the Thursday, four days later.

After I arrived at RAF Lyneham the Station Commander Group Captain Paul Atherton asked me if I would introduce myself at his open forum on Thursday morning. The Station Commander addressed the unit on this briefing and he deemed it appropriate that I stand up and give a five-minute brief on what they could expect from this policeman. So there I was in the front row with a crowded room awaiting the arrival of Group Captain Atherton. In he strode wearing his flying suit, with the demeanour one comes to expect from a Commanding Officer in the military. He spoke with a firmness that carried his stature. The words he opened his briefing with had a huge impact on me – no *massive* – and were received loud and clear.

'We do not believe at this time that the Nimrod that crashed over the weekend was a result of enemy fire.'

I replayed that short sentence in my head 'enemy fire.' To hear those words spoken in that manner were so powerful, I suddenly realised the environment I was now working in. I looked at Group Captain Atherton as he continued his address to his station, but from that moment I understood that these people I sat in a room with were directly involved in not one war, but two – Iraq and Afghanistan.

I drifted in thought as the next speaker spoke to contemplate the role I had undertaken. A policeman paid specifically to support the families of Airmen and Soldiers who were in a hostile environment, over 3,000 miles away from home. A community who fully understood the implications of conflict and enemy fire when their own RAF C-130K, XV179 Hercules aircraft was shot down in the skies of Iraq, less than two years earlier in January 2005. What a reality check that was for me and, as I was introduced to the room, I scrapped the politically correct force statement I had prepared and told them who I really was. I looked around and saw something I had not seen before, the intensity in their faces; so many, so young. These people were fighting in two wars and I spoke to them in a language they understood. It was my intention to look after their families so they had no need to worry about them at home, leaving them to focus on their job out in theatre.

Those opening words from their Station Commander was all the motivation I needed to resolve all their concerns and they were left in no doubt that I would not let them down. In my own unique way I don't think I did, but those stories are for another book and if you have seen 'Life on Mars' or 'Hot Fuzz' then my policing style was something from those chapters and known locally as 'Lyneham Law.'

I was made very welcome working in and around RAF Lyneham and quickly built an excellent working relationship with the Wiltshire Police, where I became part of that sector policing team. Lyneham law was well accepted and, with mutual respect, we delivered what we preached. Those deployed knew that I would not let them down, thus allowing them to focus on their arduous duties in Afghanistan and Iraq.

I was about five months into my new role when a date was confirmed regarding the responsibilities and duties known as 'repatriations' would be transferred from RAF Brize Norton to RAF Lyneham. A military ceremony that was carried out on a military base to bring home British Forces killed in military operations overseas. That is why with the word *military* emphasised so much, that I saw no direct impact or concern for me. My duty, as far I was concerned, was to remain focused outside the wire of RAF Lyneham, a village Bobby; to do my best to keep crime off the streets and create an ambience of security at home. Yes, I did recall the news coverage about the two big losses of life involving the C130 Hercules from RAF Lyneham in 2005, and the more recent loss of the Nimrod from RAF Kinloss in 2006, but I was totally oblivious as I guess like many others, unless directly related, of any comprehension that we had already lost 186 casualties during the Iraq and Afghanistan conflicts. I think it is fair to say, as a country at that time, we were unaware of the devastation a brief announcement on the news would cause so many, when it was reported that a British soldier had been killed.

Across the road from where I walked my beat, there was a lot of activity on the air base as the final preparations were made to transfer the repatriation operation from RAF Brize Norton to RAF Lyneham.

Probably Thursday, though I am not certain, but definitely the last week in March 2007, was the morning I received a telephone call from the PA to the Station Commander. My presence at the terminal building was requested along with many others to observe the final full dress rehearsal of the repatriation ceremony, prior to RAF Lyneham assuming the huge responsibility it would be charged with in just a few days time.

On arrival, I stood at the designated viewing area which was directly in front of the terminal building and waited for the ceremony to commence. To my left, was a recently erected marquee style tent, the front canvas removed to construct a covered viewing area. Inside that place of shelter, not just from the elements of the weather, seats were strategically placed. A setting of comfort was the intent or at least the best one could provide a bereaved family under such circumstances. Essential members of the repatriation team would be seated back from the bereaved family, to offer support to those mourning. We, the observers, stood silent to the side of that canvas structured area; we all turned and looked to our right when we heard the unmistakable sound of a C130 Hercules as it taxied onto the apron. It stopped, chocks were placed at the wheels allowing the rear ramp to be lowered and then the engines were cut leaving an eerie silence.

Movement just to our left caught our eye, the doors to the Royal VIP suite opened and a group of distressed people, with military dignitaries to their side, walked slowly towards the seats provided for them in the marquee. Those sharing an expression of grief were actors performing the presence of a bereaved family. I knew this was a rehearsal but I felt I was intruding and uncomfortable by being so close. Group Captain Atherton, alongside another high ranking officer, took up their prominent positions – as the senior military representatives they stood to the front. The silence we briefly experienced was replaced by the whimpering cries that we heard coming from within the marquee. There we stood a group of observers embraced in the solemn setting that was produced. A few moments later the military ceremony got underway and we saw the Station Warrant Officer with a Bugler, his bugle at his side, marching on to adopt their positions. They halted just to the left of the marquee and stood purposeful at attention. Without any word of command being heard, six RAF Airmen came into vision from the far side of the terminal building. Proud, present and all in step they marched in file, with their Warrant Officer at the rear, this was known as the bearer party. They were immaculate, dressed in their full No. 1 uniform – white gloves and best boots – although no headdress was worn. There must have been a noise embargo placed on the station as the only sound heard was of their heels as they hit the ground. To the right they wheeled, around the cockpit, along the fuselage, then out of sight they continued to circumnavigate to their intended destination, the inside of the C130 Hercules aircraft. There was no breaking in their step as they marched up the steep incline of the rear ramp, just the crisp stop of their swinging arms as they cut them to their sides. I was so focused on their drills, it was only as they marched into the aircraft that I noticed another Warrant Officer with a padre standing in the vicinity of that rear ramp. To my right I could see the undertaker; though his official title for the duty he would perform was in fact known as the conductor. He portrayed himself with an impressive charisma, wearing his black top hat and tails with a cane in his hand – almost a character from a past time in history – that was my initial thought when I saw him. There he stepped a few paces in front of the hearse with a gait, panache, along with every other word that describes elegance, dignity and grace. From our right to left they moved as one along the apron tarmac, which, with the atmosphere, had been transformed into a sacred ceremonial ground. The conductor halted as the hearse stopped in the designated position directly in front of where the bereaved family were sat; the engine was cut and the silence returned. The elegant gent with the cane in his hand then turned his head slightly to face the families with a bow of his head; a poignant mark of condolence. He then walked to the rear of the hearse and opened the door which gracefully rose up into position. Everything was slow, systematic, yet even though I knew it was a rehearsal, it felt extremely real.

There was a brief pause, then again without any word of command the bugler brought his instrument to his lips and the solemn sound of the Last Post commenced. My immediate reaction was to stand firmly to attention; as I did those who should salute did so in harmony to the Station Warrant Officer on the ceremony ground. I thought it felt surreal earlier, but upon seeing the coffin draped with our nation's Union flag being carried off the Hercules aircraft by six immaculate airmen, brought the ceremony to another level. Many people talk about the hairs on the back of their neck standing up, well this was one of those moments; I stood firmly to attention and absorbed all that unfolded before me. Talk about honour, dignity and respect, this was overwhelming and I really do mean *overwhelming*. I had never witnessed anything that displayed so much mixed emotion, deep sincere sadness, yet with chest-swelling pride, in knowing this is what our country does when bringing our fallen home.

I had been to military funerals and even carried the coffins of two of my colleagues, but this was something way beyond what I had ever experienced. I have no idea how long the bearer party had practised but they stood tall and proud in their duty as they carried an empty coffin, thank God, under the watchful eyes of their military supervisors. They slow marched then, wheeled to their right meticulously before proceeding towards the waiting hearse and conductor. Once in position, the bearer party were brought to the halt by their Warrant Officer; a pause nothing was rushed; there they stood directly in front of the family maybe five metres away. A word of command was executed by an inward turn, so they all faced the coffin. As they turned inward, to a man they all moved their hands to the bottom of the coffin taking the weight off their shoulders, holding the coffin just under the neck. A pause followed every move, enhancing the valued wealth they carried. Then a simple command of 'lower' saw the casket float down as if on hydraulics, stopping at waste height. The pause; but the silence is broken as the family weep – these actors were a little bit too good at their role, as their sadness was felt by all those around. The coffin then floats towards the hearse, carried five or six paces, in what the military call sideways step. No one who is observing can pull their eyes away, it was simply majestic the drills on display. Another brief pause as they reach their destination; they wait for the next words of command. Once spoken the two airmen nearest the tail of the vehicle place the coffin onto the open lip of the hearse. Slowly, systematically he is fed into his resting place and, as each airman lets go of the coffin, they cut their arms to their sides and spring upright to attention. The casket is now at peace to be secured for his journey home, and with the quietest of commands the bearer party retrace those same sideways steps. Brief pauses follow, then they are turned inwards, positioning the six airmen into two files facing the hearse. There they remained, standing proud in the duty they had just performed, while the conductor secured the casket into position and slowly lowered the glass door. He took one step back then bowed his head and gracefully walked to the front of the vehicle. Without any words of command the conductor stepped off and, with the swagger of his cane, led the hearse away; the bearer party marching at the rear. As the hearse drifted away into the distance, we watched, the bereaved family cried, we bowed our heads in sorrow caught up in the scene we had just witnessed.

To be honest I don't know what happened after that because I just watched the hearse drive off, so slowly around the nose of the aircraft and back in the direction it initially came from. After the ceremony I stayed rooted to where I was in the background and listened to the general chit chat. All the military dignitaries and advisors gave positive comments and congratulated RAF Lyneham on their preparations should they be called upon to carry out what I was then told would be known as 'Operation Pabbay.'

I had no idea why I had been invited to observe the ceremony, as honoured as I was to be included. There seemed to be no police requirement, it was a military ceremony held on a Royal Air Force station. To my surprise I was approached by Group Captain Paul Atherton and Managing Director of the funeral directors Barry Albin-Dyer and Rob Rowntree. The conversation was brief and to the point; they asked if it would be possible to escort the hearses from the gates of RAF Lyneham onto the M4, a distance of about eight miles. They explained that due to the size of the cortège, which would involve at least four other vehicles, that it would be difficult for them to leave the RAF station as a package or convoy. They believed once they reached the M4 they would have a simple enough journey travelling along the motorway eastbound, then north up the A34 to the final destination; the John Radcliff Hospital in Oxford.

I pondered the question which to me seemed a simple enough request and my reply was with emotion from what I had just seen: 'Sir after watching that ceremony I will get you to the moon.'

They smiled, but I really meant it; the impact of that ceremony was not lost on me, plus the words from Group Captain Paul Atherton still etched on my mind from September about enemy fire, how could I possibly say no.

How difficult could it be to escort a few vehicles eight miles up the road? What would it take? Twenty minutes tops. Not a problem it was a done deal. No contracts were signed. If I said anything it was that I would always deliver and Inspector Mark Levitt had told me before I went to the brief if we could help then no problem. We shook hands, I said my goodbyes and left them to continue with their discussion. I drove up to Wootton Bassett Police Station to brief Inspector Mark Levitt the Sector Commander on my observations and the request to escort the cortège if required from RAF Lyneham to the M4.

Mark is a top boss, who earned respect due to his style of management. A very sincere man, very much in touch with the community and towns he was in command of. I had only known him for six months, but he made me feel very much a part of the Wootton Bassett Policing Sector from day one. In that short time we had massive mutual respect for one another, working very closely, in fact he was like my supervisor and always available for advice. When I approached him asking if he could offer support with the odd escort from time to time should any repatriations take place at RAF Lyneham, his response was as I expected; which was just as well, because I had already told them it would be done.

Mark lived locally and besides being the Sector Commander he was part of the community when the Hercules C130 was shot down in Iraq. He experienced the impact of that on the area and, like me, he thought it was the least we could do to offer assistance to escort the cortège up the road. We chatted a little longer and decided we could manage this at a local level; the Lyneham neighbourhood policing team PC Steve Porter, PCSO Andy Singfield and me. I remember him saying to just give him a call half an hour or so before we were needed and he would pop down if no one was available. From that brief conversation our plan was formed should we ever be called upon by RAF Lyneham to assist with a military repatriation. Though his last words of our conversation would be repeated sometime later with a nervous laugh when he said, 'It'll only be like escorting an abnormal load, take us twenty minutes, we'll crack on with no one being any the wiser.'

I must admit when I went home that evening I reflected on what had been an unexpected experience that day.

CHAPTER 4

With the rehearsal of the repatriation ceremony out of the way, it was back to dealing with the normal duties one tends to expect with rural policing. Life in North Wiltshire was enjoyable, especially when you had the weekend off. It is amazing how quickly the weekend goes and you suddenly find yourself back with the thought of just another Monday morning and back to work.

However, this Monday morning was different. No sooner had I booked in at work than my mobile rang and it was Squadron Leader Dominic McEvoy. Dominic was the Officer Commanding Personnel Management Squadron (OCPMS) to give him his full title, a similar appointment to the head of human resources in an organisation within the public sector. It was his office that was my main point of contact with RAF Lyneham. Those who have either served or worked with the military will understand their phone calls tend to be almost mechanical; get the formalities out of the way such as 'good morning' then quickly moving on to the salient point. I was at the Police Station chatting and having the normal caffeine intake, when I answered his call. Then I heard the words for the very first time; words that were to be heard far too many times on this mobile phone: 'Morning Jarra its Dominic. Bad news I'm afraid. Can you prepare for Operation Pabbay, a soldier has been killed. We are looking to bring him back on Thursday, once confirmed I will let you know.'

See what I mean, brief and to the point, the MoD do not waste money on telephone calls that's for sure. No names, no units, just a short, simple message: a soldier has been killed, prepare for Op Pabbay. By the time we were notified of the loss of life the next of kin would already have been informed quite some time earlier, but even so we were requested to keep the information in house as it was not for public consumption. The delay from it being publicly announced was at the discretion of the Ministry of Defence and even after that announcement was made, the naming of the soldier killed was not released for a further twenty-four hours. The timing of the call I received from Dominic that morning meant I was already at the Police Station, so I immediately went to brief Inspector Mark Levitt.

The plan was quite simple really: ascertain the time the cortège was expected to leave RAF Lyneham and meet at the guard room half an hour beforehand. Mark would take the lead vehicle, while Police Constable Steve Porter and I would be in my marked police car at the rear. PCSO Andy Singfield would stop traffic outside the main gates, thus enabling the package to depart RAF Lyneham as a convoy. We would escort the cortège with blue lights activated, no sirens, and drive as if we were escorting an abnormal load, observing all traffic lights. The eight-mile route was clarified: turn left from the gates and drive through Lyneham, up the A3102 through the High Street of Wootton Bassett, right at Coped Hall roundabout, then up to the motorway. The funeral director would then lead his cortège along the eastward bound carriageway M4 en route to the John Radcliffe Hospital in Oxford, while we would return to normal duties. No operation orders, no health and safety brief or diversity issues, just jump in the car and escort the cortège up the road then resume normal duties. See how simple Lyneham law was. As the four of us were finishing off our cuppas, Dominic made further contact, his bullet points were noted as I scribbled them down. Op Pabbay confirmed for Thursday 5 April; timings were estimated to be confirmed later; flypast 09:00, military ceremony the repatriation 10:00; depart RAF Lyneham 10:30. Date and timings shared, we resumed our normal duties. Before the end of that working day I saw Dominic's name show up on my mobile phone as it rang, again a short sharp message: 'Bitter news Jarra, another soldier killed; plan for two now coming back this Thursday.'

Later that evening I was sat at home watching Sky News. There was the breaking news being scrolled along the bottom of the screen: 'Two British Soldiers Killed in Iraq.' I sat as if watching confirmation of what I had already been told; I knew this week was going to be very different.

Up at seven, getting ready for work, I sat watching the morning news on the TV; Sky News had already announced the two names of the recent fatalities in Iraq.

Kingsman Danny Wilson, age 28, from The Duke of Lancaster's Regiment 2nd Battalion, and Rifleman Aaron Lincoln, age 18, from The Rifles 2nd Battalion.

Unknowingly at the time, I had automatically fallen into some sort of habit: information received from Dominic, confirmed on Sky News, day or so later names of soldiers killed released. In fact to be precise it was a ritual to be added to that list that was the pre Op Pabbay brief, which always took place the afternoon before a repatriation; a meeting I was always invited to and expected to attend.

On Wednesday afternoon I attended this first pre-Op Pabbay briefing. This was a meeting chaired by the Wing Commander of the Base Support Wing RAF Lyneham; in this specific conference he was the Officer Commanding of the Repatriation Team. In attendance would always be a representative from each department or Wing in RAF language, who all had specific roles and responsibilities to assist with the smooth running of Operation Pabbay. Amongst those present were the officers who were to chaperone the family; others to attend to the needs of the high ranking Generals; the Padre would represent the chaplaincy, Catering, Media, Medical support, Air Traffic Control, Transport and RAF Police were all present in this room. Me, yes, I was also there representing the police. Although I was ex-military it was hard at times to understand what they were on about, as quite often they spoke in RAF Language; full of abbreviations, but I soon got the gist of it.

The Wing Commander opened the meeting with the family brief. The full details of both family groups was confirmed informing us of exactly who would be attending, any concerns, health, dietary, in fact any information that could assist with the support of these vulnerable people in their hour of need. This was supplied by the Visiting Officer, an invaluable link between family and military. After the family brief was digested we moved on to the logistics of how each phase of the operation was to be executed. The Wing Commander would go through the Op Pabbay order on his desk, reading through it in chronological order. He would then look at the person in the room tasked with that specific duty or responsibility, maybe ask a few questions, then move on to the next person. The families had taken the option to travel down the day before, they would stay overnight at the Hilton hotel, just off Junction 16, M4. The transport manager confirmed two highly polished mini buses would convey the families from the hotel at 08:15. That was ticked off the list of things to confirm. It was like he was automated as he went around the room, catering – confirmed tick; medical support – confirmed tick; systematically around each department. The RAF Police Flight Sergeant disclosed the security measures that would be in place. Road closures inside RAF Lyneham, particular area of interest was an inner cordon around the terminal building; where the ceremony was to take place. The briefing continued: the attention to detail was staggering. It was quite obvious that every person in that room was focused on working together; a team who would make sure they got it right. Orders were circulated that during the actual ceremony there would be no traffic movement either on the station or air traffic in the skies above their local area. The Media Officer reassured her Wing Commander there were no immediate concerns of press intrusion other than possible freelance photographers. My responsibility was straightforward enough:

1. Police presence external of the air base to deter paparazzi intrusion; confirmed tick.
2. Police escort at the guardroom for 10:30, confirmed tick.

The meeting flowed just like the phone calls with no preamble: a typical military set of orders, direct, easy to follow and what was expected of us. It concluded with all those present having a good understanding of each department's role, the attention to detail and preparations for this unique operation as getting it right was so important; there would be no second chance. But amongst that sharing of information there was something else, something I could physically feel. Yes, when I left that room it was the compassion and sincerity I felt; maybe due to the loss of their own Hercules aircraft in 2005. I saw empathy, an understanding, scars of a bereaved family preparing to offer support to their relations who served with them in our Armed Forces. Without doubt the 'Repatriation Team' of RAF Lyneham truly did care.

That morning, Thursday 5 April 2007, I drove up to the Police Station, very much aware of my responsibilities for the day that lay ahead. With the compulsory mug of coffee in my hand we sat down with Inspector Mark Levitt for the morning brief. Duties confirmed and attention to detail absorbed: meet at RAF Lyneham just after ten. 'Roger that' was my reply as I left his office to make my way to liaise with Squadron Leader Dominic McEvoy at the RAF station. The conversation with Dominic was just as quick, reiterating the bullet points of the previous night's briefing. Both meetings completed, I went back down to the main entrance of the station, positioned at which point were the RAF Police; immaculately dressed in their best kit including medals. I was standing to their side when a brisk move of their feet brought both Corporals swiftly to attention as a mini bus approached. Then I realised the reason for their sudden movement as the vehicle drew nearer; the faces of distress that the passengers displayed were those of the family of one of the two soldiers being repatriated home.

Bless them, they looked totally devastated, numb and confused as the two RAF policemen saluted to show their respect. It was awful seeing so much pain and deep, deep sadness etched on their faces. I could not begin to imagine what the last few days had been like for them, nor what emotions lay in store in less than half an hour's time when they would be standing where the actors had been the previous week. With one family already on the base I knew a second would be close behind, so I made good my escape out of sight. There was no way was I going to be present when the second family arrived. I felt it was an invasion of their privacy when I looked in their direction; honestly, it was awful to witness their pain. Once the second family had arrived the RAF police secured the gate, while I carried out a final patrol of the external perimeter to deter paparazzi or a freelance journalist who, if in the area, could gain access through the easy to penetrate open airfield. Luckily no concerns were raised, it was just as Kerry and Helen in the station media office stated at the briefing, there was no interest from any tabloid other than the local press. I certainly saw nothing on the breakfast television news when I was getting ready for work, or indeed any press interest in this repatriation. With the perimeter confirmed clear, I made my way back to the guardroom at RAF Lyneham.

I will never forget what happened next. When I checked the time on my watch it was a couple of minutes to nine. I knew the significance of the hour; I looked up to the skies and waited. The unmistakable roar of four turbofan jet engines were heard which caused confusion; I could not see or actually work out where the plane was as the noise was quite disorienting. Suddenly, it was directly above us flying extremely low. It is huge, no massive; somehow it just seemed to hang in the sky as it flew towards the terminal building. I was mesmerised by the sheer size of the C17 Globemaster aircraft as it was the first time I had seen it. A work of art, not at all what I had expected of a military design and it flew so gracefully, like an angel as it brought these two young soldiers home. The families of Rifleman Aaron Lincoln and Kingsman Danny Wilson were out of the view of prying eyes and would have been invited to witness the tribute shown from the skies. With a deft dip of the starboard wing, respects are shown to the family down below whose sons are carried in her care. The flypast was completed when four massive engines roared as the aircraft gained height, banking to the right it climbed, flying off into the distance, then out of sight to get to an altitude for the final approach.

Due to my knowledge from the pre-operation brief I knew the families would then be escorted back inside the terminal into the Royal suite. Inside they would be offered appropriate support or space to grieve after such an emotional experience; such was the attention to detail. The RAF station had televisions which would broadcast the live coverage from cameras which were situated in places to capture the aircraft landing. This allowed the next of kin and family to see their loved one touching down back in the United Kingdom, returning from this awful war.

Stage one completed, the C17 Globemaster had landed exactly on time. Stage two: the repatriation ceremony would commence one hour later. During this one-hour period was an opportunity for the bearer party to keep an eye out for each other, coming from the parent units of the two fallen soldiers, some may even have known him as their friend. Sixty minutes later they were going to carry him off that plane; for them their duties suddenly were very real. Some being so young would get appropriate words of support from their seniors and officers, while others used their fieldcraft skills and found ways to camouflage their personal emotions. A safety mechanism that is installed in so many of us men, anything to avoid thinking too deeply; adjusting their uniform and quietly polishing their medals was an example of that deflection. One thing was certain, the impact of seeing that flypast must have hit home as it was such a poignant moment. As for me, I had nipped back to the Police Station for confirmation we were still good to go at half ten.

Returning to the guardroom I looked over to the terminal and parked; with the rear ramp down, was that huge C17 Globemaster totally isolated from any other aircraft. The fly zone above RAF Lyneham was clear and there was no movement of traffic on the station. The orders given at the briefing had been enforced by Air Traffic Control and the RAF Police both in the air and on the ground. I could not see where the families would have been as the marquee was out of view, blocked by the enormity of the aircraft which totally dominated the area. I could see the two seven-man squads of soldiers, six men and their Senior NCO as they stood to attention in preparation to perform their duties as the bearer party. The station was in lock-down mode; the silence was like being isolated from the real world, almost as if time had stood still in this sterile bubble. Although just to my rear, life in Wiltshire continued in ignorance of what was about to take place some 500 metres away as traffic drove along the A3102.

The brisk movement of the two bearer parties had caught my eye when they quick marched from their start position. Exactly as the rehearsal, they set off from the side of the terminal building; from there a right wheel changed their direction as they circumnavigated around the nose of the aircraft then continued along the length of the fuselage. Two squads of soldiers marched as one; the rear bearer party are brought to a halt; those in front continue and, without breaking step, they entered the aircraft up the rear ramp then disappeared out of sight. One coffin was there waiting, the other was behind a curtain out of their sight. This prestige casket draped with the nation's Union flag, sat on trestles at peace, waiting for the soldiers to carry their brother home.

I knew these two squads of soldiers, the bearer party, had the previous day been instructed in the drill movements required in preparation of this ceremony. They rehearsed their drills over and over again until the military bosses said they were ready. However, what no one can prepare you for in rehearsals is carrying the body of someone you actually know. The emotions can, without any warning, kick in and that sensation would go to a different level when they would hear the raw grieving of a family; people they may even know. With the soldiers who carried Rifleman Aaron Lincoln and Kingsman Danny Wilson were probably two of the most important men in the whole ceremony: their two Senior Non-commissioned Officers (Senior NCOs). The experience and people skills they stored would be required for that pep talk inside the aircraft; a valuable opportunity to get their men focused so they did not let their colleague down. I learned over the years that during the Senior NCO pep talk some had a quick glass of port to share a private message with their colleague before they commenced this honourable duty. But once lifted onto their shoulders there was no turning back as they braced themselves in readiness for the words of command from their Senior NCO.

With private thoughts in their heads they lifted their brother onto their shoulders, poised at the ready for the next word of command – slow march. It was then I felt the presence of the Guard Commander with a couple of the guards standing beside me. We watched, we waited; the eerie silence all around was broken when the bugler commenced the sounding of the Last Post. No words were required when we heard that moving composition in our ears, those three serving members of the RAF and I stood immediately to attention. Glancing to my right I saw so many others had done exactly the same thing. The first soldier was brought home down the ramp. The Senior NCO was the first person we saw; slow marching backwards down the incline with the palm of his right hand firmly placed on this precious casket, ensuring it remained on the shoulders of his men. Slowly, meticulously, the bearer party moved as one, having learnt their drills from so many rehearsals the previous day. Off the aircraft the hero was carried as the music of the Last Post resounded in their ears. Two or three more steps were taken then the six pairs of feet were placed firmly on the ground. The bearer party were outstanding in their drills doing this fallen soldier proud. 'Halt' would have been the whispered command that brought them to a stop, not moving or flinching they stood on the spot. Their leader, with the most immaculate gait, manoeuvred at the slow march to his position of command, at the rear of this most valued possession in his care. A brief pause followed, the casket was then carried at the slow march, almost floating on the shoulders of the men chosen for the duty. It was a time for immense concentration for those carrying their friend; the intense training undoubtedly helped them as they lowered the coffin. The desperate sound of crying, that raw grief never witnessed before, rang in their ears. The broken-hearted family watched as their loved one was laid to rest in the hearse. Without a kiss or a chance to mourn they remained helpless, numb and most certainly confused, as he was driven away. Yet there they remained in sorrow, an unbelievable sadness, and they watched as the second soldier was brought home in exactly the same solemn fashion. As I watched my mind wandered in deep thought for what those poor families must have been going through, I honestly could not think of a more awful experience in life. Sometime later the mother of Rifleman Aaron Lincoln was quoted in a newspaper; words that I would like to share in this passage of the book. Aaron's Mother, Karen:

> 'Aaron had six months of basic training and then, the Christmas after he turned 18, he was sent to Iraq. Only once did he write or speak of the experience – on a visit home, the first time he had leave at the end of March. Even then, it took a couple of drinks in the pub before his tongue was loosened.
>
> We stepped outside, Karen continued, and he broke down crying. He said, "I've seen things you'll never see. I don't want to go back." I didn't know what to say, so I just cuddled him. We both cried. Five days later, Aaron was dead, killed by a bullet from a gun.'

It was hard to imagine a mother holding her son in her arms less than two weeks earlier, trying to comfort him before his return to Iraq. That wave, the kiss, and maybe the cuddle she gave to her son; not knowing it was to be the last time she would ever see him alive.

Sometimes you get moments in life when you witness something unique that creates a silence amongst you; that was one of those moments. I could see in the faces of Mark Levitt, Steve Porter and Andy Singfield who by this time had joined me as the second soldier was carried down the ramp, that the impact was not lost on them. Not a word was spoken between us; we just watched until the conclusion of this awe-inspiring tribute as the British Forces brought their fallen home. The sounding of reveille from the bugler reached our ears; it was time to get into our cars in preparation to escort the cortège to the M4. I think we all knew then what we had signed up to do. Yes, a small escort but one we would continue to do with the same level of respect for the two fallen soldiers we had just seen carried off the plane. It almost felt as though it was the least we could do.

Andy Singfield got into his car and drove down to the entrance of RAF Lyneham to get into position to stop the traffic on the A3102; this enabled us to leave as one. We saw the cortège coming down the road being led by the RAF police. As they approached, they peeled off and Inspector Mark Levitt was now in poll position leading from the front; slowly he headed out of the base with the cortège directly behind him. I counted the vehicles the cortège contained: first the funeral director's car, next the two hearses carrying the soldiers' coffins, a spare hearse followed them and, bringing up the rear, were two more vehicles, one was the military police in an unmarked car while the last vehicle was the undertaker's team. In total a package of six vehicles held tightly together by the police cars at the front and back. Andy had stopped the traffic from our right and we made our slow departure from RAF Lyneham main gate onto the public road. Due to the size of the cortège, Mark cruised at about 20mph to keep the convoy tight; blue lights were activated but no sirens.

Slowly we cruised through the village of Lyneham. People noticed us, of that there was no doubt, you could not fail to see them point in our direction then speak amongst themselves. Oncoming traffic slowed down not understanding why the police were going so slowly when blue lights were activated. As they went past us they saw the hearses with the draped Union flag over the two soldiers' coffins, but again possibly wondered what, who and why. Everything was going to plan. We left on time, cruised through Lyneham, then up the A3102 arriving in Wootton Bassett High Street ten or fifteen minutes later. What happened during those next few minutes was probably the first indication of what was to evolve over the next four years. The cortège remained tight as we travelled down the High Street just past the building on stilts. Suddenly we came to a halt. Initially, from my position, I could not understand why we had stopped. I saw Mark get out of his vehicle and walk towards a skip lorry that was parked across the road, this was the cause of our abrupt halt. The driver of the vehicle was out of his cab lifting the skip bucket onto his lorry using the controls on the side. He looked a little flustered, possibly due to seeing Inspector Mark Levitt heading in his direction, or possibly seeing a police car with its blue lights activated. He had no need to be concerned as Mark reassured the driver to safely secure his load onto the vehicle, then the road would clear. As we remained static I looked to my left, 20 metres away a group of people were standing at the pelican crossing, by sheer chance they just happened to be there at this time waiting to cross the road. In a small market town high street two stationary police cars with blue lights on was bound to create attention, but on this occasion it was two other vehicles that roused curiosity. By fate, the cortège had been brought to a standstill but it was where it had stopped that is the significant part of this tale. For many who do not know the layout of the High Street in Wootton Bassett, next to that pelican crossing is the war memorial; a bronze-cast sculpture of a globe held aloft by four hands. A monument to the fallen from historical wars was flanking the nation's latest fatalities from a current conflict – Rifleman Aaron Lincoln and Kingsman Danny Wilson. It was the two hearses we escorted which had caught the public eye. The lights changed from red to green to allow people to get to the other side of the road, but instead those present chose to remain where they were stood in silence; some even bowed their heads. They stayed there for the next minute or so, until we went on our way. Why? I was once asked. Well the only conclusion I could think of was that on seeing the two Union flag draped coffins those people stood in silent respect for the two young soldiers we escorted home that day. So by sheer chance, fate and circumstance I can honestly say that every single cortège we escorted from RAF Lyneham and every one of the fallen were recognised by this wonderful caring community.

The skip lorry finally pulled away which cleared the obstruction, allowing us to continue on our destination up to the M4. We stopped the traffic on the slip road to the motorway to allow Rob Rowntree the funeral director to lead his cortège safely onto the fast road heading east. We then made our way back to the Police Station for a much needed cuppa. Andy Singfield had peeled off from the rear of the escort just after Bassett High Street; his remit was to get back to the nick and put the kettle on. No, not because he was a PCSO but quite simply he really did make the best brew; that was an integral part of Lyneham law, we would never have a meeting without a cup of tea. The four of us sat down for a quick de-brief from Inspector Mark Levitt, discussing the events of the morning and the extraordinary sights we had seen. Ten minutes or so later we were still chatting away when Squadron Leader Dominic McEvoy called me on my mobile phone. Straight to the point as always he said, 'Jarra it's Dominic. How did it go?' referring to the escort. I replied that everything had gone well, but the words I heard next were difficult to comprehend.

'Bitter news, four soldiers were killed today. Can you start planning for Op Pabbay, probably towards the end of next week?'

The conversation was always as brief as that; it reminded me of my time in the Army with a pneumonic we were taught in giving orders (C.L.A.P.) Clear, Loud, As an order, with Pauses. Although I had left the military many years ago it appeared some things would never change.

I put the phone down and relayed to Mark what I had just been told. It was staggering news that left us all slightly numb. Four more killed, no names, no pack drills, just a brief call, this is what we've got and this is what we are doing. It was a very different style from what we were used to in the police. When we were passed information such as a death we were inundated with details. It was difficult to absorb. Yes, we understood the words that Dominic had spoken; it was just astonishing and difficult to digest. Especially after witnessing the sights we had seen only a couple of hours earlier. The four of us just looked at each other in disbelief as Andy said, 'Did he just say four more next week?'

It was only the first week that RAF Lyneham had assumed the responsibilities for this operation, in fact it was only five days into it and yet in that short period of time six British soldiers had already been killed.

I went home and sat down to have my dinner with Karen that evening and told her how my day at work had gone. I told her, 'You won't believe it, we have to do the same next week; four more soldiers have been killed today.' By the time I had finished my dinner the news came on the television and there it was scrolling along the breaking news bar at the bottom of the screen.

'Four British Soldiers Killed in Iraq.'

I remembered the family I had seen entering RAF Lyneham earlier that day; seeing their faces and then immediately thought of those poor people who were going to be sitting in that same mini bus next week. It was a strange feeling going to bed that night; numb yet deep in thought, feeling so much sadness for six families I did not know.

CHAPTER 5

U p out of bed, washed, shaved and showered, uniform on, then I would sit in front of the box watching the news while I ate my breakfast; that was my morning ritual. This morning the lead story was the same on all news channels. I sat engrossed by every word spoken; even from the knowledge I had gained earlier from Dominic, it was still difficult to digest. A nightmare for four families was what the country woke up to that day.

After the twenty-four hours of grace, the main news story continued to be of the latest fatalities in Iraq. The details were released and amongst the four killed in the warrior armoured vehicle, which had been blown up by a roadside bomb, or more likely an improvised explosive device (IED) were two female soldiers. From the coverage I saw on the news, be it rightly or wrongly, it was quite obvious the next repatriation was going to attract a lot of attention from the national media.

It was relentless over the next few days; the main news on every channel was that there were four British soldiers killed in an explosion. If I had one criticism over the years, it was when the press focused their attention on the volume of soldiers killed, or that it included a female soldier. For me, each and every loss of life was headline news, be it a single serviceman or woman; each demanded equal focus and attention. It was not only the news channels that focused on the loss of the two female soldiers but the national tabloids as well, specifically when the *Telegraph* highlighted a connection to Royalty:

> *Prince William has expressed his sadness after a 'close friend' from Sandhurst was killed in Iraq. The prince was 'deeply saddened' by the death of 2nd Lieutenant Joanna Yorke Dyer, 24, a statement from Clarence House said: 'Jo was a close friend of his at Sandhurst and he is very much thinking of her family and friends right now and they will remain in his thoughts and prayers.'*

Second Lieutenant Joanna Yorke Dyer was from the Intelligence Corps attached to the 2nd Battalion, The Duke of Lancaster's Regiment.

Corporal Kris O'Neill, Private Eleanor Dlugosz and Kingsman Adam James Smith also died in the roadside bomb blast near Basra, southern Iraq on Thursday.

Private Dlugosz, 19, from Southampton, who served in the Royal Army Medical Corps, was 'held in high regard by all who knew her.' The MoD said: 'Supremely dedicated to her work, she thoroughly enjoyed her soldiering and was keen to use her life-saving skills as a medic to help others.'

Also from the Royal Army Medical Corps, Corporal O'Neill, 27, from Catterick, Yorkshire, was an 'experienced and confident medic with an unflappable nature,' the MoD said. He was 'a committed family man with two small boys,' it added. His squadron commander, Major Phil Carter, said: 'I could always depend on Corporal O'Neill.'

Kingsman Smith was from 2nd Battalion, The Duke of Lancaster's Regiment. Aged 19 and from Liverpool, he was a 'popular and highly respected colleague,' Lieutenant Colonel Mark Kenyon said. 'He showed all the qualities of a reconnaissance soldier, dependable, determined and a real team player.' His family released a statement, saying: 'Adam was the most wonderful and beautiful person anyone could wish to meet. He always had a smile on his face and loved life so much; he had everything to live for. He was a loving son, brother and the best boyfriend in the whole world and he will be missed more than words can say. He will forever be in our hearts.'

Why was the media now so focused on this particular loss of life than previous ones? Well, I cannot answer for them, but what I saw as the days approached this, our second repatriation, was the increased attention on the two female soldiers. We knew from the interest in the press that the tabloids and the news channels would be present when the four soldiers came home.

The day before the four soldiers were brought home the military bearer parties arrived and carried out usual rehearsal drills. The repatriation team were called to their pre-Op Pabbay meeting to which I was invited. The briefings were vital as the RAF Lyneham team were very raw in their new role, exactly the same as we were; this was only our second repatriation. The Wing Commander chaired the meeting in exactly the same format as before, going through his orders chronologically; the family brief compiled by the Visiting Officer always the first item on the agenda. That report was invaluable to the repatriation team and assisted them in supporting each of the bereaved guests they would be hosting. There was no omission of the sincerity and duty of care felt towards the family as the brief was read out. The Wing Commander continued with his orders. As he went round the room each department's role was ticked off his list and confirmed as ready. On this occasion, one of the big concerns the military had was of press intrusion. To alleviate that, my presence was requested from 7am that morning at the front gates.

'Any questions?' was always the conclusion of the meeting as he made one last sweep around the room with a pointed hand style chop, something the military favoured when indicating to a person. Then one clap of his hands and we were done. When we left the room we fully understood the operational timings and personal responsibilities we each had allocated to us. With an early start planned for the following morning I returned back to Wootton Bassett Police Station and briefed Inspector Mark Levitt on the operational timings. Due to the media interest we tweaked our plans slightly from the previous week; still low key in the manner of an abnormal load escort. A police incident log would be created with the control room being advised of our intentions, but without the full planning of an operational order, as quite simply the same four officers who included Inspector Levitt all understood Lyneham law.

A bright and early start to the day with my morning routine, which you know by now, and yes the breakfast news crew were already live at the main gates. I watched them intently while I ate my toast. When I approached them half an hour or so later the BBC and Sky News were highly visible; TV vans with satellite dishes on their roofs, producers, sound engineers inside the vehicles, all fine tuning their equipment to beam their shots live. BBC had Robert Hall, as their reporter; he was already speaking live on their morning news programme from the entrance of the station. The Sky News producer looked slightly more anxious as he kept looking at his watch then up the road. They were set up on the grass verge outside the main gates ready to broadcast, but, as yet, without their reporter. A short while later a huge sigh of relief came from the man I was in conversation with; he was the producer of the Sky News team, his cameraman now by his side. I saw a motorbike approach where we were stood, a frenzy of activity then commenced as the chap got off his bike. He walked towards us, whipped off his helmet and ran his fingers through his hair. A nod, a slurp of tea, he then grabbed the mike and said, 'This is Geoff Meade, Sky News, live at RAF Lyneham.' I was in admiration of his professional skills as he flowed into his live broadcast. I was well impressed as he reeled off the details and accurate information about the four soldiers returning home. When they finished their live broadcast I spoke to both Robert and Geoff in an effort to build up a rapport. I remember both reporters to be decent people and during our conversation I was able to provide them with details of timings and confirmation of what they had already received from the media officer, with reference to the order each coffin would be carried off the aircraft. What I did not know then was how we were to meet far too many times over the following years. In doing so we developed a professional mutual respect for each other's needs, although Katie Stallard replaced Geoff Meade and his motorbike on the majority of times that Sky News were present.

As the clock ticked ever closer to the significant timings of the day, both news channels set themselves up outside the gates where the RAF Lyneham sign was their backdrop, basically the turning into the base from the main road. My phone rang non-stop that day, but the most significant call I received was the one informing me the families were en route from the Hilton hotel.

I reflected on what I had seen the previous week when I saw the distressed faces of the family of Aaron Lincoln and Danny Wilson as they entered the station in the military mini bus. I cannot begin to think what that journey was like for them or for the four families now on their way. However, I did perceive the last thing they would want was for a camera to be in their faces as they were driven into the base. With that in mind, I asked Robert Hall of the BBC and Geoff Meade of Sky News if they would relocate their cameras just to allow a little respect for the four families as they made their way to where we stood. The two men and their producers acknowledged the request I made and without any fuss they stood back to become an invisible presence as the families slipped through the gates. In return for this, what I believed to be a goodwill gesture, I gave them constant information as to when, and without intrusion, they would get their story. For the press, a story is quite simply what it meant for them. I also believed that the country should know of the loss of these four soldiers and if things were done in the correct manner, they could achieve it without distress to the main people, the families who had lost their loved ones.

The flypast would soon be upon us so I withdrew out of sight, leaving the TV cameras positioned in the optimum location to capture the aircraft as it appeared from the sky. The unmistakable roar was heard causing a little disorientation for the producer on the ground who was desperate to transmit the live footage when the Globemaster flew over. Just as seven days earlier, the four turbofan jet engines would not allow that angelic bird to arrive without its presence being announced. There it was, directly above our heads; the magnetism which drew our eyes to that wonderful aircraft, so low, so powerful, yet somehow just hanging in the sky, bringing these four fallen soldiers home.

Many families have told me it is a difficult moment – 'the aircraft flypast and the deft dip of the starboard wing' – so many awful yet mixed emotions that brief moment brought to the onlookers. On so many occasions I have witnessed that rawness and heard it from a distance; to see that distress in those hurting is the worst memory I still carry to this day.

I am glad I was alone when I saw that huge bird fly over because I experienced a sadness that made me feel exposed. After the aircraft landed the next hour was always where we knew there was time to sort out any last minute commitments, before we focused on our support to the rest of the repatriation. The pause between stage one, the flypast, and stage two, the military ceremony, was a guarantee. This was due to the C17 Globemaster aircraft being de-armed of anti-missile flares; reiterating that this was not a flight returning from some holiday destination. No, this was a flight that had taken off from a location that most of us could not begin to imagine.

I always went back to the Police Station to liaise with those involved in the operation for what was, in those early days, an informal briefing. Due to the intense media coverage that focused the eyes of the country on our little village in Wiltshire, Inspector Levitt thought it prudent to update headquarters of our intent to escort the four fallen up to the M4, and employed a couple more officers to assist at appropriate junctions and roundabouts.

The policing operation was to be called Op Entourage and, yes, an Op Order was provided as we said goodbye to Lyneham law, although it was the same officers involved with just a few extra colleagues at static points. During the briefing Inspector Levitt gave us, he mentioned that the Mayor and members of the Town Council along with the Royal British Legion intended to stand at the war memorial. This was something they felt very passionate about, in order to acknowledge the sacrifice of the four soldiers and allowed them to show their respects.

After the brief we drove back through Wootton Bassett High Street on our way back to Lyneham and I noticed ex-military men and women had already started to congregate around the war memorial, some wearing berets and medals. When we arrived we parked our vehicles at our layup point in front of the guardroom where we waited to escort the cortège. True to my word with the producers of both TV news channels, I informed them of the intent of the people of Wootton Bassett to stand at the war memorial. The BBC responded with that information and sent a cameraman up to the High Street.

While that happened we watched the C17 Globemaster aircraft manoeuvre onto the apron where the repatriation took place. Once in position the engines were cut and the final preparations were made prior to the commencement of the repatriation ceremony. Again, exactly as the first repatriation a week earlier, the aircraft dominated the area, offering a protective cover for the families from the cameras of the two news channels. We saw the four bearer parties march into position, twenty-four men with four Senior Non-commissioned Officers; the lead bearer party went directly onto the aircraft. When the first of the four coffins was carried down from the ramp and off the aircraft the silence was broken with the sounding of the Last Post by the bugler. We all stood to attention, in respect for those heartbroken families who were seeing their worst possible nightmare that had become a reality in front of their eyes.

As each of the fallen were carried off the aircraft the coffins went out of view and, after being laid to rest in the hearse, they were driven off the ceremony ground and away from the families. I could never begin to imagine how awful that must have felt, craving to hold your son, daughter, husband or partner for those heart-broken people, yet I could only watch helplessly as they were taken away. As each hearse left I counted them one, two, three, and finally the fourth, we then knew that a few minutes later the cortège would be making its way down into our care. It was time for us, the police, to continue the proceedings with the same reverence as the four young soldiers had been shown throughout the day. A simple escort, but one that would be carried out professionally and with the honour that Second Lieutenant Joanna Yorke Dyer, Corporal Kris O'Neill, Private Eleanor Dlugosz and Kingsman Adam James Smith so richly deserved.

Inspector Mark Levitt drove the front police car; when he sighted the eight vehicle cortège moving towards us, he slipped into pole position and the RAF police escort peeled off. I then took up the rear slot so we had the cortège held tightly between us. We activated the blue lights and slowly made our way out of RAF Lyneham. PCSO Andy Singfield had already stopped the traffic on the A3102. The cortège was now under our care and we made a dignified exit through the military gates. Our speed was reduced to almost walking pace as we entered the public road; it was so important to keep the cortège tight and at a speed which condensed the distance between vehicles. They were so well protected: the undertakers' highly polished fleet of vehicles then our police cars with blue lights flashing all combined to enhance the value of what and who we were escorting. These four soldiers were going to be recognised for the huge sacrifice they had made, and noticed they most definitely were.

First we went through Lyneham, a small village but one that was very proud of its military community and, as you have already read, sadly they really understood, as those memories were provoked from January 2005. Many stood silent as we passed, a few people walked along the footpaths, stopped, turned, then bowed their heads while the vehicles slowed down on approach almost coming to a stop.

We reached the roundabout leaving Lyneham on our way up the A3102 heading towards Wootton Bassett. Traffic had stopped as we entered the roundabout. I remember people sitting in their cars staring in what I can only describe as utter disbelief. People bowed their heads, made the sign of the crucifix across their chest or just put their hands over their mouth. Almost as if in shock they counted one, two, three and finally four as each Union flag draped coffin passed them by. Slowly and meticulously we covered the five miles up the A3102 until we entered the built up area of Wootton Bassett. We closed up again as another police colleague stopped traffic coming onto the High Street from Station Road. The road was unobstructed and the traffic flowed as we approached the war memorial; the cortège speed was reduced. I saw the town's Mayor, Percy Miles, with members of the Royal British Legion; a brief but significant bow of their heads as we slowly drove past in recognition of these four young soldiers. It was a simple gesture from a small group of people who recognised that these sons and daughters deserved a little bit of respect from a society who had forgotten our Great British Forces. And respect is what they were most certainly shown from what we all witnessed that day.

CHAPTER 6

In the first weeks since RAF Lyneham assumed the duty of returning our country's fatalities from Iraq and Afghanistan, we had already received several calls from Dominic, with that harrowing message prepare for Op Pabbay. When each of the fallen was escorted home, members of the public joined the Mayor, Town Council and Royal British Legion as they congregated at the war memorial. Although they stood for some time before the cortège arrived, the actual respect they showed was very brief as the fallen were escorted slowly through the High Street. The president of the local Royal British Legion made a request to the funeral director to ascertain if it was possible to reduce the speed the cortège travelled past the war memorial, or if indeed it was even possible to stop, so his branch members could pay a fitting tribute to those that had fallen. During their conversation they formed a plan to allow appropriate respects to be shown and, accompanied by Mayor Percy Miles, they approached the police with their proposal.

The request was approved by Inspector Mark Levitt which was for the conductor to page the cortège through the High Street, when he would then stop the fallen adjacent to the war memorial where respects could be acknowledged during a brief pause for thought. Maurice Baker of the Royal British Legion assumed the role as 'parade marshal' and would orchestrate this small ceremony with simplicity. Only two words of command were required in order to execute the minute's silence. The first was 'Up' and on hearing this, those on parade wearing their berets or preferred military headdress came to attention and saluted. Maurice would then shout 'Down', signalling the end of the respects shown; on hearing this salutes were lowered. The conductor would then tip his hat in mutual recognition and lead the cortège down the High Street where we, the escort, waited to continue on our short journey to the M4.

With the introduction of this small impromptu ceremony, Inspector Mark Levitt deemed it more appropriate to change his position in the cortège to command and control from the rear police vehicle; I would assume poll position at the front. The brief was quite simple, we drive from RAF Lyneham and on arrival in Wootton Bassett I would stop the cortège adjacent to St Bartholomew's Church. The conductor with his top hat on his head and cane in his hand would prepare to page the cortège. I would drive a further 200 metres up the High Street with the funeral director's car close behind, where we would remain. The sterile area thus created, allowed the congregation gathered to carry out their spontaneous ceremony. Once concluded the conductor would reunite the cortège and escort as one. We would then continue on our journey which, for the escort group, was as far as junction 16 on the M4.

It was early May 2007 when this second impromptu ceremony was commissioned to show respects to the fallen. I recall the date well as Mayor Percy Miles brought it up in a conversation we had much later on. Percy mentioned how honoured he was to be present wearing his ceremonial insignia, the regalia and pendant of their own little town before his tenure in office was concluded. While those who joined him on that day in the centre of the town gathered, we were five miles down the road at RAF Lyneham.

Earlier I was engrossed with the choreography that was presented in the skies with the elegance of the deft dip of the starboard wing during the flypast. It was just beautiful how it floated in from the north, slowly, unbelievably slowly, yet with humility; full of feeling, a mixture of sorrow, yet honour, as the most precious gift in life was being returned home.

Then an hour later, after our police brief, we were back to observe the fallen soldier being carried off that beast of a beauty that brought him home. As that orchestrated set of movements was completed we waited as those in Wootton Bassett were now gathered to bestow their respects. Andy had closed the road and our slow, disciplined escort from RAF Lyneham was on the move, which for me was the first time I led the cortège from the front. Once again the respects shown never wavered along the route. On arrival at the High Street I knew my brief and continued past the gathering of folk with the funeral director's car close behind.

All in position the conductor took his first steps from St Bartholomew's Church gates and paged in front of the hearse. Wearing top hat and tails and with his cane in his hand, walking with a style that I mentioned before, but believe me it was truly fitting for the occasion. Confidence, but not flamboyance as the attention was focused on the soldier resting in peace. At the war memorial that minute's silence was orchestrated through the basic command of two words, the mixture of sadness yet honour. In standing together as a united community it showed the perfect level of reverence. Initially there was ten, twenty, thirty or maybe a few more who knew we were bringing a soldier home, yet others getting on with their everyday life saw this group of people and stood by their side. But it was not about the numbers present it was about doing something that they believed to be right and it certainly made me proud to live in this town. The conductor, recognising it was time to move on, acknowledged those on parade with the tipping of his top hat to the good folk in return for their salute for the soldier in his care.

I saw Percy an Ex-Sergeant Major of the British Army, who wore his medals presented to him during his career, along with the Mayor's chains proudly hanging around his neck. But amongst all that decoration was a Wiltshire man who did not know then that he and those who stood with him had created a legacy; one they would look back on with immense pride in future years. The simplicity that this second ceremony represented was the foundation that would provoke others in time in acknowledging those who served the Crown.

Things had changed in the High Street very quickly from when we first brought Rifleman Aaron Lincoln and Kingsman Danny Wilson back home. Just as we responded in a positive manner with the requests made by those congregating at the war memorial, we did so when asked for further assistance from the funeral director. Rob Rowntree had found a more direct route that would take the cortège to John Radcliffe Hospital and asked if we could consider taking the escort a little further up the road. We looked at the map of the proposed journey which was to join the M4 as before, then come off at Junction 15, head north along the A429 a few miles, then turn onto the A420. Inspector Levitt agreed to the request and that the police escort would peel off at Gablecross Police Station, which was on the Wiltshire border of their jurisdiction with the Thames Valley police. The cortège would then freewheel to its final destination in Oxford. This extended our route from an eight-mile journey to something nearer twenty. By the end of May, only two months after the very first repatriation, so much had already changed. With increasing numbers of the public adding to those ex-military personnel of the Royal British Legion and the Town Council on parade at the war memorial, further resources were needed. Those extra police officers came from the Ministry of Defence Police (MDP) from their Divisional Support Group (DSG) and travelled up to Wootton Bassett from Plymouth, Larkhill and Aschurch, to offer mutual aid to Inspector Mark Levitt's sector. The new route, with the inclusion of escorting the cortège along the fast roads, required skills from the Roads Policing Units (RPU) from Wiltshire Police – traffic cops in old money. With all these extra resources required and at such short notice, it was the responsibility of Graham Hurst the office manager at Wootton Bassett Police Station to compile the operation order. Graham was not a police officer but support staff and, if I am to be honest, I am not really sure what his role was. All the years I knew him he never wore uniform, but was immaculately dressed perched in the front office as you walked through the door. A very proud man who had also served the Crown as a Warrant Officer; an illustrious career in the Royal Air Force with the British Empire Medal; though he seldom would tell. However, once he was handed the baton this was one operation order that he was not prepared to let go.

Then we received the tragic news released by the Ministry of Defence confirming the death of Corporal Mike Gilyeat from the Royal Military Police in Afghanistan on Wednesday 30 May 2007. The operation administration went straight into action requesting resources from both the MDP and Wiltshire RPU. There was never a shortage of officers volunteering for these duties. The MDP officers came from Larkhill near Salisbury and the two motorway patrol cars from Chippenham Road's Policing Unit (RPU); all were advised of the timings required at Wootton Bassett that day.

One of the first to volunteer was PC Jim Torrie from Chippenham RPU, an ex-Scottish soldier who was a character and a half and had a daughter who was presently serving in Afghanistan with the Royal Military Police. His rational was one of wanting, on behalf of his daughter, to perform this duty for Corporal 'Gily' Gilyeat who she may well have known as a friend or colleague. Jim's actions were typified by so many who carried out this police operation. Yes, it was a duty, but we really did care. The military ceremony of the repatriation was carried out with what is known as two magic words 'military precision.'

This was the first occasion we escorted the cortège with the Roads Policing Unit, which extended our initial escort from eight miles to nearer twenty. During that journey, heads bowed, cars stopped and the conductor paged through the High Street, where those congregating at the war memorial stood in the salute. Then, out of the town en route to the motorway, we followed PC Jim Torrie in the lead patrol car, who knew exactly why he was there. We travelled down lane one of the eastbound M4. This was a first for us as we had never escorted the cortège up the motorway before. Everyday traffic in lane two and three were unsure if they should overtake, especially when they saw the hero honoured in his Union flag draped coffin. Our final destination as the escort group was Gablecross Police Station and, as we peeled off, the cortège drifted out of sight along the A420.

As each month passed more bitter news followed and the congregation grew to honour each hero home. Without a doubt the tide was starting to change and our fallen were being recognised in the most respectful way.

At the end of August the escorting of the cortège was reviewed by the Roads Policing supervisors Inspector Ian Stevenson and Sergeant Craig Hardy who deemed that they would replace the front motorway patrol car with outriders. The number of outriders resourced for the escort would depend on the size of the cortège, but always a minimum of two. They would clear our route; where a hold on traffic was required one bike would remain at the road closure until we had passed through, then with their skills they would overtake us to once again lead from the front.

Once they led us onto the motorway into lane one, the inside lane, the outriders would drift into lane two, the middle lane, and the rear motorway patrol car would hold traffic back, alleviating the dilemma of whether everyday traffic should overtake or not.

Once again this had an impact on police resources with all three of Wiltshire Roads Policing Units – Salisbury, Gablecross and Chippenham – supporting Operation Entourage. Those resources, just like the rest of the police were never slow in volunteering their services, many were ex-military and deemed it an honour to be involved in escorting the fallen along the road.

The local newspapers, the *Swindon Advertiser* and her sister newspaper *The Gazette* and *Herald* were often the only tabloids covering the repatriations during this time. The coverage they gave to the fallen was highly respectful; I think they knew they were starting to witness something completely different and something which had not been seen before. When one of their journalists made a request to witness the respects from within my car, I had no hesitation to invite her along as a front seat passenger.

Privates Aaron James McClure, Robert Graham Foster and John Thrumble from 1st Battalion The Royal Anglian Regiment were killed in Afghanistan on Thursday 23 August 2007 and eight days later they were brought back to UK soil. With the journalist Hayley Court by my side I am able to refresh my memories from an article she wrote in the *Swindon Advertiser* in relation to the day we escorted these three 'Vikings' home.

Friday 31 August the flight had been delayed which meant it was early evening when the police outriders led us out of RAF Lyneham main gates onto the public road. A soldier carrying his burgan on his back turned his head to cross the road, to his surprise we approach; the kit bag is ditched as he comes to the salute. I note the surprise in Hayley's eyes and say, 'What else do you expect but to show respect, it is the last thing he can do,' and quickly the journalist scribbles her shorthand notes.

The cortège is flowing smoothly; the introduction of the outriders is a huge success in particular with Friday traffic at a peak. Yet slowly, methodically, we enter Wootton Bassett for what Hayley tells me is the twenty-third time. The public have turned out and others stopped on their way home from work as the conductor comes to a stop at the war memorial. The salutes are made and more shorthand notes are written in my car. Haley calculates that the combined ages of the three heroes in our care does not equal those of the veterans on parade. The High Street was closed as the small ceremony took place, but no one who was stuck in traffic complained as one by one the motorists stepped out of their vehicles and bowed their heads as we pass by their side. The cortège is then escorted along the M4. The plan has worked perfectly; it's a smooth transition getting onto lane one, the outriders move into lane two and the rear police car holds back traffic at the rear. At Gablecross we peel off knowing these three soldiers have been shown the utmost respect. It was the end of the fifth month and from Hayley's research she tells me we had already escorted fifty-four fallen home.

But things did not always go to plan, as you can imagine, with such a major operation as bringing the fallen home. During that first year there were quite a few interesting and challenging moments for all involved. With the flights of the incoming C17 initially being around 9am the families travelled the day before and were put into the Hilton hotel in Swindon to alleviate extra stress. As the months went on flights were moved back to around 13:00 hours, this was because the fallen were not only coming back from Iraq, they were now also brought home from Afghanistan. Although hotel facilities and accommodation was always an available option, some families preferred to remain at home and travel to RAF Lyneham on that morning. The link between the Repatriation Team and the family was a person who carried the title of 'Visiting Officer' (VO); a person who had huge responsibilities. A chaperone, a confidant, a fixer, someone who would make it happen; a person who many of the bereaved would look upon as a sincere friend in this awful place they now found themselves to be in. One of the priorities was for the VO to accompany the family to RAF Lyneham for the harrowing experience that lay ahead. Maybe to travel from home on the day, instead of staying in the unfamiliar surroundings of a hotel, was the preferred choice, but a decision that had to incorporate factors such as time and distance to RAF Lyneham. Whether the family travelled on the day or stayed at the local hotel, the timing of that flypast was the most important schedule they had to meet; to be present when their loved one returned.

On two occasions this caused somewhat of a challenge as one family left from Bulford in South Wiltshire to travel north of the county. The C17 Globemaster was always on time and to make sure that happened it would circle around the Fairford air space, then make its final approach as per the timings of the operation order. So there we were, half an hour to go before the flypast and the family are stuck in heavy traffic on the A345 about five miles south of the M4, 18 miles away from RAF Lyneham. The RAF Repatriation Team, who were at the terminal building waiting for the family, were getting rather anxious when news was relayed to them by the VO of their predicament. My phone rang; it was Flight Lieutenant Claire Adamson, as always polite, no panic, but again brief:

'Jarra, we have got a problem, can the police help?

Three salient points: 1. Family should be here they are not. 2. The aircraft is circling running out of fuel. 3. Both need to be at RAF Lyneham within the half hour can you make it happen?'

The beauty of technology, police radios, mobile phones and a hell of a lot of luck, two Road Police Units were already waiting to make their destination to RAF Lyneham as part of the escort group. Fortunately, that day they were coming from Gablecross Police Station and were heading south towards the same M4 junction as the family were en route to. Details were passed and they were diverted to locate, trace and escort them to RAF Lyneham. Once they were collected they made progress with sirens, blue lights and flashing headlights, the full works, to get this family to the terminal building on time. Make it they did, but with only a few moments to spare allowing the family to gain some composure before the aircraft made its final approach. With relief and immense sadness they stood and saw this huge aircraft gracefully flying in their direction; with a deft dip of the starboard wing, the family were there when their loved one was brought home.

Sometimes you hope lessons are learnt from experiences such as travelling to a location and allowing plenty of time, especially for such an occasion, but you would not believe what happened a few weeks later. On this occasion, we the police, were having our meal break at Wootton Bassett Police Station at around 12:00 with the flight due to fly over at 13:00. My mobile rang and I saw the name flashing up on my phone. Flight Lieutenant Claire Adamson, this time a little rattled and sounding slightly annoyed, for obvious reasons as I was about to learn:

'Jarra, we have a major problem the family are in Lyneham and the aircraft is due on the hour.'

The obvious question, 'What was the problem?'

The answer was one that I found hard to believe. The Visiting Officer, who was responsible for the wellbeing of the family and, possibly the most important role, was to get them to RAF Lyneham for the repatriation. However, not being familiar with the area, he had programmed the sat nav in the vehicle to Lyneham and this distraught family were at the wrong location. Yes, Lyneham, but one in Oxfordshire! Fortunately the Visiting Officer had realised the significance of his error and was heading towards the correct Lyneham in Wiltshire as fast as possible with the family in his tender care. After the dilemma was brought to my attention I informed Claire we would do our utmost to get this family to RAF Lyneham for the designated time. Although the challenge would be tight, her parting gift was to provide me with the mobile number for the VO so we could have comms. PC Lee Maplesden was my colleague with me that day and he nipped out to my car to grab the road map as neither of us knew where this other Lyneham was. When he returned I was in contact with the VO who, as you can imagine, was somewhat under pressure.

The distance between the two locations was about 40 miles away, a mixture of country roads, A Roads, the M4, then through Bassett to Lyneham. I spoke to the Visiting Officer and there was no need to say anything other than to offer our help, so I gave him an option which he gratefully accepted and we made our way to the rendezvous point. If there was one glimmer of encouragement, they had made good progress since initially informing the RAF of their error. However, on this occasion there were no RPU available so a basic plan was hastily put together. The plan was simple, collect the family, sandwich their vehicle, a people carrier, between the two police cars and make progress to cover the eight miles through Bassett and get to RAF Lyneham for the flypast. While we sat at the RV point the car phone relayed a constant commentary from the VO. We told him the plan and asked if he felt his driver was up to the task to follow us. He confirmed he was, not that that would have helped me 'on a discipline' if it had gone wrong. My colleague, PC Lee Maplesden was on his mobile to the RAF who, in turn, gave us updates on the status of the flight. The feedback wasn't great, the plane could possibly delay the flypast by fifteen minutes but after that they were on fumes and would have to come into land.

'No pressure then,' was my reply.

As we waited, Lee and I agreed there was no way we were going to let that family down – if they get to us before 13:00 we could do it. Our chat was hushed when we heard the words from the Visiting Officer that they were now on the M4, about ten minutes away. I looked at my watch, it was cutting it tight, so we knew we had a difficult challenge ahead. Ten minutes can go fast or slow depending on your dilemma; those ten minutes seemed to go very fast and still they had not arrived. Then suddenly, yes, I saw the flashing headlights of a people carrier in my rear view mirror. I pulled out, pressed a few buttons which activated my lights, sirens and anything else I had, warning the traffic in front to get out of my way. Rear police car in position, confirmed, the package in our care, affirmative. With a deep intake of breath and fingers crossed I looked at Lee and said, 'Best let the RAF know we are on our way.'

Let's just say it was interesting driving at those speeds. Yes, both I and the other police officer were trained to do so, but on this occasion we had a people carrier sandwiched between us, with a military driver who was not. With the roar of the sirens, the flashing lights and maybe someone upstairs looking after us, we covered the ground and roared into the approach road to the main gates of RAF Lyneham. Lee updated the anxious Repatriation Team at the terminal we were one minute away and the message was relayed to that aircraft circling in the skies above us. We parked up at the end of the terminal as the family were supported out of their vehicle into the warmth of the RAF Repatriation Team. No doubt shaken, but the better of the evils as they would have been devastated not being there when their own fallen hero had come home.

The military driver, whose name I wish I could remember, drove over and parked next to my car. He jumped out of his vehicle somewhat the worse for wear and came over to where we stood. He reached in his pockets for something he badly craved that white stick of nicotine, which he brought to his lips and tried to light with his shaking hands. Due to the adrenalin of our short, but memorable, journey he found the simple task of lighting a cigarette too big a challenge. I'm not a smoker but I removed it from his lips and put it in mine and lit the thing for him. He looked as relieved when he inhaled deeply as I did when we finally reached our destination. We had one narrow miss when his vehicle nearly hit mine but that was not his fault, that sadly was down to the RAF policeman at the gate who had not been briefed, causing us to make an emergency stop.

No sooner had his cigarette been lit than we looked up to the skies to see that huge aircraft perform the honourable ritual of the flypast. When I saw the deft dip of the starboard wing in respect for the mourners, I felt relief and satisfaction that the soldier's family were there waiting for him when he came home. With the aircraft now landed it was time for us to move on; a shake of the hand was all that was needed as we went our separate ways. But I hope one day the driver of this family gets to read this short passage as for him I am sure it is a day he will never forget. So if you do see these words my dear friend, stand tall, stand proud, you performed skills well out of your comfort zone in getting this distraught family to RAF Lyneham in one piece.

With those two experiences out of the way word must have filtered back along the chains of command as we never had to do any more last minute escorts again. Although some families still chose to travel declining the offer of the facilities provided at the hotel the night before.

That first year was a steep learning curve for all of us involved in this delicate and sensitive operation.

On this particular day a set of circumstances occurred that to be honest we never envisaged, when we responded to a call for assistance from the RAF Police. If I am to be honest, disorder at the terminal building was not what I expected to hear. The brief circumstances relayed to PC Steve Porter and I were that the Visiting Officer was adamant that the family he was responsible for was not leaving anything to chance and had set off early; they were ahead of schedule so had stopped off on route. This group had two mini buses full of extended family and they travelled with the next of kin. When they stopped off for lunch an element of them consumed alcohol leaving one young lad emotionally charged and in that emotion was anger. On arrival at RAF Lyneham terminal the family were given a briefing and either it was not understood by the young lad or the alcohol was affecting his judgement, but when the aircraft carried out the flypast his emotions were provoked.

The padre tried to offer some comfort with reassuring words to the lad as he was very distressed, fortunately with nimble feet and with the grace of God in his corner, the padre dodged the reply – a right hook in his direction. The RAF police were already in the area and, with their skills, tried to defuse the situation. Their attendance, however, was not well received, in fact it was more like a red flag to a bull. The lad was wound up and had no qualms or hesitation in putting his size nine boot into their car door. As you can imagine when we turned up there was a bit of confusion, but I am glad to say a family member had grabbed the lad and managed to shepherd him away in an effort to calm him down. While everyone waited for the repatriation ceremony, I was briefed by Wing Commander Dave Collinson and told they did not want any police action, but requested we remain in situ but out of sight, in case this young lad reacted aggressively again. A short time later the C17 Globemaster was in position, ramp down and the bearer party ready to perform their duty. PC Steve Porter and I were stood at the side of the building; the marquee was slightly to our right where this distressed young man was standing with the grief stricken family. As the Last Post sounded and the Union flag draped coffin was carried down the rear ramp the lad darted from the marquee and away from the ceremony ground. When he ran around the corner he saw our presence which resulted in him changing gear and sprinting further away from the building. We remained where we were as he ran 200 metres away and caused us no concern, allowing the bearer party to focus on their duties. Being so close, it was horrible hearing that rawness of emotion, a family breaking their hearts when their loved one was brought off the aircraft. I don't think I had ever heard or witnessed such a scene of desperation like it; the crying, it was awful, so raw, so painful and so crushing. By the time the ceremony had finished I walked up to the young lad who had fled who was now sitting on the grass, his head in his hands and obviously having trouble dealing with his emotions. Some people do find it really difficult to cry and are almost embarrassed to do so in front of other people. We chatted and I asked him about the soldier being returned that day. It was his cousin, not much older than his own late teenage years. As we talked he broke down. Then a family member who came looking for him gave him a hug and the two walked away. Yes, such was the raw emotion, for some anger was the way they grieved.

Following this repatriation, observations were made by the military who decided to enable the smoother running of Op Pabbay they would restrict the family attendance to eight. Extended family and friends were to be encouraged to attend the war memorial in Wootton Bassett High Street; and that was how and why the families started to join the community five miles up the road.

As each loss of life took place, be it in Iraq or Afghanistan the people of this market town never failed to line their High Street. In all weathers the numbers grew; there was no media other than the local papers. They simply congregated for the right reasons as they stood there in recognition of the fallen who had paid the ultimate sacrifice. These humbling sights which we witnessed on each occasion were so moving in their simplicity. In an age when society just moves so fast, this town just stopped for that short period of time and welcomed those extended family members and friends to stand with them in their High Street.

Spring, summer, autumn, we saw so much sadness and now we were in the winter months. As many in the country were preparing for their Christmas, in December 2007 the body of Sergeant Lee Johnson of the Yorkshire Regiment 2nd Battalion was repatriated into RAF Lyneham. Sergeant Johnson, 33, was killed by a mine in Helmand Province on 8 December. Full military honours and respects were shown as the fallen hero was carried by his comrades off that huge Globemaster Aircraft, and on completion of the flawless ceremony we escorted his cortège out of RAF Lyneham.

The Union flag draped coffin was illuminated in the glass showcase of the hearse as we slowly made our way along the Wiltshire roads. The High Street in Wootton Bassett once again came to a standstill as the conductor paged Sergeant Johnson's body through and stopped at the war memorial for the one minute's silence. Maurice Baker, the parade marshal, brought the Royal British Legion to the salute as others bowed their heads. Once these respects were shown the cortège reformed with the police escort vehicles and we slowly made our way out of town. The outriders led the way and, as we followed, I saw many oncoming vehicles stop and activate their hazard lights in a mark of recognition. On arrival at Gablecross we peeled off as this, as you now know, was where our destination ended. The cortège was now in the care of the funeral director although they had no blue flashing lights on their cars. They, as again you know, formed their own guard of honour for the remaining 26 miles.

The following day, after each repatriation, I used to read the local newspaper *The Swindon Advertiser*. The reporters always wrote an article in relation to the fallen with compassion and sincerity, which included many tributes to show how much the soldier was valued. Lieutenant Col David O'Kelly of the Yorkshire Regiment said he was touched by those who stood in the bitter cold to pay their last respects to Lee. He continued, 'I know the family will be touched by the compassion of the people of Wootton Bassett who stood in the cold winter weather to show their sincerest respects to Sergeant Johnson. He will be greatly missed but it is a comfort for those who knew him to know that his repatriation didn't go unnoticed. We are honoured by the people of Wootton Bassett and their actions shall not be forgotten.'

With the change of Commanding Officers in the same week, Group Captain Paul Atherton moving on to pastures new, this would have been the first ceremony under the command of Station Commander Group Captain Mike Neville. One wonders what private thoughts went through his mind as he was the Officer Commanding 47 Squadron, when RAF C-130K XV179 Hercules aircraft was shot down killing all ten on board. One thing that was clearly evident at the start of his two-year tenure as the Station Commander of RAF Lyneham, he certainly had an understanding of what each bereaved family was going through. The traumatic experience of January 2005 could never have been forgotten by anyone who had witnessed such grief at close quarters. It was possibly due to those memories he recognised the heart-warming respects that were shown by the community of Wootton Bassett and why he joined them at the war memorial in showing mutual respect.

Throughout the last nine months, since 1 April, British Forces fatalities in Iraq and Afghanistan recorded 74 dead. The vast amount of them were repatriated back to RAF Lyneham, the few who did not, died in hospital in the UK from their injuries sustained in theatre. But on each occasion we escorted the fallen home, those standing in that High Street never wavered; in fact they grew.

So much change in this last year for so many and also at Royal Air Force Lyneham as the station began a new chapter under the leadership of Group Captain Mike Neville. Nevs, the name on his flying suit, was fully aware of the extra pressure on his prestigious station, with the repatriations on top of the immense operational commitments of keeping his fleet of Hercules Aircraft work horses in the sky.

Something that was very important to any working unit was morale and this station oozed it; almost an unwritten motto 'work hard, play hard and party when you can.' One thing I witnessed in my tenure was the team ethos that they all signed up to and boy could they party. They needed no encouragement when it was time to get into the Christmas spirit; just ask anyone who served there about 47 Squadron's 'Guinness and mince pies.' After work there were the end of year inter unit-mess sports matches and of course the Christmas functions; those not on essential duties departed for two weeks leave. But the impact of seeing so many caskets carried off aircraft had to take its toll. I know for me personally as this year came to end I sincerely prayed that the repatriation of Sergeant Lee Johnson would be the last.

CHAPTER 7

The best part of three weeks into the New Year, then my mobile rings and it was a message I was hoping not to hear: 'Prepare for Op Pabbay' were the brief words spoken; a soldier killed but no other details. The limited information was relayed to Graham Hurst the Admin Manager at Wootton Bassett Police Station, who was tasked to resource the police operation. Twenty-four hours or so later the British soldier killed in Afghanistan was named by the MoD as Corporal Darryl 'Daz' Gardiner, an exceptionally brave soldier as you are about to read. Sky diver and instructor, a member of the Royal Electrical and Mechanical Engineers, attached to the 5th Regiment Royal Artillery and 52 Brigade's Reconnaissance Force. On 20 January 2008, he was just 2 kilometres from Musa Quala – a town he helped liberate from the Taliban just before Christmas – when a vehicle from his unit was hit by a mine. Corporal Gardiner, aged 25, drove to the troops, rescued a badly wounded soldier and was ferrying him towards a waiting helicopter. He got to within 100 yards and then a mine went off under his vehicle. The impact of that explosion killed Corporal Gardiner instantly; he died in an act of immense bravery and it was his actions in recovering that soldier that helped save his life.

Due to operational reasons, the actual date of this repatriation was changed a couple of times, then finally confirmed it would take place Monday 28 January. This meant that the rehearsals would take place on Sunday the day before. This was the first time I met Station Warrant Officer Nick Dale who was observing the ceremony before his tenure in post in March. He watched with intense interest as this was a role he would soon command. Some jobs you learn from the book, others on the ground. This one would be learned out here now as he absorbed the soldiers responding to the words of command during their rehearsals. It can never be underestimated how much preparation is given to this ceremony as this was a duty that you did not get a second chance to get right. On the day prior to the repatriation, as on previous occasions, I watched the bearer party carrying out their training as I was on my way to attend the Op Pabbay briefing.

As I watched, I saw the Army Warrant Officer give his words of advice to this band of six brothers, technically skilled soldiers from the Royal Electrical Mechanical Engineers who were to be taught new drills to look like guardsmen performing the duties as the bearer party. I thought to myself, were they possibly the friends and comrades of the fallen soldier? All young men often struggling with their own grief and facing the most arduous of tasks. The Army thrives on discipline as I knew from my years in service and that's why they rehearse over and over again. The Warrant

Officer shouts his words of command to take them through their paces before they carry out this sombre duty for real and most importantly in the close proximity of the family.

'Slow, steady as you come into view,' he calls out across the tarmac.

Some feet away these six men in uniform are heeding his words of advice, the encouragement and genuine support to those carrying a 6 foot by 2 foot 6 inch wooden box. Yet twenty-four hours later on their shoulders would be a precious casket, which was not lost on them as they focused on their drills. Step by step, inch by inch, they moved perfectly down the constructed iron ramp representing the exit from the giant Globemaster aircraft. In unison the men move slowly, methodically aiming for the painted markers on the ground which will guide them to lay their colleague to where he will rest. The choreography during the ceremony is exactly the same for all those who are returned home, with the identical attention to detail in what is known as 'military precision.' There was no doubt when you heard the Warrant Officer speak to his men he did so with a vast amount of knowledge, understanding, compassion and genuine pride in what he wanted to achieve at the rehearsal. When they were stood down that day they had a full understanding of the task and commitment that lay ahead.

Corporal Darryl Gardiner was repatriated back to RAF Lyneham on Monday 28 January 2008. Due to circumstances, this flight arrived later than usual from Afghanistan which created a knock-on effect to the timings of the original operation order. Visibility was good which allowed the C17 Globemaster to complete the honourable flypast mesmerising all as it seemed to hang in the air floating rather than flying a couple of hundred feet up. The deft dip of the starboard wing was executed to honour Corporal Darryl Gardiner in his care. That angelic bird really does seem to fly in slow motion, then with a burst of power in those gigantic engines the aircraft gains altitude to circle the Air Station for the final approach.

It was a typical winter's day, dry, cold, but fortunately no snow as the aircraft came into land. The defusing of anti-missile flares and preparation of the aircraft for the ceremony gave us that golden hour to prepare for our planning of the escort. As this flight was delayed many police officers were due to finish their shift, but such was the impact on us who had been involved in these humbling scenes, there was no shortage of volunteers to extend their tour of duty. Then the military repatriation ceremony commenced and you hear the Last Post sound in the distance; you know from previous experiences exactly where the bearer party are. Fully trained to perform as guardsmen when the time came, as it did on this cold January day, they get it right and return their hero home in the presence of his family. That preparation had paid off and the repatriation of Corporal Darryl Gardiner was yet another immaculate ceremony that reiterated the efforts of all involved as the six soldiers laid their colleague to rest in the rear of the hearse. Briefly he remained there until, with the bow of his head, the conductor leads the soldier away from the grieving family to take priority in the waiting cortège.

On this occasion I had no knowledge if any of Darryl's family were aware of what had previously taken place in Wootton Bassett during 2007. Although locally it was well known what respects were being shown at the war memorial, I was not sure how far afield this information was being passed on. In fact it had been some five or six weeks since Sergeant Lee Johnson was repatriated just before Christmas, so we did not know what to expect when we went through Wootton Bassett. Would the novelty of showing respect dwindle on a cold winter's evening? There were no media news bulletins reminding the public that yet another soldier was returning home.

When we left RAF Lyneham escorting the cortège out onto the public road you could not fail to notice our nation's hero in the hearse; interior lights on, illuminating the casket of the fallen soldier. The image that was created was like a priceless treasure on display, placed in a highly polished glass cabinet, with lights so bright they draw the naked eye to the colours of the Union flag – the red, the white and the blue. A flag that is fitted tightly in a perfect fold, no crease in sight; yes, another example of military precision. Corporal Darryl Gardiner was a hero and as dusk went into night the illuminated setting where he was at rest, enhanced his honourable presence. We drove slowly through Lyneham village where the locals stood at their vigil points, many in RAF uniform creating the bond between the military and civilian residents of this rural community. Along the high tree-lined country road we continued up to Wootton Bassett; two outriders way out in front, blue lights flashing paved our way, sending a message – sadly we are back. Oncoming traffic reduced their speed, some even stopped, hazard warning lights indicating they had seen us. My response was one of mutual acknowledgement as I slowed the cortège down. Over Skew Bridges we were now in the built up area where the glow of street lights and people's homes lit up our route. Many on their way home from work would suddenly stop as they saw us approach and lower their heads; a simple gesture of their sorrow. Arriving outside St Bartholomew's Church we come to our planned stop; here we would wait for a brief moment while the conductor prepared to commence the impromptu ceremony.

With the subtle tipping of his top hat, we know he is ready. This is my signal to separate from the cortège and, with the funeral director's car, we make our way 200 metres along the High Street where we will wait.

That short, slow journey is one that I will never forget. The town truly felt the loss of each of the fallen, as again they stood shoulder to shoulder along the side of the road displaying so much warmth and compassion. It was a gratifying sight for me, particularly when I recognised some of the, how can I say, mischievous young characters standing alongside the ex-servicemen and women. This show of unity really had transcended both society and generation, as normally it would be the elderly contacting the police complaining about these youths, but tonight they stood with one common purpose, to show respect for this British soldier.

Once we, the escort, adopted our holding position at the far end of the High Street, we cut our engines then sat in silence. However, this evening the silence was broken when I heard for the first time the unmistakable sound of the tolling of a Tenor Bell.

I learned at a later date that due to the timing the conductor had paged through on that Monday evening, it had spontaneously introduced the addition of the Tenor Bell of St Bartholomew's Church to this unrehearsed ceremony.

The bell is one of the four oldest in the tower, cast in 1663. It weighs almost a ton and bears the inscription: 'Come when I call to serve God all.' Roger Haydock explains that the tolling of the bell started because that was the time when the cortège came through on that Monday. He explained, 'That's when we normally start bell-ringing practice. It felt inappropriate to let that racket go on so we started tolling.'

And that is how on each occasion when the conductor paged along the High Street he was joined step by step with the tolling of the Tenor Bell.

On this particular evening it was by fate and as the cortège was halted at the war memorial the respects were shown accompanied by the sound of the toll of the Tenor Bell.

I'm not sure if any of the funeral team, in particular the conductors and Roger the bell ringer, ever met? But perhaps with the blessing of God the two of them were always in unison as between them they enhanced the ceremony with an ambience, that unless you stood there it was difficult to describe.

But on this cold winter's night I wanted to share with the families and friends of Corporal Darryl Gardiner who were unaware; to send a message on to be remembered in years to come, that so many of whom you did not know recognised your loss.

As fate has so many hands to play in the happenings that took place during those years it now seems to have transpired into these pages. Through the transparency access of the internet I received an e-mail from Paul Gardiner who serves with the RAF; he had become aware of this chapter that I had written. He asked if he could add his own personal tribute; heartfelt words from a man who is missing his younger brother. It is with great honour and privilege I wish to share Paul's words:

'I hope you don't mind but I will try and summarise our feelings and thoughts, as a family, on how we felt during that most terrible of days. Prior to the repatriation we had had an awful time as a family trying to come to terms with what had happened. We had lost all sense of time; for the first twenty-four hours none of us ate or slept. I remember feeling all over the place when we were told on which day Darryl would finally be coming home, as we had been previously told a few different dates. We were informed that we needed to meet at the Hilton hotel on junction 16 of the M4, on 28 January. When we arrived at the hotel, two REME (Royal Electrical Mechanical Engineer) officers met us and discussed the incident in which Darryl had been killed. We were also met by the Station Commander from RAF Lyneham, I knew him quite well as I had been on a course with him. There were a few other RAF officers present, the OC Ops and the station Padre. The room in the hotel was a conference room; it felt large and cold. We all sat around on chairs talking together in a circle, at times there was complete silence as we thought about the gravity of the situation we had found ourselves in. We sat there waiting for the call to say that we were being picked up for our transfer to Lyneham. We then moved to RAF Lyneham on a coach provided by MT (Military Transport). This was a strange moment for us as a family, because we had been an RAF family for such a long time and knew the area very well. I can remember being based at RAF Lyneham only six months prior to Darryl's death and knew that the base would be eerily silent and that members of my trade (Movements) would be there to greet us into the VIP lounge. In the lounge the officers from the Hilton were there, as well as the REME Brigadier. We then chatted ('hob-nobbing') and waited for the C17 to land. My sister and I were talking to the Station Commander and although a truly horrendous day, we tried to make a horrible situation light-hearted and were telling stories about Darryl. Like myself and Darryl, Laura serves the country in the West Midlands Police. We are all used to banter and I am so proud of her for the way she conducted herself on that day. We tried not to think of ourselves, but to make it as comfortable for my Mum, Dad and Lucy.

We were given a five-minute warning and went outside to watch the flypast. When it did, and this will be something that will live with me forever and something I never hope to see again, my Mum collapsed to the floor. We then watched on a TV screen as the aircraft landed and I remember us as a family collectively saying, "Welcome Home Darryl." This may sound strange, and as I write this I feel it is strange, but at the time it was such a relief to have him home. We had waited so long to get him home as the repatriation date had changed a couple of times. We then had to wait for the aircraft to be offloaded. Again we moved outside to wait for the aircraft to park up and start the ceremony. This was the point we were relieved, but the moment we were also dreading. To this day we all hate hearing the Last Post; whenever any of us hear it we cry. I knew it would be horrible seeing the coffin coming off the aircraft, but the pall bearers were brilliant and had been practising for days. After the ceremony we had asked to meet them, as they were friends and colleagues of Darryl from his unit. They were very respectful and my Mum put them at ease and had a hug and a smile for each of them.

I remember on the day we were allowed nine people at the repatriation ceremony, so there were some family members who were disappointed to not be there. However, they had been told about Wootton Bassett and they set up camp there. We didn't do this, however, we met up with them later at a pub next to the Hilton hotel. At this point we as a family went to see Darryl in the station's small chapel of rest. I remember his coffin was draped in the Union flag and I went into the chapel with my wife, my sister and her to be husband. I remember asking everyone to put their hand on his coffin and say a few words. After seeing the coffin we went to say our goodbyes to the officers and waited to get on the coach back to the Hilton hotel. I remember on the journey back as we were going through Wootton Bassett, crowds were dispersing from the High Street. At this point we saw family members and friends in the crowds. The coach driver then told us that this was normal for repatriations and it was a symbol of respect from the town. Finally we met up at the pub with our friends and extended family next to the Hilton and had a drink to Darryl after such a hard day. So seven years on does it get any easier? The simple answer is "No". But I love it when I hear Darryl's name mentioned, it gives me a boost, a great glow; he genuinely was my hero and some days I miss my Brother so much it hurts.

I would also like to finish this short personal passage to say "Thank You" to the Bell Ringer for tolling the Tenor Bell at St Bartholomew All Saints Church in respect of our legend, my Brother. For the people of Wootton Bassett, what can I say that's not been said before, but maybe simplicity with sincerity is all that's required? The comfort it has brought knowing what happened the day Darryl was brought home and that he was then and still is now in so many people's thoughts is genuinely comforting to know.'

CHAPTER 8

What became very clear during the bleak winter months was that the weather would not deter those coming out onto the streets to show their respects, as they did during the month of February. Corporal Damian Stephen Lawrence of 2nd Battalion The Yorkshire Regiment was killed on Sunday 17 February and Corporal Damian Mulvihill of 40 Commando Royal Marines on Wednesday 20 February 2008; two more fatalities of this war and both were shown a huge amount of respect when they were returned home.

With old fashioned communication such as talking, word would cascade throughout the town; the initial sombre message initiated by RAF Lyneham to the Town Council and the local Royal British Legion. Not through e-mail, but from one friend to another; a voice that spoke with empathy during a personal phone call, sharing sadness, reiterating the genuine bond between the local community and the military. That is why when those that stood at that war memorial portrayed so much compassion; the loss of life was truly recognised, the ambience created could not be described as anything other than sincere.

The same, and much more, was said in relation to the Repatriation Team at RAF Lyneham who were described as an outstanding and dedicated group who were awarded so many accolades for their professional approach in dealing with the most arduous of duties with such sensitivity. Care, compassion, a true understanding and a thousand words more, would be needed to try to explain the etiquette they offered so many bereaved families over the years. Each person knew their responsibilities and many brought their own personality to the team which complemented the family ethos. One of those who certainly brought his character to the team at the end of February/beginning of March was Station Warrant Officer Nick Dale. How can I describe the man? Those who have served will know that the role of the Station Warrant Officer is similar to that of a Garrison or Regimental Sergeant Major; the man with the big stick that would kick you up the arse when needed. With his immaculate gait, that stick in his hand and a moustache you could spot from a thousand yards, he would command so much respect from his station, not through fear but with pride. A man who had Royal Air Force engraved within him like a stick of rock, who epitomised the honour and glory in serving as a Gunner in the Royal Air Force Regiment for more than thirty years. Yes, Mr. Dale would make his presence known by bringing his own personality to the proceedings; professionally I had seen none better in the way he worked with those involved in returning the fallen home.

Very shortly after his arrival the skills of everyone were required when it was confirmed that the recently announced fatality in Iraq was from a Royal Air Force family, whose personal links evidenced the bond between the military and local community here in Wiltshire. Sergeant Duane 'Baz' Barwood died on Friday 29 February, after a rocket attack on the Contingency Operating Base in Basra. The RAF serviceman based at Brize Norton in Oxfordshire was a well-known First Responder with Great Western Ambulance Service in Swindon. The *Swindon Advertiser* wrote in their paper: 'He leaves behind his loving family: wife Sharon and two daughters, Leanna and Rebecca.' The newspaper made mention of his dedication to the local community from his voluntary work as a first responder for the ambulance service. I knew from the many contacts I had within RAF Lyneham that they had lost a genuine friend and were deeply saddened. To be fair it was more than that, many people were in shock as they knew 'Baz' really well. Further tributes came from the Royal Air Force. Group Captain Malcolm Brecht, officer commanding RAF Brize Norton, who said: 'An enthusiastic, loyal and dedicated member of the RAF, he was a willing volunteer for his tour of duty on operations in Iraq. A caring and diligent man, with a larger-than-life personality, Sergeant Barwood was admired and respected by all those he led.'

The words were echoed by many of those wearing the proud uniform of the Royal Air Force, as they stood side by side with those congregating at the war memorial the day Sergeant Duane 'Baz' Barwood was repatriated home. There was also a large presence of green, not of the military, but that of the NHS; equally proud of a friend they knew, not as a man of combat, but as a volunteer who saved lives. Many openly wept that day as the conductor paged the local hero home. The public, the military, the paramedics, the friends; a community stood in silent recognition of a man who had given his all, and also in support of a family who had lost someone very special to them. There were hundreds present that day yet, even though the size of the congregation grew, it was always carried out within the boundaries of our sombre British mood.

As previously mentioned I would get the early heads up from Squadron Leader Dominic McEvoy once he had been made aware of a loss of life. At the weekends it was Sky's *Breaking News* that was my first source of information. As it was on Sunday 30 March, when further bad news scrolled on our TV screens 'Two British Soldiers Killed in Afghanistan.' A day or so later the names of the fallen were released to the public. Lieutenant John Thornton, 22, and Marine David Marsh, 23, both serving with 40 Commando Royal Marines, were conducting a patrol near Kajaki in Helmand Province when their vehicle was caught in a blast.

Behind the scenes the military focus on the preparation of 'Op Pabbay' for the Police 'Op Entourage' where Graham Hurst requests the resources from Wiltshire and the Ministry of Defence Police (MDP). We often use the term as 'routine' in the police when you do something frequently. Although we had done this operation sadly on far too many occasions and though there were similarities, never once did we treat these duties with a blasé attitude. That's why so much attention to detail was carried out in the planning and preparation by us and even more so with the military, so we all remained focused.

Following the initial announcement of the most recent fatalities the day of the repatriation soon came around. Briefings concluded, information shared, then a perimeter patrol completed, I parked my patrol car in the lay-by on Chippenham Road.

On the last few occasions I had tweaked my own responsibilities slightly in that after carrying out a security patrol to deter unwanted guests through the perimeter fence, I would be a highly visible presence parked in the commonly known aircraft viewing area on Chippenham Road. There, I often met friends and extended members of the family who wished to observe the flypast, as they did when Sergeant Duane Barwood came home.

On this particular morning a van was present, connected to the network of news feeds for television, with a satellite transmitter on the vehicle's roof. I'm sure it was Jon Kay, but alas my memory may have faded; a reporter for sure with the local BBC news team. This was not unusual for a regional news team to be present as on this occasion they were reporting the return of Royal Marines from Norton Manor, Taunton. The location where they were set up created an excellent viewing area where, without intrusion into RAF Lyneham, it was a place to capture the images from the skies as they would unfold. I had an excellent relationship with the BBC and Sky News teams always sharing information. Usually it was me passing on appropriate dialogue to them such as timings, the order the fallen would be carried off the plane; details that were so important in reporting the facts. Later that day they were to return the favour and pass some information my way, in relation to a journalist with his own agenda.

A glance to his watch and the producer gets his cameraman in position; a link is confirmed as their pictures are beamed directly to the studio in London, the remit is simply to capture the live footage of the aircraft as it arrives at RAF Lyneham. At the precise hour just as scheduled, the Globemaster announces its arrival with the roar of the turbofan jet engines; such a picture of elegance it is overhead, low, slow and with the deft tip of the starboard wing Lieutenant John Thornton and Marine David Marsh were returned home. I stood once again mesmerised by its beauty; a ritual I had seen many times before but which never fails to move me. Height is gained to an altitude required in preparation for the final approach, then to my right some 100 metres away the wheels touchdown as it lands. With the aircraft safely down I made my way to Bassett for the police briefing. The BBC would relocate to the main gate of

RAF Lyneham; it would be from here that they would capture the images as we escort the cortège away.

Back at the Police Station we sat around in preparation for the Op Entourage briefing. However, all was not well back in Lyneham as I was just about to find out. A London journalist from the big city with an agenda and described as someone who had pounced with excitement at the thought he could sell a story to his editor, said the informant on the other end of the phone. The message I received from that person was one that I found quite disconcerting. A journalist was snooping about wanting timings of the cortège leaving RAF Lyneham. It was his intention to then follow the escort and produce a story that would not be favourable to the respects shown along the route from the repatriation ceremony to the coroner's office. To evidence his story he would draw a comparison between Britain and Canada on the way the fallen are returned home. I paused for thought with the words I had just been told running through my head. I did find it very sad; for some unknown reason there will always be someone or some organisation who, for their own reasons, have the ability to dissect anything that is good and find a negative, instead of focusing on a positive. Then again how many positive stories sell papers?

Thanks to the informant, we had the heads up of the intent of the journalist from the *Mail on Sunday*. That information was relayed and Inspector Mark Levitt made contact with Thames Valley Police (TVP) in an effort to arrange an escort from Gablecross Police Station to John Radcliffe Hospital. If that could be achieved at short notice it would avoid this story being produced and the potential of negative press to our neighbouring colleagues would be a wasted journey. While that dialogue was carried out I was tasked to tracing the journalist and given a simple brief – to encourage him to join the cortège then contain him within the escort between the rear funeral car and police vehicle. Our rational was to keep him in a confined space so he could not disrupt the proceedings and witness at first hand the huge respects that were shown. It was not long before I found the gent as he was hovering outside the gates of the Air Station and introduced himself as Peter Almond. He did confirm he was writing an article for the *Mail on Sunday* in relation to the respects shown to our fallen. I relayed the invitation for him to join the cortège in his own private car which he eagerly accepted. He agreed to the terms and conditions of our offer which was for him to remain in the cortège from RAF Lyneham to Gablecross where we would peel off.

Meanwhile Inspector Levitt had received a negative result; Thames Valley police explained they could not resource units which meant the cortège would be escorted to Oxford with the undertakers from the A420 road for the remainder of the journey.

About an hour or so later the repatriation concluded with immaculate drills from the Royal Marines during this sombre military ceremony. Once completed the cortège wheels slowly rolled to where we waited. With road blocks outside the gates, the A3102 was clear for us to enter. Blue lights activated, outriders in front, the cortège was ours – Lieutenant John Thornton and Marine David Marsh the two commandos in our care. We made a brief stop as we left the base to put the journalist in his place, although if I had put my thoughts into words I would probably have needed a federation friend for discipline proceedings. But after that brief lapse that makes me human, a more professional thought came into my head. Maybe he might review his initial agenda and report on all that is good in the respects that are shown; something which was about to stare him directly in the eyes. Methodically the cortège goes out the gate where the two old boys at the corner who are always on parade there stood and then saluted. One Royal Navy, the other from the RAF, enhancing the honour from one generation to another as they had both served the Crown was evidence enough of the respect, unless of course the reporter chose to ignore it. St Bartholomew's Tenor Bell is tolled as the High Street is closed for the heroes' coming home, the conductor paged with that awesome gait; this is the story that should be told. The silence is loud if that makes sense. Even the birds stopped singing as you heard the sound of the conductor's heels hit the ground. The word of command by the parade marshal is only one, but they all understand, as they raise their right arm in salute. Heads are bowed, standards dipped, a time for reflection during the one minute's silence as friends and family sob in sorrow. 'Down' is ordered as the arms come down from the salute and the standards are raised while numbness lingers all around. The conductor, with one final bow, turns and leads the cortège to where we wait, to escort it another three miles to reach the M4. The wheels once again slowly turn as many watch us drift away, but as each set of eyes say goodbye, another set comes into sight. The accustomed spontaneous reaction is performed so many times along the route with a brief stop and a bow of a head. Along the M4, no more than 50 miles an hour says the speedo in my car, this is a journey I want our guest to savour for his editor, for him to be honest and tell what he *really* saw. With saddened eyes we watch our separation as we peel off at Gablecross Police Station, and the cortège continues on its journey. But have no fear the fallen are not alone, Albins Funeral Directors will escort them to their destination, not with blue lights front and rear, but still with dignity and honour.

Two weeks later it was difficult to believe the journalist had been on the same journey as I had been on, as these were the dramatic words to be read that Sunday morning on the front page of the *Mail on Sunday*. A story that had been created by Peter Almond whose name was printed bold and proud.

Pictures that should shame us all reveal the shabby way Britain treats its fallen heroes.

The *Mail on Sunday* publishes extraordinary pictures that contrast the final road journeys:

In Canada, there is a police escort and crowds line the route; in Britain, the hearses are denied outriders and go unremarked. In Britain most of the journey is spent ignored and stuck in traffic? Because Thames Valley Police refuse to provide an escort as they 'focus on community safety rather than ceremonial roles.' Their two black hearses and an empty spare hearse accompanying them were initially escorted by Wiltshire Police. The cortège first passed through the village of Wootton Bassett where locals, forewarned by the RAF base, gather at the war memorial to pay their respects. But for much of the rest of the trip to Oxford, where the bodies undergo a post mortem before being returned to their families, the hearses are on their own, led only by an undertaker's car. They were cut up by impatient motorists at roundabouts, stuck in traffic and generally ignored by the public, their significance lost because of a lack of the gravitas that a police escort would provide.

So on, so forth, the article continued on the front page and the centre pages. The journalist must have been rubbing his hands with glee, getting so many inches to tell his story in the tabloid.

One thing for sure my informant was good, as the article he wrote was exactly in the flavour he said it would be – a comparison between Canada and Great Britain being his main aim – almost to the point of discrediting any respect for our fallen. I was aware of the respects shown in Canada due to the availability of sharing information so freely in this modern age. I, along with many others in our country, had been sent the document *Highway for Heroes*. We could all see from the slide show images that were produced, the huge admiration from a massive nation, who rightly honoured their fallen from Afghanistan in a manner they felt very proud of. When I read the article and saw the images, not for one moment did I think to myself we should do this for our fallen. The image created by the Canadians lining the route is powerful, flags waving, thousands making their presence known on bridges and along the roads; fire engines, police vehicles, the works, one nation's way of showing appreciation. However, for me, respect is not about scoring points over different communities, nor trying to out-do one another in comparing the respects shown between two proud nations. Maybe in the pressurised world of creating a newspaper story it escaped his mind this was a time of devastation and that two families had lost their sons.

So in contrast to what Mr. Almond states, that the cortège was cut up by inconsiderate motorists, then let me reassure those families whose loved ones were not escorted by the police, that this is just one journalist's perception. My own perception will differ greatly based on what I know and indeed from the images I saw produced in that particular article. The hearses were not in disarray, it was a cortège very much in the care of a funeral team who were probably the best in the land and they arrived in a dignified fashion when they entered the John Radcliffe Hospital. Yet I wonder what the families, the colleagues and friends of Lieutenant John J.T. Thornton and Marine David Marsh thought if they read Mr Almond's proud testimony; his version of events. Something only they will know I suppose. But I hope one day to share the words I have written with regard to the day their sons came home and reassure them they were recognised with so much respect. As for Peter Almond, I appreciate you have a job to do and what you wrote we had to take on the chin, but I hope you are as equally gallant when you read my own observations from that same day.

There is one area that we probably would agree; your scoop on the front page was an article that would most certainly provoke a response. I think it's fair to say on the following Monday morning we were about to find out.

CHAPTER 9

Monday morning the ripple from the *Mail on Sunday* front page story caused a reaction, I would not say a tsunami, but yes, if we hold the thread as in speaking in terms of water, throwing a pebble in calm water caused a wave. Inspector Mark Levitt got the brunt of the calls, but that was batted back to his headquarters once they realised he had communicated with the Thames Valley Police to advise them of the journalist's agenda. The calls I received were from my main points of contact at RAF Lyneham responding in a manner of disappointment, a sentiment that we all felt and shared. Though the most valued call I received that day was from my Divisional Operations Manager, Chief Inspector Phil Lowe. Phil was a great boss, he talked in a language I understood, clipped my wings when they needed trimming, he also had the most wonderful set of one liners that always made me laugh. I think he went to the 'Life on Mars Police Training Academy', some would argue he was the first recruit, but you get the picture, he was 'old school.' One thing I do know he could do, was walk the talk and he was a significant sponsor to the policing resources that came from the MDP in support of Operation Entourage. On this particular day as he was on the phone to me, no doubt chain smoking at the same time, came his opening words:

'I've seen the papers,' he always took a pause or drag of his cigarette. 'Some twenty-minute escort that nobody would notice, you said to me twelve months ago; tying up my resources every week and now front page on the Sunday papers, eh Jarra Brown.' Another pause for nicotine intake. 'Do not sign up to anything else again without my say so, do you understand?' He laughed as I could imagine him shaking his head; I knew he didn't mean it. Phil fully understood what this was all about having attended a few repatriations; the impact and gravity was never missed on anyone. Though on a serious note he did say it does look like it's catching a bit of attention up there and assigned Sergeant Mark Venning to give me direct support as my line manager, to keep the flack off my back. The call was finished with another wonderful phrase out of his book of one liners, 'You're having a good year, do not fuck it up,' then the line went dead. Needless to say Sergeant Mark Venning did make that call to arrange his visit, I could not have wished for a better chain of command, as he was another man I had a great relationship with.

Phil and I were similar in style doing things in an old fashioned way, though he earned a lot more money than me. Mark was the perfect hinge that stopped the door falling off. He was not a student from the training school inundating me with phrases full of force policy, but one who got the job done without any fuss. A very professional policeman, who knew how to play the corporate card when we needed to get a result.

So as my own chain of command within the MDP was formed, a far higher ranking officer from another force had responded to the newspaper article.

Sara Thornton CBE QPM, Chief Constable at Thames Valley Police, confirmed that unlimited resources would be found to escort the fallen through her jurisdiction. That decision created as you can imagine a surge of activity, which identified the main players who would form a plan to make the escort run smoothly. Thames Valley Police, Abingdon, Roads Policing Unit, made contact with Inspector Mark Levitt and arranged a meeting to be held at Wootton Bassett Police Station later in the week. It was confirmed at the next repatriation they would be ready, what they had not realised when they signed up just what short notice they were about to be given.

By lunchtime and so many phone calls that my mobile was glowing with overuse, the next call was about to start another flurry, as Squadron Leader Dominic McEvoy's name was displayed on my screen. You know the routine, no preamble his words from the MoD book of communication. 'Bitter news, start planning for Op Pabbay,' he was telling me as reports were coming in that two more British Forces had been killed on the same day the *Mail on Sunday* was publishing its story. Inspector Mark Levitt was updated and the meeting with Thames Valley Police was brought forward to the following morning, as they would be required to fulfil the second leg of the escort they had signed up to do.

I have mentioned that so many things during this period of time happened by fate, the same could be said for those involved in every aspect of bringing the fallen home. So many people came together from every corner of society: military, public, community and the police all complemented each other, in fact in time the whole nation pulled together to do something right. This was also my first impression when I met Sergeant Mark Ponting and Rob Langton from Thames Valley Police, Abingdon Roads Policing Unit, they had all seen what takes place at Wootton Bassett and were chomping at the bit to get involved. Both ex-servicemen, Rob served his time in the Royal Air Force and Ponters, as he was fondly called, with the Army Air Corps. Two great blokes who I feel I know now as sincere good friends. It was quite obvious at this first meeting chaired by Inspector Mark Levitt, we were all singing from the same hymn sheet. On conclusion the finer details of the escort were confirmed; we would escort as per Op Entourage to Gablecross Police Station and peel off. Ponters and Rob would organise TVP resources to escort the remainder of the journey into the John Radcliffe Hospital, under there Op Order Operation Return. With a shake of hands and contact details exchanged we went our separate ways.

As we held our meeting, the names of the two fallen were being released by the MoD confirming the deaths of Senior Aircraftman (SAC) Graham Livingstone of the Royal Air Force Regiment and Senior Aircraftman (SAC) Gary Thompson of the Royal Auxiliary Air Force Regiment.

Within a few short days the hour had arrived when SAC Graham Livingstone and SAC Gary Thompson would be flown home in the honourable style that angelic bird in the sky produced. Knowing that Station Warrant Officer Dale was at the helm of the ceremony it was no surprise to hear that the repatriation was conducted with confidence in an immaculate display of honour and respect for men who proudly served the Royal Air Force. But for five young ladies standing huddled with their mother, there was no comfort gained in that; what they wanted was their father back home with them. I read so many tributes written about these two men on how they were so loved and respected by family and friends, both of whom were from different backgrounds and in different chapters of their lives, but who both proudly served. I knew that day from the stories I read in the press that a lot of people would be hurting real bad. There was nothing any of us could do to take away their pain but I promise you we brought two fathers back with compassion and you were all in our thoughts.

This was the first time we were to drive the 46 miles as Operation Entourage amalgamated with Operation Return, to provide the appropriate police escort that these two heroes deserved. From leaving RAF Lyneham to arriving at our final destination in Oxford hundreds bowed their heads in a very British way as they mourned your loss. The old boys, yes, they were always present as we left RAF Lyneham, standing tall and saluting as we went past. Up at Bassett High Street, adjacent to the war memorial, many wearing the RAF headdress from different generations, did exactly the same. They were joined by a community who unashamedly wept in sadness enhanced with the tolling of the Tenor Bell. The escort went smoothly, how could it not, when everyone is on the same side. I'm sure Rob and Ponters saw, as we led the cortège along the Oxfordshire roads, just how much chest-swelling pride at times like this our country produces.

I want to finish the memory of this day with an article I read in the *Telegraph*.

Senior Aircraftman Gary Thompson, who at 51 is the oldest serviceman to be killed on current operations. He leaves behind, his wife Jacqui and five daughters: Laurie, 24, Aimee, 22, Jordan, 20, Jade, 17 and Kelly, 16 – who he said inspired him to serve in the war against the Taliban. He was quoted in the Rutland and Stamford Mercury as saying: 'I have five daughters, three of whom are at university. I want women in Afghanistan to be given the same opportunity that my daughters have had. It means I can come back and say I have played my part in trying to make that happen.'

Sir, from one of those who escorted you home, I salute you for your values.

CHAPTER 10

Spring moved into the summer months and sadly further calls were received from the same mobile number advising us to prepare for Op Pabbay, but through a change of personnel it was not Dominic who relayed the message, it was from a new member of the team.

Squadron Leader Katherine Rand with her own style took command of the administration of the repatriation team and was always at the front. She was once described on Sky News as 'Chief of Staff for repatriations' in what was a massive team effort both inside and outside the base. It was a title she may not accept, but as the Sky News reporter carried out a fifteen minute inside story about the repatriations at RAF Lyneham, I could see where they were coming from. Katherine was the central link for all the countless people involved – the different branches of the military, undertakers, coroners, caterers, flower arrangers, drivers and the police – for me she was my point of contact and I welcomed her to her new office. There was no settling in period, as sadly our losses continued when we would receive that harrowing call, that a further fatality of this conflict was returning home. So many names, so many stories, which all deserve recognition, but it is just not possible to write about each and every one of our nation's fallen heroes. I do hope though, that those who are not spoken of cause no distress; they have not been forgotten. The day your own very special person was repatriated home, they did return in exactly the same manner I have described, with a vast amount of honour and respect.

Every single one of our fallen was recognised; let there be no doubt in your mind, in all weathers, no matter what day of the week, the crowds continued to grow to show their respects. The national media was mainly confined to the tabloids and local news channels except when they focused on a particular angle, a statistic, or a story that they found of interest.

Not for me or my colleagues, we were never interested in statistics, or the media and their overriding story. No, for us, we never lost sight of the person or persons in the cortège; to us each was somebody who was very special to someone, who was hurting real bad. For that family member, whether a father, mother, wife, sister, daughter, husband or son, their life had instantaneously changed leaving a huge void. I also recognised that it was not just the family who had lost their precious person, but those who still served the Crown, who by now were joining the congregation at the war memorial. There were occasions when you could not fail to recognise that a particular military unit was hurting deeply too; losing multiple brothers from a regiment has got to have a massive impact. Over the years we saw this far too many times. It was on occasions such as these, that standards came from all over the country to stand alongside the people of Wootton Bassett. Members of different associations joined the standards of the Royal British Legion and you would see their Corps or Regimental standards fluttering in the wind as we approached.

This we first saw when the bodies of five Paras were returned in June 2008. The men, all from 2nd Battalion, the Parachute Regiment based in Colchester, Essex, died in two separate incidents in Helmand within a week. Privates Nathan Cuthbertson, David Murray and Daniel Gamble died in a suicide bombing. L/Corporal James Bateman and Private Jeff Doherty died under Taliban fire.

Such was the tide of change in support of our Armed Forces; towns across the country began to recognise the sacrifice their local troops were making. A prime example of this was on the Friday following the loss of the five Paras killed; the garrison town of Colchester paid tribute to them with a ceremony in their streets. Paras from the 2nd Battalion marched through the town's high street to applause from watching shoppers. Crowds gathered outside the town hall and held a two-minute silence, while a Union flag flew at half-mast. Recognition such as this will always have a massive impact on the morale of our forces and this type of acknowledgment was long overdue, but once it arrived it was greatly received.

The day we escorted those five Paratroopers home, many words and tributes were said, but a quote that was brought to my attention is so fitting in every way for those who served in the Parachute Brigade:

> What Manner Of Men Are These That Wear The Maroon Beret? They are firstly all volunteers and are toughened by physical training. As a result they have infectious optimism and that offensive eagerness which comes from well-being. They have 'jumped' from the air and by doing so have conquered fear. Their duty lies in the van of the battle. They are proud of this honour. They have the highest standards in all things whether it be skill in battle or smartness in the execution of all peacetime duties. They are in fact – men apart – every man an emperor. Of all the factors, which make for success in battle, the spirit of the warrior is the most decisive. That spirit will be found in full measure in the men who wear the maroon beret.
>
> Field Marshal Bernard Montgomery

These five men were certainly that and were truly honoured, along with so many more in the following weeks as the loss of life continued.

Whenever I watched the military ceremony from afar, when the wind was blowing in my direction, it carried with it the cries and distress. For the next of kin, the family, it was almost to the point of cruelty; the emotions on seeing their son, daughter, brother, father, or indeed wife. The same applied when Corporal Sarah Bryant was brought home in June 2008. Watching, they stood confused, numb and so many other words to describe how they were lost in a new world they did not understand. The Last Post sounded, then their own hero was brought towards them, carried by many who resembled their own loved one, yet he was on their shoulders. Then, after being gracefully placed into the hearse they were escorted away; no kiss, no cuddle, no private words could be said. Yes, they came home with a vast amount of honour, but none the less they were gone.

This is why whoever was instrumental in the construction of the Chapel of Rest at RAF Lyneham deserves recognition for their sensitivity, compassion and understanding of the needs of the bereaved family. Bringing this building into the equation of the repatriation ceremony, brought precious moments to so many people who were hurting so badly. It was a wonderful gesture when RAF Lyneham found the funds to construct this building, which was so valued by the families in their hour of need. The building on the outside was just a prefabricated structure, but on the inside it represented the church; a place where for many of us, we only go when in need of comfort and to have our faith restored. It also allowed the families to grieve or do whatever they felt appropriate, away from the prying eyes of strangers.

It was on Monday 11 August 2008 that the Chapel of Rest was officially unveiled by Air Chief Marshall Sir Clive Loader. On the same day some 3,500 miles away Signaller Wayne Bland, from 16 Signal Regiment was killed by an explosion from a suicide bomber, in Kabul, Afghanistan.

In days to come the family of Wayne Bland were to stand where all these dignitaries had stood and they were allowed to spend a private moment before he was escorted to the John Radcliffe Hospital.

Maybe the importance of this building can be better explained by Reverend Colin O'Dell who was at that time a Chaplain at RAF Lyneham:

At the Chapel of Rest, the coffins are laid in private rooms and the families are brought down. I speak to them and ask what they want from the day. This will be the first time that they've had a chance to be close to their relatives; for them to have a private time. Grief isn't a normal process and it has no normality, some may take a few minutes or it may be forty-five and that really is down to the family. There is no pressure for them to conform to our time pattern. We just go with whatever they want to do at the time. The Chapel of Rest has six private rooms and whilst there's no expressed limit on how many family members can attend, a figure of seven has become the accepted number of mourners allowed on site. In a way, that explains the numbers of family and friends who appear at Wootton Bassett, the High Street is their first chance to see their loved ones and so becomes their open air Chapel of Rest. Once families have said their goodbyes at the Chapel, they'll be given the choice of going on to Wootton Bassett, where a large crowd traditionally waits. Most families do see the North Wiltshire town as an important part of the grieving process. Invariably, it's become a hub for extended family members to meet up so Wootton Bassett provides a really important part of the whole day.

Certainly from what I observed the Chapel of Rest was an appropriate addition to the military ceremony. As we left summer and we entered into the autumn there was no relent in the loss of life in conflict; the use of the Chapel of Rest proved to be a place that was gratefully accepted for the distraught family to spend some private time. As the padre mentioned, there was never a set time that any family would spend in this sacred building and over the years we incorporated that unknown factor into our operation.

We, the police, involved in Operation Entourage or further along the route in Operation Return would always stand at the ready waiting for the time we were required to convey the cortège along the 46 miles. With the Chapel of Rest, that could not be quantified into the timings of Operation Pabbay, there was never a certainty of exactly when we would be required, yet no one complained or indeed nor was it ever mentioned, when we had gone over our duty time. To be honest if we could not give a little of our time to the families whose loved ones had paid the ultimate sacrifice, then something was deeply wrong.

During the latter part of the summer and into the start of autumn of 2008 a major change took place in the policing operation when Inspector Mark Levitt was promoted and commenced his new role at Wiltshire Police Headquarters. It can never be underestimated the input and foundation that Inspector Levitt gave to the policing operation, he was instrumental in everything that took place. Many people smile on promotion, my perception was that Mark left dragging his feet; leaving a sector he had moulded into something a little bit special. A lot of that sadness was also in leaving . . . how can I say . . . unfinished business. Something which he started and knew was to continue until the planned return of the repatriations to RAF Brize Norton sometime in 2011. I'm sure if offered the choice at the time, he would have seriously considered relinquishing his promotion, to conclude his career as the Sector Commander for Wootton Bassett.

Sometimes, a person who is so well respected by a community, when he leaves there are huge shoes to fill and you may hear the terminology the mould was broken when they made Mark Levitt. The man who had to face the challenge of replacing an exemplary Sector Commander was Inspector Steve Cox.

So Inspector Steve Cox arrived and, yes, maybe that mould was broken, but the one Coxy came from was equally as good. Coxy, not Steve, had an amazing skill in man management approach, a great character, yet you knew he was the boss. Coming from a Roads Policing background, he immediately put his own footprint onto the respects shown by adding various aspects. Operation Entourage was now in his care; he tweaked and changed a few things the same as any new boss would do, but nothing drastic. He settled in quickly with his unique personality and those people like me, who did not know him previously, soon appreciated his style. That's why whenever he requested additional resources from the MDP he was amazed at the numbers who volunteered to assist.

That request was made almost immediately a fatality was known, such was the volume of people attending to show their respects. Also the length of time they spent in the High Street was extended due to the inclusion of the Chapel of Rest, meaning that further policing resources were required.

Wootton Bassett Sector PCSOs, police officers and special police constables of Wiltshire police who were in the town, were supported by police officers from the MDP Divisional Support Groups (DSG). These officers came from Aschurch near Tewksbury, Larkhill just outside of Salisbury and Devonport, Plymouth some 160 miles away. Sergeant Mark Venning, my recently appointed Line Manager came from the South of the county in Bulford. He had a team of fourteen officers working for him, all with their own responsibilities. Many of those officers over the years also came up to support the operation, not because ordered to do so, but volunteered, reiterating again just how many did care. The word of what was taking place in Wootton Bassett had become well known locally and, occasionally, when the respects were shown a few times on national television, people took note. It was, however, most certainly recognised by the Troops on the front line and those in the Repatriation Team who had supported so many families this last year and a half. The military wanted to do something to let the Wootton Bassett Community know that they appreciated them showing respects to their fallen brothers and sisters. A card or letter to the Town Council would have been gratefully received, but no, our British forces wanted to say thank you in their own unique style.

CHAPTER 11

The military had noticed the respects shown, no one more so than the Station Commander at RAF Lyneham. Group Captain Mike Neville many a time was sighted alongside the Mayor and Royal British Legion members saluting during the minute's silence. It was that mutual respect for the support the community gave to the Armed Forces which possibly motivated him into being influential in the organisation of the appreciation parade. I had an excellent relationship with Group Captain Neville and he talked with so much pride of what the local community did week in week out as each of our fallen were returned home. He was so enthusiastic of the Armed Forces to give a reciprocal tribute to a community that had never wavered in its support. The Wootton Bassett Appreciation Parade was the name he had proposed for the event for the Tri Services – the Royal Navy, Army and Royal Air Force – to thank the people of Wootton Bassett for their recognition during the multitude of repatriations through the town.

Sunday 12 October 2008 was the date confirmed when a lot of planning would come to fruition from those serving the Crown to give the Wiltshire town a day to remember.

Word spread around so much so, that when the day arrived thousands of smiling faces lined the High Street as they were entertained by marching bands, speeches by military and local dignitaries, flyovers by a C130 Hercules and a C17 Globemaster. Such was the attention to detail and organisation, the station Padre even booked the weather; they always did tell me when I served in the Army that the Chaplaincy had a lot of clout. It was stunning blue skies and such a contrast from the sombre scenes observed so many times over these last eighteen months. Air Chief Marshall Sir Clive Loader presented a parchment scroll to the town's Mayor, Mike Leighfield, which expressed the 'Heartfelt gratitude and appreciation of the Armed Forces for the people of Wootton Bassett.'

Group Captain Neville read a message from Princess Anne praising the community. Yes, the Royals had noticed too.

Mayor Mike Leighfield responded during his speech:

'This parade is a wonderful gesture by the Armed Forces and further cements our very close relationship with them. It is a day not just for the people of Wootton Bassett but all across Wiltshire to be proud of how we support the military. Hopefully, we can serve as an example to the rest of the country.'

That last line of his brief speech was almost a challenge, but the tide was certainly turning in the relationship between the country and its Armed Forces.

The event was on Sky News and covered by the national tabloids which reached many households throughout the country. The public started to understand just exactly what was taking place in Wootton Bassett. What they did not know, however, was that the respects being shown to our fallen was rippling along the full 46 miles.

Rob Langton and Mark Ponting from Thames Valley Police were feeding back to us that they were now getting pockets of people lining their route from Gablecross to the hospital. This was quite interesting as not long after the appreciation parade I had a conversation with Group Captain Mike Neville, who wondered how long the scenes that we had witnessed in Wootton Bassett would continue, or would they in time start to dwindle.

My reply was that far from any signs of the support dwindling, it was if anything growing. The public support was like an animal which had grown legs and was now making its way along the A420 to Oxford.

Mike or 'Nevs' as he was referred to on his flying suit, wanted to witness what was unfolding in this new chapter of respect from the country to the British Forces and in particular the fallen. So, following on from that conversation, arrangements were made that he would be the front seat passenger of my vehicle, in escorting the fallen the full route when the inevitable sadness occurs.

A week or so later Katherine Rand's name lit up on my mobile phone and once again it was one of those eighty per cent bad news calls. 'Jarra, can you start planning for Op Pabbay next week, possibly Wednesday 19 November; further details to follow.'

Following that call I relayed the information which was standard practice to Inspector Steve Cox and Graham Hurst of Wiltshire Police so they could start requesting resources from their own force and request mutual aid from the MDP. I then made similar calls to Rob Langton and Mark Ponting so they could prepare the resources of the Thames Valley Police.

That evening when I went home I found myself waiting to see the scrolling breaking news at the bottom of the TV screen; it wasn't long before I saw what I already knew.

The names released twenty-four hours later were: Marine Neil Dunstan and Marine Robert McKibben both from the UK Landing Force Command Support Group, Royal Marines. Later that week my wife received a call from her sister who was quite distressed. It turned out that the fiancée of Neil Dunstan was a school teacher at her son's primary school, Holy Cross Catholic School in Plymouth.

This reflects the impact a fallen soldier had not only on the immediate family but also on those who are indirectly linked with them; in this case a classroom of primary school children in her daily care.

We returned to work on the Monday morning and confirmed with Graham Hurst that we had notified all resources required for the return of the two Royal Marines.

Katherine's name popped up on my mobile, 'Plan for three now Jarra' as a further soldier had been killed over that weekend. There were probably a few more words said than that, but by now I was tuned into the way the military got straight to the salient point. A day or so later the third soldier was named as Colour Sergeant Krishnabahadur Dura of 2nd Battalion the Royal Gurkha Rifles; he would be coming back with the two Royal Marines. She also confirmed that Group Captain Mike Neville would accompany the police as previously discussed.

By this time the repatriation of the fallen had been established, for many of us who had been involved from the start, both those at RAF Lyneham and us in the police knew what to expect. Yet down the road no matter how many times they had carried out Op Pabbay the military were focused, so much detail in the pre-op briefing and rehearsals drills carried out over and over again; that's why they always got it right.

To emphasise this attention to detail in the police operation; two further factors were incorporated by Inspector Cox. Coxy had created a five-minute PowerPoint presentation for his briefing, which covered all individual duties, Intel and details of any actions to be carried out in the event of unexpected security incidents.

The second brief which he implemented was that I would liaise with the undertakers prior to the C17 Globemaster flypast. It was an informal brief where we would exchange information, the route would be confirmed as no concerns at that time, or, if there were concerns such as the extensive roadworks on the M4, what the plan would be. The drivers of the vehicles were encouraged to keep focused and tight within the cortège as it was a long day for them, especially so close to the raw emotions. The conductor would confirm he had carried out the duty previously, if not he would be reassured as to exactly what would take place at the war memorial. Finally, the funeral director would feed back any information he felt appropriate on his return from the family brief at the Hilton hotel. This informal briefing always took place in the hangar at the rear of the terminal building where we all waited for the return of Rob Rowntree, who had not yet come back from the family brief. While we waited I received a call from the president of the Royal Marines Association, Brigadier Charlie Hobson, who informed me that 500 Royal Marines would be lining the full 46 miles. He made one simple request: when the cortège approached the vigil points along the route, could we slow down so the appropriate respects could be shown? I reassured him that his request would be executed and I would brief my colleagues in the police and the undertakers. The timing of the call was almost co-ordinated with the return of Rob Rowntree who had just parked his car in the hangar. We slipped straight into our dialogue, while the hearse drivers and conductor closed up to hear what was being said. I initiated the brief; the route was confirmed there were no concerns and I told them of the intent of the Royal Marines to line the full 46 miles and at the places they intended to stand, we would slow down. Rob confirmed the order of the hearses: senior service first, hence the Royal Marines would lead Marine Neil Dunstan, Marine Robert McKibben then C/Sergeant Krishnabahadur Dura. The feedback from the briefing he attended at the Hilton hotel included just one request. The family of Colour Sergeant Krishnabahadur Dura wished to place a white flower as per their Nepalese traditions on the coffin. There was slight confusion which maybe got lost in translation as to whether the family wished to lay flowers on all three coffins, or just their own relation. To alleviate any embarrassment the plan was drawn up so that when the hearses had been escorted by the conductor to the war memorial the drivers would then get out of their vehicles and open the rear door. They would remain standing and, once the flowers were laid on the coffin, they would secure the door and then return to their vehicles. They would remain static until the conductor paged the cortège to join the escort group at the far end of the High Street. I looked at each of the three hearse drivers who acknowledged that their orders were understood. The briefing finished and it was time to move on. For me a patrol of the external perimeter fence and park on Chippenham Road while the undertakers polished their fleet of cars.

Once parked up with a few others from Bradenstoke Village we looked up to the skies over Wootton Bassett, a dot in the sky was one we recognised while we waited for the clock to hit the hour.

Then there it was the C17 Globemaster flew over, a sight that always brought a degree of emotion with it, just by its sheer size hanging in the sky, as it so gracefully flew low to honour the return of these three men, from their very proud fighting units.

A circuit around, then the wheels hit the ground as this aircraft's engines roared announcing its arrival. The routine would never change. It was then back to the Police Station for the operational brief and a bite to eat before we returned back to RAF Lyneham.

Briefing complete, we the police escort group, formed up at the Guardroom at RAF Lyneham where we waited for the cortège to arrive. During this time we were getting confirmation from our colleagues on the High Street that the Nepalese had once again turned out in force and were congregating at the war memorial. In the Cross Keys just over the road 'Royal' were present proudly wearing their Green Berets and medals, many displaying their Commando crest on their blazers.

Once we received information that the repatriation ceremony had concluded we entered the phase where the families spent private time with their own fallen hero. The families were now present with their loved ones, the two Royal Marines in the Chapel of Rest and the Gurkha in a specially prepared prayer room to meet the requirements of the Nepalese religious beliefs.

Half an hour or so later, we were informed that the families had left the Chapel of Rest and that the cortège was now making its way to our location. The police outriders set off; the road blocks were on allowing our safe exit onto the public road as we took possession of the six vehicle package. On this occasion I was tail-end Charlie, a term I used in the Army meaning I was at the rear.

Normally I would be at the front, but on this escort I was to drive the full route with Group Captain Mike Neville, who I would collect at the war memorial after he had shown his respects.

As soon as we entered onto the public road from the RAF station there, standing on the junction was a member of the Royal Marines Association (RMA) with his standard lowered in salute. We turned left and headed to where the shops are situated in Lyneham village centre, again Royal were present but this time joined by members of the public. Methodically we drove through the village and headed towards Wootton Bassett; another group of locals who I recognised had formed at the roundabout that took us out of Lyneham with Royal in front taking the salute.

We entered Bassett High Street and stopped at St Bartholomew's Church. Standing with a Royal Marine standard was another member of this very proud organisation, and yet again not alone, as members of the public had joined him.

The conductor prepared to page towards the war memorial; this was the first time I had seen him this close up, normally I was in the lead car and would be parked up waiting for him after the respects had been shown. As he strode off with the cortège following him, it felt like his feet were synchronised to the tolling of the Tenor Bell. At his pace we rolled behind the cortège making our slow, dignified approach along the High Street.

Members of the public standing alongside the Royal British Legion and Council dignitaries who were chaperones to the Nepalese. Such contrasting colours to the sadness felt by those wearing traditional national dress and Gurkha soldiers in their best kit and medals.

On the opposite side of the road formed up en mass was the unmistakable sight of the Royal Marines Commando Green Berets. Some were still serving, but the majority were those who had done their time. Yet past and present with standards on parade, they stood with the two bearer parties who had carried their brothers home.

We halted as the Parade Marshal gave his one word of command; a High Street in Wilshire came smartly to attention. The Gurkha soldiers and Royal Marines needed no encouragement to join the Royal British Legion as they raised their arms in the salute. The minute's silence then followed when that simple word 'Down' was called out.

A pause, a silence, but we knew what was coming next as the drivers carried out their duties in preparation for a family's wish. Escorted by an Army Officer, a Nepalese lady graced us with her presence. Step by step with so much dignity displayed, she made her way to the rear hearse; a symbolic white floral tribute held so tightly in her hand.

C/Sergeant Krishnabahadur Dura this lady did you proud as she laid the floral tribute that came from her heart. Hundreds of eyes watched with so much curiosity yet all that time her composure never failed. Respects completed, a reassuring arm placed on her shoulder by the knight in shining armour, an Army officer who then escorted her back.

Once the hearses were secured, the drivers returned to their vehicles and Group Captain Mike Neville got into my car. A final bow of the head and the conductor led us away on the remainder of our journey and one that I can still see vividly to this day.

The wheels once again turned with our escort at the front resuming command out of the High Street to the M4, the green we sighted was not of the grass verges or fields, but those of the berets that formed up to salute. Along that stretch of road there must have been a Green Beret on parade every 400 metres and on every roundabout there were standards which were slowly lowered. We entered the M4 and headed east, on each bridge Royal stood to attention in the salute and down the A419 in each lay-by there were more. Next onto the A420 where there were more and where they stood locals from the nearby housing estate had come out and joined them. We approached Gablecross Police Station where Thames Valley take over the escort. As we approached we could see the slip road into the station full of police officers, this was a first. The Divisional Commander, on discovering that a band of Royal Marine brothers were standing proudly outside his Police Station waiting for the cortège, ordered all on duty to join them on the roadside.

As the cortège approached, the Chief Superintendent called his station to stand to attention. The Royal Marine brothers, on hearing the word of command, stood as one at his call. The next word of command was to salute and the Senior Police Officer and those wearing their famous Green Berets saluted as the standards were lowered, the respects were shown in unity to both who served the Crown.

The Wiltshire police escort peeled off and TVP took command for the next 26 miles where we saw exactly the same. Every roundabout, every garage forecourt and lay-by there were further members of the RMA and where they had stood for hours waiting, they had been joined by so many members of the public.

On the Watchfield roundabout that leads to Shrivenham, there must have been about 30 Royal Marine Officers from the local Defence Academy standing to attention in their Lovatt uniform and with them were members of the RMA from Poole.

At the 'final turn', as it was commonly known to those forming up just outside the Hospital in Oxford, there were just far too many to count. For me the most heart-wrenching scene was actually inside the hospital by the entrance to the morgue, with what can only be described as a guard of honour. Two rows of standards were on either side of the road, Union flag bunting was fluttering in the breeze with a large photograph of each of the three fallen. It was a sight that had a massive impact on me in the showing of so much dignity, honour and respect and one I will never forget.

Was I proud to be British? Damn bloody right I was; but even more so to have once worn the Green Beret.

Although words cannot possibly do justice to this heart-wrenching experience, I thought it important for my observations to get back to the families so that they could be aware of the overwhelming – and I really do mean overwhelming – respects shown along those 46 miles. I did not know, but hoped that it might give those hurting some comfort to know that their loved ones really did come home as heroes. I found a quiet area in the hospital grounds away from prying ears and phoned the president of the RMA. I remember the conversation so clearly:

'Charlie, PC Jarra Brown here' ... A pause as I tried to compose myself as these were words I wanted him to hear.

'Charlie, you told me there would be 500 Royal lining the route.'

'Were they not there?' was his shocked reply.

'You underestimated mate, there were hundreds more, it was awesome. It took almost two hours to get here and such were the respects we saw. If it is possible can you please somehow let the families know their loss was truly recognised.'

As I hung up I realised I had tears in my eyes as I was speaking to him; the emotions and humbling scenes we had witnessed all day had caught up with me. I may have worn the Commando beret and served in the police, but one thing I also knew and a phrase you now know – I was *not* made of wood!

I think it had a similar impact on Nevs, as he was deep in thought as we drove back to Wiltshire; so much so he got us lost in Oxford and it took us another two hours to get back. Mind you it broke the solemn atmosphere in the car when I ribbed him about being a navigator in the RAF as we made our second lap round this University city.

What this repatriation did though was raise the benchmark up to another level, because from that day on never did a fallen hero come home unnoticed for the full 46 mile route. A network of informants would warn the next vigil point to 'Get on Parade' as the cortège made progress along this journey of respect.

I have told so many mothers, widows, fathers, children, extended members of the family and indeed friends of the fallen, what we witnessed that day. You can see in their eyes the comfort it brings knowing that people genuinely did care about their loss. I also mentioned earlier that it is impossible to mention each of the fallen and the respects they were shown, but believe me when I tell you again, this is what took place on each occasion.

The *country* and this *46 Miles* recognised your loss.

CHAPTER 12

ollowing the repatriation of Marine Neil Dunstan, Marine Robert McKibben and
C/Sergeant Krishnabahadur Dura, a significant addition to the ceremony at the
war memorial developed. The Nepalese lady laying her floral tribute appeared
to be the catalyst for others in the future to bring flowers. Predominantly they were
brought by extended family members and friends, who would place a single red rose
on the roof of the hearse. It was their personal gesture of representing their love for a
special person who lay at rest in their presence for a few short moments. If the family
wished to lay a floral tribute or a personal memento on the coffin or inside the hearse,
this could be done whilst at the Chapel of Rest.

The impact on what so many observed and indeed felt when we escorted those
three men home was not lost on anyone who lined that route. Members of the Royal
Marines Association, the Royal British Legion, the RAF Police Association and so
many others, had made it known they also wished to stand at vigil points along the
route should any further loss of life occur.

This was coordinated by members of the Royal Marines Association; their point
of contact with the police was Derek Boorn a former Royal Marine and Metropolitan
Police Officer, although many like me soon got to know him as 'Blondie' a member of
the RMA Poole and District Branch. On our first meeting he explained that his branch
members would congregate at their vigil point which was the Watchfield roundabout
on the A420, just outside the Defence Academy. He made it very clear that they felt
very passionate about acknowledging all who paid the ultimate sacrifice. The journey
for this particular group would be a 200-mile round trip from South Dorset and back
and the average age was 70. These Dorset people would always be immaculate in
their attire – white shirt, Royal Marines Corps tie, beret and medals, to accompany
their demob suit, which was a blazer and grey slacks. They say behind each good
man is a better lady, well these wonderful women all proved that statement was true,
because on each of those four-hour journeys they came too. Blondie volunteered to
be the point of contact for all these organisations with the police. The information he
would then circulate was to advise everyone at the vigil points the estimated time the
cortège would pass each location. However, to make that happen he made one small
request to me during our first conversation:

'Could you let us know when you would be leaving RAF Lyneham so those wishing
to get on parade had good time to do so?' How could we possibly not. From that day
on the last thing I would do before we escorted the cortège from those gates was a
brief call to Blondie informing him we were on our way.

With less than eight weeks until the end of the year and many families across the country planning their Christmas gifts, there were many more praying for spring. For them the greatest gift of all would be the sound of the voice of their loved one as they walked home safely through their front door.

Tragically for twelve families before the end of 2008, those prayers were not to be answered. Their biggest fear had arrived – the day the notification officer delivered that harrowing message.

On the 24 November 2008 Royal Marine Alexander Lucas was killed by a blast in southern Afghanistan; he served with 45 Commando who were based in Arbroath. Three days later Royal Marines Tony Evans from Sunderland and Georgie Sparks from Essex, were killed, both served with 42 Commando Royal Marines. They died after their foot patrol near Lashkar Gah, Helmand Province, came under fire from insurgents.

On 12 December, Royal Marines Damian Davies, 27, Sergeant John Manuel, 38, and Corporal Marc Birch, 26, were killed in an apparent suicide bomb attack by a 13-year-old Afghan boy, close to the town of Sangin.

An hour earlier Lance Corporal Steven Fellows, 28, of 45 Commando Royal Marines was killed in a roadside bomb attack a few miles away.

And on 15 December, Lieutenant Aaron Lewis, 26, from 29 Commando Regiment Royal Artillery, died near the town of Gereshk when the gun battery he was commanding came under enemy fire.

The story that dominated the national news was that this conflict had stooped down to a level not many of the British public found easy to comprehend, when a 13-year-old suicide bomber became the new weapon of the Taliban.

The fact that a child could be used as a weapon when at the same time of year our own 13-year-olds are begging parents for an X-box game for Christmas, demonstrated an example of how hideous and disgusting this attack was on three men who were trying to bring stability to a country.

On 18 December, a week away from Christmas Day, the two trees either side of the building on stilts were strung with festive lights along the market town High Street. The ambience was changed for that day when Christmas was put on hold in Wootton Bassett as five young men came home from this bloody war. A thousand people or more stood silently on the streets to honour the fallen, some in the crowd clutched gifts for their families and shopping, maybe deep in thought. I know I was, for the men's families who will endure this Christmas and possibly forever more in a mist of deep sadness.

Just as it was earlier in the year when five Paras returned through the streets of Wootton Bassett, you could see the distraught emotions from many wearing the famous Paratrooper Maroon Beret. On this day those emotions were to be found on many wearing the Commando Green Beret.

As the Tenor Bell tolled, the town came to a standstill, with shops closing and members of the public, including many veterans, standing in solemn silence. The salutes were made, the standards were lowered, and as the conductor paged many were in tears as he led the cortège through. A brief pause for a minute's silence at the town's war memorial, then calm is broken as the overwhelming grief ripples through each person as they lay their flowers on the hearse. For some standing there that day and forever more, the season of goodwill will be just another reminder of when their loved ones passed away.

The following day I remember seeing a photograph in a national newspaper of the cortège as it came to a halt at the war memorial. In the middle of the High Street front and centre stood a young Royal Navy Lieutenant wearing her white hat, she was the military media officer. Her job that day was to supervise her team in capturing the images and then to pass them onto the families of the fallen. This was her first time in Wootton Bassett though she had, like many others, witnessed the spontaneous ceremony on TV on many occasions. She suddenly found out being present was a totally different experience. As a media officer in the military, it is almost taboo to be captured on film when you are actually there to report on the event. On this day, along with so many others, she just got caught up in the emotion.

Some weeks later I met the Royal Navy Lieutenant and in conversation this photograph was mentioned. She explained that as the cortège was being led by the conductor she was encouraging her photographer to get into a better position where they could capture the appropriate images. However, unknown to her, all the regular photographers and even her team knew as the cortège approaches the war memorial, out of respect, they dress back. As they dressed back she remained absorbed and rooted to the spot and quite literally, like a rabbit caught in headlights, she raised her right arm and saluted.

I wish I could recall her name but sadly I can't, but I told her, it just looked so fitting to see her standing to attention in the salute. It presented her not as the media officer doing her job, but a Royal Navy officer showing compassion for the moment four of her Royal Marines and a Commando soldier came home.

With the contacts I made within the media, I was able to get a copy of that photograph which I sent to her as a memory of the day she stood proud to serve.

Sadly, three days later, we were all back again as the conductor paged Rifleman Stuart Nash from the 1st Battalion, The Rifles, up to the war memorial where the Australian was shown the utmost respects.

It had been an awful week, in fact even less, as in a period of just six days six families were seen standing on our High Street sharing so much grief. I was certainly ready to go home that night after another very sad day.

I had just got back to the Police Station when I saw on my mobile phone that

Katherine was calling me, I was shattered and prepared for more bad news.

I have mentioned earlier whenever I saw the name of Katherine Rand light up on my mobile, eighty per cent of the time it was a call to say 'Bad news Jarra.'

As I put my ear to the phone to my surprise it was a call that came in the twenty per cent bracket. Bless her, she had found the time to see if I was OK and said in the most softly spoken voice, 'Merry Christmas, Jarra.' I replied back the same.

I realised just how exhausted I was emotionally, as I walked home under a cloud of sadness. We are not made of wood believe me, seeing that raw sadness almost week in week out was taking its toll. I never told anyone that before, being a macho man that we all like to think we are at times, in reality I quite often just used to lock down and find a quiet corner to be alone.

I strode home that chilly evening back along the High Street of Wootton Bassett knowing Karen and I would be travelling to spend Christmas with the girls, which was only three days away.

The following morning we were all packed and ready to head down to Devon for a week's quality time and the excitement of seeing the grandchildren was just what I needed. Then sadly the job mobile phone rang, it was Katherine and we were back in the eighty per cent bracket planning for 30 December.

This meant our week's stay was to be reduced, but as I played with my grandchildren Charlotte and Chloe on Christmas morning I really appreciated how lucky I was. That short break was the perfect deflection from the sadness that I knew I was going back to. The break away had given me the time to distance myself from the environment I had found myself in.

We had, as you can imagine, a pre-Op Pabbay brief before we went away for Christmas leave, hence why I had my works mobile phone with me. On my return I knew exactly what to expect.

Graham Hurst had created the op order and all resources had made their way to the Police Station for the brief; Thames Valley Police were ready and would be waiting at Gablecross.

On 30 December the crowds gathered for the last time that year to pay their respects to the final two fallen servicemen repatriated through Wootton Bassett in 2008.

It was the 61st time this year residents had stood along the roadside, heads bowed, mourning the loss of Corporal Robert Deering from the Commando Logistic Regiment Royal Marines and Lance Corporal Benjamin Whatley, of Lima Company 42 Commando, Royal Marines. And, yes, all the vigil points along the route were present and correct as Blondie confirmed after we finished their escort home.

The following day for me is the greatest evening, New Year's Eve. There is something special, the hope I feel, that fresh start, new opportunities to look forward to and as I was deciding whether to go into town or to a friend's house party I saw on the TV the

Breaking News. 2009 was hours away and already carried much of the same sadness that we saw in 2008.

It just didn't seem right to shout out loud 'Happy New Year' when somehow I knew 2009 was a year that I was not looking forward to. So for the first New Year's Eve when I was not on duty, I was in bed before the bells chimed midnight.

CHAPTER 13

With the news already received on New Years Eve that Corporal Liam Elms, from Wigan had been killed, I found celebrating the incoming year had left a bad taste, so it was for the first time in quite a few years I woke up without a sore head. I lay on the sofa and watched the highlights of the news showing the bells tolling in London and the massive firework display that followed. Unknown to me at that time a family in Plymouth were to be getting that dreaded knock on their door after an even bigger explosion killed Serjeant Christopher Reed from The Rifles when his vehicle hit an improvised explosive device (IED) in Helmand Garmsir.

A week later, on Wednesday 7 January 2009, the repatriation took place of the first two fallen heroes of this year: Serjeant Christopher Reed of the 6th Rifles and Corporal Liam Elms of 45 Commando Royal Marines. After the military ceremony and Chapel of Rest the respects were shown once again along the full 46 miles where, despite the cold winter's day, these two men were truly recognised having paid the ultimate sacrifice.

I was not to know how awful this year was going to turn out for so many more families as each month passed, but for me personally, just five days later, I was to get an insight into the impact caused when that harrowing message was relayed to a friend's front door.

It was on Sunday 11 January 2009, John Thurlow, a police officer I knew from my days working at Plymouth and a former Colour Sergeant Royal Marines, was at home.

His son Michael was following his father's footsteps serving with 42 Commando and was out on the front line in Afghanistan. He also had a daughter Laura whose boyfriend Travis Mackin, was again another outstanding young Royal Marine who was on his second tour.

John was at home on the day he received a brief phone call from one of Laura's friends to tell him that something tragic had happened. John, one of the old school like myself, believed that when things were done they should be done correctly. He could not comprehend hearing the news in this way that it could be true – especially learning it had been distributed on a social network site. Therefore, as anyone would in these circumstances, he reassured the young person, 'I'm sure that's not right.'

John pondered, deep in thought, surely that can't be right as he sat at home all alone; his wife was out at work. Then a knock at the door and his fears were confirmed when a man he knew stood before him and broke the tragic news. I cannot begin to imagine the fear it brings to a person when they see the bearer of the worst possible news approach them. Then, as the words are spoken, the harsh reality slowly begins to sink in. The man knocking at John's door was the partner of Debbie Mackin, the mother of Travis, the message he had heard earlier was actually true. Hearing through a chain of messages on the internet the traumatic news that Travis Mackin, his daughter's boyfriend, had been killed showed just how quickly news could spread at the press of a button. The news is shattering and even knowing John I cannot begin to imagine how he felt nor would I ever intrude, but I did know his own son was still out there serving on the front line.

It's an awful feeling when the war on terror leaves its footprint on your own carpet. John was frantically trying to get his thoughts into gear to deal with what he had been told so he could offer some support to his daughter.

Travis died in an explosion while on patrol in Kajaki; he was leading his team in an operation between Victor Company, 45 Commando Group, and the Afghan troops.

What started off as a ripple soon became a tsunami via the internet and mobile phones, the rumours were being confirmed. The news was sinking in, the network of close friends were being informed that it was true; their friend had been killed. One of those who learned of the tragic loss of life was my own brother Peter, a colleague of John in the Devon and Cornwall Police. After hearing the news, Peter had his own moment of reflection as the words sunk into his head.

Once the information was absorbed he picked up the phone and dialled his big brother to share the tragic news and also craving information on what happens next. We have shared many calls between the two of us, but I never ever thought it would be him breaking the news to me that we would soon be planning for another Op Pabbay. I was shocked and I could feel the loss and hurt that this particular ripple was causing; it was affecting my family and friends I had known for quite a few years.

After passing on my deepest condolences I answered the many questions he raised, but reiterated that the next of kin would receive all details first prior to us at this end.

Obviously, due to the experiences we had over the last couple of years some questions were answerable in relation to both the Operations Pabbay and Entourage; relevant information that would help with their planning to attend Wootton Bassett.

The next day at work I was not surprised to see the incoming call from Squadron Leader Katherine Rand and, once received, I passed on the information to my colleagues in the police.

I was also aware that my brother would be coming up with quite a few of our friends to show their respects at the war memorial when Travis would be brought home.

I spoke to Graham Hurst asking him to plan the escort without me. I felt it more appropriate to be standing along with my friends and show respects on this day.

As Graham was waiting for the positive responses as to who was available, we were waiting for confirmation from the RAF of the date when the next Op Pabbay would be. Normally, if circumstances allowed, the fallen were brought home within the week.

However, Travis did not come home until Tuesday 20 January some nine days later.

Sadly, in that time two more front line troops from 3 Commando Brigade were killed: Captain Tom Sawyer, 29 Commando Royal Artillery and Corporal Danny Winter from 45 Commando Royal Marines.

Having been advised by RAF Lyneham that the date was confirmed for the repatriation, I contacted my brother to find out what plans were in place for the extended family and friends of Travis to make their way from Plymouth up to Wiltshire.

The immediate family of Travis, along with his girlfriend Laura, were all staying the night at the Swindon Hilton hotel. What I also found out was that Corbin, the younger brother of Travis, would be on the same flight as his brother, as he was also serving in Afghanistan with The Rifles.

To lose a brother when you are thousands of miles away from home, lonely and isolated must have been an awful experience and one which I cannot begin to imagine nor the heartache when you had to bring him home.

Fortunately someone was able to offer support to Corbin on that flight to bring his brother home, when it was arranged for Michael Thurlow to return on his mid tour leave and fly back with him.

On the morning of the repatriation I booked on duty as normal and confirmed that officers from the Divisional Support Group would drive the front escort in my place and I would stand with my friends at the war memorial.

Once I had completed my duties I arranged to meet the extended family and friends of Travis in Lyneham. When I saw them I was drawn to the obvious distress in their faces and even two years down the line since I had become involved in the operation, it was still a sight I had seen far too often. But when it's your own suffering, words are just inadequate. I tried to explain what was going to happen but as I was attempting to do so, all I could see were the tears in their eyes. For me, trying to string a sentence together was nigh on impossible. I knew then that I had made the right decision not to escort the cortège that day.

One thing was certain, Travis was a popular lad, as was testament to the number of his friends who made that journey from Plymouth to be present when he was returned back to UK soil. As more and more of his friends turned up you could feel the love and comfort they gave each other, but amongst it also the hurt and the pain; images I will never forget.

Once all this young Royal Marine's friends had arrived at Lyneham I brought them to the Neighbourhood Policing Team Office. This was a married quarter house that had been allocated to us, a place to bring community policing back into the hub of this village. It was never planned to use this property for briefings like this, but it turned out to be perfect and over the years many were drawn to its front door for guidance on the days their loved ones were coming home.

After making the large group comfortable I was able to gather them into one room and brief them on the chronological order of events that would unfold during the day.

It was very difficult to explain to them what was about to take place over the next couple of hours or so without getting emotional, but somehow we managed and as they held each other's hands they had an understanding of what lay ahead.

After confirming the flight was on time for the flypast, PCSO Andy Singfield came down to the house. Together we escorted the group to the viewing point on Chippenham Road at the edge of the runway where they could witness the C17 Globemaster bring their friend home.

I had stood there many times before, but I knew that particular day would be very personal with some thirty plus people who I knew standing by my side.

I had briefed them and pointed to the black dot in the sky that was making its way in our direction and I explained exactly what would happen as the aircraft made its approach to RAF Lyneham. Each and every one present was transfixed watching that aircraft fly first over Wootton Bassett then over Lyneham village just to our right.

I knew the impact of raw emotion that angelic flight would bring and saw the despair etched on their faces as the daunting reality of what they were witnessing had just started to sink in. I had to walk away and find a quiet place to compose myself; it was heart breaking and it was the first time I felt the same pain they did.

Although I did not know Travis, I knew many who were close to him and seeing them hurting so much was difficult to distance myself from the feeling of devastation.

From where we stood the C17 Globemaster floated in the sky to our right and out of our sight to carry out its honourable flypast. The three families stood in front of the terminal building spellbound at the approaching aircraft with so many emotions floating around their heads. That image will never leave them and one they prayed they would never see, but with a deft dip of his starboard wing that heart-wrenching message is passed – their loved one is home.

Many people have told me over the years that this was the moment of awakening, suddenly realising that this was not a bad dream but in fact a living nightmare as they saw the aircraft approach.

They knew that inside that huge aircraft was a very precious person, a person they loved and a person who had been killed fighting in a war many of them did not understand. Many would breakdown and crumble, it was a moment where big strong men stood totally absorbed in personal emotion, unashamed at shedding tears, yet trying to comfort loved ones as they did.

With a roar of the four turbofan jet engines, those standing in the viewing area saw the aircraft climb back into their sight. Majestically it climbed and flew off into the distance as it circled RAF Lyneham flying south then coming back north for the final approach.

It seemed to go in slow motion and, with each turn of the plane, everyone's eyes followed its flight path; then it comes into land. It was so close we could see the face of the pilot as he brought their Travis home; this vivid picture of that day is so clear even now.

As the wheels touchdown on UK soil the group of friends are left in their own personal thoughts, nothing is spoken, just the sound of distress as they hug each other in desperation praying for their pain to ease.

The aircraft then taxied out of sight and, after the roar of the engines, everything returns to silence. For some thirty or so people, including myself, time was frozen, for those few short moments we reflected on what we all had just seen.

Once the aircraft was down then all the timings would be as per the Op order, so we had about a two-hour window prior to the cortège arriving at the war memorial.

It was cold and many were numb with shock and we needed to get them into the warmth of a sheltered environment; none better than the one provided by the Cross Keys public house in town, so we set off and made our way to Wootton Bassett.

This was another first time experience for me as I had never been in the town waiting, or as in this case finding myself inside the Cross Keys public house, amongst the hub of the extended family and friends of the three men returning that day. The landlady Kirsty Lambert and her staff had taken note of the many families who travelled into the town and made sandwiches and light refreshments with true Wiltshire hospitality.

This was done because Kirsty is quite simply a really nice person who wanted to do her little bit, just as the bell ringer did by tolling the Tenor Bell. It was those spontaneous acts that made this town just a little bit special. It was a genuine goodwill gesture to offer a cup of tea or coffee and a bite to eat for many who were in need of nourishment on this emotional, cold winter's day.

Once we were all secured inside the premises we each grabbed a hot drink, or for those who needed something stronger, they sought their personal tipple.

Many gathered in this small public house, the extended family and friends of the three men who were being honoured that day, military personnel in uniform were present, along with the likes of the Royal British Legion and other ex-service organisations.

There was such a feeling of support for the people who were hurting. I certainly felt that people genuinely did care for the loss of the three young servicemen. We sat in the warmth and comfort of the Cross Keys and more people arrived, many carrying flowers wishing to place them on the hearses. I was able to tell them the order the three soldiers would come back so they could lay flowers on the vehicle that carried their loved one home. That order was not done as per rank but as per military protocol, senior service will always be first, then the Army followed by the Royal Air

Force. On this particular day this meant that head of the cortège would be Corporal Danny Winter, Royal Marine Travis Mackin in the middle and Captain Tom Sawyer, 29 Commando Royal Artillery, at the rear. I realised while I was sitting in the Cross Keys that many people, in particular the friends and extended families of Corporal Danny Winter and Captain Tom Sawyer, were oblivious to events that had and would be taking place in relation to the return of their own special person. Yes, they all knew that at some stage the hearses would be halted adjacent to the war memorial but there was so much more detail. So I approached them and after introducing myself, briefed them with the same information as I did for the friends of Travis. It was important to share this information, explaining to them what had already taken place and the huge honour that would be carried out during the repatriation ceremony. I was able to reassure them that their family and friends, who were with the next of kin, were being well looked after. We knew from sad experience the next of kin on many occasions were totally drained by the time they reached the war memorial, but reassured them they were in good care. Then after the Chapel of Rest they would be escorted up to where their family and friends were standing. It was there that they could comfort each other and offer the huge support that many families craved; those are the times when a cuddle is worth its weight in gold.

It was important for them to know that each family was placed in relation to the order of march and where the three coffins would stand at rest. I told them of the significance of hearing the tolling of the Tenor Bell which would be in acknowledgement of the three men who were so special to them had arrived in the town. The conductor would then walk in front of the hearses, stop and turn to face the cortège as the drivers of each hearse would close up to him at the war memorial. The conductor would turn slightly to his right, raising his hat in respect to those who were hurting. This would be the signal for them to move towards their fallen hero, place a flower on the hearse, say a prayer or just feel close to him as he lay in his coffin.

I mentioned that time would stand still, there was no rush, there was no need to throw their flowers, and in fact they were encouraged to place them on the roof of the hearse. It was their personal moment, an opportunity to walk forward and show their love and respect for a very special person to them.

For many, it would be the first time the significance of the day would hit home, in exactly the same manner as when many of my friends had seen the aircraft approach them an hour or so earlier. The emotions would be raw and I emphasised the need for them to look out for each other. As I spoke to these people, none of whom I knew previously, they appeared to absorb the content of information in exactly the same fashion as my friends who mourned Travis.

To finish off, I was able to share my experiences of a few months earlier to explain that the full route would be lined all the way to Oxford to honour these three men they mourned. I had received confirmation from Blondie that those vigil points that stretched the full 46 miles were already manned.

From the feedback I received, I made a personal note to make sure that on any future repatriation I would do the same again. I would make the time to offer my condolences to those extended family and friends and brief them in the same manner as I had on this day.

It was emotionally draining to see so much despair in so many people I did not know and by the time I finished I was ready for the cup of coffee my brother had waiting for me. We sat together in the Cross Keys, while the ceremony took place five miles down the road at RAF Lyneham.

It would be an untruth to say we all sat in a state of depression, as mixed with the deep sadness was a great feeling of purpose and honour, even pride that these people were all here for their friend. There were the sounds of raised voices amid the typical military banter, even humour deflecting the inner emotions they were trying to keep hidden.

Periodically, people would break down in the pub, but there was never a shortage of comfort for those who needed it. While those people were being supported in the warmth, the next of kin were being well cared for by the amazing team at RAF Lyneham.

Even though on this day I was not involved in the escort, my friends in the Albins funeral team were aware this particular repatriation was close to home for me. As a result of this they gave me constant updates as each stage of the repatriation was completed. The calls flowed that day and allowed me to keep everyone updated; the ceremony has started; the next call it was completed; the bodies have been placed in the Chapel of Rest. This was always an unknown period of time during the ceremony, some families would spend more time than others inside this sacred building. As that private family grieving process was taking place we started to make our way outside to join the vast numbers of the general public who were already congregating. The bearer parties by that time had made their way up from RAF Lyneham and were forming into their six man squads. The Mayor, the Royal British Legion and their standard bearers took up their positions on both sides of the road adjacent to the war memorial. There was an ambience, a feeling of pride on seeing so many people already lining the street. The old boys who had served in years gone by, proudly wore berets and displayed their medals on their blazers. The family and friends of the three men were clutching flowers, a simple red rose but which for them carried so much love.

It was a cold, dry, winter's day as we waited; the paparazzi were forming up behind the standards, some carrying step ladders to get that one photo demanded of them by their editor. The South West news channel BBC Spotlight was present to get their coverage for that night's opening news story: 'Three Plymouth Heroes Returned Home.'

As we waited I took in so much around me as previously I had driven through in the lead escort vehicle. That was very different, you just saw a volume of faces as you made your way through the High Street; here you could feel and taste the sadness.

Then out of the corner of my eye I saw the RAF police car coming into view from the other side of the building on stilts; the old town hall. Behind them were the vehicles carrying three emotionally drained families.

When I saw the mini bus carrying the faces of friends that I knew, I approached them as they got out of the vehicle. They were all numb and I saw Corbin approach his friends and shake their hands when he recognised so many people in the crowd from his home town. Laura was carrying a teddy bear which was dressed in a combat uniform and even wore a green beret.

I had not seen Laura for a few years, I think the last time I saw her was at 'the music of the night' in Plymouth in the summer of 2006 when she was on duty with the Royal Navy Reserve. When she saw me she looked drained, she said two words 'Jarra Brown', fell into my arms crying and then gave me a really tight hug. I didn't know what to say, so I just held her and gave her a kiss on the forehead.

As I held her, I saw her mother Debbie Thurlow across the road. She was hugging her son Michael who had returned home on his mid-tour leave, or R&R as we used to call it, which had been brought forward due to the circumstances. I don't think I have ever seen a mother hug a son so tightly and bless her, she was breaking her heart.

The families were invited to stand in the same order as the three fallen were being escorted, so that once the cortège stopped their loved one would be directly in front of where they stood. In the streets, seeing people showing respects with humility was humbling. Then the arrival of the broken-hearted families raised the ambience to a whole new level. I was so proud of this community I now lived with, how they created this second ceremony was, yes, done spontaneously, but my goodness me the comfort they unknowingly gave to the families by doing this was so genuine.

Corbin looked shattered! What do I mean looked, he had to be! To bring his older brother home in a Union flag draped coffin for his mother. How does anyone deal with that at such a tender age, but he did. He stood silent, shoulders slumped, hands in the pockets of his desert combat uniform and head down. He wasn't standing with his hands in his pockets out of disrespect, Corbin was the image of a broken man. An image of someone in stark contrast to the members of the Royal British Legion who were from a generation who were taught to show the stiff British upper lip, compared to a kid whose generation were not afraid, nor ashamed to bare their soul. This young man was saying loud and clear he's my brother and I'm hurting real bad.

I know which band I was in and especially if it was my brother. I tell you this Corbin, I would have been hurting just as much and have been just as broken as you were, I could not begin to imagine that pain.

Sometime later I spoke to Corbin and from what he told me, my observations were not too far wrong as the words came out of his mouth loosened by a couple of beers:

'I will never forget as I got off that mini bus in the middle of Wootton Bassett, I saw the faces of so many I knew, greeting and shaking friends and family's hands who had come all this way up for the repatriation; I found it really bizarre. My brother has died in Afghanistan and it's as if I am in deep shock and utter disbelief. To me my actions were so confusing and not of one who has lost not just his older brother, his role model, but also his best friend and, yes, there I stood as the hearse neared, shoulders slumped, hands in my pockets not in disrespect, honestly Jarra, I was fucked.

That's how I remember the events Jarra and how I felt from the moment I stepped off the plane. I felt so awkward and not right that I'm coming home and my brother isn't, the regret and guilt I had felt. Wondering how to confront my family and friends knowing that he was the better man and superior brother, it should not of been me there alive, but it should of been reversed. Honestly mate it should have been me in that wooden box, and Travis there to be strong for my family.'

As Corbin stood amongst his friends I saw Debbie Mackin their mother who looked as if her life had been drained from her. She was grey, standing on a planet she no longer understood, as family and friends stood around her offering their support.

If I tried to describe the pain that I saw I would be doing an injustice to a grieving mother, because no matter what was visible on the outside, it could be nothing like the trauma beneath the skin. I did not know Debbie Mackin and felt even standing in close proximity that I was intruding in her grief and forgive me if I was wrong for not offering my condolences, but I quite simply did not know what to say.

It's strange when you are so focused you become oblivious to everything around you, but it was the silence that woke me out of my trance. I had not even noticed the traffic had stopped and amongst that eeriness the tolling of the St Bartholomew's Tenor Bell sounded. I woke up, the cortège was in town, and standing with the families I almost felt as if it was wrong so I moved back discreetly to find a place of safety; I was well out of my comfort zone. It was so silent you could almost hear the footsteps of the conductor as he approached.

As he got closer the atmosphere was full of so much respect, so much honour and dignity, the love was immense and with it the heartache as the emotions were being released. The voice of the parade marshal, Maurice Baker called the Royal British Legion to the salute and the standards were lowered.

The conductor tipped his hat in recognition of that respect and, on reaching the war memorial, bowed his head in acknowledgement of what the monument stood for.

There in front of us were the three coffins all draped in the Union flag of our proud nation and for that brief moment, there they remained. Friends, families and loved ones all overwhelmed by their presence broke down and offered what comfort they could to each other. Those who wished to, walked up to the hearse and laid a flower. I have witnessed crying, hysterical screaming, but the raw grief and pain I saw at close quarters this day was an experience I never wanted to repeat; it was awful, truly awful, to see so many in so much pain.

The conductor remained still watching all that was unfolding before his eyes, as he saw wave after wave of broken hearted people approach the three hearses.

As the last person stepped back having shown their love to their fallen hero, he once again tipped his hat and slowly stepped away from the war memorial with his cortège following his lead. Once the escort and cortège coupled as one, the wheels slowly turned as they continued on their journey to the John Radcliffe Hospital.

Maurice Baker brought the salute down and dismissed his parade; many of the family made their way into the Cross Keys where Kirsty and her marvellous team had prepared refreshments for the next of kin.

I was just about to set off back to the Police Station to get changed out of my uniform because after the emotions I had seen and felt that day I was ready for something a little stronger than a cup of tea, when Stuart Harrison, the photographer for the *Swindon Advertiser* approached me.

'Jarra the girl you greeted off the mini bus,' he said tilting the viewing screen of his camera for me to see. Stuart showed me the image he had captured. 'That's Laura isn't it?'

I confirmed that it was and saw the heartbroken face clutching her commando teddy bear.

The image was personal, yet at the same time spoke a thousand words; a picture that was going to be the front page story of his tabloid. Stuart had in his own words captured the image that his editor had craved for and later it was awarded recognition in a national photograph competition.

We all have to accept at times that the media have a job to do, sometimes that job can be perceived as intrusive, but I was grateful that he had the compassion to ask me to approach Laura and ask if she was comfortable with it. Laura also appreciated Stuart's compassion and gave her consent for the photograph to be used.

Seeing that image had a massive impact as it captured so much emotion that even now as I close my eyes I can still see it.

I really was glad of that slow walk back to the Police Station, sometimes the best company is your own and this was one of those moments. I dragged my heels getting changed out of my uniform, then made my way back to the Cross Keys along the same

High Street where less than an hour ago so much emotion had poured.

As I walked back the only indication that the ceremony had taken place were the newly placed flowers on the war memorial. I briefly stopped to read the messages. After reading them and digesting the words I was now ready to join those who shared the odd glass or two of port, where many a toast was being made in memory of three outstanding men.

It had been a very long day for them all, emotionally charged, probably like no other day any of them had previously experienced, or would want to again, but between them all they were there for each other and get through it they did. Once the decision was made to start the journey back home to Plymouth our goodbyes were said and I walked home totally drained.

The following day, the front page story in the local newspaper the *Swindon Advertiser* showed the headlines which read something along the lines of 'The True Face of War.' The image captured of Laura tightly clutching her commando teddy bear as her tears flowed, dominated the front page.

On 29 January I went to Plymouth for the funeral of this outstanding Royal Marine Travis Mackin. I came to learn he was so outstanding through the tributes I read from the men who served with him on the front line.

These are just a few of those words and remember as you read them they are talking about a young man who had just turned 22, a character without a doubt but also a dedicated and focused Royal Marine so proud to serve the Crown.

Sergeant Lee Collins said:

'They broke the mould when they made Travis. His energy and enthusiasm for life knew no bounds; he was the biggest bag of morale I have ever known in the Corps, always smiling, always laughing. Always looking for a new pet, Travis befriended cats, dogs, snakes, spiders and was raising two chickens in the FOB (Forward Operating Base). Travis was always willing to go further, carry more, and do his bit and then a bit more. He died doing the job he loved. The Corps will be a much quieter place without him.'

Major Nigel Somerville said:

'A talented, popular and exceptionally courageous individual, Marine Travis Mackin died supporting his colleagues in the face of hostile enemy action. Brave, calm and always measured under enemy fire, Travis was synonymous with leading his team from the very front to support his colleagues around him. This is how he died and how he will always be remembered. The dedication, loyalty and pure courage shown by someone so young is truly humbling.'

Company Sergeant Major, Victor Company, Robert Millman said:

'Marine Travis Mackin was a true Marine; his sense of humour intoxicated all around him, and even when put in extreme situations, he could lighten the moment with a practical joke. He even arranged for Santa Claus to visit his Sergeant Major on Christmas Eve, a feat still unsurpassed by others – he will be in my good books forever. He was an inspiration to all young Royal Marines in the way he conducted himself on operations and at home. He will be sorely missed by all the Men of Victor Company Group and throughout the wider Royal Marines. The thoughts of all the men of Victor Company are with his family at this time of extreme grief.'

The funeral, as you can imagine from so many powerful words spoken, was a fitting ceremony for the young Royal Marine, but as I have previously stated, behind every good man is a wonderful woman. For Travis Mackin that wonderful woman who was always there for him was his mum.

CHAPTER 14

To Debbie Mackin, Travis was her eldest son, a brother to Corbin and Milo and it is fitting the mother who brought this hero into this world has the opportunity to tell us about the other side of her beautiful boy, who was born on the 9 December 1986.

This is her story:

Yes, while living up in the Wirral area of Merseyside, a cute little bonnie baby with long dark brown hair, weighed in at 7lb 7oz on the 9 December 1986 and the name we had chosen 'Travis' an unusual name suited this little bundle of joy.

Over the early years Travis developed into his own character and became a polite well-behaved child. Was Travis a shy boy? No, not at all, he had good social skills and would talk to anyone. He was reading and writing before he started full time schooling and he had a passion for all sports, reading and the outdoors were his joys. Travis was never a 'day dreamer' just the opposite, he was a very energetic child who was quite boisterous at times; he liked a challenge, with a mind of his own he was focused and could be quite stubborn.

For a child of such a young age, he was very particular with his appearance; his hair always had to be immaculately groomed, his shoes had to be shining and his shoe laces had to be a certain length and if they were to trail he would refuse to walk. His dress code had to be smart, his school tie had to sit with a perfect knot and he never liked getting his hands dirty.

By the time Travis reached his teens some of his little traits changed; he became very competitive, he grew a stronger personality; mischievous, humorous, opinionated, loving, caring and was classing himself as a 'free spirit' never to be a follower, only a leader. He lived by his strong adopted family values, principles and morals, but also pushed home boundaries because of his beliefs. Travis went through high school achieving his academics and during his A-levels was when he decided to leave school to join the Royal Marines.

Travis joined the Royal Marines on the 5 July 2004. He was 17 years of age, baby faced, slim and was one of the youngest of 53 new recruits; all of mixed ages, who were a part of an 880 troop. Travis described his marine training as sheer gruelling – hard work, mentally and physically. During his training I was always his first port of call when things were getting a little tough or he was running on empty and needed a little support emotionally.

March the 18th 2005 soon came around, as it was the day Travis passed out as a Royal Marine gaining his Green Beret or another word he used was the 'Green Lid.' Travis looked rather handsome and dashing in his uniform; he was as proud as punch, not only to receive his green lid, but also to find he was one of only 12 recruits that passed out, when they started with 53. Throughout Travis' training I had every confidence in him passing out because he was NEVER a quitter and had an inner belief not to be beaten.

Travis becoming a fully-fledged Marine meant he was away from home for quite some time, though when he came back I did see a massive change in him, not just physically but also in his personality, he had become quite macho and also a lot cheekier. He was nearly reaching six foot in stature, his shoulders were a lot broader and his muscular physique was well defined. Oh and his smile just got a whole lot bigger and being a Marine was just right up his street.

Over the five years Travis spent as a Marine he always looked smart going off to work all suited and booted. He worked hard, played hard and always maintained he would be part of the Special Forces by the time he was 25 years old. I didn't doubt for a second that he wouldn't achieve his goals.

Travis, being the eldest sibling, was mostly competitive with Corbin 17 months younger, not so much with Milo the quieter one, who, being six years younger than Travis, is the youngest of my three boys. Corbin is also a cheeky chappy and was just as mischievous growing up but wasn't as boisterous. Corbin also enjoyed challenges hence why he eventually joined the Army '1 Rifles' and worked alongside the Royal Marines. Travis focused more on Milo with his academics and was always supportive and pushing him to do well academically, which Milo has achieved. Growing up together Travis was quite bossy and over protective towards his brothers but only wanted the best for them. The bond they created between them was one not to be beaten; no one could break the closeness and understanding all three of them had gained as brothers.

Raising my three gorgeous boys single-handed certainly didn't go without its challenges. Yes, we have been through hard times, emotionally, mentally and physically; with some lows but just as many highs as any family would experience.

My boys are my world and despite the obstacles, I have always considered the four of us a strong family unit.

September 2008 Travis was deployed for the second time to Afghanistan and soon to be followed in October 2008 by his younger brother Corbin who was out there on his first tour.

The day Travis left he said to me in his humour:

'Mum if anything happens to me make sure I'm cremated as ya know I don't like spiders and I want *Staying Alive* by the Bee Gees played at my funeral.'

I shrugged his comment and said, 'I'll be seeing you in February my boy.'

While both of my boys were serving overseas in the north and south regions of Afghanistan, I tried not to think about the fact that they were both living and fighting in a war zone that was classed as the front line. Air blueys (airmail) from Travis and Corbin often dropped through my letterbox, which always put a smile on my face, and the non-frequent phone calls kind of reassured me they were doing OK. As each day passed my home was rather a quiet place to live, I thought about them every day and Milo and I were missing their presence immensely.

Christmas 2008 was soon approaching and I decided to buy and wrap only stocking fillers for Travis and Corbin with the best intentions of treating them to something more luxurious on their return in February. A week before Christmas I had a really weird feeling, I became sweaty, felt a little weak and anxious due to the fact I had this terrible thought; one of my boys was not going to come home. For the life of me I cannot tell you where this feeling came from, but I soon pulled myself together and kept myself busy to pass this awful feeling. The festive season came and went and I must say Christmas was not the same for Milo and I without Travis and Corbin at home, their cards and presents under the Christmas tree a clear reminder they were absent.

January 2009 arrived and it was getting close for my boys to return to the UK for their R&R (rest & recuperation). I was rather excited with the thought that my boys would be returning home soon and we would all be a family again. On Sunday 11 January I decided to do an agency shift on Lynher Ward at Derriford hospital where I normally work as a staff nurse. At that time I was not a familiar face to this ward; the morning shift was going well and some of the elderly patients were asking me lots of questions with regards to my family life. They were quite intrigued when I replied that I had not only one but two sons fighting in Afghanistan.

'How do I cope with that situation?' one asked.

With a huge grin I replied, 'I try to stay positive.'

At 10:05am someone telephoned the nurse station to ask if I was working on that ward. I thought at that point I was going to be moved to another ward around eleven o'clock, which was often the case. At 10:15am a lady in civvies approached me on the ward and told me two gentlemen were here to see me and waiting in the nurse's staff room; she didn't give anything away.

I walked into the staff room with a smile, looked at these guys and asked them twice 'What can I do for you?' But before they could reply I started to realise what I was looking at, two men, one wearing black with a white collar around his neck the other wore a Green Beret. As seconds passed on the clock I started to realise something wasn't quite right. I yelled, 'Something has happened to my boys or one of them . . . which one?'

My words became a little mumbled and within seconds my hands reached my head, my heart felt as if it was pumping outside my chest. I was perspiring and going into panic mode, my blood pressure felt as if it was dropping to my boots, I felt nauseous and my legs gave way and I fell to my knees. The man wearing the Beret was a Marine Major who stood up and told me Travis had been killed by an IED (improvised explosive device) and Corbin had been flown from his territory to be with Travis. I kept repeating, 'You've got the wrong man' only because I had spoken to Travis the night before, therefore, I couldn't see that his death was a reality. The man in black with the white collar was a navel padre who tried to comfort me as the reality started to kick in. Within minutes my whole world collapsed around me and it felt like the floor beneath me had opened and swallowed me into this dark hole, feeling totally in despair, disorientated and traumatised.

Two hours later I returned home; the Major and the Padre came with me to tell Milo the sad news; his oldest brother had been killed. Within minutes of arriving home I had a phone call from Travis' best friend Lloyd; I was reluctant to answer but I did. Lloyd was quite reserved as he asked me innocently, 'Has anything happened to Travis, he's OK isn't he?' I told him the scenario, he screamed 'No' at the top of his voice . . . To this day I still think of his reaction.

That same morning I also had a visit from a Marine welfare officer by the name of Stuart Mason. Stuart was assigned to us for eighteen months. Stuart was my rock; he had such empathy and fantastic listening and organisational skills. His timing on everything I had to organise and deal with was spot on.

The day arrived for us to attend RAF Lyneham for Travis and Corbin's return to the UK. Corbin was accompanying his brother something he had done from the moment Travis was killed. I can't imagine how Corbin must have felt spending nine long days with his brother, then bringing him home in a wooden box.

I remember clearly standing with my head held high and holding a large red rose waiting patiently for the aircraft to fly in and land. I could see the aircraft at a distance, what a feeling of pride I felt for my gorgeous boys as the aircraft flew by with its roaring engines. The aircraft landed and Travis was brought onto the tarmac and put into the awaiting hearse. My head dropped, my heart pounded, I couldn't speak, and the tears dripped and all I wanted was to hold my boys and tell them how much I loved them. Once Travis had left the runway we were then escorted to a room within the terminal to see Corbin. Boy I sure was pleased to see him. Corbin's face was tanned and his hair was really long; quite blonde in colour. He just smiled but showed no emotion. From Lyneham we went to a small Chapel of Rest to spend a short time with Travis.

Moving onto Wootton Bassett, sitting in a mini bus we entered the High Street, but by this time I was pretty much in another world physically, emotionally and spiritually. I stepped off the bus, still holding my rose, to be completely overwhelmed as I saw hundreds of people who had taken the time out from their busy daily lives to line the streets in order to pay their respects to Travis. I could see lots of familiar frozen-looking distraught faces between the crowds. The hearse that Travis was travelling in slowly approached and my rose I had held so tightly before now in left my hand was now ready to be placed on top of his hearse. At this point it felt like my heart had stopped beating I couldn't breathe very well and I cried like a baby... many other flowers from mourners had also been placed on the bonnet and roof of the hearse. I met lots of people on that day from family members, friends, including strangers, all of whom were supportive and passing on their condolences. This was where I briefly met a lovely kind policeman called PC Jarra Brown.

Although our visit to Wootton Bassett was short and, under the circumstances rather traumatic, it was rather humbling too. I cannot thank everybody enough from Wootton Bassett for their support and hospitality. I wouldn't have wanted Travis' repatriation to have taken place anywhere different.

I returned to Plymouth from Wootton Bassett and two days later Travis had also arrived back in Plymouth. Going off to see Travis without telling my welfare officer was not a good move. Seeing Travis lying in his casket for the first time at the Chapel of Rest was frightening as I didn't know what to expect having no knowledge of his injuries. For me personally, Travis did not look like the same boy. His face seemed a different shape, his left leg was missing and he had also severed his left arm. His hair was rather long and he had too much make up applied by the mortician. I was horrified to see Travis in that awful condition and I was not prepared. I guess I was in denial and was expecting to see my first-born all intact and unblemished. Overall, despite the discrepancies, in a weird kind of way Travis was still my boy and he still looked dashing in his blue uniform.

At first I was reluctant to hand over his blue uniform, as I wanted to keep it. It is Royal Marine tradition for the deceased Marine to dress in their No 1 uniform and I couldn't deny Travis that privilege; after all he worked so hard to achieve what he had accomplished and so deserved being a Royal Marine. This was certainly a big reality check for me that Travis was never coming back home in the flesh to be a part of the Mackin household.

I never slept much after visiting Travis and spent many hours during the following days preparing for his funeral. On the day of Travis' funeral the attendance overspilled St Andrew's Church. Yes, more than 500 people attended. All I can say is WOW! What a turnout. Travis' wake was no ordinary wake as we kind of threw a party with over 300 guests at the Duke of Cornwall. By the end of the night I think most people were a little drunk to say the least, all mixed up with thoughts of sadness and happy times spent with Travis. His closest friends and family gave speeches and sang independently. Corbin couldn't help himself by stripping off on stage, performing as he does to the Bee Gees classic of 'Staying Alive.' Travis had a fantastic send off and along with his 'only' two wishes, both of which were granted, I know he wouldn't have wanted his funeral organised in any other way.

Since Travis passed away no changes have been made apart from moving house less than a quarter of a mile. Travis' clothes still hang in his wardrobe, his much-loved books are still on display along with his skiing equipment and his Christmas stocking fillers remain unwrapped. A briefcase stands on his bedroom floor which holds the abundance of condolence cards, letters, media clippings and Travis' personal belongings such as passport, iPod, wallet, cash etc. including a clipping of his hair. Many photos and memorabilia of Travis are displayed in every room of the house. His ashes remain in the base of a statuette which sits very proudly alongside his Marine cap in the living room. Travis' 'Green Lid' and medals are mounted again proudly on the wall with other parts of his kit.

Six years on we as a family are still traumatised by the loss of Travis and we find it totally impossible to ever regain normality as our lives have never been the same since. As his mum the pain I have suffered and still feel, is inarguably hard to describe, and the emotion that runs so deep within my heart as my heart bleeds. Many times I have felt totally in denial of his death and had visions of him walking through the door. The daily sadness I feel I'm sure shows upon my face and my behaviour; I often feel I want to be alongside him so that he's not alone. I so wish we could bring him back into our lives not only for myself but for Corbin, Milo, his closest friends and for all that knew him because Travis, along with his groomed hair, huge smile and character leaves such a massive void. There is never a day goes by I don't think of him. I cannot get it out of my head what Travis has lost and what he will never experience or achieve again. Memories of good and bad, regular reminiscing, work commitments and the often-played 'Staying Alive' still plays a part in disrupting my day.

As Travis is loved beyond words, missed beyond measure, I know he'll be walking beside us today and forever ... but underneath our skin we are a broken family living without him.

For those that say it will get better in time then Jarra they lie my friend, they lie, they truly do not understand and for all that accept my words – thank you for keeping my oldest son's memory alive.

CHAPTER 15

The last death of a British Serviceman serving in Iraq brought attention to the hidden enemy – the trauma of mental health. Alarm bells throughout the Ministry of Defence were sounding very loud to the fact the last three soldiers that died in Iraq were from gunshot wounds with no evidence to suggest that anyone else was involved.

Private Ryan Wrathall serving with the Princess of Wales Royal Regiment was found dead on the 12 February 2009. In December 2008, two British servicemen died at the same base from gunshot wounds which are thought to have been self-inflicted, Lance Corporal David Wilson, serving with 9 Regiment Army Air Corps, died from a wound on 4 December. Corporal Lee Churcher died a week later.

This huge concern about the trauma of mental health at the time of the last soldier returning from Iraq activated an unprecedented 'suicide watch' which had been launched by commanders at Britain's main military base in Iraq. An investigation was launched to discover whether the soldiers who died from self-inflicted gunshot wounds were suffering from Post-Traumatic Stress Disorder (PTSD).

Following the third death in February, commanders launched a poster campaign calling for troops to keep a close watch on colleagues who appeared to be exhibiting suicidal behaviour, mood swings and symptoms of PTSD. One of the posters stated: 'Never let your mate fight alone. Worried about someone in your team? Be willing to listen. Not all wounds are visible.' The posters then called on troops to: 'Talk to your medical officer, Padre . . . Tell someone in your chain of command.' Another poster adds: 'Never accept defeat. Getting help is a sign of strength. No soldier stands alone. Your medical officer or Padre can help. Talk to someone in your chain of command.'

Although it is possible that the wounds may have been self-inflicted accidentally, sources at the base believe all three were suicide. Suicide is a recognised symptom of PTSD and many former servicemen who have seen active service have taken their own lives. At least 15 military personnel are believed to have taken their own lives after serving in Iraq and more veterans of the Falklands War have committed suicide than were actually killed in the war. I found that statistic staggering. We can only hope that lessons have been learnt and those suffering from PTSD do not have to suffer in silence. It is imperative they get the support they deserve as they should not have to rely on charities for that help.

Between February and the end of May, 24 further British Servicemen had been killed and with each loss of life brought recognition to our fallen like never before. With the public, came the media who would report on these sombre occasions; with the fallen, came their heartbroken family and friends. It was not unusual to see a contingent from a community attend and each did their hero proud. There were of course those who were still serving who stood smartly in uniform; they really did understand what a loss of life meant to them. The impact was massive on every corner of our country – Liverpool, Nottingham, Yorkshire, Cornwall, Plymouth, Lincolnshire, Lancashire, North and South Wales, Somerset, Gloucestershire, Oxfordshire, London, Norfolk, Scotland and Ireland. And on each sad occasion those communities made the journey down to that small market town in Wiltshire which was becoming a representation of respect to our nation's fallen heroes.

But there were not only soldiers from the home counties serving our proud nation, as part of the British Army we had Gurkhas and Fijians too. Amongst those who died was Corporal Kumar Pun 1st Battalion, The Royal Gurkha Rifles and Fusilier Petero Suesue, 2nd Battalion, The Royal Regiment of Fusiliers.

It was a time of much change to the small market town as the media interest intensified. Both Sky News and BBC News became regular attendees as well as the national tabloids, all initially focusing their attention on the people of Wootton Bassett.

It seemed almost weekly you would see an interview in the local and national newspapers from the newly elected Wootton Bassett Mayor Steve Bucknell, or Anne Bevis talking on behalf of the Royal British Legion.

The media attention also brought along with it resentment; some were using the word circus, as all the cherry pickers and telescopic TV cameras were set up early in the morning to gain the best advantage spot. It did shock some people, even Chris Wannell a member of the Town Council was quoted as saying: 'It took away the dignity of the tribute. The silence of it all is very important. With so many journalists there it was no longer a silent affair.' Many felt that the tone of the reporting was wrong and there was a growing concern that what had been a modest acknowledgement of the fallen was being hijacked by the media and turned into something quite different.

I recalled a conversation with Katie Stallard of Sky News over a cup of coffee in a side street café during which she mentioned the 'under the breath' whispers she heard as certain individuals walked past. Mutterings of people chuntering 'disgraceful have you no respect', an individual's perception that the reporters were intruding on their High Street with all the cameras.

Those people muttering had the right to voice their opinion, but I wished they could have looked at the situation holistically; for the positives this coverage had for the family who had lost a loved one that was coming home in a wooden box.

Many of those young men and women had families who were elderly, maybe even disabled or frail, or due to circumstances were unable to travel and be present; for example when their grandson came home. But due to the media coverage they could witness the huge honour that was being shown on the television in their front room.

Also the comfort for some that this news coverage could be saved and shown again for example to a child so small they were oblivious when it happened that they would never know their father. Also something the public did not know was that both news channels often used to send me copies of the coverage they had taken and recorded onto DVDs so they could be sent to the family via the Visiting Officers. It was not possible to do this for each family but for some we were able to and the letters they sent back all began with words similar to 'Thank You.'

Many families avoided the media on the day which was very understandable, but never did I see or hear of them being harassed. Some even wanted to stand tall and proud as they told the world about their husband, just as Christina Schmid did in November 2009.

What better platform for her than live on the National News and why not? Just look what this one man had done in saving so many lives, by doing his job with skill and determination while staying focused in appalling heat and conditions. Staff Sergeant Olaf Schmid, 30, of the Royal Logistic Corps, was a British soldier responsible for making safe 64 bombs during five months in Afghanistan. He died as he tried to defuse another.

His wife, Christina, said: 'She had lost her soul mate. Oz was a phenomenal husband and loving father who was cruelly murdered on his last day of a relentless five-month tour. The pain of losing him is overwhelming. I take comfort knowing he saved countless lives with his hard work.'

So for me stories that were spoken from the heart deserved to be heard and well done to the journalists and news reporters for doing so in a manner that did not, in my opinion, intrude but paid a fitting tribute to these fallen heroes.

If I was critical of the media it would be to say they should be reporting on each and every one of the fallen as they returned home, not due to a story about the volume of fatalities or, dare I say, that a female had been killed.

With so much attention being focused on this small town due to the repatriations being on many occasions beamed out live to the world, could we be seen by some terrorist organisation as a legitimate target?

Well those concerns were raised at the right level. The risks were continuously being assessed and reviewed by the appropriate agencies. The findings were that we were a low risk, but a decision was made to execute a reassurance search of the area in and around the High Street and the vicinity of the war memorial prior to each ceremony.

This once again required further police resources including the specialist search dogs. Due to the volume of repatriations, dogs needed to be resourced and there was never a shortage of offers to support the policing operation. The MDP had the dogs required. One of those to regularly attend was PC Dai Williams such was his fondness of the community. When he retired from the police he linked in with the town council as their CCTV operations manager. Other forces heard of the assistance that would be gratefully accepted and at no cost travelled from forces such as Devon and Cornwall, Cheshire, Avon and Somerset; even the prison service contacted Wiltshire police volunteering to support the Operation.

Although we were always briefed on current intelligence in relation to terrorism and had plans in situ in the unlikely event, I think many of us were surprised when three British Islamic extremists, including a Muslim convert originally from Dorset, were jailed for terrorism in 2013.

Richard Dart, the son of teachers from Dorset, and his co-conspirators, Jahangir Alom and Imran Mahmood, were sentenced at the Old Bailey for engaging in conduct in preparation of acts of terrorism.

They admitted the offence, which took place between July 2010 and July 2012.

Former BBC security guard Dart discussed bomb making with Mahmood and the town of Royal Wootton Bassett, which had held repatriation ceremonies for several servicemen and women, was marked as a potential target.

Dart was jailed for six years, Alom for four years and six months and Mahmood for nine years and nine months. If those three were hostile then the presence of friendly forces was soon to make an appearance in late spring/early summer of 2009.

This unique group of people who made their grand entrance and which for many enhanced the occasion, was the Royal British Legion Riders who were motorbike enthusiasts.

They are predominantly ex-service personnel and between them have raised thousands of pounds for military-related charities each year, but to the naked eye some of them looked rather scary.

Initially many of the public did not recognise the rig they wore, some just saw a big motorbike amongst many more, but when they looked closer they could see they proudly wore on their bike leathers, badges displaying who they served with during their military careers.

I've reviewed video footage and I was unable to establish exactly when they started to form up on parade for want of a better word. They certainly were not present in January when Royal Marine Travis Mackin came back, but between spring and summer of that year they started to congregate. During this period of time they were seen initially in small groups and, like their foot soldiers of the Royal British Legion, their representation grew in numbers – 20, 30, 40 or more, many carrying pillion passengers.

They would park their highly polished motorbikes at the rear of the old town hall, the building on stilts. They lined them up side by side parallel to the footpath running all the way to the rear of the war memorial.

Like the Royal British Legion had their media officer, the riders had their own; he was Steve Blundell or known by his members as 'Big Steve.' Just like Mrs Bevis, he was also very proud of his organisation and was not shy coming forward to express his views in front of the camera. Strangely enough they both had similar titles for the spontaneous ceremonies that took place at the war memorial, introducing themselves to be the Royal British Legion Repatriation Liaison Officer and in the case of 'Big Steve' he added the word Riders into his title. And liaise they did, with the many families who made their way to Wootton Bassett.

There was a period during that summer that I took a step back and was quite concerned that some people attending were losing touch of what the reality was. Their focus seemed to be on getting on the TV or flying their own personal flag. Maybe they had become blasé; seen the draped coffin so often that it had no impact anymore. What is the word to describe this behaviour? Pride maybe? As it is the antonym to humility that I saw long before the press arrived, I do not know, but I did think some, not all, lost direction.

For me, I can honestly say I never lost sight of what the impact was on my brother and friends when Travis was killed. Having that picture on my office wall of Laura Thurlow, made damn sure this copper was not going to become blasé.

I heard the rumblings amongst individuals and it was not only the journalists who upset some of the town's people. I understood some genuine concerns, but to hear complaints that clapping and throwing flowers did not fit into what some considered the British way of showing respect, seemed to me so narrow minded.

If the friends and family wished to express their grief, love and emotion in that manner then, seriously, what was the problem with that?

Something else that caused concern was the clamour to have the town and its people honoured in some way. Many thousands of people have signed a petition supporting a campaign launched by a former soldier from the north east of England to rename the High Street the 'Highway for Heroes.'

Another suggestion, again from outsiders, is that the town ought to be known as 'Royal Wootton Bassett.'

Yet a third idea was to give the place some sort of medal, perhaps a George Cross. Many of the townspeople found such ideas a little dramatic and most certainly ill-timed.

So the council leader, Mayor Steve Bucknell, MP James Gray and the president of the local branch of the British Legion, Maurice Baker, wrote to the national papers asking for restraint from the media – and dismissing the idea of the town receiving any formal accolades.

'We are proud that in a way we stand proxy for the grief of the nation,' they wrote. 'But we are simply the ordinary people of a very special town standing still and quiet for a few moments in a mark of sorrow and gratitude for those who have given their lives.'

The letter goes on that the town is 'proud that the national media has broadcast our moment's stillness to the world' but adds: 'We would be grateful for slightly less intrusive media coverage in the future.'

It continues: 'We welcome visiting generals and senior politicians if they would like to come and simply mingle with the crowds, but we'd prefer no pomp, nor militarisation. It's the people of the town; no more or less than that.'

When I saw that letter, I thought there would be repercussions as the wording could easily be misconstrued that generals were welcome but the foot soldiers were not.

That last passage did, as I believed, have a knock-on effect as after that letter some troops who proudly wanted to stand in their uniform, combats or best kit and medals would still do so. If that meant standing at the other end of the High Street, then there they would stand and that's exactly what happened the week after that letter was published.

The letter concludes: 'We'd also much prefer that there was no further discussion of any recognition for what we do, or at least not until it's all over and that happy day has arrived when there are to be no more of these "repatriations". The power and pathos of the occasion is its simplicity; its peace and quiet in an angry world. And we, the people of Wootton Bassett, want it to stay exactly like that.'

Mayor Steve Bucknell fears anti-war protests could be the next stage in the Wootton Bassett story. 'That wouldn't be appropriate at all.' He does not voice it but others do – might Bassett also become a terrorism target? For now, the town council will be talking about whether it needs to control what happens – setting up barriers or asking reporters to stay away.

These were all genuine concerns by many people and it was deemed appropriate that a meeting should be held.

In attendance was Group Capt. Mike Neville who chaired the meeting with his media officer and Head of his Repatriation Team; three members of the RBL with their spokesperson being Mrs. Bevis; the Town Council were represented by Mayor Steve Bucknell and the Town Clerk Johnathan Bourne; I was present to represent the police.

Many points were raised in a very amicable meeting and all the concerns were individually discussed. The conclusion was that the great thing about what was happening was the freedom of it, the spontaneity. If control had to be exerted something would be lost. For that simple reason the spontaneous ceremony that was, remained. Without ownership or direction and with the dignity of a community who were once again focused as one to show respect to the fallen.

It was an important meeting to tweak and focus the attention of all onto the fallen as the front line that summer was a very dangerous place to be. During those months in Helmand Province, British forces would request 'Op Minimise' sadly far too many times.

As each fatality occurs a further military operation takes place out in Camp Bastion. It is called 'Operation Minimise', an order from headquarters in southern Afghanistan to restrict communications. British troops in Helmand Province dread Op Minimise. They know commanders will be phoning the UK, and a chain of events will lead to a family being told that their very precious person is dead.

That chain of events would also include a phone call from Katherine Rand: 'Prepare for Operation Pabbay.' That summer we were to witness scenes that brought our country together as one, in almost shock, seeing the volume of fatalities that were walked through the High Street of this small market town in Wiltshire.

CHAPTER 16

Operation Panthers Claw was launched around midnight on 19 June 2009 with the aim of securing control of various canal and river crossings and establishing a lasting ISAF presence in an area described by Lieutenant Col Richardson as 'one of the main Taliban strongholds' ahead of the 2009 Afghan presidential election.

In what the Ministry of Defence described as 'one of the largest air operations in modern times', according to BBC News, more than 350 troops from The Black Watch, 3rd Battalion, Royal Regiment of Scotland (3 SCOTS), (2 Rifles) were transported by 12 Chinook helicopters, deployed into Bābājī Faşal, northwest of the provincial capital Lashkar Gah, in Helmand Province.

The operation, which involved 13 other aircraft – including Apache and UH-60 Black Hawk helicopters, Harriers, unmanned aerial vehicles, and an AC-130H Spectre gunship involved both British and American air power, and was supported by more than 150 ground forces from the Black Watch and Royal Engineers.

Taliban fighters in the area launched multiple attacks against British forces, all of which were repelled, and 3 SCOTS secured three key crossings – the Lui Mandey Wadi crossing, the Nahr e-Burgha canal and the Shamalan canal – by 23 June.

To restrict movement by Taliban forces, British troops also constructed several checkpoints to be manned by 3 SCOTS but eventually ceded to the Afghan National Police.

According to Lieutenant Col Stephen Cartwright, Commanding Officer of the Black Watch, 3 SCOTS established a 'firm foothold' in the area of the operation despite encountering resistance.

Lieutenant Col Richardson reported that British forces killed several insurgents during the course of the operation, which was dubbed the 'Battle of Babaji.'

On 23 June, the MoD reported that British troops involved in Panther's Claw discovered 1.3 tonnes of poppy seed the day before, as well as improvised explosive devices (IEDs), which they disabled. Analysis of a sample of the crop by the Food and Agriculture Organisation of the United Nations in Kabul, however, revealed the haul to be that of mung beans.

On 25 June, the 1st Battalion, Welsh Guards, pushed up Shamalan canal securing 14 more crossing points, cutting off the insurgents' supply route and thus preventing more Taliban fighters coming into the Babaji area.

In the third phase of Panther's Claw, more than 700 British soldiers from the Light Dragoons and 2nd Battalion, Mercian Regiment supported by soldiers of the Danish

Battle Group, launched a ground offensive, backed by fire support, against Taliban-held areas north of Lashkar Gah.

The assault was timed to coincide with Operation Khanjar, or Strike of the Sword, launched on 2 July, by American forces against Taliban strongholds in the Helmand River valley.

The BBC reported that British troops had by 3 July, 'taken some key towns', but that their progress was impeded by insufficient resources.

By 4 July, British forces had encountered 'little resistance', in contrast to American and Afghan forces to the south participating in Khanjar who were engaged in 'fierce' fighting against the Taliban.

As of 5 July, around 3,000 Task Force Helmand troops from the United Kingdom, Denmark, Estonia and Afghan government forces were involved in Panther's Claw, with the British MoD reporting close quarters combat with Taliban fighters.
That fighting came at a cost:

BATTLEFIELD CASUALTIES

19 June: On the first day of the operation, one British soldier, Major Sean Birchall, from the 1st Battalion Welsh Guards, was killed in an explosion near Lashkar Gah.

23 June: Lieutenant Col Richardson of Task Force Helmand reported that British forces killed several Taliban fighters during operations in the vicinity of Bābājī Faşal.

1 July: Two British soldiers – Lieutenant Col Rupert Thorneloe, commanding officer of the 1st Battalion Welsh Guards and Tpr Joshua Hammond of the 2nd Royal Tank Regiment – died, and six were wounded, near Shamalan Canal, at Lashkar Gah, when an IED exploded under their BvS 10 Viking armoured vehicle.

4 July: Two more British soldiers were killed, Private Robert Laws, from 2nd Battalion, Mercian Regiment by a rocket-propelled grenade and the second L Corporal David Dennis from the Light Dragoons, by an IED, near Gereshk.

5 July: L Corporal Dane Elson, a member of the 1st Battalion Welsh Guards was killed in an explosion near Lashkar Gah.

6 July: In an unrelated incident to panther's claw; Captain Ben Babington- Browne, from 22 Engineer Regiment, Royal Engineers, died alongside two Canadian troops when their aircraft crashed in Zabul province. A safety investigation 'determined that the crash did not occur as a result of enemy fire.'

7 July: Trooper Christopher Whiteside, A member of the Light Dragoons was killed in an explosion near Gereshk.

9–10 July: The Ministry of Defence announced that eight British soldiers had died within a 24-hour period. Rifleman Daniel Hume 4th Battalion The Rifles was killed in a blast while on foot patrol near Nad Ali on Thursday afternoon, Private John Brackpool Princess of Wales's Royal Regiment, attached to 1st Battalion Welsh Guards, was killed during an engagement with insurgent forces near Lashkar Gah later that day. On Friday Corporal Jonathan Horne, Riflemen Daniel Simpson, Joseph Murphy, James Backhouse and William Aldridge of 2nd Battalion, The Rifles and Corporal Lee Scott of The 2nd Royal Tank Regiment were killed in two bomb blasts.

16 July: Rifleman Aminiasi Toge, A member of 2nd Battalion, The Rifles, was killed in an explosion near Gereshk.

As the fighting continued from one operation to another throughout that summer in Afghanistan the support for the troops back home was getting stronger than we had ever seen before.

It really knocked the silly nonsense of a few who complained about the clapping, the flowers, and the amount of standards that were turning up. The word 'circus' was never heard of again as people focused on one thing only, those men who paid the ultimate sacrifice.

Yes, these fallen, as well as the previous ones demanded recognition and by God they got it.

That summer of 2009 was awful, we had escorted cortèges of one, two, three, four and five; now we were to escort eight.

Eight is an easy number to say, but when we escorted Corporal Lee Scott, Corporal Jonathan Horne, Riflemen William Aldridge, James Backhouse, Joseph Murphy, Daniel Hume, Daniel Simpson and Private John Brackpool, it was a devastating sight.

We left RAF Lyneham that afternoon on Tuesday 14 July 2009. The four outriders were leading the way; we turned left onto the A3102 at walking pace. Immediately, as we came out onto the public road, hundreds of people had gathered. Heads bowed in sorrow and to my left the two old boys' arms were raised in the salute.

Slowly, methodically, I lead the cortège out of the main gates. I looked into my rear view mirror and started to count the hearses, one by one as they came into my view.

One, two, three, four, another one, then another, seven, the eighth and finally the rear police vehicle. We had the cortège tight stretching the length of a football pitch and crawling along the streets of Lyneham village.

In the middle of this little village centre is a mini roundabout on one side of which are a couple of stores and on the other the primary school. On the grass banks leading to the school many of the children had gathered with their teachers and parents. Some of the younger ones recognised me from my many visits and waved, such was their innocence; I nodded my head in their direction to acknowledge them.

Then without warning or prompting the children started to clap; the clapping got louder as the adults joined in, following the lead of those aged between six and eleven.

I was confused at first but the following day the head teacher told me the children's clapping was their way of expressing themselves and of recognising that those eight soldiers were heroes. It really caught me off guard and the tears were blurring my vision. Yet, at the same time, I looked in my mirror, at the coffins behind me and realised that inside there were lads only seven years older than these children in primary school uniform.

The constant flow of radio messages from the Police Bronze Commander let us know that they were ready for our arrival and to prepare for thousands of grieving people lining both sides of the road. The eyes of the nation watched our progress from the images being broadcast from a BBC helicopter hovering directly above us to millions of people in their front rooms. Those images were also being seen by the eight families who remained inside RAF Lyneham and were being supported by their Visiting Officer and the outstanding RAF Repatriation Team. As we entered the built up area the helicopter peeled off, out of sight and sound, so as not to deflect attention from the eight young men behind us.

We were warned there would be thousands and they certainly did not exaggerate. We stopped adjacent to St Bartholomew's Church for that brief moment while the conductor prepared to make his slow, dignified page of the fallen up to the war memorial and I looked around. Ten deep I counted; people on roof tops, looking out of windows, all wanting to share compassion and sympathy towards those families who were hurting with so much pain. Then we made our way through the crowd, slowly squeezing between the 51 standards on parade on the right side of the road, running the entire length of the High Street. On the side of the war memorial it was a mass of people: some wore T-shirts of their loved one; others held banners high; all were heartbroken as those raw emotions broke free.

We were concerned about how to manage the respects to be shown at the war memorial with such a massive number of people expected. It was decided the most appropriate decision was to stop for one minute and for those involved in the brief ceremony to be forewarned. This would allow respects, be it saluting or indeed laying flowers, and all the extended family members and friends would have been made aware.

Normally, we would have remained until everyone had had the opportunity to place their flowers but it would have taken hours, such was the volume of people in attendance.

After the one minute concluded the conductor raised his hat to acknowledge the respects shown and slowly made his way towards where we were waiting to re-unite the cortège as one.

As he walked and the cortège wheels slowly turned I heard something that sounded like running water. The public, the military and all, were following the actions of the Lyneham pupils, when they spontaneously brought their hands together and applauded.

It really was emotional. As I stood to attention at the bottom of the High Street, I looked around and saw many people openly caught up in their own emotions, not ashamed to shed their tears.

Karen, my wife was standing some ten metres away from me, she looked deep into my eyes and I knew she could see the impact the respects were having on me almost weekly. She mouthed the words I knew so well, 'Are you alright?' I nodded my reply and smiled as she said, 'I LOVE YOU.' I then focused again on my duties and saluted as the cortège led by the conductor approached me.

Once the flowers that had fallen on the hearse windscreens were removed and placed inside the vehicles the conductor confirmed we were ready to continue on our journey.

Forty miles further on the cortège would travel along the M4 and then down the A419, next onto the A420 from Wiltshire into Oxfordshire where the Thames Valley police assumed their duties all the way to the John Radcliffe Hospital. Thousands stood and waited hours for those eight young men, 46 miles in total, which took three hours to complete, such was the outcry of respect from our proud nation. Our country was hurting not in a manner that can be anything near the trauma the young men's family and friends were suffering, but the genuine compassion was overwhelming.

Sadly it never stopped there as 24 more fallen heroes were to make that same humbling journey through July and August. Whether the repatriation was single like on Friday 7 August when craftsman Anthony Lombardi, 21, from Scunthorpe, came home, or multiple losses, the respects were always shown from a nation who truly recognised their fallen sons.

Thousands of people made their journeys to the town of Wootton Bassett, from every corner of our country and some even from foreign lands. How things had changed in a few short years when the public never even knew our fallen had been returned. We now had a nation travelling many miles to stand along that route to show so much respect.

They would travel in cars, coaches or any transport available as a community to show how much they cared. Once I even saw a cyclist who did not make it to Bassett quite on time. He sighted the outriders in front of me and quickly jumped off his bike. With two hands he threw the bike into the hedge then whipped out his Paratrooper Maroon Beret, quickly placing it on his head. Then as smart as any guardsman on Horse Guards' Parade, he came to attention and saluted. I had seen his efforts, so slowed the cortège down to walking pace to show mutual respects. How far he had cycled I had no idea, but his respects were appreciated by the two Royal Engineer Corps Sergeant Majors in my car.

Yes, it was an awful summer, the worst the country had experienced so far. Sadly though there was more breaking news on the horizon as my phone continued to ring with Katherine's name on display.

Friday 4 September 2009: 'The bodies of two British soldiers who died in Afghanistan, Sergeant Stuart 'Gus' Millar from Inverness and Private Kevin Elliott from Dundee were killed in a blast in Southern Helmand on Monday, will be flown home into RAF Lyneham later today' were the opening words I heard on the early morning news as I prepared to go to work that day.

I made my way up to the Police Station that morning just before eight. I saw kids in uniform dragging their heels, just like I did, on their way to school, each wearing their respective school colours and badges. At the same time, I also knew many more uniforms, not from school, but from across the land would be heading in our direction, making swift progress as they wanted to be present in plenty of time.

I was always in deep thought as I walked up the road on repatriation days and without fail I would have a brief stop to read the words on the cards that remained neatly placed at the war memorial. Some beautiful words, so many, so young; I knew more tears would be shed later that day.

The media teams were already setting their mobile studios for periodic live broadcasting throughout the day. I would always share a few words with them as they waited for their reporter to arrive. The invasion, we had heard, was on its way from north of the border and by 10am they had started to arrive. They were welcomed by this Wiltshire town who were ready to show compassion to 'Scotland the Brave.'

Yes, in exactly the same manner as with so many others, when one of their own was returning home, they travelled to show their respects on mass. As one they would gather later to lay their floral tributes and today the 'Flower of Scotland' would be laid with sadness for their two fallen heroes. But amongst the sadness was the pride, as so many stood in full military regalia proudly wearing that famous Black Watch uniform.

Dozens had made this distressing journey and Colour Sergeant George Murray of the Royal Regiment of Scotland was one: 'We've seen this various times, but when it's one of your own it really hits home and you're here seeing it for yourself. All the civilians have come out to show their respects – it's very emotional and the boys will agree it's a sad, sad day.'

Many have seen what has taken place before, watching it on TV in the comfort of their military mess or sat at home. But stood in this High Street when the fallen are being paged towards them to the tolling of the Tenor Bell, it is a different matter. I think it's the silence that catches them off guard; to be broken only by the sound of that raw grief. There is no escape, as they stand to attention in the salute. No, that raw grief had no respect for brave soldiers who proudly wore their hard earned medals across their chest; the tears were difficult to control, so in the end they just flowed.

After we escorted the two Scotsmen out of the High Street some families remained at the war memorial, others walked away across to the Cross Keys; a safe haven where no press are allowed to invade.

But amongst a sadness that only those hurting knew, many found the time to share their love and pride for their hero as they tried to take in the events of this emotional day. Some did speak to the press and many tributes could be read the following day, in the national and local tabloids.

Forty-year-old Sergeant Stuart Millar, from Inverness, known as Gus to colleagues, joined the Army in 2000 after serving in the Territorial Army leaves behind his wife Jillian and daughter Grace. His family said the father-of-one had 'always wanted to be a soldier' and 'passionately enjoyed his job.' He was very brave and is a credit to both our family and the Army. We are really proud of him as a father, son, brother and soldier.

Twenty-four-year-old Private Kevin Elliot, from Dundee, was the loveable rogue in his regiment. His Commanding Officer, Lieutenant Col Stephen Cartwright said: 'He was on the verge of leaving the Army earlier this year but his inclination to be in the thick of the action was too tempting and he caught the last transport to Afghanistan with his mates. It was no surprise to hear that in this tragic incident, he was the first man on the roof in the defensive position, the first to volunteer to protect his colleagues in a dangerous area.'

Private Elliott had previously served in Iraq and Northern Ireland. His family paid tribute to the 'life and soul of the party who lived life to the full. He chose to go to Afghanistan to be with his mates and to give his life for them. The whole family loved Kevin and we are devastated by his death.'

The many tributes written about this young Scottish soldier are there for all to see and without doubt the men who trusted him with their lives in conflict thought there was no better a man to cover their backs. But that was Private Kevin Elliott, 3rd Battalion, The Black Watch, Royal Regiment of Scotland.

His Father Sandy Elliot continues:

'That's how the Army knew my son; it's not how I knew him. My son Kevin joined the Army in 2002. He served in Northern Ireland and Iraq and finally in Afghanistan where he died on 31 August 2009. He was 24 years old.

Kevin was due to leave the Army in March 2009. He had passed his medical and was ready for civvy (civilian) life. At the last moment, he decided to stay. When asked why? Kevin answered that he couldn't let the guys go to Afghanistan without him. So Kevin went to Afghanistan, but didn't return.

That's when my nightmare started . . . from the moment I heard Kevin had died I questioned myself. Why didn't I try to convince him not to go? Why couldn't I protect my son?

Those questions and many more went around my head for months; my son had given his life for his country.

When we went to Royal Air Force Lyneham for his repatriation . . . That's yet another awful day in a long journey.

To know the flight coming home had your son on it, but you can't see him or hold him ever again. He was in that flag-draped box; his comrades carried off the plane and marched to the hearse.

15 September 2009 was the day of his funeral – our chance to say goodbye. It was a military funeral which was Kevin's right. At the funeral, Kevin's humour came to the fore as his mate turned up in a lime green dress and orange stockings. They had made a promise if one of them was to die the other had to attend the graveside in a dress. His mate kept his promise and the funny guy, Kevin, came back to us in the most spectacular way. Kevin wasn't perfect and as a dad I wasn't perfect, but we loved each other and that's what mattered. It's been a long, hard journey from that day to this and I realise it's a journey that will never end.

No one can replace my oldest child. No one can fill the hole in my heart. No one can bring Kevin back to me or our family. Kevin will never be forgotten. I have learned throughout this journey that no one, except another grieving military family, can understand how I feel. It's a different grief . . . it's one that can only be shared among other families who have lost their son or daughter in the military. I have been lucky to have the support of many families here in the UK, and in October I realised the journey we are facing here is the same journey families in the US are facing. Having met a few families from TAPS, I have made lifelong friends to travel this journey with. I'm not alone and neither are our loved ones.

So many years have now passed and still the hurting goes on; something that I know will never stop.'

Sandy has had many changes in the new world he stepped into the day he started to mourn for his son. Some things have surprised him immensely and, like me, another who believes in fate, he feels strongly that since Kevin died he has been pushed by him to offer support to others in this similar new world.

Today five years on, he has dedicated his life to the fallen as the Chairman of SSAFA's Bereaved Families Support Group a very dedicated team offering support to so many families.

I felt it was only right that I included this tribute to a man who has moved no further on with his sorrow, yet has the compassion in helping so many others; some I have met and all of whom speak so highly of him.

CHAPTER 17

Throughout that summer into autumn there was no relenting as the loss of British personnel continued. That ripple of devastation was activated weekly with the sounding of Operation Minimise that would send shock waves throughout our country.

On 3 November 2009, we were to hear even more appalling news when an enemy from within, not PTSD that was often invisible, but one that was highly visible feigning to be a friend. It brought into the equation in this conflict the word 'trust.'

Five British soldiers had been shot dead in Helmand Province, in an attack the UK military blamed on a 'rogue Afghan policeman.'

Warrant Officer Class 1 Darren Chant, 40, Sergeant Matthew Telford, 37, and Guardsman Jimmy Major, 18, from the Grenadier Guards, died alongside Corporal Steven Boote, 22, and Corporal Nicholas Webster-Smith, 24, from the Royal Military Police.

The soldiers had been significantly advising the Afghan National Police and the Afghan National Army in training, tactics and patrol methods. Besides mentoring they also lived together in the compound. The individual responsible for this evil act of violence opened fire injuring eight others before fleeing the compound.

The British casualties were evacuated to the field hospital at Camp Bastion in Helmand by medical emergency response teams using a Chinook.

Those seriously wounded soldiers from that incident were flown home by that awesome aircraft the C17 Globemaster that had been converted into an intensive care unit. Flight Lieutenant Niv Phoenix was one of those pilots on that C17 Globemaster.

Nivan was a friend of mine who lived in Lyneham and many times we would catch up for a coffee or the odd glass of beer. Quite bizarre really, I would be walking my beat and he would be off or have just returned from a flight predominantly from Afghanistan, when I would hear, 'Fancy a coffee, Jarra?' I was never one to refuse and we chatted as friends do. Sometimes during our conversations he mentioned some of the harrowing sights he saw. I heard what he said and even with the most vivid imagination I had difficulty visualising the scene he mentioned, especially when we sat in his home in rural Wiltshire. The human devastation he spoke of was almost surreal, like something out of a Second World War movie. Tens and dozens of seriously injured soldiers with blood-stained dressings, wounded with life-changing injuries; many who had lost limbs. They would be brought onto his aircraft, many plugged into machines hanging in there with the support of outstanding medical teams and it was his job to fly them home in his converted air ambulance.

Some time later the words he spoke at that time were to be seen by all, as the return of those seriously injured by the Afghan rogue policeman was shown on Channel 4's *Cutting Edge* documentary 'Air Hospital.' This documentary can be found on 'YouTube' and I cannot encourage any reader enough to sit down alone and watch the programme.

Two days after that awful incident, Serjeant Phillip Scott, 30, of 3rd Battalion, The Rifles, was killed by an improvised explosive device near Sangin, in Helmand. His loss of life resulted in him coming home with the five who were slaughtered in such a cowardly manner.

Katherine Rand confirmed that Tuesday 10 November 2009 was the date for Operation Pabbay, which was also a significant date for the Wiltshire Roads Policing Unit. On the morning of this repatriation, further south in the county respects and tributes were being paid to Police Constable Bill Brown at his funeral. Bill had led the cortège on many occasions as an outrider and on this sad day it was he who was laid to rest, with his coffin draped in a Union flag, his white traffic peak cap on top.

With the emotions of close colleagues from Wiltshire Road Policing Unit carrying their friend Bill on their shoulders, Thames Valley Police (TVP) offered the assistance of their outriders to escort the cortège the full 46 miles. Sergeant Mark Ponting and Rob Langton liaised with Inspector Steve Cox and planned the logistics. In my vehicle that day was Sergeant Mark Venning and two police officers from TVP, who were school friends of one of the fallen soldiers.

Thousands stood side by side and paid a silent tribute to the six servicemen who were brought home that day. There were always so many who would line the route, but possibly today, due to the sickening circumstances, there were a few more. Even though the media story was focused on the five killed during the one incident, Serjeant Phillip Scott was equally recognised for paying the ultimate sacrifice.

This was the second time that I had escorted the fallen the full route, almost a year to the day since the previous one. It was humbling to see the volume of people lining the streets. I knew what to expect at Wootton Bassett, but no matter how many times we carried out this operation it was always carried out with sincerity and compassion. My recollection is very vivid. I recall the white T-shirts worn with the picture of 18-year-old Guardsman Jimmy Major with the bold lettering 'Jimmy R.I.P' and a banner displayed 'Welcome Home Our Hero Steven.' Others were just too heartbroken, numb and confused to comprehend what was taking place. The ambience was something that could never be transmitted onto a TV screen, as the Tenor Bell tolled and our nation watched the conductor page the six heroes to the war memorial.

For the Thames Valley police officers it was their first experience witnessing the raw emotion that took place throughout Wootton Bassett. They saw the family and friends laying their flowers on the hearses of the six soldiers and heard the grieving of so many broken people. The impact though for two of their officers who travelled in my vehicle was very personal; Corporal Nicholas Webster-Smith, Royal Military Police, was their friend.

The respects flowed and continued as you now know from what I have previously written. The rain, the drizzle, even the cold crept in, but had no inference on the thousands who lined the route, except to provide the sombre setting. At each vigil point and so many others, there they stood for many hours until we reached the 'final turn.'

God bless our country, we might be small but at times like this we are simply a very proud kingdom; stood in sadness, united as one.

Throughout our journey no words were spoken in my vehicle as the two Thames Valley police officers sat in silence. Having seen the sadness in my own friends when Travis came home, I understood their subdued presence, when so much of their mind was focused on a friend. A shake of their hands, was how we said our goodbyes, words were not needed on a day like this. The impact of what they witnessed was clearly seen on both faces, so much emotion does cause confusion when you mix sadness with chest-swelling pride.

For Mark and I it was back to Wootton Bassett, though this time he drove and I switched on my mobile phone. It was almost tranquil; the two of us sat together giving us a chance to reflect on what we had witnessed, because on many occasions after these sad events we had no chance to have a conversation. I enjoyed Mark's company because by this time he had become more than just my supervisor; I looked upon him as a friend. Our de-brief on our journey was not to last too long, as no sooner had I switched on my phone than the incoming call ring tone activated. It was confirmation from Katherine: plan for a further Op Pabbay, the following Monday, as two more soldiers would be coming back.

I finished work this wet November evening, my big black coat on, hands in my pockets to keep them warm. I truly valued the half hour serenity on my walk home. How quick the town had changed from one of mourning as the High Street returned to normal. I stopped at the war memorial as per my usual ritual; a private reflection on the tears that this monument had seen earlier. I stood up straight, there was no one around, then a slight bow of my head and I moved on. Although with Katherine's recent message fresh in my mind the reality was we would soon be back.

On walking through the front door into the comfort of my home and my wife, we sat down for our own little de-brief, though she liked to call it a chat. We would reflect on the extraordinary scenes I had seen, though if I am honest I was shattered and I would be laid out on the couch. A bit like a counselling session before the soaps would begin as even I could not compete with *Coronation Street* and *Eastenders* on the TV.

The phone rang, it was Chris Pearn, a really good friend of mine who always brought a cheer and who would often ring to see how things were going. That evening as he spoke his voice was unusually gloomy, which I soon realised was a reflection of his sadness, an emotion also felt within his small Cornish community. The shock wave of devastation that Op Minimise creates had entered Cornwall by the Torpoint Ferry. I offered my condolences to this lovely town and made arrangements to meet Chris on Monday as the Cornish Army would be present for their own hero who would be coming home. On putting down the phone, I felt exhausted, it had been a very long day and I knew I was ready for bed.

On Monday 16 November 2009, I met up with Chris and his dad who I always used to call the 'Mayor.' Mike Pearn, who was honoured with the MBE for his dedication to Torpoint Town Council, epitomised community spirit and, yes, he had been the Mayor. Chris, his son, and one of my best friends were two of the many people I recognised as Cornwall stood side by side with Wiltshire to honour Rifleman Samuel John Bassett, age 20.

From further along the south coast they also came, this time from Dorset in recognition of their own hero Rifleman Philip Allen, again a 20-year-old adding to the ever growing list of fatalities within The Rifles who were sustaining heavy losses. The Dorset Rifleman Phillip Allen, had only completed his training in April, deployed to Afghanistan in October and was killed the following month.

Both these young men had in their very short military careers left their footprint in their units, 'Swift and Bold' they had both proudly served with The Rifles on the front line. I always read the tributes that were written for the fallen as I always felt it was important to know who we were escorting home.

I hope those words I read gave the two grieving families I saw at the war memorial that day a further reason to be so proud of their loved one.

Lieutenant Michael Holden, 1 Platoon Commander, said:

'Rifleman Bassett was a true Rifleman; in camp a nightmare, always up to no good. However, in Afghanistan, a real professional, a master of his trade. When Rifleman Bassett first joined the platoon in May of this year he was thrown straight into pre-deployment training. It is full on with very little time to relax, and it is taxing on a young Rifleman and causes a lot of stress and hardship on family and friends. Throughout pre-deployment training he always gave us reasons for concern, he seemed to have the ability to be in the wrong place at the wrong time with, most certainly, the wrong kit.

He became a unique test of his Platoon Sergeant's patience. Outside of work he definitely enjoyed his play, at home in Torpoint, either surfing or motocross, there was always something to amuse him.

Rifleman Bassett really came out of his shell, he was proud of his job and a true team player. He worked hard, continually developing his skills, thinking on his feet and taking on the task of clearing routes for the rest of his section and platoon. This takes immense skill, patience and most of all courage. Rifleman Bassett had a great sense of humour, always quick to try and outwit his fellow Riflemen. Every day in Afghanistan Riflemen are asked to do things that require a lot of nerve.

Rifleman Bassett always stepped up to the challenge without a second thought. Through the ups and downs it has been my absolute privilege to have known him as well as command his platoon. My thoughts go out to his family and friends in this difficult time. He will always be in 1 Platoon's hearts and minds and he will be truly missed.'

Warrant Officer Class 2 Freddie Fryer, Fire Support Group Platoon Commander, said:

'Rifleman Allen's arrival in my platoon was a blessing. He had been operating with 2 RIFLES for three weeks in Forward Operating Base Inkerman, which was three weeks more Afghan experience than I had. It was clear from the start that his experience and positive attitude was nothing less than a massive bonus to my platoon in its early days on tour. Everything he did was to an amazing standard for a soldier so young. He was such an asset to the platoon that I did spend many days trying to 'nick' him from 2 RIFLES and I spent many hours trying to persuade him to stay for a full tour and come back to Bulford as a fully-fledged member of my platoon. We have lost an outstanding Rifleman, a valued and close friend, a brother-in-arms. Rifleman Allen will be sorely missed but never, ever forgotten.'

One thing I guarantee he will not be forgotten if you read the interview with his mother Karen Charman-Allen *The Life of a Soldier* by Patrick Barkham in *The Guardian*.

I also read 12 months later at a Remembrance Service the words of Coline Bassett the Mother of Samuel Bassett, who spoke to a reporter about the harsh reality of a front-line infantry soldier.

'When Sam passed out in April last year he was one of 18. Two of them are now dead and five have lost arms and legs – four of them are double amputees and one is a triple amputee. It is just awful.'

A picture that is never mentioned in the recruiting brochures when these young lads join up is the true cost of conflict is massive.

Having read so much on these two 20 year olds I am immensely proud to tell their mothers, their family and their friends, your sons were truly honoured by thousands along those 46 miles.

Sadly that was not the end, those 46 miles were to be lined several times more, as 11 further British soldiers were killed and returned home in 2009. On each of those humbling occasions communities made their way to Wootton Bassett in support of the heartbroken families. They let each one of those families know that from the sights I observed the country truly cared as they recognised the loss of your loved one.

By the end of 2009 the British public had seen the huge respects that were shown and made their feelings known they approved by nominating Wootton Bassett for a national award.

The Sun Military Awards, organised by *The Sun* newspaper in close association with the Ministry of Defence, recognise the excellence of the Armed Forces and supporting civilians. Prince William and Prince Harry were guests of honour at the event held at the Imperial War Museum in London on the 15 December 2009. They were joined by military chiefs, senior government, political figures and stars from the worlds of entertainment and sport. In ten categories, the awards, affectionately known as 'The Millies', recognised the bravery and professionalism of service and civilian personnel working in today's Armed Forces around the world. They also celebrated members of the public who provide unstinting support to the military in various ways.

Prince William presented the award for 'Support to the Armed Forces' to representatives from Wootton Bassett. Those selected for the honour were Mayor Steve Bucknell, two members of the Royal British Legion: 'Parade Marshal' Maurice Baker, with Anne Bevis and landlady Kirsty Lambert of the Cross Keys pub, who provides refreshments for the families of those being brought home.

When handing over the award, a silver and gold statuette, Prince William said: 'One of the most remarkable things is that the people are so modest, they refuse to accept any praise.'

Those awards were recorded on ITV and shown on the 21 December 2009, I can only account for my own household, but as we watched the 'Tribute to Wootton Bassett' we could not disguise the mixture of pride and sadness as we reflected on the last two years.

Did I cry? Of course I did. I told you I am not made of wood and before this awful year was to draw to a close so many others were to shed tears, as four more soldiers were killed. It was no wonder our country was feeling the strain when you realised the total of fatalities of British forces during 2009 was the staggering figure of 108.

Yes 2009 was truly an awful year; insurmountable was the devastation it caused to so many families and their friends, some of whom I knew. It also brought to an end the two years command of Group Captain Mike Neville as Station Commander at RAF

Lyneham. He was an outstanding man, a huge personality who cared deeply for his station and the surrounding community who all looked upon him as their friend.

Group Captain John Gladston MBE, DFC, was the new Station Commander at RAF Lyneham. I had met him briefly on a media course, which gave me an opportunity to introduce myself to him prior to his appointment in post. He was the third Station Commander during my time working up in Wiltshire. He, like his two predecessors Mike Neville and Paul Atherton, was another great Commanding Officer and a very approachable dynamic leader. All three had a different style in commanding their station, and each had their unique nicknames in, Nevs and Gladis, although now that Paul Atherton is an Air Vice-Marshal I will keep this under wraps.

Gladis though was an action man pilot, he was military through and through and a very much respected man both in the Royal Air Force and the higher echelons of some important places. Yes, I liked him from the off; a top man and immediately into his two-year tenure we knew we would continue with our excellent relationship between the station and the police. I think it is fair to say we had the utmost mutual respect, maybe due to us completing the arduous commando course we both knew we wore the dagger of trust on our upper left arms.

So the continuation of RAF Lyneham remained in good hands with a pilot at the controls, to take on the pressure of running his station which was never far from front page news.

He stood his station down so they could enjoy their Christmas leave which they all so richly deserved. Yet before we finished our final repatriation that year and Big Ben had the chance to sound the bells, we knew that our hopes for peace and goodwill for 2010 had fallen on deaf ears.

Two soldiers, Rifleman Aidan Howell of 3rd Battalion, The Rifles and Sapper David Watson from 33 Engineer Regiment Explosive Ordnance Disposal were 3,500 miles away, waiting to come home.

CHAPTER 18

I f there was one thing guaranteed in this small market town which had been recognised by the country for showing its respects to the fallen, it was always expect the unexpected. Just after the bells had tolled and we were preparing to resource the first repatriations of this New Year, we received intelligence to suggest a political protest was being planned.

These were the same concerns raised by the Mayor Steve Bucknell back in the summer of 2009 during the meeting that was called. He suggested that anti-war protests could be the next stage in the Wootton Bassett story.

'That wouldn't be appropriate at all,' he was quoted as saying and how right he was for raising those concerns.

Word was received that an Islamic group was planning to march through Wootton Bassett to mourn the thousands of Muslims they claim had been murdered in conflicts in Afghanistan and Iraq.

The Town had been chosen by Islam4UK, a platform for the global front Al-Muhajiroun, because of the part it plays in the repatriation of Britain's fallen service personnel. The group published a statement on its website, announcing its plans to march on the town, which had honoured 108 troops killed in theatre last year. The statement read:

> 'Islam4UK would like to announce the launch of a momentous march that is scheduled to take place in the following weeks, details of which will be released shortly Insha'Allah (God willing). The destination of this very special event is the small market town of Wootton Bassett.'

Needless to say this news created a reaction locally and nationally. The local response from dignitaries was one to be expected as their stance had always been that the repatriations have never been political.

It had been previously stated that Westminster was the place for political argument and debate, not this 500-metre stretch of road; Wootton Bassett High Street.

Home Secretary Alan Johnson said he would have 'no hesitation' in supporting a ban on the march if the police or the council requested one.

The debate continued for some time and many high ranking politicians voiced their concerns, where as those at Wootton Bassett stood back although a little concerned about what could unfold. The public were whipping up a frenzy on a Facebook site dedicated to preventing the march; in days it was to attract nearly 300,000 members.

Among those sharing their comments and taking the opportunity to fly their own political flag and views was the English Defence League.

The sheer thought of the English Defence League and Anjem Choudary, leader of Islam4UK, with his 500 followers coming together on Wootton Bassett High Street was a serious concern to everyone.

One word, carnage, and as the arguments and political debate over this proposed protest was taking place at Westminster our focus was on the return of two more soldiers coming home.

After three days of controversy surrounding the proposed Muslim march in Wootton Bassett, townspeople once again gathered to show their respect to the two soldiers recently killed in Afghanistan.

The bodies of Rifleman Aidan Howell of 3rd Battalion, The Rifles and Sapper David Watson from 33 Engineer Regiment Explosive Ordnance Disposal were flown into RAF Lyneham. Sapper Watson died of wounds sustained in an explosion caused by an improvised explosive device (IED) on New Year's Eve near Patrol Base Blenheim in the Sangin region of Helmand Province.

His family described the 23-year-old, who was brought up in Whickham, Newcastle-upon-Tyne, as a true hero who 'lived his dream' and 'did what a true soldier is ready to do for his country.'

Rifleman Howell, 19, was killed after an explosion near Forward Operating Base Zeebrugge in the Kajaki area of Helmand province on 28 December.

Aidan Howell, who was born in Sidcup, Kent, was nicknamed 'Sunshine Boy' by his family.

Hundreds of people, as expected, stood alongside the friends and families of the soldiers on the streets of Wootton Bassett that day.

Steven Stratford and Pete Bell travelled over 100 miles to the repatriation to pay their respects to close friend Rifleman Aidan Howell. Mr. Stratford said, 'Aidan was an excellent boy. You could not meet a nicer, better gentleman. It's very difficult to be here. We came over 100 miles to get here but we would have walked. If these Muslims come to protest here it will be carnage. If they want to protest they shouldn't do it here. This is where the soldiers come back as heroes.'

Mr. Bell said, 'If this Muslim group want to protest they should go to London or go to the Government – it is completely disrespectful and anti-British. Everyone who comes to see the soldiers through Wootton Bassett are themselves heroes. The people in Wootton Bassett are the best and treated us so kindly.'

The repatriation of these two fine young men was concluded with the same dignity and respect as this market town's High Street had become accustomed to. Never again were political views debated on the day a British hero was returned home.

After the repatriation, however, the debate and public reaction continued as the latest comments by Anjem Choudary, leader of Islam4UK, said it was 'full steam ahead' for the march, campaigning for the withdrawal of British troops.

A date for the event – to feature 500 people carrying symbolic coffins – has not been set. But it will not coincide with a repatriation, Mr. Choudary said. Islam4UK, a branch of the extremist al-Muhajiroun movement, claims its 'momentous march' will honour the thousands of Muslims who have been killed in Afghanistan. The arguments continued for a further few days until the Government stepped in and, with the appropriate powers, banned the organisation Islam4UK. In doing so it gave the power to the police to arrest and detain any protester descending on to Wootton Bassett.

Although those powers had been granted to the police the rumours continued that the protest was still going to take place and the date for that march was to be, Sunday 10 January 2010. As a result of that the police had a planned response in place.

The English Defence League did attend that day and formed up at the war memorial. Once they arrived, a mobile police presence was visible, not to antagonise, but to reassure the local community. And there they remained as rumours continued to flow that busloads of Islam4uk protestors had been arrested. These were rumours which proved to be totally untrue. The reality of the situation was finally recognised by the English Defence League; they were neither wanted nor welcomed in this High Street, and they retreated to wherever they had come from.

It was with a huge sigh of relief from all that the fears of carnage had not materialised. The only ever political protest that raised its ugly head during these humbling days had failed and was never to be seen again. Although sadly the fallen did continue to return and many of the personalities who turned out regularly were once again present on parade. Among the many proud personalities I had got to know over the years that never failed to catch my eye, were two men of honour. These two men epitomised the sincerity and integrity of the Wootton Bassett community. I found myself on many escorts looking out for, dare I say, two 'old boys'; both very proud men who wore the cloth, chip bag style hat of a Second World War veteran, one Army the other RAF. John Beauchamp, RAF, always stood alone at the end of the High Street by the small mini roundabout which led to Sainsbury's and our route out of town. He was always immaculately turned out and in the winter months wore the greatcoat of an Officer which proudly displayed his campaign medals. As we drove the cortège towards him, he would stand to attention and salute; in doing so he gave the impression that he was one man who knew what a loss of life really meant in conflict. I often wondered what images were provoked amongst his many memories of comrades he knew but who were never brought home.

The other was another gentleman from the same generation as Mr. Beauchamp. This man was Mr Ken Scott a man I always had aspiration to be. I mean how many men are there at the age of 92 with their own set of wheels and always with one of his lady friends giving him a lovely warm kiss, do you know? But that was Ken Scott, frail on his feet, but he would always be smart as he went around town on his mobility scooter with his personalised registration – KEN S1. I would often see him tidying up the flowers and tributes around the war memorial. Ken was a character who I never tired of listening to. He won't know me as there were many police in the town, but there was only one Ken Scott; a man I will always remember long after he does pass away. He had his own routine on repatriation days which he spoke of in our conversations. He would hear of the timings through the grapevine and he would always wait at home in the warm until he saw the aircraft had flown over. Ken was always immaculate in his attire wearing his chip bag style hat, but for his own reasons and ones I did not ask, he never wore his Second World War campaign medals. A man not caught up in any romance, he knew the true cost of conflict. Maybe those shiny things that were in his home also brought back so many sad memories and were better locked away.

On that bitterly cold January day, the two men who really understood the meaning of paying the ultimate sacrifice, waited with many hundreds who were not just the locals, but who travelled from all corners of the country.

I remember the day well, a group of friends and extended family of Captain Dan Read were chaperoned by an Officer (I am sure his name was Eamon) from 11 Explosive Ordnance Disposal Regiment. They all turned up at the police house in Lyneham. Once again we turned our skills to hosting them all with hot drinks and giving them some warmth as they had arrived early. One young chap in the group was a nephew of Dan Read. When he left our office that day I gave him a print of the C17 Globemaster Aircraft, a symbol of the Angel that brought his uncle home. We braced ourselves as we knew what to expect when we stood with them as the three men were flown home.

Then up to Wootton Bassett to the Cross Keys where we handed the heartbroken group over to Kirsty and her team, while I resumed my duties.

The Tenor Bell tolls announcing we have arrived in town. Captain Dan Read, 31, 11 Explosive Ordnance Disposal Regiment, Royal Logistics Corps, Corporal Lee Brownson, 30, and Rifleman Luke Farmer, 19, both of 3rd Battalion The Rifles are in our care.

It's an extraordinary scene which I have seen many times before, yet each is unique in its own way. I clearly recall the banners that are displayed with Captain Dan Read for all to see. By their side, not alone in the crowd, was a broken hearted pregnant wife, whose unborn child will never see their father Corporal Lee Brownson smile. Two hundred or more travelled down from Yorkshire in a tide of colour – the red and white checked shirts – no chance they could have been missed. Rifleman Luke Farmer, you must have been one outstanding man, as the community of Upton had relocated and brought the Rugby League Club with them.

The wailing starts, there is no holding back the tears, as the shock of seeing the flag-draped coffin for the first time hits the soldier's extended family and friends. The next of kin are numb and distraught and step forward to lay roses and other flowers on the three vehicles carrying their men. There the three heroes remain whilst those who travelled do the same; one final bow of the head after respects had been shown and the conductor paged towards where his escort waited. As we drive off the town remains silent and numb for a short period of time to reflect. The standard bearers adhere to the word of command, a sharp turn to the right, they move as one, three quick paces, they are now dismissed. The Legion Riders get their mounts roaring then drive away as the mourners take refuge in the Cross Keys, a safe haven for family and friends.

A town that cried wipes away its tears, as a 92-year-old man stands alone in sadness. He starts to view the many cards and tributes he wants to protect. There are no words I can write to better describe the sincerity of Mr Ken Scott than the ones he spoke when I saw him on television being interviewed by the BBC:

'I do know what it is like for these soldiers in Afghanistan, I really do. I spent all of my young life at war, from 21 to 28. I know what it is like to see people die in front of you, for them to be taken off to hospital. People these days don't have a clue what it's like to be in a desert, where there are so many flies and heat and desert storms. This is what these lads experience. We did our best for those who were killed. We did not know the name of the poor soul, we scrapped a grave and lay him to rest; built a cross and said a prayer, that's all we could do. I feel so sorry for a mum who has lost her son, for a father, for a little boy or girl who won't have their dad to take them to school, or a football, or cricket match when they grow up.'

He shakes his head slowly from side to side. While that clip was shown you see the man with a tear in his eye sat in his front room chair with the album open on his lap. He turns the pages in an orderly, precise fashion, as you would do with any prized possession, and there is no mistaking how much the album means to him. So many cards with heartfelt words written on the cards and tributes he has collected from the war memorial. This is a memorial book that Ken created, as he felt the beautiful cards he had seen written were too precious just to allow them to blow away in the wind. Inside the album are photos of soldiers holding baby children in their arms, of others in dress uniform, or in desert camouflage on the battlefield. There are notes that say 'Never forget you, you're my best mate' and 'You will truly be missed, you're a braver man than any of us.'

It is mesmerising to watch Ken speak as he continues:

'These messages are sacred. They shouldn't be blown away on the High Street, I want the mums and dads and granddads to know that the messages are here and that when I have passed on they shall go to the museum.'

I think it would be fair to say that history will show that Wootton Bassett respected the fallen that passed through their town. It will also know of you Ken, a man who had the vision to keep sacred so many beautiful messages for many generations to come.

CHAPTER 19

It really was full on in this small market town; at the end of the month Prince Charles, The Prince of Wales and his wife, Camilla, Duchess of Cornwall were to pay a visit to Wootton Bassett to thank the town for its support for the Armed Forces.

As all Royal visits are thoroughly planned well in advance, it was hoped the date would not fall on a repatriation day; the Royals had insisted they would not wish to distract any respects shown on such an occasion.

Sadly, as the volume of the fallen continued to increase, Lance Corporal Daniel Cooper, 21, from 3rd Battalion, The Rifles and Rifleman Peter Aldridge, 19, from 4th Battalion, The Rifles, were repatriated home on the same date as the Royal visit. Clarence House did not cancel or change the dates for the Royal visit, but the itinerary was altered for Prince Charles and his wife, to arrive after the two soldiers were honourably returned home.

Their bodies were flown into RAF Lyneham on a bitterly cold day; an hour later the prestige ceremony commenced. With full military honours L/Corporal Cooper and Rifleman Aldridge were carried off the aircraft with so much respect. The repatriation, once completed, allowed the privacy of the two families to spend time with their sons in the sanctuary of the Chapel of Rest. That time was precious to them to be alone and share that moment with their loved one. When the time was right they made their way up to Wootton Bassett to stand with their friends and joined the hundreds of people who lined the streets, in the extreme cold, gripping their flowers tightly. The chatter stopped, a sombre silence is the response as St Bartholomew's church bell announced our arrival. Once again those in mourning were supported by people they did not know, as respects were truly shown and continued all the way to the final turn.

A couple of hours or so after the town had shown its respects, they prepared to welcome their Royal guests. The media were present but on this occasion they were penned in a press cordon, due to the security upgrade which is normal on such occasions. The itinerary for the visit was for Prince Charles and Camilla to each lay a wreath during a simple ceremony. Then the Royals were to be escorted into the Cross Keys public house to be introduced to Kirsty, her staff and various other regular attendees, such as the Royal British Legion Riders.

They would then be ushered to the Conservative Club where other personalities representing the Royal British Legion, the Town Council, Police and RAF Lyneham Repatriation Team, were to be introduced.

The crowds patiently waited, huddled closer into each other, not just because they are friendly folk in Bassett but it was freezing! Then, without warning, the Royal party arrived turning onto the High Street from Station Road, catching many onlookers by surprise. The arrival almost coincided unexpectedly with a downpour of snow. Like I said previously, in this small market town the unexpected was always just around the corner and it was no different on this Royal occasion.

The National Anthem sounded and people strained their necks to gain a better view of the couple as they stood at the side of the war memorial. A few words were said by the Reverend Canon Thomas Woodhouse who always carried off each service with his unique and sincere charisma. After this short service, a very brief pause, then the first few bars of the Last Post brought those who wished to respond immediately to attention.

During the last post the Union flag would be lowered on the newly presented flag pole adjacent to the war memorial, something that had been rehearsed over and over again. A young Sea Cadet was given the honour of lowering the Union flag as the Last Post was sounded on the cornet of the town bandsman. The snow continued and with it the icy wind chill factor took its toll, getting the better of the young Sea Cadet's gloveless fingers. They must have gone numb because no matter what he tried to do he could not undo the slip knot and the flag remained flying at full mast. There he stood isolated, possibly a feeling of vulnerability, desperate for his task to run as smoothly as the rehearsal. The bandsman looked at the Parade Marshal Maurice Baker, who in turn looked at the Mayor; there was a moment of panic as everyone looked at the young seaman who stood there in despair. Seeing him flustered, there was a feeling of confusion in the town; how could this possibly happen on all days in the presence of the future King?

For me though, this is what made Wootton Bassett special. Ceremonies were not done with military precision, it was the sincerity and innocence of this remarkable town just doing its best in what they thought was right.

Then one of the Town Councillors came to the aid of the young Sea Cadet, placing a comforting arm on him and giving the 15-year-old a feeling of safety in numbers. The slip knot was released and the Union flag was lowered. It was wonderful to see the smile of relief on the young Sea Cadet's face which was returned by those who saw his satisfaction, not just in holding the Union flag, but he now was wearing the Councillor's gloves.

Prince Charles and Camilla both laid wreaths at the war memorial during the service and the unveiling of the new flagpole, which had decided it wanted to be the centre of attention. Camilla, who is Colonel-in-Chief of Rifleman Aldridge's regiment, had written to his family, a Clarence House spokesman said. Her wreath, which had red flowers in keeping with the regiment's colours, read: 'With deepest gratitude, Camilla.'

Prince Charles's wreath read: 'In grateful and everlasting memory, Charles.'

Once the wreaths were laid the National Anthem was played to conclude the small ceremony as the flagpole this time allowed the Union flag to resume its position at full mast.

The Prince of Wales enjoyed a glass of whisky after stopping off at the Cross Keys pub to thank landlady Kirsty Lambert and her staff for the hospitality they showed to the bereaved families on repatriation days. Whilst introductions and recognition was being carried out to those present in the Cross Keys, I joined those invited to the Conservative Club who were to be introduced to the Royal couple. The invitation was for those who were involved in the repatriation ceremony at RAF Lyneham and the spontaneous ceremony in the town. There must have been 200 people present, it was wall to wall with many people I had never seen before, but who was I to dampen their wishes to be present on this day. The town was proud, so what if a few extra were sneaked in, it's not every day you get the chance to have a chat with Prince Charles and his wife.

I was sitting next to Inspector Mark Levitt. He leant forward to speak to me and reminded me of our initial conversation when we had prepared to carry out our very first escort.

'It'll only take twenty minutes Jarra, no one will notice.'

'I think they did Mark,' was my reply, as Prince Charles made his way to be introduced to the four of us who, back in April 2007, escorted the first two soldiers home. Not in our wildest imagination did we realise that simple gesture would be the foundation of everything which had taken place since.

After being introduced to all present Prince Charles told the 200 guests at the town's Conservative Club:

'My wife and I have come here today really to express our sincere and heartfelt gratitude to the people of Wootton Bassett for their unstinting support of Britain's Armed Forces. Only an hour or so ago you lined the High Street for what must have been the 110th occasion to pay your respects to Lance Corporal Cooper of 3 Rifles, and Rifleman Aldridge of 4 Rifles who returned home from Afghanistan to their final resting place. As a father myself I can only begin to imagine how agonising and devastating it must be for the families of Daniel and Peter and indeed the families of all those who have lost their loved ones on operations overseas. As they come to terms with their tragic loss, however inadequate they may be, our thoughts and prayers are with all of them. Above all, this country owes these brave men and women a great debt of gratitude which is why it's wonderful to see the good people of Wootton Bassett honouring that debt time after time when our boys and girls come home on their final journey. Your actions have come to symbolise our nation's grief. We would like to express our profound gratitude to you all for your support.'

As the Royals left that day it was yet another chapter in this story that has unfolded before our eyes. In the first month of 2010, we had seen some astonishing scenes, often finding ourselves as the lead story of the national news. Unknowingly to this community, at that time, there were a lot more extraordinary chapters to follow.

CHAPTER 20

During all the activity we had in the first few weeks of January I received a message from an ex-59 Commando colleague of mine, Tommo Thomason. Among the normal conversations friends have, was a brief comment about some bike ride that he was going on that would take place in our area. Tommo was a keen motorbike rider and he brought to my attention a page that had been created on Facebook, of an event he was planning to take part in.

I logged onto the page and read that an 18-year-old biker Elizabeth Stevens planned a ride to call in to Wootton Bassett and had an open invitation for others to join her. Julia Stevenson was one of the first riders to apply to take part in the initial Facebook message from the college student. Here she describes her initial contact:

'I was the 16th person to reply to her. Lizzie explained to me that she put the message on Facebook to see if anyone fancied going on a bike ride to Wootton Bassett with her and a few friends. Her plan was to call in at a local pub, have a bite to eat, a drink and say thanks to the locals for what they do for the fallen and then ride home.'

However, people started to accept Lizzie's invitation to join her on this bike ride and soon she realised she was out of her depth and was grateful of the support offered by Julia. Between them they discussed the basic details of such an event: routes, meeting points, dates and to raise funds for a suitable charity.

Julia describes how the charity was chosen:

'I Googled Heroes and the first thing that came up was "Afghan Heroes", a charity that had been put together by a group of mothers after their sons had been killed in Afghanistan. Their eight sons were repatriated together at RAF Lyneham in July 2009 and it is there that some of the mothers who founded this charity met for the first time. Contact was made with Denise Harris, one of the founders, whose response was one of absolute delight that the bikers would donate to their charity.'

With the Charity chosen, next on the agenda was to find a suitable date for Lizzie and Julia's ambitious event to take place. Well, there could only be one date, as it was a charity set up by mothers who lost their sons, it was agreed that Mothering Sunday, the 14 March 2010 was the most appropriate date for the event.

With the basic plan formed in their minds they sat down and amended the Facebook page and this is what had caught the eye of Tommo.

'A charity bike ride will gather at the Leigh Delamere services on the M4 (Junction 17 – eastbound) then ride through Wootton Bassett to RAF Lyneham where the fallen were repatriated into the UK. Each rider will pay £5 (on the day) and receive a special commemorative Afghan Heroes wristband, which will be their entry pass to the RAF base. All proceeds raised from the ride will go to the Afghan Heroes charity, which helps our service personnel in theatre, families of the fallen and our returning troops.'

After planting the seed in people's heads they sat back waiting for a response and I brought it to the attention of Inspector Steve Cox. Coxy did not know anything about it, so tasked me to liaise with the newly-appointed Station Commander at RAF Lyneham, Group Captain John Gladston.

On speaking to Gladis he confirmed it was a charity he was aware of and that the station had indeed been approached by the organisers with the request for 50 bike riders to come onto RAF Lyneham. The event he agreed to was that these bikers would seek security clearance through the RAF Police prior to the date, then ride onto the station. The bikers would then present RAF Lyneham with a symbol of their gratitude in recognition of how they honoured the fallen when repatriated to his Air Base.

He confirmed that he most certainly had not agreed to the mass of bikes that was being promoted on Facebook to drive onto his station runway among his aircraft for a fiver. He had delegated one of his Squadron Leaders as the project officer for the event to liaise with the organisers. It was to be made quite clear that they would honour the initial request of the 50 bikes to enter his station and not one bike more. With peace of mind that we were not to be invaded by bikers trying to get into RAF Lyneham, I reported my findings back to Coxy and around mid-January that's where it was left.

The weekend after the Royal visit I was contacted by another friend Phil Warren; another ex-Squadron mate of mine. Phil had also signed up to the event advertised on Facebook. I found it strange that out of the 50 bikers I knew two of them, so I logged onto the web site.

Staggering is one word to describe the numbers. By the end of January over 5,000 names had already registered to attend the event; with still about six or seven weeks to go it was rising daily.

On Monday morning I suggested to Coxy he might want to check out the Facebook page. He knew from reading it he was once again looking at another major policing and planning operation. I was to liaise with the RAF project officer, while he made contact with the Town Council.

I shall never forget the look on the Squadron Leader's face when I went to see him that morning. He confirmed he was the project officer and I asked him if he had viewed the website or contacted the organisers. He replied in the negative to both questions but stated he was in charge of the station Bike Club, so he thought with that experience he would look at the event a little closer to the time.

I laughed at his comments saying, 'I think you'll find it's a little bigger than a Bike Club.'

When he realised that the numbers who had already signed up were not in hundreds but thousands, there was a brief moment of concern. That initial panic soon turned to relief, when he eagerly accepted the invitation to join the newly-formed multi-agency planning group, which would liaise with the organiser Julia Stevenson.

As the bike ride was being organised behind the scenes, the loss of life continued in Afghanistan with a further 15 servicemen killed during February 2010. Each was escorted through the High Street in cortèges of single and multiple hearses carrying their bodies in those flag-draped coffins. Veterans, servicemen and townspeople were united in mourning with family and friends as they were brought back to the UK. It was not uncommon for communities to travel to Wootton Bassett, many the bereaved friends of the fallen while others had served with him: Soldiers, Marines and Airmen all stood dignified, yet hurting. There they stood, shoulder to shoulder, from every corner of our proud nation with the residents, shopkeepers and ex-servicemen local or from afar. People who had never met before, united on each solemn occasion, in lining the High Street to pay their respects.

From Scotland, Wales, Northern Ireland, England, North, South, East and West they came; towns, villages, cities and communities all united in support for their very special man. Many of those who travelled arrived early and made their way to that lay-by adjacent to the runway where they could see the C17 Globemaster bring their loved one home. As each person witnessed that honourable homecoming, it will be a vision they will never lose, nor be able to fully explain as they release the raw emotion that image provoked. It was private, personal and insurmountable to anything they had ever experienced and painfully so.

My goodness me they were all proud of their man, and they so much wanted to tell us about him. They paid tributes, told stories of the good times; many would break down no matter how hard they tried to get the words out. Cousins, aunties and uncles spoke with a sparkle in their eyes; a mixture of pride and with tears that many were unable to shed before. Possibly they just could not believe he was dead. Yet seeing that aircraft fly over opened up the heartbreak they could never have imagined possible.

In that lay-by, as they spoke we listened, as did the people of this remarkable little town when they returned back to the Cross Keys and the High Street to await the cortège a few hours later.

Week in week out through February the town's folk listened to each story, each dit, which needed to be told by those hurting. Just by listening it gave comfort to those in need.

Wootton Bassett Mayor Steve Bucknell once said during his year tenure:

'Each one is different; each soldier that falls is different. We always have a lot of family and friends coming down to Wootton Bassett to pay their respects. Part of why so many local people turn up is to offer whatever support we can to them. They will be going through so many emotions – grief, sorrow and a huge amount of pride. They have a lot to be proud of and the people of our own proud community were always there as we believed it was the right thing to do.'

At the same time, on each sad occasion out of the media eye, many hundreds more stood at their own vigil point in recognition to the fallen. The Wootton Bassett factor had rippled along the 46 miles; it was also having an impact on the 'Afghan Heroes charity bike ride.'

The Facebook page was accepting applications on a scale never before seen and was about to create another chapter in this remarkable story. The number of registered bike riders had now reached the staggering figure of 15,000; all making their own arrangements to head to Leigh Delamere service station, eastbound down the M4.

It was at this stage that the Multi-Agency Committee of the Town Council, Police and others, told the organisers that the monster that had been created by this Facebook promotion needed to be reviewed urgently. With only a few weeks to go they had a huge headache to try and resolve; time was not in their favour. The first thing they had to do was stop recruiting others as 15,000 bikers were enough of a challenge.

Firstly, the intended start point was a non-starter. I mean, how can you accommodate 15, 000 bikers at a busy service station on the M4? No chance. Secondly, the distance from Leigh Delamere to RAF Lyneham was 12 miles; the length of a thousand bikes on a motorway is one mile. 15,000 bikes = 15 miles; initial route planned 12 miles; yep, that's a problem, gridlock with still 3,000 bikes parked up.

So without going into the logistics, a start point, holding area, routes, resources and a plan was required and required rather urgently. If – and at that stage there was an 'if' – this event was going to happen then a lot of people were going to have to focus and work together. Failing to do so would leave two other options, cancel or have complete mayhem.

By the end of February that plan became an operational order with huge support being offered by so many agencies and for us, other police forces were volunteering to assist at no cost. Without those individuals, forces and agencies this event would not happen, but the Wootton Bassett factor had this impact on so many people.

That factor brought many groups, organisations, families and individuals into the town to pay gratitude to the community. Most would make their way to stand by the war memorial where many laid a cross, a flower, or a card with a message on it. Some of these cards will be held in the album that Ken Scott had created and secured.

The whole country had heard of Wootton Bassett and indeed further afield across the Atlantic, it was certainly noted by the most powerful man in the world. President Barack Obama of the United States of America referred to it in a speech he gave his country, in relation to respects being shown to all the fallen:

'We want to honour our fallen warriors with the respect and gratitude they deserve whether it's here or in the small British town of Wootton Bassett. People line the streets there in a solemn tribute that represents the best of British character.'

In early March, a choir formed up at the war memorial as once again hundreds were waiting to pay tribute to four servicemen. Sergeant Paul Fox, of 28 Engineer Regiment, Rifleman Martin Kinggett, of 4 Rifles, Senior Aircraftman Luke Southgate, of 11 Squadron RAF Regiment, and Rifleman Carlo Apolis, of 4 Rifles, who were being repatriated to RAF Lyneham.

The Welsh male voice choir sang in tribute at the war memorial, before the cortège passed through. I have no idea if it was planned to coincide with a repatriation or if it was coincidental. Nevertheless it was their own personal tribute to the town and our Armed Forces.

Nick Rogers, the conductor of Swansea's Gwalia Singers, said: 'We thought we would pay our respects to the troops.'

After doing so, the choir to a man stood humbled as so many others have in response to St Bartholomew's Church as the Tenor Bell is struck. The tolling of that Tenor Bell has a massive impact on every person attending especially the first time and I am sure the silence that always followed provoked deep thought.

The hearses were brought to the resting place adjacent to the war memorial and once again that raw emotion broke the silence. As they wept, they moved forward, all wanting to have their own private moment to lay a flower or tribute on the roof of the gleaming black vehicle carrying their loved one.

For a few minutes the world appears to stop as we all feel so helpless in seeing so many people lost and overwhelmed in the one place they had possibly prayed never to be.

As those people left that day others were planning their own visit, but for happier times, as the date was rapidly approaching for the 'Afghan Heroes Charity Bike Ride.'

No other ride of this magnitude had taken place in this country before and a lot of planning had gone on behind the scenes. Resources, routes, timings; in fact everything that could be humanely possibly in preparation of this event was done. The weather – well that was up to him upstairs – but we were ready for 15,000 bikers to fly their flag in tribute to the fallen. Yes, there were a few mutterings in the town as plans for road closures were published, some were concerned they would not get their Mothering Sunday lunch. Although in comparison there were a lot more mothers who would never see their soldier sons or daughters again, which put their complaints in the appropriate place. The vast majority of the town was excited as the day got nearer; I was certainly looking forward to the event. The bikers, well, they were busy making their last minute plans to confirm hotels, routes and to meet up with others and descend on North Wiltshire. Although as they did, Katherine was sharing more bad news and we were to start planning for a further Operation Pabbay.

Even as this huge event was coming towards us and the excitement was building up, no one ever lost sight of where our priorities lay. On the day of repatriations everyone was focused on one thing and one thing only – the fallen and their family.

Three days before the bike ride no one would have even known it was on the agenda, never mind planned for the 14th, as on Thursday 11 March 2010 a further five soldiers who were killed in Afghanistan were repatriated home.

Amongst the thousand plus mourners on the High Street was the distraught fiancée of a fallen British soldier who watched as his body returned home from Afghanistan; in her arms the newborn son he never met.

Grieving Michaela Lindley, 18, and 18-day-old Jaden were among hundreds of mourners who lined the streets to pay tribute to her husband-to-be Rifleman Liam Maughan and four other comrades.

The 18-year-old soldier, of 3 Rifles, killed during a gunfight in Sangin, Helmand, was due home just days before his death and never even saw a photo of son Jaden, who was just 13 days old when his father died. Liam had excitedly told colleagues he could not wait to get home and hold his child with fiancée Michaela Lindley. After his death, she wrote on a website tribute: 'I'll always love you and I'll be the best mum I can be to our son xx.'

Liam's body was repatriated alongside four comrades who died in six bloody days as part of the new offensive against the Taliban. Corporal Richard Green, 23, from Reading died from small arms fire near Sangin in Helmand Province on 2 March. Riflemen Jonathon Allott, 19, from Bournemouth, died following a bomb blast near Sangin, on 5 March. Both Corporal Green and Rifleman Allott served with Rifleman Maughan as part of 3 Rifles. Corporal Stephen Thompson, 31, from Bovey Tracey, was serving with 1 Rifles when he was killed by a bomb 3km south of Sangin district centre on 7 March. Lance Corporal Thomas Keogh, 24, from Paddington, London, of 4 Rifles, died on the same day during a firefight in Sangin.

I watched in silence as the grieving families laid their flowers on the hearses and I found myself deep in thought. What does a mother tell her child when he or she is a little older to understand that their father was killed in a war and explain to them what a hero is? Well maybe Jaden, when the time is right you will get to know that your father came home as a Great British hero with four other equally outstanding young men. Hundreds and hundreds of people lined the 46 mile route to honour them, where they stood for hours as a mark of respect.

Why did they stand? Well because the country woke up and recognised that each and every Soldier, Airman, Marine and Naval rank who paid the ultimate sacrifice deserved to be honoured as the true hero they were. That is why you and every other person who has lost a father, son, daughter, brother, sister, husband, wife, fiancé or partner should always know that the country truly recognised your loss. Always stand tall telling the world how proud you are of them. So many, who were so young, with so many unfulfilled dreams are gone, but not forgotten by a nation trying to support those poor families with compassion and care.

Some four years later I met the mother of Jonathon Michael Allott, Andrea Johnson, at her home, which can only be described as a shrine in memory of her son. One cannot mistake the trauma that is etched on her face as she told me of her beloved oldest son, brother to Nikki, Marc and Daniel, who has followed Jonathon into the Rifles. It is with sadness and pride she fights the tears and wants people to remember her son; like so many others of the fallen.

During our conversation I learnt that Jonathon was a fighter, a proud man to serve the Crown as a 'Barma man' (one who searches out IEDs). He was always at the forefront of every patrol, clearing the way for his fellow men who were protecting his back. Yes, The Rifles were an elite front line infantry unit. That band of brothers I mention so many times transcends each rank. No better example can be shown, than when Captain Mick Robinson, the Quartermaster of 3 Rifle Battle Group made a visit to Andrea Johnson to tell her about the day her son passed away.

As Jonathon slipped away, the Captain vowed to the young rifleman he would visit his mother at the end of this gruelling tour. This was a vow he honoured when he made his way to Bournemouth and kissed the forehead of a very grateful mother, saying it was from Jonathon. Then he sat before her as she took in each and every word he spoke. Captain Mick Robinson created a journal during his deployment and opened the page dated Friday 5 March 2010 and explained the day her son Rifleman Jonathon Michael Allott, B Coy had been wounded by an IED blast. In graphic detail he describes the catastrophic injuries her son had sustained, but even though unconscious and not breathing, with severe wounds this young rifleman did not leave without a fight. When the harrowing decision was made to switch off the life support machines, Jonathon's colleagues and friends came in to say their final goodbyes.

The padre stood on one side of the bed with his crook in his hand saying a prayer, asking God to take Jonathon from this life and offer comfort to his family. When the machine was turned off, Captain Mick Robinson was holding Jonathon's hand while stroking his head, a nurse placed a hand on Mick's shoulder to offer some comfort and the captain, a Quartermaster, who had gone right through the ranks from an illustrious career, turns his head.

He tells Andrea, to his surprise he saw the room full of the nurses and doctors who tried to save her son's life; all their faces engraved with deep sadness, their eyes full of tears. It gave him comfort that he was not alone as Jonathon passed away. He kissed his forehead and said, 'Goodbye my brother – be with God.'

Those words were so important to a mother who lost her oldest son; to know he was not alone as he passed away with the man now sat before her at his side. A Quartermaster who looked upon her son as one of his own, along with so many other Rifleman brothers, 'Swift and Bold.'

I was overwhelmed by the words written in the journal by Captain Mick Robinson, which he had handed to Andrea. Words failed me in how to respond after I read such words of compassion, that were for a mother who was now holding another picture in her hand. I looked up at her and just shook my head knowing that my eyes were welling up. Andrea placed the photograph in my hand which was of her son's headstone. The images I have seen in the last hour are still so vivid in my mind. A blast has erupted, I see the trauma in trying to save a life, the last rights are given and now I am at a graveside with the photo in my hand. A heartbroken mother's message was so poignant and truly meant; I just held the photo in my hands and felt the pain in each of the words she wrote; unashamedly I felt the tears run down my cheek as I read:

I'd gladly take your place; your life had just begun
Sleep my little Soldier
Sleep tight my little son

When I left her home that day I said, 'God Bless you Andrea; I will never forget you or your son.'

CHAPTER 21

The day after those five men came home was the start of more extraordinary scenes. Scenes on a scale never before witnessed in the country, never mind Wootton Bassett, as the bikers started to descend on this small market town for the weekend. The initial fifty bikers that requested permission to ride onto the station of RAF Lyneham were approved, although that date was changed to Friday 12 March. They would congregate at the war memorial then ride down and onto the Air Station but only 50; their 14,950 friends were asked to come in spirit only.

I made my way up to the war memorial around lunchtime to find that Julia and her followers were together chatting away with a mixture of excitement and emotion. Many were pinching themselves to make sure it was not a dream; that this idea of young Elizabeth Stevens to pop down to Wootton Bassett for a pint had indeed arrived.

Julia's invited party of 50 formed up and just before they set off I noted that the RAF Lyneham Padre had joined them on his Harley to make the number up to 51, but with the good Lord on his side I was sure he would get into the Base.

I nipped down to RAF Lyneham before they arrived and met up with Group Captain John Gladston, the Station Commander. He was waiting at the front of one of his C130 Hercules aircraft for the arrival of Julia Stevenson leading these 50 plus one bikers.

Just as you always heard the roar of the engines of the C17 Globemaster before you saw it, so we heard the rumbling thunder of bikes heading through the village of Lyneham making their way to RAF Lyneham.

They arrived proud as punch, riding up from the main gates like a long snake; turning towards the terminal and then onto the apron where Group Captain John Gladston was standing with his project manager. Once there the engines of these powerful machines were turned off as each of the riders closed up to hear the words of Julia Stevenson. A brief speech concluded, she then presented the Station Commander with a commemorative inscribed shield from the bikers. A final handshake and best wishes for Sunday were passed to all that had the honour to be the 50 chosen, before they left the sacred ground where so many fallen had been returned home.

On Saturday, the day before the main event, I worked a day shift predominately in Wootton Bassett High Street; flying the flag as we used to say in the police. It was a glorious day with the sun shining down on us and one that could so easily have been mistaken for an English summer's day. It really was nice and remained so for the whole weekend. They say God works in mysterious ways, well, if this weather was a gift from him, it was gratefully received.

The preparations had been going on for sometime prior to their arrival as road signs were placed on major routes to advertise the event. Anyone travelling east and west along the motorway between Bristol and Reading would notice the RAC signs, or hear on the radio news the continuous updating for the local community. It was another example of the behind the scenes activities that were taking place with everyone trying to do their best to host the event without causing unnecessary disturbance to everyday life.

You have to chuckle really, this huge amount of activity, must have had an impact on so many thousands of people besides the 15,000 participating on the ride. The brainchild of Elizabeth Stevens, a young student who just fancied popping down to Bassett for a pint with a few mates on their bikes to say hello and thanks to the locals. If I keep in tune with the Facebook terminology I guess I have to put lol at the end of that sentence, but that was her initial plan.

Nick Spargo, Jim Wale, Andy Singfield and I were on duty in the High Street and each time the traffic lights changed from red to green we saw another wave of bikers arrive.

The magnet that drew them into the town centre was the building on stilts, which everyone arriving recognised as the most prominent object they had seen when watching the spontaneous ceremony on television. Within a short period of time, that area was a flood of leather-jacketed men, women and children, who changed the ambience of the small market town that day around the building on stilts to a place of hallowed ground. Throughout the day they walked up from any place they could park their bikes and paid their own personal respects at the war memorial, many capturing their presence with photographs. A photograph that to them which said: 'I was there.'

It was only two days earlier that five soldiers were brought to rest for a short period of time, where flowers were laid on their hearses where so many people had wept. That fact was not missed by anyone who stood paying their personal respects looking down at the many floral tributes that were laid along with the many cards and crosses that had messages from loved ones. For many I think they realised where they were and what it signified to them personally. A few tears were shed as they read poems, cards and crosses, everyone caught up in the atmosphere that they themselves had created with their presence.

They travelled in their hundreds that day, from every compass point as I found out during the many friendly conversations we had with the bikers. One group I met had travelled from the States arriving at Heathrow Airport and then hiring their bikes to take part. They shook hands with the local people who were carrying out their everyday shopping, the pubs, the cafés; the shops were full to bursting point. Yep, the bikers were making their presence known with the hallmark of everything Wootton Bassett had to offer, with honour, dignity and respect.

The planning team had decided that the old runway at Hullavington was to be the designated start point and it was awash with activity as tents, reception areas, toilets and refreshment facilities were being erected. I drove up there with PCSO Andy Singfield and what a sight. Would I be exaggerating to say a million cones? Probably, yes, maybe five less, but they were placed in row after row stretching the length of the former runway. A runway that was used as a flying training school at the beginning of the Second World War, where top officers from allied nations came to share ideas and ways of using the aircraft. How fitting that this route was bringing generations together, a chapter in the history of a past war at the start and to conclude at Wootton Bassett; a representation of a modern conflict. Two separate generations from our proud country who remembered her fallen.

So as we left the runway just as the sun was going down and the last cone was laid, everyone who was involved in the planning and preparations could take a deep breath; they were ready. There was an air of excitement as we drove back along the designated 12-mile route for the event. Bikes were everywhere going in all directions, as they carried out their own preparations for the following day. Residents were hanging bunting and Union flags in their gardens and you could feel the exhilaration building up. It was almost like a virus spreading rapidly through the community, along the A429 to Malmesbury, turning right to Brinkworth on the B4042 down Callow Hill turning left to White Hill Lane to the final turn left; onto the A3102 where Wootton Bassett was buzzing in anticipation. This was going to be huge.

The day had arrived: Sunday 14 March 2010, Mothering Sunday. Julia Stevenson recalls her thoughts, when she rode her own wheels of thunder onto Hullavington Runway for that first time:

'It was so exhausting; I felt so humbled and proud to be associated with this event and the way that the whole of the biking community came together. We worked with so many different agencies, with one goal to say a simple thank you to so many who deserved to be thanked. To the fallen: to show we do remember them; to their families: to show we care and to the town of Wootton Bassett, a thank you for the respects that they have shown.'

Julia glows as she speaks:

'I was immensely proud when I actually arrived at Hullavington, I could not believe how it had all come to fruition. From 7.30am on the day seeing the airfield as just a mass of cones (see I told you there were a million). Then the thunder started rumbling. Through the gates they came in their hundreds, as the bikers made their presence known heading towards the registration area. I think I grew ten feet tall watching them heading in my direction, looking from them, then seeing my own family brought me almost to my knees. My grandchildren were walking towards me carrying orange buckets with flags in; I just broke down in tears. I was so proud to be a Great British biker and believe me these were the first tears of many to be shed by me and many others that day.'

Then with the shake of her head and running her fingers through her blonde locks, standing in her leathers, there she was live on Sky News. There was no mistaking her passion for our country, of being able to be a part of something a little bit special; in supporting our troops in conflict. Who knows it may well have been seen in Camp Bastion and if it was I am sure it was a nice tonic for the very important morale tablet that is so often needed when deployed so faraway from home.

The plan was for the bikers to gather at Hullavington Airfield with the reception area allowing for 500 bikes to be parked in rows, each group being called a pulse. Each pulse would be led by police outriders for the 30-minute ride along the rural route through Wootton Bassett and disperse at the roundabout at the north of the town.

Julia was at the front of the first 500 bikes as she followed the two marked police outriders leading each pulse, and describes that memorable journey:

'Let the thunder roll, I roared as I led the first batch of bikers out of the airfield and along the country roads en route to Wootton Bassett. I was amazed at the amount of people on the roadsides along the route, hundreds stood on the verge proudly waving flags and clapping. I really had to focus on riding as I could feel the emotions once again building up. This was real rural England on a glorious sunny warm day and what a fitting route for such an event. People were everywhere; you would come round a bend where there were more people setting up picnic tables, establishing their viewing points for the day. The happiness we all shared, them seeing us, us seeing them, especially the older people with their carers, sitting in their wheelchairs with blankets over them outside their nursing homes, waving to us as we passed. I cannot describe what feelings and emotions this gave me and I know I was not on my own. Then we started to climb the hill that leads up towards St Bartholomew's Church into Wootton Bassett High Street and you just saw a mass of faces all looking in our direction. I find words inadequate to fully describe my emotions going into Wootton Bassett, seeing the building on stilts, thousands of people lining either side of the road. The tears flowed and I could do nothing to stem that flow, it really was one of the most emotional moments in my life. Did I feel proud? Yep, that's one word I could use, amongst many others that best describe satisfaction in being involved in something very, very special. It was our little way of saying thank you. After riding through the town, we stopped at a lay-by and I practically fell off my bike. I was shedding tears as I looked through the glazed vision that were now my eyes, I was surrounded by many other riders reliving that last 30 minutes' experience. One that neither they nor I will ever forget.'

Being on point duty that day with my colleagues in the High Street was, as Julia says, incredibly emotional; thousands of people lined the road. The crowd were trying to touch the glove of a rider to high-five them in recognition of mutual respect. People were smiling, people were buzzing and they were shouting so loud to try and make themselves heard or shouting even louder to get their mate to get them a pint. There was every make and model of bike ever seen on the roads of our country that day and even a couple from the *Mad Max* movie, when I saw a few of the trikes. I also had a brief chat with my mates Phil and Tommo who both expressed their own pride in being involved in this half hour ride of respect.

The last pulse though was around 2,000 bikes as a decision was made to let all that was left on the runway go at once; else we would have been there all night. Yet, as the clock was approaching 6pm, the town's people remained and applauded the last man on his bike through.

It was another extraordinary day, started almost innocently with Elizabeth Stevens and her mates wanting to pop down to Bassett for a pint and a bite. Although we were extremely busy, I could never get that image out of my head. I heard Elizabeth had taken part as a pillion passenger on a friend's bike, probably one of the ones she invited to join her initially. Well, if I had met the young lady, I would have bought her that pint myself. Her imagination and guidance from Julia had created this event, and in doing so raised over £100,000 for the charity. An outstanding achievement, but this was far more than raising funds on this special day. It was for the mothers who founded the Charity Afghan Heroes. We can only hope they took some small comfort that so many thought of them that day. It was a day the country recognised the sacrifice they and so many others had borne, as they will never hear from their son or daughter, the words many take for granted: 'Happy Mother's Day Mum.'

CHAPTER 22

The roar and thunder of that amazing weekend in Wootton Bassett was something that will live in the memories of so many. It was the topic of conversation in the town; there were thousands of messages on Facebook and many clips put on the internet. It was lovely to see the 'town that weeps', as it was regularly referred to, become a town who once again smiled. Yes, that 'thank you' was very well received and the bikers were the latest group of people to fall in love with our small market town.

Rich Bond, my colleague from Plymouth, who had travelled up with the Ministry of Defence Police, Divisional Support Group phoned a couple of days later. He was thanking us up here in Bassett for inviting them to assist in policing the event. This was echoed by so many others and was something unheard of; thanking us for working on a Sunday! By the time they got back home they had worked around 14 hours that day and without pay.

The town was buzzing. Popping into the Town Council offices, the mood was one of great satisfaction because all the hard work behind the scenes had paid off. This was a great community, working with each other and the other agencies, it was only right that they celebrated the great success of the Afghan Heroes Charity Bike Ride in raising over £100,000.

However, the smiles of happiness were not going to last for long as two days after that amazing day, Katherine's name flashed up on my mobile and I was to hear those familiar words again. The people of Bassett at least could have 24 hours of happiness before they would see the news scrolling along their TV screens with the headlines: 'Two British Soldiers Killed in Afghanistan.'

It was such a confusing time, our minds were an emotional mess, even an element of guilt for celebrating on Sunday, then two days later knowing that someone's family had just received that awful knock on the door.

Ten days later the hand clapping of the bikers' hands and the roar of those powerful engines was replaced with the sounding of the St Bartholomew's Church Tenor Bell. Lance Corporal Scott Hardy, 26, and Private James Grigg, 21, both from 1st Battalion The Royal Anglian Regiment, died after being hit by a Taliban roadside bomb in Musa Qala, Helmand Province, on 16 March. Hundreds of people stood in silent tribute under grey skies as the two soldiers were returned to British soil.

I cannot begin to imagine the worry those at home had whilst their loved ones were away on deployments on Operation Herrick. That was the operational name for British operations in Afghanistan. To have one son or daughter deployed in that hostile environment was worrying enough, to have three sons out there in a front line fighting unit, beggar's belief the sleepless nights that would have provoked, in what must have been the longest six months of any parent's life. Rodney and Tracy Holkham from the Isle of Sheppey in Kent were the proud parents of three frontline soldiers serving with the 3rd Battalion the Rifles. Their sons: Riflemen, Andrew Holkham 18, Daniel Holkham, 19 and Matthew Holkham, 20.

On Saturday 27 March 2010, the three brothers were in the last couple of weeks of their deployment when tragedy struck. Rifleman Daniel Holkham, the middle son was killed in an explosion when he tried to intercept a suicide bomber near Sangin Bazaar in Helmand.

Three days later there they stood, mum and dad with their oldest and youngest sons at Wootton Bassett war memorial; one son missing, killed in action. United in grief, I saw them as I drove the lead police vehicle to the end of the High Street, a family watching, waiting, clutching their flowers, distraught as the body of their son and brother is led towards them. Rifleman Daniel Holkham, 19, was one of three soldiers whose coffins were driven through Wootton Bassett that day.

Just as the Holkham family were huddled together watching the conductor page towards them leading the three fallen heroes, so were the family and friends of Serjeant Steven Campbell and Lance Corporal of Horse Jonathan Woodgate.

The Ministry of Defence had stated Serjeant Steven Campbell was killed by an IED while on foot patrol in Sangin. The 30-year-old was also from the 3rd Battalion, The Rifles. The third soldier to be brought through the town was 26-year-old Lance Corporal of Horse Jonathan Woodgate. This Household Cavalry Regiment soldier was fatally wounded by a grenade having previously survived a notorious US 'friendly fire' incident in Iraq in 2003.

Family and friends placed yellow, red and white roses on the hearses for several minutes while the cortège stopped at the town's war memorial. The standards and regimental banners were lowered and church bells tolled in respect.

From where I stood you could hear the grief as the town stood still. The conductor slowly made his way towards us. Then I would salute, raising my right arm in my own personal recognition of the three soldiers before we continued on our route.

One could easily be misled to believe that this was a full time job and no other policing duties were carried out. Yes, it was a priority, but alas just as in any other neighbourhood, we had other duties to perform. One day, whilst carrying out a day shift duty unrelated to Operation Pabbay, I received a call from the RAF Police requesting my attendance at the main gate to RAF Lyneham. On arrival I was introduced to a couple of women who were slightly flustered having driven to Lyneham from Somerset. One lady was the manager or owner of an elderly person's residential home. She told us that one of the residents had gone missing and she thought that he would have come to our area.

It appeared from the information she shared that the missing gentleman had watched many of the repatriations on the national news in the confines of his cosy chair and in the warmth of the residential lounge. During those humbling scenes on the screen he had mentioned to the staff that he had served in the Army and wanted to go to Wootton Bassett to show his respects. Sadly, for whatever reason, his wish was never fulfilled.

However, there is no such thing as 'no' if you're determined, focused and had once worn the Beret of a British soldier. Age and frailty are just a challenge, one that he had decided he was going to overcome. I circulated the gent's name and description over my police radio, having got further details from the somewhat embarrassed informant. One of the town's PCSOs heard the information and description of the missing gent being circulated on the police radio and was on the High Street. Within minutes the elderly gent was located proudly standing at the Wootton Bassett war memorial with a man and lady.

It turns out that the couple were driving in their car and came across the former British soldier hitchhiking on his way to Wootton Bassett.

He told them who he was and his intent; the couple were so overwhelmed with his story and determination that they changed their plans and drove him to the war memorial to allow him to lay his own personal tribute.

How he absconded we never established and who knows maybe he returned to be present at a later date to salute the fallen. Although what he did show was the massive impact this small market town was having on so many people in our country, in recognising the huge loss of those serving.

My one regret in relation to that gentleman is that I am unable to name him; his details remain in my old police pocket book, locked in a cupboard with my old uniform; discarded, but like you Sir, not forgotten. I salute you with the utmost respect.

CHAPTER 23

S adly, as we all now know, 2010 was as devastating as the previous years and never a month passed without those awful words being received: 'Prepare for Op Pabbay.' April and May brought more families from across the nation down to Wootton Bassett when they travelled from their own communities.

They would travel from major cities such as Newcastle, Manchester, Stoke and Swansea, but also from the small towns. I will never forget the people of Dipton, Co Durham who stood there breaking their hearts; proudly wearing the T-shirts of their local hero, Royal Engineer Daryn Roy, when he came home.

It was a relentless chapter for our Armed Forces, as one battle group was planning their return from their six month gruelling tour the final preparations were being made by the units to replace them.

However, before any unit deploys the training prior to this is intense. Refreshing skills and making sure they are as prepared as possible for the challenges that lay ahead of them. Many of those preparing to deploy to Afghanistan would even find time in between the intense training to lead normal lives, perhaps fit in a holiday abroad and some even found the time to get married.

One of those that took the plunge into marriage was Royal Marine Adam Brown who, with his childhood sweetheart Amy Tardelli, made Christmas a little bit special by getting married on the 21 December 2009. Not a bad Christmas gift for either couple, a dashing young Royal Marine and a beautiful blonde bride, full of happiness and excitement as their dream comes true; the day they both said 'I do.' No time for a honeymoon because the training was full on, with courses to be completed in preparation for a six-month arduous tour.

It was so important to be finely tuned for this tour, but with great leadership and experience each unit was always ready on time. Besides brushing up on all the skills that were required, administration was also a very important part before they set off from home.

Of the many aspects in preparation of a tour that was to take place was the attention to detail should one be killed. As unpleasant a thought as it was, it could not be avoided as everyone was going on this tour fully aware of the dangers they would encounter.

Letters were written, wills were made and photographs of each serviceman or woman taken. These were the photographs that would be presented to the media, when making the announcement that they had been killed.

It was vitally important that those words were written, but once completed they were to be omitted from their thoughts, hoping they would be destroyed when their tour was safely completed.

Many returning to Afghanistan were on their second or third tour and with other conflicts were time served veterans by the time they were in their mid-twenties.

Royal Marine Adam Brown was on his third combat mission having served in Iraq and Afghanistan previously.

He had joined in October 2004 and passed for duty as a Royal Marine Commando in September 2005. Men like Adam were the rock you needed in a unit who, from his previous experience, would be looked upon by his peers for guidance in stressful situations. He stood out from the crowd, tall, rugged, handsome and athletic, an action man with huge drive and determination. With him being on his third operational tour and with all those natural skills, he was looked upon as a natural leader, a team player who had the respect of all. The other vital ingredient for those deploying was the support of your family so you could focus on the job in hand and he certainly had that. Amy and the family understood exactly what worry was in store when they would wave him off, from their own experiences of his previous tours.

Once away the letter writing would begin; the greatest comfort for a person at home or deployed was when the postie drops that bluey through your door or in Afghanistan on your pit.

Since my days in service, communications have improved with the ability to make a satellite telephone call. Those having been on previous deployments knew the quality of those calls and that you could be cut off without warning. So Adam and Amy both made a pact before he deployed that once a call got through the opening words would always be to say 'I LOVE YOU' in case the call was terminated. Just hearing that simple message would make life so much more bearable.

With the last hugs and kisses, the coaches depart on the first phase of this long journey from the green hills of Somerset, to the bleakness of sun-drenched Afghanistan.

The fear, the worry, the nightmare in each and every person's mind that was there to wave the Marines off must have been noticeable on each of their faces. How does a person left at home get through the day, the weeks, the months, until the safe return is reached? I cannot begin to imagine.

Yet manage they must, as it was another awful year for fatalities to our Armed Forces in Afghanistan and it was impossible not to be aware when that sad news broke. Another soldier killed, another family heartbroken and another reason for the country to mourn the loss of one of our own.

40 Commando had been out in Afghanistan just weeks into their six-month tour when they sustained a fatality. Corporal Christopher Harrison described as a 'legend' by his Commanding Officer, was killed on the 9 May.

So much sadness and raw grief would follow. It was impossible to imagine their loss, even though we saw it with our own eyes when they came through to Wootton Bassett. It was impossible to forget the scene of devastation when two heartbroken women; a wife who lost her husband and a mother who lost her son, broke down and were inconsolable as they held onto the hearse.

There, Corporal Harrison's wife Rebecca and his mother Gill remained oblivious to everything around them, lost in a world that was so difficult to understand. It was awful to see so much pain as they touched the glass window that separated them from their special man.

And sadly it was a scene that was to repeated because by the end of that month a further five families would be equally devastated with the same message which followed that awful knock on their door.

Friday 21 May 2010 Corporal Stephen Walker, 42, of 40 Commando, died from an explosion while carrying out a foot patrol in Sangin, Helmand Province. Five days later Corporal Walker's body was brought home to RAF Lyneham alongside that of Navy Petty Officer Andrew Brookes, who died in a traffic accident in Bahrain on 16 May.

Standards were lowered, Marines and British Legion saluted while the tearful family and friends placed orange lilies onto the hearse as it stopped at the town's war memorial.

For many it was difficult to distance yourself from that deep sadness, and many who never knew Corporal Stephen Walker felt the grief and despair of his family.

It was shattering seeing the innocence of a six-year-old girl breaking her heart as she was picked up to place her floral tribute on the vehicle that carried her dad. Such raw, emotional sadness from a daughter that no stranger could ever experience, as she looked down at the Union flag draped coffin that contained her hero long before he died. When all respects had been shown her father was escorted away; the little girl stood with her mother and brother hating to say goodbye.

That sadness stayed with us all as we escorted the cortège away, leaving a mother to comfort those left behind.

Leona Walker was full of dignity on the day she spoke so proudly of her husband: 'Steve was a fantastic dad to his daughter Greer and son Samuel, he was passionate, loyal and determined. He enjoyed the role he had in the Marines but he was a family man at heart. Although this is a very sad time, Steve would want us to be positive, to remember the good times, the happy times.'

Those words were spoken by a woman, a mother, a grieving wife distraught over the loss of her soul mate, but also having to help her children cope with the start of their new life. That courage and determination to tackle each new day showed that not every hero went to war; many were at home coping with the new world that they and their family had to face. A new world that all at home feared to enter, as their loved ones were in a conflict which continued to have no mercy and inflict further devastation on yet more families.

Marine Scott Gregory Taylor, from Alpha Company, 40 Commando Royal Marines, was killed within the area of Sangin, Afghanistan on Sunday 30 May 2010.

Operation Minimise was activated in Camp Bastion, while in the UK two Royal Marine officers and a Padre carried a message of despair to an address in Buxton, Derbyshire.

In Afghanistan, another military officer was waiting the arrival of an aircraft, carrying more commandos from RAF Brize Norton, who were flying out to begin their own six month tour. That military officer was to meet only one man; one man he had specific orders for.

Royal Marine Liam Taylor was just getting off that aircraft to commence his own operational tour in Afghanistan. As he stepped down from the aircraft he was to hear the tragic news and a set of orders that it would have been difficult to take in.

Those orders were to return home with the most important piece of property he would ever be charged to carry throughout his whole career, in fact possibly in his life, his younger brother Scott. His new orders would have been delivered with compassion and the empathy one would expect when such a harrowing message had to be passed onto the Royal Marine.

The military seem to have an operation name for everything they do – op this and op that – but even they have no op name for a Marine escorting his own brother home. Possibly because no word or op order could ever describe the numbness, the hurt and pain that only those brothers felt or understood when they endured the duty of carrying out that unimaginable task. A task bestowed upon many during this conflict.

As preparations were being made in Camp Bastion to return Scott with his older brother Liam to RAF Lyneham, I would always find the time to read the tributes of the men we were escorting back in a few days' time. I can never emphasise enough how important that was for me as each of the fallen was a person from a family. I never looked upon them as just a name, or number, or worse still, a statistic. The tributes I read came from colleagues as well as friends and most importantly his family.

Helen English, a close family friend wrote, 'Scotty was the whole package – kind, loving (devoted to his family and friends), generous and full of fun and mischief. As well as being extremely brave and strong in mind and body. He was truly selfless, showing respect for all he came into contact with. He had the highest of morals and was a true and loyal friend to our James from the day they met over 15 years ago.'

The warmth, love and sincerity is shown and you know they were written from a broken heart; not just her own, but also carrying the pain felt by her son James who had lost his best friend.

His Commanding Officer said: 'Marine Scott Taylor was everything I needed in a

Bootneck; proud but not arrogant, loyal but still independent, courageous but not foolhardy, he was an outstanding Marine. He was an utterly selfless man who was often unassuming, preferring instead to let his actions speak for him – and they spoke with power and tumult. He was a giant in the gymnasium, a consummate professional in the field and a true mate to his friends.'

Many of those words were reiterated by his comrades who felt the loss of their friend, who loved his cups of tea. Described as having a great sense of humour and dependable when times were tough, the hurt was clear to feel as you read every word. Everyone mentioned him being awesome in the gym, from the Commanding Officer through the ranks. You do not need much of an imagination to understand exactly what they meant by his physique, when best described in the tribute written by Marine Tino Hotine and also how they all felt:

'Scotty "The Back" – due to the fact that your back was massive! This was but one of your many qualities, the others being the rest of your body: abs like a cheese grater and a chest that Lucy Pinder would be proud of. As well as this, you were professional through and through and although I didn't know you for long, I really enjoyed the time we spent together.

You never complained about a thing, every time something needed doing you were the first volunteer no matter how bad things got. You carried out your job with the utmost pride and you were proud to be a Bootneck. It is terrible that you are no longer with us mate and I hate to write in the past tense, but our memories of you will be shared between us for as long as I live.

Our thoughts are with your family buddy, but if they are as strong as you were, I am sure they will get through these hard times. We'll be sure to have a drink with them back at Norton Manor, and the obvious hoofing dits about you will be spun.'

It was also very evident that Scott was a family man when those Marines hurting said: 'How much he spoke proudly of his older brother Liam.' I have no doubt their thoughts would have been with Liam, knowing he was bringing Scotty home.

To a home that was devastated in grief which was insurmountable, far worse than anything they had ever known and yet bravely his mother said:

'We were blessed to be Scotty's parents as Liam was to have him as his younger brother. He was loving, caring, kind and loyal. Material things had little value to Scotty; the love and respect of his family and friends meant so much more. He lit up our lives with love and laughter, and made the world for us a better place. He will live on in our hearts and memories forever, but our lives, they will never be the same.'

Scott was to be repatriated home on Thursday 3 June and his family accepted the offer to stay in the Hilton hotel on the Wednesday night rather than travel down to RAF Lyneham on the same day. This allowed those in the role of support, be it the Visiting Officer or RAF Lyneham Repatriation Team, to try to prepare the family the evening before as best they could for a hugely emotional day.

On Wednesday, Jayne and Steve Taylor were at home when their Visiting Officer had to break some further tragic news before they made their journey to Swindon. The Visiting Officer is their protection as they make their progress through unknown territory, yet there was no easy way to relay the words other than with sincere compassion. Their son's comrade Royal Marine Anthony Hotine, 21, of 40 Commando, had been killed. It is impossible to imagine what must have been going through their minds on hearing more shattering news. Tino Hotine, who wrote that personal tribute about Scott, would not be making it back for that drink at Norton Manor. Inconceivable as it was, he would be on the next flight home.

It almost seemed too far fetched, yet sadly it was true. Inside three days, they had found themselves in a completely different world, one that was awful, cruel and which brought so much agonising pain.

It was the correct decision to deliver that tragic message to Steve and Jayne in the privacy of their own home; on Thursday morning it was being announced on the morning news. Their day was emotional enough with their thoughts on both their sons, as Liam their oldest was bringing his younger brother Scott home.

On that Thursday 3 June 2010 two other outstanding men would be repatriated home. I could not help but get drawn into what I read about each person who we escorted home and these are a couple of statements that allow me to use words such as 'outstanding men'.

Lieutenant Colonel Paul James, Commanding Officer, 40 Commando Group, Combined Force Sangin, said:

'Corporal Stephen Curley was the very best of his generation; bright, fit, charismatic and supremely brave, he was a man who genuinely inspired others. Based with me in FOB Jackson, I saw in him a selfless, loyal, utterly dedicated and natural leader of men. He died on patrol in Sangin leading the men he loved, and alongside the men who loved him. His sharp wit knew few limits, particularly in the gymnasium where he reigned supreme, with both the RSM [Regimental Sergeant Major] and I regularly in the firing line. As a Marine he was professionally unrivalled – a Mountain Leader, a consummate tactician and a brilliant Section Commander who cared passionately for his men.

Our thoughts and prayers are with his wife Kirianne and new-born son William, his family and his friends. He will be desperately missed by everyone in 40 Commando. Corporal Stephen Curley was, and always will be, a Royal Marine Commando.'

The third soldier who came home that day was Gunner Zac Cusack, of the 4th Regiment Royal Artillery, from Stoke-on-Trent. When I read of this outstanding Gunner it was the words of his family that caught my eye:

'Zak was a courageous, compassionate and charismatic young man. We are justly proud of not only the job that he did, but of the complete person we all knew and loved. For such a young man, Zak's infectious sense of humour, appetite for life and truly romantic heart inspired so many others. Zak's loss leaves a hole in our hearts, a chasm in our lives and many, many other broken hearts behind. He had a fire in his soul that will burn brightly in all our memories. He is our beautiful boy, loving son and best friend, in Zak's own words, "he is a ledge" (Legend).'

And, yes, in the words of a heartbroken family three legends were in that huge aircraft when it flew low and slow just hanging in the sky. Then with so much grace the deft dip of the starboard wing showed so much honour, with a message that they were home.

As hundreds started to form up at the vigil points along the 46 mile route the three heroes were carried off the aircraft with the utmost honour and pristine drills during the military repatriation ceremony. Then for some the most personal time, where they would be alone with just their family in the Chapel of Rest before standing with friends, family and communities who wanted to comfort them in their grief.

The spontaneous scenes that had been started by so few and now caught the imagination of so many, were once again shown. Unfaltering support was displayed along the streets of Wootton Bassett as they were lined with people who wanted to pay their respects. There was no doubt from the scenes I saw that the nation stood together in recognising the loss of three outstanding men.

Seven days later they were back when the repatriation ceremony was held to bring home the bodies of four more servicemen who had recently lost their lives in Afghanistan.

One of those as you know, was Marine Anthony Hotine, 40 Commando, Royal Marines, who wrote such a personal tribute about his friend Scotty and was equally respected by members of his unit. If I can be so bold to summarise some of the quotes I read from a Commando that was hurting from so many recent fatalities.

Tino was described by his Commanding Officer: 'A brilliant young man who was at the height of his profession; bright, selfless, dedicated and keen-spirited, he was an outstanding Marine.'

His colleagues loved his personality, his character, the dits he used to tell and immense professional skills he displayed, but one thing that was repeated by many was from something deep inside: 'Tino's strength came from the heart and it really did radiate outward to the rest of the lads.'

With each tribute that was written there was a similar end – Anthony Hotine was another who will not be forgotten by his colleagues, families or friends.

So many wonderful words written in relation to each and every one of the fallen that are worthy of being read, but alas it is just not possible to do so in this book. So as you read the name of the three other heroes who came home this day, I challenge you to read what was said.

Corporal Terry Webster and Lance Corporal Alan Cochran were both from the 1st Battalion, The Mercian Regiment. They were killed in an exchange of small arms fire with insurgent forces in the Nahr-e Saraj district of Helmand province on the 4 June.

Lance Bombardier Mark Chandler, 3rd Regiment, Royal Horse Artillery, was killed by small arms fire in a contact with insurgents in the Nad Ali area of Helmand province on the 8 June.

I often used to wish I could record the scenes of respect we saw whilst escorting the cortège and send copies to each family. There were so many images that could be shared, but this one was witnessed by PCSO Andy Singfield which was particularly unique.

Andy was in the rear police escort vehicle with Inspector Steve Cox as the cortège made its way out of Wootton Bassett. A radio message is passed to another police patrol car on the M4 motorway a few miles short of Junction 16. That message was to commence the rolling barrier, a term used by police in slowing down traffic on a fast road. What it also did was create a void in the traffic, to allow the cortège to enter onto the motorway, almost creating a sterile bubble. The outriders would lead the cortège down the slip road and then they would move into lane two, the middle lane. Leaving the front police patrol car leading the cortège on the inside lane, lane one. Once the cortège was all on lane one, the outriders would drop back and place themselves at an equal distance apart and ride parallel to the hearses carrying the fallen. The rear police car in the cortège commanded by Inspector Cox would close up tight. The police patrol car executing the rolling barrier would be about 200 metres to the rear of the cortège, holding back three fully congested lanes of traffic. This highlighted the importance of who was being escorted and established a guard of honour as they drove along the motorway at 50mph.

It was an awesome sight of respect as the cortège was escorted along the motorway with all the blue lights activated, a spectacle not missed by the vehicles travelling in the opposite direction, as it drove gracefully on this five-mile stretch of road. But not only did it catch the eyes of people on the ground on this particular escort, it caught the attention of those above. The skies were clear until two Apache helicopters were seen to be flying over the motorway from the north. Although it was not an unusual sight seeing military aircraft from RAF Lyneham some eight miles away and Salisbury Plain to the south, however, it would have been interesting from their height to see what this scene looked like from above.

PCSO Andy Singfield recalls that day:

'Unexpectedly both aircraft swooped to their right taking a starboard turn and approached the cortège from the rear. The pilots then manoeuvred their aircraft so that the front Apache was over the lead hearse; the second Apache flew up above the rear police vehicle.'

Andy spoke with such clarity how he and Coxy were mesmerised, watching the aircraft fly above them for the few miles they were on the M4. Those who were in regular attendance on the bridge over the motorway also saw this flight of respect. One person was seen to take a snapshot of the sight they all observed. Andy saw this and said to Coxy, 'That's tomorrow's front page story in the local evening paper.' Sadly the image of that extraordinary scene never did surface into the public domain, which was a great pity. I am sure it would have given those families whose loved ones were being escorted that day something very special to treasure. It is moments like that which show those who lost loved ones that the level of honour shown went a lot further than the humbling scenes on the High Street in Wootton Bassett.

I was unable to clarify exactly when the Apache escort took place as this was one of the few Op Entourages I was not involved in, but the day is one Andy will never forget.

CHAPTER 24

I t truly was once again an awful summer as the harrowing news of each loss of life rippled throughout each community connected with this conflict. The fear of so many who had loved ones out in Afghanistan grew; praying they would not be the next to receive that knock on the door.

As towns and communities came to Bassett to show their respects, so did many of the wives from their military estates, sometimes arriving as a group on a coach just as the wives did from Taunton.

There is no tighter community than that of a military family unit, particularly during the time when their men were overseas in conflict; those women stood in support of their sisters. The wives of those at Norton Manor, Taunton, were no different to the wives living on other military estates, be them Army, Royal Navy, or Royal Air Force, they each had their own network of support for each other.

Thirty-six more times during the months of June and July that summer those communities and families activated their own networks of support.

The phone calls from Katherine were frequent: 'Prepare for Op Pabbay' and sadly more often than not, it was for multiple losses.

I recall Monday 21 June, the initial call from Katherine when Royal Marine Paul Warren had been killed; by the 23rd, two days later, the number returning had risen to seven.

Seven more lives lost and the tsunami of devastation affected thousands more people across our country.

It was a difficult time to try and remove the fear floating in their heads when their loved ones were deployed. Although these people were resilient and if there were to be good times, then they would grab them with both hands, tightly.

Amy Tardelli Brown, a newlywed young lady, was certainly planning to do just that as confirmation had reached her that her husband Adam was soon to be home for his two weeks R&R – the *military* slang for rest and recuperation. If only there was a magic tablet to close the mind down and forget what horrific scenes those on this deployment had witnessed. I am sure each returning member of Her Majesties Forces would sign up for that particular prescription so they could unwind and relax for two weeks with their families.

As that wonderful day of expectation came around Adam was at Camp Bastion loitering with intent, desperately craving to get home to his beautiful wife and spend some quality time with his parents, brothers Stephen and James, along with his sister Laura; even the in-laws, he got on famously with John and Susie.

The excitement that is felt when you are due home is a personal experience. During my military career it was like being a four-year-old child waking up on Christmas morning; it almost made going away worth it for the feeling it provoked on coming home.

So there he stood, the excitement starting to build, when one of his bosses pulls him to one side. 'Darbs has been killed,' he was told, referring to Sergeant Steven Darbyshire. Gutted does not even begin to tell the tale. A huge blow to this close unit of men as the other great leader that they all looked up to, 'Whiskey' Corporal Stephen Walker, had been killed just a few weeks earlier. And there he was preparing to go home, 'Let your hair down and come back refreshed after a nice little holiday said the R&R brochure', yeah right, this really was turning into a tour from hell!

He was stunned by the news, maybe even feeling a bit guilty knowing as a senior Marine that some of the younger lads might be struggling without Darbs and Whiskey, while he was on his way home. Adam rang home from Camp Bastion. His mother Jenny answered the phone telling her he was devastated about 'Darbs' having only just left him in the compound. It must have been a heart wrenching phone call for a mother wanting to hold her son who was hurting so badly as she reassured him he had to come home. The family needed to see him as much as he needed to have a break. He was also reassured by his boss to go home which his heart was telling him to do, and yet his leadership qualities were arguing inside his mind. With the reassurance of his two families, those at home and those in Camp Bastion, the correct decision was made and some hours later he was standing in the arrivals lounge at RAF Brize Norton.

There waiting for him was his beautiful wife. It's such a special moment when time stops still, when you first catch sight of each other across a crowded room. There could be a thousand people in that room, but when you see the face of your loved one your vision sends everything else into oblivion. After the hugs and the kisses from the missus, his kit thrown in the boot of the car, he was on his way home. The family were there to meet him, all lining up for their cuddles from this giant of a man.

For the next two weeks it was their time; their very precious time to try and cram in as much as they could.

His parents had booked Amy and Adam a belated mini honeymoon at Mudeford Quay. There was also a further surprise as friends of Adam and Amy wanted them to be the godparents of their baby who would be christened while he was on his two-week break. They were delighted with the huge honour bestowed upon them.

Although one thing Adam really needed to do was make his way to Wootton Bassett to be there when his friend, his leader, 'Darbs' would be brought home. Less than a week after Adam had returned home for his R&R he and Amy made their way to Wiltshire. The day had arrived when 'Darbs' was coming home. They were two of the thousands who turned up to honour the seven fallen heroes: Sergeant Steven Darbyshire, Lance Corporal Michael Taylor, and Marine Paul Warren, all of 40 Commando Royal Marines, Lance Corporal David Ramsden, of 1st Battalion The Yorkshire Regiment, Colour Sergeant Martyn Horton, Private Alex Isaac and Private Douglas Halliday, all of 1st Battalion The Mercian Regiment.

I have mentioned the reason why I read the tributes in relation to each man. They were about heroes – someone very special – and it is only right I share a fraction of what I read.

Sergeant Steven Darbyshire

Lance Corporal Ratcliffe, Company Medic, 3 Troop, Alpha Company, 40 Commando Royal Marines, said:

'Darbs was a Royal Marines Sergeant who I looked up to immensely. Always being behind him in the patrol I learnt a lot from him that I will remember for my whole career.

I have lost count of the amount of times I have laughed with Darbs on patrol; I remember when he fell over in an irrigation ditch and I couldn't stop laughing, but then neither could he and that was the kind of guy Darbs was.

A northern lad like myself, we got on well; I will miss my smoking partner. He never stopped talking about his two beautiful little boys Ryan and Callum. Our thoughts and prayers go out to his partner Kate and their two young children.

Darbs, it was a pleasure and an honour to have served with you and I would just like to thank you for everything. I will miss you and you will never be forgotten.'

Lance Corporal Michael Taylor

Sergeant Al Grant, 9 Troop Sergeant, Charlie Company, 40 Commando Royal Marines, said:

'Words cannot describe the sadness I feel for the loss of Mike. He was someone I admired and a true friend without a fault. You don't meet many people in your life like Mike, men who have these attributes.

Mike was a true Welshman to the core and a Bootneck through and through. With his two distinctive large red Welsh Dragons on each shoulder and the Commando Dagger in the middle, these were his dual love and passion – work and country.

He was a pillar of strength to the section and the troop, and the trust I had in him was paid back ten-fold. Mike wanted more and more responsibility, showing he was up to the task; proving what a vital individual he was to the safety of the young lads in the section.

His DIY skills were second-to-none and would amaze me. It was like watching a 60-minute makeover; he would be able to build anything around the patrol base to make life easier and more comfortable. This was the selfless nature of Mike.

Mike was a family man who loved his partner Sonia and their three boys. We would talk about them, telling stories of each other's families. I will miss those times greatly. The troops' thoughts are with his family at this difficult time. You will be missed, but you will always be in our minds.'

Marine Paul Warren

Corporal Simon Schofield, Section Commander, 9 Troop, Charlie Company, 40 Commando Royal Marines, said:

'I was proud to have served with Paul, as we all were; a hoofing Marine and a top bloke who kept our section safe.The most 'switched on' guy I have ever met, it gave me great confidence to follow Paul as I always knew that he'd make the right decisions and lead us on a safe and true path.

I will always remember Paul for his quick wit and his dry sense of humour; he was always keen to share the news if I had made a wrong decision, and always referred to his idea being far better.

Paul was a true fighter in every sense of the word, always keen to lead if there was a scrap. An immensely brave man, a quality he proved on countless occasions as point man in Sangin.

He leaves behind a massive hole in 9 Troop and an even bigger one in 2 Section, but I know he would want us to go on and continue to take the fight to the enemy.

I had the pleasure of meeting Paul's parents at the Families Day prior to deploying to Sangin. They were immensely proud of their son and all of his achievements. Our thoughts go out to them at this heart-breaking time. Rest in Peace Royal.'

Lance Corporal David Ramsden

Captain Ben Stephens, Intelligence Officer, 1st Battalion, The Mercian Regiment (Cheshire), said:

'Lance Corporal Ramsden possessed a quiet and sincere disposition. He executed his duties with a consideration for others not always seen in soldiers.

As a reservist volunteer for operations in Afghanistan I had the utmost respect for him and his dedication to the cause. He was highly committed to his job and hoped to re-enlist back into the Regular Army to continue his career. It was for these reasons he was such a popular figure amongst his peers.

His passing will not be forgotten amongst those who served with him. My honest and heartfelt sympathies go out to his family and friends whose loss we cannot comprehend. Stand Firm and Strike Hard 'Lizard' Ramsden, your memory lives on.'

Colour Sergeant Martyn Horton

Captain Julian Clayton, Support Company Second-in-Command, 1st Battalion, The Mercian Regiment (Cheshire), said:

'I have known Bobby since he joined the regiment as a young tom, and I knew his father who served in the regiment before him.

I first noticed Bobby when I was Company Quartermaster Sergeant of A Company and he was sent to me as a very reluctant arms storeman. He hated every minute of it because to him it wasn't front line and he wanted to be out there with the blokes. Me and Scooby Doolan used to rip him because his writing was shocking; happier days looking back.

Both of us have moved on since then, and it was to my great satisfaction that I found him as the Reconnaissance Platoon Second-in-Command when I took over as Support Company Second-in-Command.

Reconnaissance is a job which always suited him. Small teams, maximum responsibility, reduced supervision, and the chance to do things your own way – that was Bobby's style. He was happier in the field than in camp, a true recce soldier with an astute tactical brain.

He was also without doubt one of the fittest soldiers I knew, able to tab with extreme weight despite his size, and also run with the very best in the regiment – he had it all. To lose anyone is terrible, but when you start losing people like Colour Sergeant Horton, there just aren't the words.

He had such a bright future ahead of him. My thoughts and sympathies go out to his family and friends back home; he will be remembered and acutely missed by us all. God Bless. Sleep well Colour.'

Private Alex Isaac

Captain Ben Stephens, Intelligence Officer, 1st Battalion The Mercian Regiment (Cheshire) said:

'Private Isaac was an enormously likeable character. His quiet nature, wry smile and willingness to complete all that was asked of him marked him out as one to watch.

It is such a tragedy that his future has been stolen from him. His passing will be felt keenly by his friends in the Battalion, many of whom grew up with him in the North West.

I extend my most sincere condolences to his family; I know your son was a man of courage and honour who fought with great spirit. He will not be forgotten by those who knew him. Stand Firm and Strike Hard Alex Isaac.'

Private Douglas Halliday

Captain Ben Stephens, Intelligence Officer, 1st Battalion The Mercian Regiment (Cheshire) said:

'Private Halliday possessed a boldness and confidence of someone far more senior. He completed all tasks set for him with a smile and aplomb. His positive nature was infectious and this will leave a hole in his team that will not easily be filled. The fact that he went about his duties with such competence and a positive outlook, was testament to his courage and character. He will be sorely missed by his friends and colleagues in the Battalion but we know that this pales into insignificance compared to the feelings of his family at this difficult time. I wish you God's Speed Doug Halliday, you will not be forgotten. Stand Firm and Strike Hard our Mercian Brother.'

After reading those tributes from their colleagues it emphasises just how special these seven men were; not just to their family and friends but to the brothers they left behind. They were not statistics, they were real people serving the Crown and that is why, for me, it was so important to know a little of them as we escorted them home.

It was a long day as multiple repatriations always were and we used a benchmark to try and estimate timings for the cortège to leave RAF Lyneham. If the repatriation was a singleton then we would estimate the time to be about one hour from the start of the ceremony. For every additional one of our forces to be repatriated add an extra half an hour. We were never far out as on this occasion some four hours after the ceremony started, we made our way to form up at the guardroom. There we waited to escort the cortège while the families were with their loved one in the Chapel of Rest.

As they slowly filter out; a last look over their shoulder towards the room which allowed them the privacy to release words that were not for world consumption. Words that were personal to only one man, the one who lay inside the Union flag draped coffin; who they would never see again.

I was asked earlier that morning by one BBC reporter where my thoughts drifted during my duties on a repatriation day? I was unable to answer, but as I reflect, let me try and express where my thoughts drifted in what I saw and knew to be happening in relation to this day.

The police all formed up by the guardroom with the outriders and escorts, where we would stay until the family were ready to leave RAF Lyneham after such an emotional day.

The call from Albins confirms that the families will soon be en route; we wait, we look, to see them escorted to the gate.

They approach and we stand up smart to show respect to these families we did not know.

As they pass us one by one, we see the emptiness, sadness and grief etched upon their faces as they weep.

Out of the Air Station in convoy they go, off to Wootton Bassett the town they will forever remember.

On arrival friends and family lay in wait to hold them tightly, wanting to take away their pain and share their grief.

Whilst at the Chapel of Rest, Albins removes the heroes from their brief resting place to the hearse with dignity and so much grace. Once all secured, the cortège rolls slowly towards RAF Lyneham exit gate.

The outriders are perched and ready to go, as the St Michael's Church Bell tolls to let the village know.

Lyneham stops to form up on mass, overflowing off the footpath and with the children outside their school on the grass.

The cortège comes into my sight; to acknowledge them I activate my lights, the hand brake is released, I turn my wheels; my radio message to all is solemn and brief – the cortège is ours, we are on our way. The roads are closed as heads are bowed by the many hundreds in the crowd.

The commentary on the radio flows at the same speed as the cortège moves; methodically we escort them along the road with their seven precious heroes.

As we make our way along the route, cars stop as the drivers sit and weep, it is a sight I so much want to share, to let the families know the country did care.

Then we enter the town where thousands pay their respects in the High Street they never knew.

With honour, dignity and respect, the St Bartholomew's bell tolls to salute the heroes who we behold.

The cortège is stopped, the conductor is braced as we leave him to page the heroes with his usual panache and grace.

I make my way to a place that is safe, 200 metres up the street, and wait.

The Royal British Legion lead in the salute that started so small, but now has the warmth to invite the military, bikers, the public and everyone who wants to take part in this special ceremony.

I stand looking around feeling so proud to have been involved, the way this ceremony spontaneously evolved.

Pride, compassion and honour to help ease the grief, I hope what we did gave the families some small relief.

I stand helpless as I watch the grieving and hearing the sounds of raw emotion. The sights I see make me feel so very sad and I ask myself why our world is so mad.

I watched far too often the flowers laid as the woman cries, then hear the innocent voice of her child asking, 'Why, mummy, why?'

A lady makes her way down the line with her flowers gripped tightly in her hands. She turns finding her loved one and is clinging onto his hearse, breaking her heart and in so much pain.

After her flowers are laid she stands with pride, her flag telling the world how proud she was of her hero; his name displayed for all to read.

The conductor turns to us with so much style, but I wonder when the town will again smile.

Step by step he makes his way to where we wait; he enhances the respect with his immaculate gait.

I raise my right arm to the salute; the heroes are drawn together to continue on their route.

As we leave the town that so often weeps, I silently prayed, 'Please Lord, please no more. Let these poor families sleep.'

How did I feel, I was asked that day?

To have been involved in showing so much honour, dignity and respect to our nation's fallen; I hope from the words I have written inside this book will one day show: 'That quite simply I was immensely proud to see our fallen recognised.'

The next day's newspapers stated the lady I saw holding the banner was 'Helen Fisher'. Inconsolable was the word the reporter used to describe his observations as she kissed the glass window of the vehicle carrying her cousin, Douglas Halliday. Inconsolable she most certainly was, bless her, it was awful seeing such anguish.

Yep, on days like those I found it so difficult to distance myself from the scenes of immense pain.

And as the sun went down that night and Bassett said goodbye to the thousands who came to show their respects, we already knew the date when the town would weep again.

CHAPTER 25

As we planned for our next Operation Entourage and the military Operation Pabbay, Amy and Adam were enjoying their last few days before he had to return to his duties in Helmand.

As good as it feels to come home, it's not a great feeling knowing you are going back. If only the days went as fast out there as they did during the R&R.

It was a job only half done and the emotional farewells started to begin: the last kiss, the final wave, the sleepless nights missing the man you crave, until you finally cry yourself to sleep.

Then you start again; brush yourself down, put on a brave face and start crossing off the days on the calendar until your loved one returns. That's how you cope, I was told.

So Adam and those others returned back after their two-week rest and recuperation. Back home the families got back into their routines praying for their safe return. Back to the letter writing, the parcels being sent and, with the benefits of technology, the great bonus of hearing the voice of your loved one over the phone.

Adam phoned when he arrived in Camp Bastion; sadly on this call his mother Jenny was out. However, Adam knowing the importance of the family hearing his voice left a message on her answer phone. In the message left that day were those three important words 'I LOVE YOU.' Words most of us take for granted as we leave to go to work each day, but when these families are apart, they were always spoken from the bottom of the heart.

Whilst in Wootton Bassett for the second time in 72 hours, hundreds from Sheffield, Great Yarmouth and many towns in between made their way to our High Street. On this occasion they were honouring Trooper James Leverett, aged 20, of the Royal Dragoon Guards who was killed in an explosion whilst on vehicle patrol in Nahr-e Saraj in Helmand Province, three days earlier.

The C17 Globemaster had completed its honourable flypast and had landed. I made my way back up to Bassett. When I arrived at the war memorial I was called over by 'Big Steve' Royal British Leaders Riders Repatriation Liaison Officer. He had been handing out his contact details on cards to a group of people around him. Amongst this group was a feeling of concern that two grandmothers of the fallen soldier should have been at the repatriation ceremony and not where they presently stood.

The Liaison Officer had informed them he would get them there to see their grandson come off the aircraft; sadly he had built their hopes up as the numbers of family members were restricted. I offered my sincere condolences straight away knowing the restrictions for the next of kin inside the Air Base and the attention to detail by the military; I knew there was no mistake.

I encouraged them to take a seat in the Cross Keys across the road from where we stood and should they be required at RAF Lyneham for the repatriation ceremony, I would drive them there in my car. Comfortable that they now knew where they should be, the group of around ten made their way to the comfort of Kirsty's hospitality.

After making the appropriate call and confirming this with Katherine Rand I walked over to share this information with the ladies, to explain the reason why they should remain where they were.

Inside the Cross Keys I sat amongst this family, but predominantly focused my attention on the two ladies, the grandmothers of the young soldier coming home.

I fed them as much information as I felt appropriate. Their grandson was to be returned home a hero, explaining everything including about the day before when the bearer party went through their drills rehearsing.

Then I briefed them on the chronological diary of timings to make them feel part of the day. Even going into detail about what happened after we left the town and of the respects that would be shown along the full route.

One of the grandmothers, Linda Mason, gripped my hand as I went to leave; again heart wrenching to see someone hurting so badly. She looked deep into my eyes and spoke with so much sincerity to say thank you for the words I had just said. Although broken hearted she was extremely proud of her grandson and was comforted by the fact that he was being treated with so much honour. The tears in her eyes sparkled with love as testimony to that as I listened to every word she said.

An hour or so later numerous flowers were placed on the hearse from the many relatives and friends of the soldier. Amongst them I saw that poor grandmother breaking her heart over the hearse which carried her precious grandson James Leverett.

I mentioned earlier that this summer was equally as bad as 2009. We were still getting far too many calls from Katherine and her repatriation team due to 36 fatalities that occurred during these months.

The next loss of life I heard of was not by the usual telephone call from Katherine; this time it came directly from J treble C: Major James Joshua Bowman, Lieutenant Neal Turkington and Corporal Arjun Purja, all of 1st Battalion, The Royal Gurkha Rifles, were all killed by a rogue Afghan soldier. Major Bowman was shot as he slept; his comrades were shot in their command centre and four others were injured.

Such were the horrific circumstances which challenged the relationship between The International Security Assistance Force (ISAF), Afghanistan Army and Police that the President of Afghanistan held a press conference to the world's media.

During his speech he passed on his condolences to the families of the three British soldiers killed. This was not overly helpful to the Ministry of Defence as they were frantically trying to contact the next of kin before it was announced on the news. On this particular morning I was dealing with a complaint in a property in Lyneham when I received a call from Rob Rowntree. Rob by this time had moved on from Albin Funeral Directors and was employed by the MoD at Joint Casualty and Compassionate Centre (J treble C) and needed urgent police assistance to locate and trace the next of kin of Lieutenant Neal Turkington.

'I need help Jarra,' were Rob's opening words as he began to explain the circumstances. His notification officers were outside the deceased's address in Portadown, Northern Ireland. The young Lieutenant's parents, Ivor and Marie, brother Gareth and sister Cathy were not home and could the police help find them?

Now this was a challenge he laid down before us. Initially when Rob asked could we help locate the family, I assumed they would be in our policing area or at least in Wiltshire, but no they were in Northern Ireland.

With hastily made phone calls to the ever dependable Graham Hurst in the front office at Bassett Police Station, he was able to provide me with a number for the Police Service Northern Ireland (PSNI). The family I was dealing with at the time, being from RAF Lyneham, immediately understood the importance and challenge that had been placed on my lap and suddenly their front room was my call centre. They gave me their landline number so Rob could have contact with me on that line and I used my mobile to make contact with PSNI. Rob phoned me back on the landline and at the same time I had PSNI on the mobile explaining to the operator the full circumstances as they were being relayed to me by Rob.

We had a connection so we were not going to lose the momentum by explaining everything to another operator. Faxes were sent providing the all-important information that was required by PSNI to action the 'locate trace search' for the Turkington family.

Once received, logs were created and I was then transferred to another Police Station covering the area where the Turkington family lived. Next the voice of a very strong Irish accent confirming he was the Duty Sergeant announced that units were deployed and finally it was the appropriate time for Rob and the Sergeant in the PSNI to exchange numbers. There was a huge sigh of relief in Rob's voice as we once again successfully completed the latest challenge he gave us.

As I terminated both calls there was a deep sadness felt by the family who kindly allowed me to use their front room as a call centre. They had worked out the basis of the conversations I had had between J treble C and PSNI.

Within an hour that Sergeant who had tasked all his available units to find the next of kin of Lieutenant Turkington phoned me back on my mobile to update me that they had found the family and they were now being briefed by the military.

The parents of the young Lieutenant were now being spoken to by the military officers and fortunately they had avoided hearing the worst possible message via the condolence speech spoken by President Hamid Karzai on the news.

There was almost a feeling of relief in the front room after I shared the information that the family had been found. The mother of the complainant I was dealing with brought me a much needed cup of tea and her husband switched on Sky News. We sat there in silence and saw the press conference that had been broadcast earlier by President Hamid Karzai. The words he used were that of a politician; the words the parents of Neal Turkington were hearing in their home were heart wrenching and passed with the utmost compassion.

This was still the main news story in the country the day the repatriation took place. Their names were on the front of everyone's minds as were the cowardly circumstances on how they were executed.

Major James Bowman, Lieutenant Neal Turkington and Corporal Arjun Purja Pun – all victims of a rogue Afghan soldier

Coming home with them was Marine Matthew Harrison. He died in a field hospital just one day before his 24th birthday after he was wounded in a firefight while on foot patrol.

The conductor, having paged his cortège to the tolling of the Tenor Bell, brought the four men to their families as they lined up by the war memorial. Then the emotional scenes took place again, on this occasion led by the innocence of a small little girl. Comforted by her mother Durga, Corporal Pun's eight-year-old daughter Eva was lifted up so she could place a bunch of yellow roses on the roof of the vehicle carrying her father. As she did so the others followed suit. There were hundreds present and amongst them was Gurkha Private Pirthraj Thapa, 25, who lost his left leg in Afghanistan in a mine explosion. He was pushed up to Corporal Pun's hearse in his wheelchair to lay his own flowers.

So many mixed emotions on another desperately sad day but amongst them a sense of pride in the honour that was bestowed upon these four men, something which continued along that honourable 46 miles route.

CHAPTER 26

As July was ripped off the calendar and another day ticked off those 'days to do' charts, 3,500 miles away the start of another month was to bring more devastating news.

Sunday 1 August 2010 Operation Minimise is activated as a signal is sent to Joint Casualty and Compassionate Centre (J treble C) Insworth, with the name of the latest fatality killed in Afghanistan.

Service No. PO61555T Royal Marine Commando, Adam Robert Brown: date of birth 25 February 1985.

Marine Brown was conducting a reassurance patrol as part of 3 Troop, Alpha Company, 40 Commando Royal Marines to provide security for the locals in the area. At approximately 1750 hours on Sunday 1 August 2010, there was an explosion in the vicinity of his patrol base and Marine Brown was killed instantly in the blast. This was the second fatality confirmation signal J treble C had received that day. Earlier, the notification officers had been tasked to inform the next of kin of Lance Sergeant Dale Alanzo McCallum of 1st Battalion Scots Guards.

Lance Sergeant McCallum, who was serving as part of Combined Force Lashkar Gah, was killed by small arms fire whilst commanding his men in an operation to provide security to Afghan local nationals in the Lashkar Gah district of Helmand Province. At approximately 1320 hours, the sangar at his checkpoint came under effective enemy fire from insurgent forces. Lance Sergeant McCallum quickly moved to the sangar and, as he was moving into a position to engage the insurgents, he received a fatal gunshot wound.

These deaths would activate a chain of events which enabled the next of kin to be informed in a sensitive and compassionate way.

Adam was the 14th and final fatality that 40 Commando had sustained in this gruelling tour. The notification officers were briefed from the information that was contained in the sealed envelope. Their orders from Adam were read and absorbed by the Royal Marine officer and Padre and so began the harrowing duty of informing the next of kin.

With the details and information read and re-read they knew what was required to share as the burden of the messenger, to commence the first leg of a journey that would bring despair to the home address of the parents of Royal Marine Adam Brown.

Jenny, Rob and Laura were at home that day relaxing; in fact having a lovely BBQ with friends they had not seen for some time. Like all mums, when visitors come over the photograph albums often come out and there was no difference this day. During the afternoon Jenny had taken great pride in showing her guests the images of her giant of a son on his proud day, the marriage to his beautiful childhood sweetheart Amy.

It was a lovely, enjoyable afternoon. Then with the hugs and kisses that follow such a visit, they said their goodbyes.

Jenny looked out of the window watching her friends drive off. She was reflecting on Adam's wedding day and maybe the call she had had with him the previous night which as always finished with those three powerful words 'I LOVE YOU.'

Yes, that day in December, some eight months earlier had brought her so many happy family memories. Unbeknown to her at that exact moment, another memory that will never leave her for the rest of her life was walking up her street.

Jenny saw the man dressed in a green uniform. Initially he was running up and down their street, first one way then the other. She mentioned it to Rob, saying how strange it was, as he looked so out of place.

What she did not know at that time was the man in green was looking for house No 2. To add to the stress of the message he was carrying, he was confused as there were two No. 2s for some unknown reason to him in the same street.

As Jenny came away from the window she saw the man disappear out of sight along the road again and for that brief moment thought nothing more about it.

Laura was upstairs, Rob was in the front room and Jenny was tidying a few things away following her friends' visit.

Bang! Bang! Bang! On the front door was the sound of the deafening knock. It's the knock that even if it's nothing, makes your heart beat overly fast when you are not expecting anyone, particularly when your son is in Afghanistan.

Jenny remembers those next few seconds:

'Rob went to answer the door while my head was working in slow motion trying to put the pieces together, rewinding what I had seen. A man in the street, what were the words I used to describe him to Rob? Yes out of place, wearing green, running up and down, a loud knock moments later.

I was screaming inside. No!!!! Please God No!

Rooted to where I stood, desperate to hear what's being said yet at the same time praying not to. While my heart was beating so fast and I was in a trance, Laura was coming down the stairs as her father opened the door; they both saw the man in green. Then the most unimaginable distress as the worst nightmare is there on your doorstep and you know, and they know you know, but nothing is spoken.'

But speak he did.

I heard the words as did Laura, though Rob asked them please don't say anything yet. 'The world has just stopped, I collapsed in a heap, there are no words to describe those first few minutes after hearing the news that your son or, for Laura, her brother is dead.'

Having delivered the death message on a few occasions, I have seen the devastation those opening words produce from a sentence that is already expressed on your face.

Anger, numbness, hysteria and total disbelief are among just a few of the emotions as the tears pour from a pain that hurts like none ever before, when your heart has just been ripped out.

There is nothing the messenger can do, only answer any questions that may be asked when the grieving family are able to or ready to talk.

It's an awful experience standing watching that raw grief unfold before your eyes, even though you want to run and escape from this intrusion. But they need you there with them as the tidal wave of questions start to trickle through, desperate to know the answers only you have. You have to do your best to facilitate this, not with spin or what they might prefer to hear, but honest sincerity and with compassion, because you genuinely cannot help but to care.

Jenny reflects back to those minutes after hearing the words spoken: 'The man in green was a Royal Marine Officer, with him was the most wonderful sincere Padre and as we asked they answered.'

The Padre and the Marine officer would answer with the utmost integrity; one from the Church the other from the Corps. But under these circumstances Jenny and Rob not only had to ask the questions, they had to take in the answers as they were soon to contemplate the unimaginable task of bringing the distressing news that had just crippled them to Adam's brothers Stephen and James and, of course, to his wife Amy. There was only one way to inform Amy and that would be through her own mother and father, which was Adam's wish.

Rob took a deep breath as he picked up the phone to dial the home of Amy's parents. 'There was no easy way,' Jenny said.

Amy's parents, John and Susie were sat at home in Yateley that Sunday evening with their oldest daughter Luisa. It was around 10 pm when the phone rang. As Rob spoke John listened; his face went grey and Susie cried as she knew why.

Rob quickly got sorted and with the Marine Officer set off on his journey from hell, one which would inflict awful pain on Stephen and James. Jenny and Laura remained at home comforted by the Padre, as they contemplated making those harrowing calls to the rest of the family and close friends.

As Rob was making his way to Yateley to inform his sons, another car carrying the same message left that Hampshire village en route to Burtle, the home of Adam and Amy. The baton of the messenger had now been passed onto John, Susie and Luisa.

To carry the message that only a couple of hours ago had activated Op Minimise some 3,500 miles away; news that they knew would shatter Amy's world.

Setting off on a journey that none ever wanted to make, en route to their daughter Amy who was about to have her soul crushed by the words that were spinning round in her father's head.

It must have been the longest two-hour journey ever. Then finally they arrived. The front door opened, Amy smiled, her dad cried and no words were needed.

Her only small comfort was the fact she was told by her mum and dad along with her sister Luisa. They were all going to need the love that they had for each other on this journey from hell upon which they had just embarked.

It is a journey that has a start, but for many, never finishes.

In life you sometimes need a knight in shining armour or a guardian angel, someone to lead you through troubled waters. The military call them a VO– a Visiting Officer – and at times like this they are worth their weight in gold. The Visiting Officer allocated to Amy, Jenny and Rob was a serving Royal Marine. So many others like him were serving members of Her Majesty's Forces. All had one thing in common they had all volunteered for these duties. For the family, the guidance and support they gave these vulnerable people on this epic journey and their devotion to duty could never be undervalued.

From what I was told the Visiting Officer they had was excellent; the most caring genuine man they could ever have wished for. Amy and her family were immensely grateful for his support and guidance, as he walked them through each day and answered the many questions they had for him.

No sooner had the family and friends of both Marine Adam Brown and Lance Sergeant Dale Alanzo McCallum been informed of the loss of their lives then the planning started for the repatriations. I got the call first thing Monday morning on my mobile, 'Sorry Jarra can you and your police friends start planning for Thursday, two at the moment.'

Strange, even though the humane deliverance of the messages received from the RAF from the early days were brief, short and straight to the point, they still took their toll as the message was passed with empathy and sadness. During these years there were a lot of others who also found they were not made of wood as the humbling scenes we had all witnessed were felt by everyone involved.

The operation was having an impact on us all but it was nothing compared to those who were coping with their loss. By Wednesday afternoon the pre-Op Pabbay briefing was held where the military went through their briefing orders in preparation for the following day. Flight, catering, family needs – the briefing went on – the toll remained at two returning with no further increase in the loss of life.

The poignant flypast with that honourable dip of the starboard wing brought Marine Adam Brown and Lance Sergeant Dale Alanzo McCallum home on the hour stated on the operational brief.

And, just as the importance of the pre-Op Pabbay brief was to the military, so was the Op Entourage brief for the police, which always took place after the plane had landed. This was always presented by Inspector Steve Cox, the Sector Commander. Even though every officer in the room had heard the briefing almost a hundred times and could possibly even have given the orders, it was an example of the importance never to get blasé. If you become blasé you make mistakes and for these families it was important to get it right. Due to the constant attention to detail, we did get it right on each and every occasion.

The 5 August was a gorgeous day – well the weather was – although the mood as always on these days was respectful and sombre.

I parked my car at Sainsbury's car park amongst the coaches, mini buses and many cars carrying friends and family that had travelled from all corners of the country. Having put on my hat I made my way up through the small shopping arcade and spotted a group of about eight people in their early twenties smartly dressed with one thing in common, they were all wearing black.

They sat outside a café and as I approached I stopped to offer my condolences to those mourning their friend. They were the friends of Adam Brown, travelling from Yateley and as there was a spare seat I joined them. They thought I was just being nice but I was starving and saw an opportunity to blag a sandwich. If they read this they will confirm that's just what I did.

But seriously, yes, I did join them, to give them an idea of what would take place. The order of march for the hearses and answer any questions they had, although most of all to advise them to look after each other as they were about to experience emotions that will be forever engraved in their memories. As they listened I could see the mixture of confusion as for some, until they saw tangible evidence, it was almost surreal that on such a beautiful day they were waiting for a friend, a friend they would never see again. But as time was not an issue they talked and I listened.

The stories they each told were of a young man growing into an adult and of his wedding only eight months earlier, yep, Adam, they loved you.

So often I had seen over the last few years groups of young people sitting in the same seats as these eight were that day and, just like those previously, these young people from Yateley were hurting just as badly. They were lost, confused and were seeking comfort. That comfort was only a short walk away, a place of safety where Kirsty and her girls were always present to show some true Wiltshire hospitality.

As I walked over to the Cross Keys with them they saw friends and relations of their friend Adam, who were congregating around the war memorial.

It always seemed to comfort those coming to Bassett under these circumstances to see a friendly face they knew in an unknown location.

I left them to chat as I made my way to the Cross Keys for a valuable cuppa and a cake, dropping my pound coin in the 'Help for Heroes' charity box on the table. The room was full of the Royal British Legion Riders all wearing their leathers and proudly displaying badges of Corps, Regiments and insignia. The banter and nervous laughter was good and another way of dealing with uncomfortable situations.

For some who had not been in the military they may have thought it was disrespectful, but it really was a safety mechanism, which goes with the saying, 'best I laugh before I cry.'

The group from Yateley came over and once inside the Cross Keys they felt the warmth and took the opportunity to grab something a little stronger than tea.

As I walked around the rooms of the pub I spoke with many who carried flowers.

One man I met that day has become nothing short of a legend and a man I hold with the greatest respect. In different circumstances Mike Crankshaw would have become a genuine friend; an inspiration to others in drive and determination in raising thousands of pounds for a very special charity. A charity I was to find out a lot more about the following year. Mike, the uncle to Adam, was with his wife Jo, his daughter Hattie and son William. I took the time to tell them what would take place, where and when and a general conversation on how the rest of the day would unfold. I also was able to reassure Mike that his sister Jenny, Adam's mum, would be well looked after and not to worry about her care. The adulation RAF Lyneham Repatriation Team had received throughout the military was one described as a pillar of excellence in the care and compassion they showed each family. I never met a family who would not second that.

Mike's wife Jo was clutching flowers. I explained that she should take her time when placing them on the roof of the hearse as everything was about showing dignity, honour and respect to the two lads returning. I looked at their son who had in his hands a scroll rolled up and out of curiosity I asked what it was.

Being a little shy he passed it to his father who opened it up. The scroll was a large Union flag, hand drawn by William, age eleven, and in bold letters were written the words:

ADAM BROWN
ROYAL MARINE
MY HERO FOREVER

It was quite obvious that this was not only an outstanding work of art created by William, but it was something very personal and done with so much love.

Mike told me that William wanted to put it on the hearse that carried his cousin when his mother laid her flowers. Of course he could do that, but this was too valuable a tribute and raised my concern. With a further 40 miles to travel after we leave the war memorial en route to Oxford, it would blow off in the wind or get damaged. So I suggested that if he gave it to me I could place the scroll of honour inside the vehicle carrying Adam. After a brief family conference this is what he agreed for me to do.

While we were speaking, a friend of Adam's, a Royal Marine not in uniform, introduced himself to me and sought advice. I never knew his name so I will refer to him with the utmost respect as 'Royal'. This chap sensed that he might be the worse for wear through drink by the end of the day. Knowing he would be unfit to drive he was concerned that his transit van parked on the High Street could get a parking fine. To alleviate his concerns he gave me his van keys as I was leaving and I told him I would park his van at the Police Station for him to pick up the following day. I would return his keys to him after I completed my involvement in escorting the cortège to the Thames Valley Police border.

So with his keys and William's scroll I resumed my duties, relocating the van, then making my way to RAF Lyneham to liaise with the outriders and Coxy the cortège commander.

While both families were in the Chapel of Rest I made my way to where the empty hearses were parked. It was there that I passed the scroll of honour to Graham Cook the Funeral Director of Albins, making sure he understood the importance of this property. When the time was right to do so, the two families made their way out of the Chapel of Rest to their vehicles and were escorted by the RAF police to where their extended family and friends stood in wait on the High Street.

The order of the coffins in the cortège was senior service first and inside Adam's Hearse, on the near side of his coffin, was displayed the scroll of honour William had created. It was in clear view so that as each person laid their floral tributes they could see this loving message for Adam from his little cousin.

Thirty-seven days earlier, Amy had been standing on this same High Street holding Adam's hand tightly, praying silently in her subconscious never to return on the day 'Darbs' had been brought home.

I write now wondering if throughout that day, Adam and I spoke or even saw each other. We must have been in close proximity for a short time either on the High Street or in the Cross Keys when I briefed the extended family and friends. I don't know, I can only hope I had as it would have been a great honour to have shaken his hand.

For Amy, however, on this heart wrenching day, she could only imagine Adam's hand which had given her so much love and comfort and which she so desperately wanted to hold again instead of the sunflower she held that day as a final floral tribute.

After the individual respects were paid by the many friends and family and the floral tributes placed on the two vehicles completed, then the cortège was escorted away.

As we left the town the tributes were frantically being scribbled in shorthand by the journalists who had pen and paper ready to grab the quotes to accompany their photographs for the following day's newspapers.

Some could not be there in person but I am sure their thoughts were with both the families and gave press releases some 3,500 miles away.

Lieutenant Colonel Paul James, Commanding Officer, 40 Commando Group, Combined Force Sangin, said: 'Marine Adam Brown was a superb Marine – courageous, supremely fit, hugely professional and utterly selfless; he was a model Commando and true Alpha Company Saint.'

Lance Sergeant Dale Alanzo McCallum was born in Hanover, Jamaica. He was 31 years old, was a father to Kevin, a son to Lurline and Paul and a brother to Sandra, Rodney, Denise, Milissa and Montel. Lance Sergeant McCallum quickly gained a reputation for being an immensely strong, fit and robust individual. At the time of his death he had been selected for promotion to Sergeant and was already performing the duties of a Platoon Sergeant with the Fire Support Group.

Commanding officer Lieutenant Colonel Lincoln Jopp called him: 'A noble warrior who died protecting his men under heavy fire. A hero soldier described as the coolest Scots Guardsman to walk the Earth, who was known for his love of dancing and had a crusade to teach white men to dance.'

As the press hurriedly made good their exit in time for the following day's headlines, I returned to Bassett with the keys of the transit van belonging to 'Royal'.

The Cross Keys public house was a familiar scene after the war memorial ceremony and always packed full. A mixture of locals, ex-servicemen, comrades of the fallen heroes and quite often the bearer party. A familiar scene, in fact the only thing that was different were the faces of the latest family and friends to be present. Of course there was deep sadness amongst all those present, but possibly just for that short period of time there was an atmosphere of immense pride.

They all mixed with everyone, no divide by rank or uniform and with the vast majority of family or direct friends of the fallen still present, they sipped their drinks reflecting on an extraordinary day.

Drained of tears, emotionally shattered, yet feeling absorbed in warmth and support from so many people they never knew. Maybe, just maybe, for some, they found some very welcome reassurance in the knowledge that their own hero had been truly recognised.

There I was stood, still in uniform, drawn to this unique mixture of emotions, whilst trying to find 'Royal' whose transit keys were still in my pocket. I felt a tap on my shoulder and turning around I saw the face of a man for whom words were not required as his face just, like a picture, spoke for him.

Mike Crankshaw grabbed my hand, held it tightly and as his eyes filled with tears we looked at each other. No words were needed. He squeezed my hand tightly and nodded whispering that word of gratitude, 'Thanks.'

The impact of doing something as simple as placing William's scroll of honour alongside his nephew had given them all a little comfort to know that in spirit their presence was still with Adam.

That Scroll of Honour from William never left Adam, just another example of the level of care and professionalism of Albins Funeral Directors. Where Adam went, that gift from his little cousin followed, as it did when he arrived home to his final resting place in Yateley.

'Royal', well yes, I found him; well to be honest he found me. As he knew he would be he was well on his way to being drunk, hurting, but using the art of camouflage he managed to disguise it extremely well. Our eyes drew together in mutual respect and in each hand he held a small glass of port. He knew my past life of proudly wearing a Green Beret from our initial conversation and as I gave him his keys he handed me the glass of port.

I stopped, I thought, I looked around. Drinking on duty is strictly taboo the rule book says. I saw Mike standing with his family; Jenny with Rob, James and Stephen with their sister Laura, Amy with Susie, John and her sister Luisa. I looked back at 'Royal', nodded my head and as we raised our glasses in unison as a salute we both said: 'Adam Brown, Royal Marine' and I threw the port down my neck.

'Rest in Peace Adz' were the last words I heard from 'Royal' as I walked back into a world that Adam's family and so many others no longer understood.

CHAPTER 27

O ne thing I could clearly understand was the relationship between the military and the country. A relationship that felt like togetherness, rippling through the Armed forces, just as it was through our towns, cities and villages; uniting our Great Nation in showing respect for all our heroes.

So many people were pulling together to do their little bit. Charity events were being organised up and down the country to raise funds for our forces who were now getting the support they truly deserved.

Just locally to us we had so many events, with everyone wanting to say their thanks to the town and acknowledge our troops.

Not every event caught the attention of the press so were not highlighted, but each raised further funds for military-related charities.

I recall one Saturday morning waiting for the latest visitors to show their respects, but this group were not coming up the road past the building on stilts. No, this crowd were flying through the skies, when more than 100 microlight aircraft flew over, their own unique and symbolic gesture to recognise the bond between the fallen and the town.

Another time we had more than 150 Mini enthusiasts drive in their Mini motor cars that raised money for 'Help for Heroes'.

Choirs would turn up and sing, cyclists would ride and some came on foot, all raising funds for military charities. If *X Factor* was a show to find the most patriotic town in England, I think Wootton Bassett would have taken some beating.

We even got involved in one event that the West Midlands police organised. They invited police forces to join them at RAF Brize Norton in a charity event to raise funds for BLESMA (British Limbless Ex-Service Men's Association), a national military charity that supports servicemen who have lost limbs or the use of limbs or eyesight.

As we were caught up in the emotions during our escorts through Wootton Bassett, West Midlands police were equally aware of the impact this conflict was having on them. They would escort the seriously injured from the C17 Globemaster in its role as an 'air hospital' after it landed at Birmingham International Airport to the Queen Elizabeth Hospital.

Whilst our escorts were slow and dignified, they were making progress using their driving skills to get these seriously injured to hospital safely on the 'hurry up'.

Once at the hospital further amazing skills were being used by the medical profession to save so many lives with such challenging injuries.

Sadly, even with the miraculous skills of the medical profession, technology, science and the prayers of the families at their bedsides, some of those reaching Queen Elizabeth Hospital were unable to be saved. Heroes each and every one of them and another family began that journey of grieving.

The headlines on the BBC News stated a soldier had died in a UK hospital a month after he was wounded in Afghanistan. He was named by the MoD as Lieutenant John Charles Sanderson of 1st Battalion, The Mercian Regiment (Cheshire). It is so important to remember all those who paid the ultimate sacrifice.

Two others who also lost the fight to survive their injuries were: Captain Andrew Griffiths, 25, from 2nd Battalion, The Duke of Lancaster's Regiment (2 LANCS) Theatre Reserve Battalion who died in Birmingham on Sunday 5 September and Kingsman Darren Deady from 2nd Battalion, The Duke of Lancaster's Regiment, was shot in southern Afghanistan on 23 August. The 22-year-old from Bolton, sadly died in hospital on Friday 10 September. Kingsman Deady's family were with him when he died at Queen Elizabeth Hospital.

His family said in a statement: 'Darren was proud to do a job that he loved and most of all believed in. His little brother once turned round to him and asked him, "Why do you fight?" Darren simply replied, "To make a difference." That statement concluded with these important words. "There is only one thing left to say now – please don't forget him."'

Well, I guess this is what this book is all about – for the reader to be aware of the names of so many soldiers who selflessly gave up their lives and so that they are NEVER forgotten.

As the hearses were driving those three heroes to their final resting places, we continued to escort those coming back to our home country through RAF Lyneham. The repatriations continued from mid-August to the end of October when a further 12 soldiers came home. As they came home, hundreds gathered to show unity with the grieving families who had travelled from not only every corner of our country, but from Nepal with the loss of a further two Gurkhas.

Another news headline we were beginning to see on the front pages of the national media over the last few years was the home-coming parades. I, like many, had only witnessed them from the armchair in my own front room as I watched the evening news. The parades were full of pomp and swagger, images of happiness, not that a war had been won, but the simple relief they had returned home safely.

One evening when I was walking my beat around the small village of Lyneham I met Wing Commander Paul Weaver-Smith. He was home on R&R and in our chance meeting he asked me what I thought of an idea which was floating around in his head. He was considering a homecoming parade through Wootton Bassett, when those he was in command of completed their tour. That group of units were No 4 Force Protection Wing, including 1 Squadron Royal Air Force Regiment, elements of RAF

Police, 16th Regiment Royal Artillery and personnel from RAF Lyneham. Quite a few different elements to pull together to make it work, but that was his challenge. Mine was simple, what did I think of the proposal? My personal thoughts and response were positive.

Through the grapevine a few weeks later, I had heard a whisper that plans were well under way to indeed have this homecoming parade. Well, if I am honest, it was a little more than a whisper as I sat in Station Warrant Officer Nick Dale's office when he told me of the plans. Leaving Nick's office with a smile on my face, I thought I best prepare Coxy for the next event. With the influence Mr Dale had within the Royal Air Force and the station, this parade would happen. The only thing left for discussion was the date.

Yet the pleasure of looking forward to the homecoming parade was put on hold as the sadness continued.

Corporal David Barnsdale, 24, from 33 Engineer Regiment (Explosive Ordnance), was caught in a blast from an IED which resulted in his death. His girlfriend Helen McEvoy stood beside his mum Wendy, dad Stephen, and sister Vanessa on the High Street, where so many had stood before. And, just like all those others, they were not alone. On this particular day the Hertfordshire community from the town of Tring descended on Bassett and showed their support. When they said their farewells to our town they left their message engraved on my brain – David was their hero and just like I told them on that day, he is a soldier that will not be forgotten. Although I have not yet had the opportunity, I would be honoured to fulfil the invitation I was offered by Matt Yelland, the landlord of The Bell, to share more stories about David in his favourite bar.

But for us left in Bassett the date had been confirmed that the day for the first homecoming parade would be on Armistice Day, 11 November. This gave us something to look forward to, a tonic we were all happy to accept. Although sadly the tonic did not last long as a week later we were all coming back.

On 5 November the town gathered and paid their respects to Sapper William Blanchard, 101 (City of London) Engineer Regiment (Explosive Ordnance Disposal), who had been killed by small arms fire while investigating a suspect device in the Nahr-e Saraj district of Helmand Province on the 30 October.

As the hearse entered the town to the toll of the church's Tenor Bell, standards from a variety of Service Associations were lowered in salute. The flowers were laid, hearts were broken, and the cortège drifted away for further respects to be shown.

With the words 'military' and 'respect' often being associated with Wootton Bassett, there was a further honour to be bestowed on the town. Well more due to the town itself, the 'Field of Remembrance' that the Royal British Legion created was sanctioned to be in the beautiful grounds of Lydiard Park, Swindon. That great honour was to be enhanced when it was confirmed that on 8 November, Prince Harry would be present for the official opening. When that day arrived, his Royal Highness planted a cross to stand along with the other 35,000 crosses that were planted. Each cross carried a dedicated message, some with a photograph and many with the names of people that had been honoured in the High Street just a couple of miles away.

The Prince also met service personnel taking part in The Royal British Legion 'March for Honour'. A journey organised to raise funds and to commemorate servicemen and women who had fallen in Iraq and Afghanistan. Four groups of servicemen from the Royal Navy, Royal Marines, Royal Air Force and the Army, had marched from the North, South, East and West. With them they carried 'The Book of Remembrance' to its final destination, the Royal Albert Hall. This most sacred manuscript would be returned into the care of the Royal British Legion during the 'Festival of Remembrance'.

I briefly met the Royal Marine contingent as they gathered in the Cross Keys the previous evening. They had stopped at the war memorial, a bronze-cast sculpture of a globe held aloft by four hands for their own moment of reflection. It was a monument which had witnessed so many mixed emotions in recent years, those men 'marching in honour' and pride being the latest to show their respects. Three days later it was to be witness to more.

CHAPTER 28

They arrived a day before the homecoming parade – 200 personnel from various units – No 4 Force Protection Wing, including 1 Squadron Royal Air Force Regiment, elements of RAF Police, 16th Regiment Royal Artillery and a contingent of Royal Air Force Lyneham personnel, all of whom had recently served in Afghanistan.

I guess it was one of those moments when it seemed like a good idea at the time, especially after the first drill session was completed. The challenge was there, but to turn the basics into something with a little bit of pride and swagger they would need a little touch of that magic lotion 'military precision'.

That lotion was to be provided by Station Warrant Officer Nick Dale RAF Regiment, who was charged with coordinating the finer details, along with the Officer Commanding, Wing Commander Paul Weaver-Smith.

Behind the scenes and prior to Thursday 11 November 2010, a lot of work had been completed. With half a day to go the man with the big stick that shouts and the most recognisable face in the Royal Air Force, was ready to whip this group into shape. It was quite a challenge not just in getting the drills correct, but in getting the balance right. This was a unique parade, in fact almost a duel ceremony, a mixture of Remembrance followed by marching with pride on returning home. Yes, a difficult set of ingredients to get right without confliction, yet the following morning they arrived in Bassett and disembarked from their coaches. Out of sight, the men and women all formed up in their combat dress ready to march on parade.

All stood at ease, braced, waiting for the words that would commence this unique parade and like a starter's gun those words of command caused 200 left legs to move as one. 'Parade, Parade, Shun' – a pause, then the Officer Commanding moves them off with the command 'By the left quick march.'

We saw them making their way down the High Street the opposite end to the building on stilts. The pride and swagger was enhanced by the military music played by the band of the Royal Air Force Regiment as Wing Commander Paul Weaver-Smith proudly led his 200 combat-weary troops. Howling winds and heavy rains did not deter the crowds who turned out in their hundreds to welcome the troops home and to pay their respects on 'Armistice Day'. Families travelled from all over the UK to see their loved ones on parade. Many spoke of their immense pride and relief that husbands, sons, partners, wives and daughters had returned safely home.

I felt privileged to be present on duty. I stood well back and as I looked around I saw Station Warrant Officer Nick Dale, standing adjacent to the war memorial.

It was a total contrast to the heart-breaking sights that unfolded before his eyes almost weekly during the repatriations. Today was a little bit special, in seeing his beloved 'Gunners' marching through Wootton Bassett back to the safety of home. For me there was no better sight than when you saw the homecoming parades, the flag waving, the smiles, the relief as families, towns and communities welcomed their troops back. The parade stood to attention facing the war memorial in three files, waiting for the Remembrance Ceremony. The ceremony commenced with a dedication given by the Reverend Canon Thomas Woodhouse and Padre, Wing Commander Tim Wright of RAF Lyneham, followed by the Last Post to mark the lead into the two minutes' silence. This two-minute silence was poignant to both the local community and very meaningful for the military on parade. In particular those of the RAF Regiment as during their tour they had lost two of their young men.

Senior Aircraftman Kinikki 'Griff' Griffiths, from the RAF Regiment, was killed in a vehicle accident in Afghanistan on Friday 16 July 2010 and was repatriated whilst his colleagues completed their tour. The second loss of life sustained was almost incomprehensible to imagine, a tragic accident which was for many so very raw and still had not sunk in. It was reported by the Ministry of Defence that their comrade had died after being hit by a power boat operated by the Military Training Wing at the Cyprus Sovereign Base Area. Senior Aircraftman Scott Hughes, 20, from Gwynedd, North Wales, had survived a six-month tour of duty battling the Taliban and taking part in demanding and dangerous operations, including evacuating wounded soldiers.

The gunner with 1 Squadron Royal Air Force Regiment died in Cyprus on 7 November four days before this very parade that he should have been a part of.

Inconceivable and almost beyond belief that after completing six months of arduous combat in appalling conditions, he leaves Afghanistan to have a short stay at a decompression centre especially adapted for troops to start to unwind after their deployment, and is killed.

When I stood to attention I wondered what must have been going through some of his colleagues' minds when the Last Post signalled the start of the two-minute silence. God alone knows; but they held their composure and emotions while the service was completed.

Wreaths were laid by the military on parade, the Mayor Mary Champion, the Royal British Legion and other dignitaries within the community. I looked around the drenched community on either side of the road and could feel the sombreness in the air. It almost felt quite fitting, the overcast clouds in the sky creating the ambience of sadness especially during the two-minute silence. I always thought Remembrance services in this town had so much meaning and an understanding from the public; they were knowledgeable enough to respect the duties that these young men and women in front of them had completed. They also understood the huge sacrifices that had been made after having witnessed so many Union flag draped coffins which had been brought home in front of where they now stood.

The Mayor, Mary Champion, presented a framed Crest of Wootton Bassett to Wing Commander Weaver-Smith, and then a few words were spoken.

The parade was once again brought to attention and reformed ready to march off with the words of command 'Left Turn, Quick March.' The sombre atmosphere followed the 200 men and women as they left what had once again felt like sacred ground.

As you know this parade had to be orchestrated with sensitivity to create first a solemn, sensitive presence, yet followed with that of elation; I think it is fair to say it was a challenge to get the oxymoron balance right. Most certainly a difficult decision to incorporate a homecoming parade on 11 November of any year, but even more so after only a few days earlier Scott Hughes had died.

The first stage was completed and the serious mood reflected what that service was about. The challenge now was could they turn the frame of mind in the crowd around, to welcome these 200 troops back home?

As they marched down the hill past the building on stilts the words of command from Wing Commander Weaver-Smith were: 'Parade Halt, About Turn.'

The silence in so many could only be matched with the sounding of the Tenor Bell when it was used to announce the cortège had arrived. No one spoke, we just waited in anticipation. Could they get it right? The Commanding Officer and standards were reformed. The words of the Band Master were heard to order 'Band Ready.' This was a moment when once again I found myself in a world that had stopped spinning. Mr Dale braced himself. Had they got it right he would soon find out? Then the silence was broken with the words of command from Wing Commander Peter Weaver-Smith: 'Parade by the left; quick march.'

Boom!! Boom!! Boom!! the unmistakable sound of the military bass drum being thumped as the left heel of the troops hit the ground. That was all that was needed to ignite the musicians in the band. I kid you not, each and every one on parade grew six inches taller, the RAF Band played a rousting beat that put the swagger in their stride, that only a British serviceman or woman can pull off.

Pride, passion and honoured to serve the Crown, was what I saw as they made their way back along the High Street; that was all the encouragement the vast crowd needed. The spirit of the homecoming parade was achieved. Flags were pulled out of pockets and waved, mums, dads and children cheered, and the partners of those marching on parade had never felt so proud. Not a dry eye was in sight, but this time not of sadness but tears of happiness having that special person back home.

I just love the pomp and ceremony our country pulls off time after time in our own British way, as flags were waved proudly on such occasions. I clapped as proudly as all the people along the High Street that day.

It was wonderful to see another side to this horrible conflict, one of relief almost shouting 'We are home.' When those very proud men and women were ordered to first halt, then dismiss, it was a privilege to witness the hugs and kisses they received.

It was an even greater honour to give the ones I saw staggering down the road later that evening, a blue light taxi home after a few beers that they truly deserved.

CHAPTER 29

The following morning, Friday, the cloud of sadness which had briefly been lifted descended once again when confirmation was made that Senior Aircraftman Scott Hughes would be repatriated four days later.

However, before that it was Remembrance Sunday, where I always attended both services that took place on this poignant day.

In the morning was a service at St Michael's Church in Lyneham village, and then in the afternoon I would be on parade with my colleagues from Wootton Bassett Police Station. I have no idea the history behind Wootton Bassett having its Remembrance march past and service on a Sunday afternoon, but that's what they did.

After the morning service at Lyneham and prior to the parade we were having a cuppa in the Bassett Police Station when a police officer from headquarters walked in dressed in his normal attire of a suit. I was quite surprised to see him as he is usually present with a specific remit in relation to the protection of a VIP. On this occasion he dismissed his presence, stating he was intending to attend the Church service. I never thought anymore of his presence and walked down the road with Inspector Cox, Sergeant Martin Alvis and PC Nick Spargo to form up with the rest of the community.

It was a parade that typified many that had taken place earlier in the day in small towns across the country. A band at the front led the members of the Royal British Legion, then the Military Cadets, Scouts and Brownies along with the emergency services marching along the High Street. At the war memorial we were formed up for the brief ceremony where traditional respects were shown while the Last Post sounded; the two-minute silence followed and wreaths were laid. On completion, we marched down to St Bartholomew's Church. The close protection officer was already present outside the gates. I thought he was keen being one of the first there as we walked passed him to take our seats in preparation for the service.

I was sitting at the rear of the packed Church waiting for the Reverend Canon Thomas Woodhouse to begin his service, when I saw the head of a latecomer enter and quickly make his way to the front pews.

The door was closed and The Reverend Cannon Thomas Woodhouse began his service of Remembrance. An incredible character with a huge personality and a great sense of humour, and someone I never tire of listening to. He welcomed some of the invited dignitaries who had joined us this afternoon.

However, the presence of the latecomer was causing a great deal of curiosity and fidgeting in seats. This was obviously noticed by The Reverend Cannon and he decided to put them all out of their misery and announced: 'Due to the lack of Church funds we could not afford the fees of an impersonator, so we opted for the real thing and we welcome Prince Harry to our service.'

Heads were straining to catch a glance of his Royal Highness and when the Canon requested the community to please stand for the first hymn one would have thought he had fired an Olympic starter gun, such was the enthusiasm to stand.

It was moments like this I cherish seeing the pure innocence of this wonderful community and of the great respect both the Royal family have for the nation and vice versa. It was a wonderful service, but then how could it not be as The Reverend Canon Thomas Woodhouse was simply, as always, outstanding.

The following day we were back to work and already knew our plans for the week; two separate repatriations were to take place, and as each sad occasion took place the country stood by the side of those hurting.

On Tuesday 16 November, Senior Aircraftman Scott Hughes, 1 Squadron, Royal Air Force Regiment was repatriated home with the immaculate drills executed by the Queens Colour Squadron throughout the ceremony carrying the gunner home. Yes, it was a particularly sad day when we escorted this cortège through Wootton Bassett, where so many like me had gathered in silence finding it difficult to comprehend the most cruel set of circumstances that led to his death. While we were deep in thought, Scott's parents Emma and Michael and younger brother Adam placed white roses on top of the hearse as it paused at the war memorial. Around 20 of his school friends had travelled from North Wales to pay respects to their friend.

It was yet another scene we had seen so many times before, no matter what the circumstances; a nation recognising another loss of life. It was a chapter in our lives that needed to be remembered and that was exactly what the BBC planned to do. Earlier in the summer they had indicated that they were planning to produce a documentary on the respects that were shown for the fallen and had commissioned American Henry Singer, a documentary filmmaker who produced *The Falling Man*, to head this project. Over the last four months we had seen their presence as they carried out their research. Henry and his team were never intrusive, always polite, enthusiastic without being excitable, wanting to capture the warmth and support this small community had created.

On Friday 19 November the sombre setting was again present in the High Street and on this occasion the friends and family of the fallen came from Northern Ireland. Twenty-three standards were lowered as the cortège of Ranger Aaron McCormick of A Company, 1st Battalion The Royal Irish Regiment came slowly to a halt in front of his family and friends who stood silently at the war memorial.

The dignified and honourable repatriation ceremony that took place that day was captured by Henry Singer for his documentary with the consent of the parents of Aaron McCormick.

As the McCormick family were leaving the town, another family were already aware that they would soon be standing at RAF Lyneham when their loved one came home. Operation Minimise had been activated two days earlier and that ripple of despair was felt for the hundredth death this year. Guardsman Christopher Davies, 22, from 1st Battalion Irish Guards was shot in an ambush while patrolling in the Nahr-e-Saraj district of Helmand Province.

I knew it was an awful year, but I had not realised until then just how bad and how much desolation it had caused was impossible to calculate. That same devastation was clear as I read the tributes from the family and friends, of 'a cracking lad' with an 'invincible personality'. After I had read such wonderful words, there was no surprise to see so many from St Helen's present when the Guardsman was escorted home. One by one, with broken hearts, the flowers were laid, a symbol of love that we had seen so many times before this dreadful year.

Not everyone brought flowers when their loved one came home, and I know some felt so guilty when they reflected on the occasion because they had not. But they should feel no guilt, this was an extraordinarily emotional day which no one could plan for. Your grief was traumatic, your heart was ripped out, but more importantly, your son did not need flowers to know you loved him. It had been a devastating year for many and as those from St Helen's left the town they knew our deepest condolences went with them.

Wootton Bassett was at times a bizarre place to live as the people would brush themselves down a day or so after their respects had been shown and then with Christmas on its way they got on with the festivities as in any other community. The town that the country often referred to as an extraordinary place was quite simply, a small Wiltshire market hamlet, but with a wonderful community spirit.

One of the most enjoyable events on the town calendar which epitomised this spirit was on the first Friday in December when the Christmas tree lights were switched on. The High Street is closed until 9pm and the road is full of fun. The brass band plays carols, local butchers sell burgers, hot dogs and hog roasts, and traders and charities set up stalls. The excitement in the air is intensified with children dragging on the arms of their parents to see the arrival of Father Christmas on a sleigh pulled by a team of real reindeer. Just as the Church welcomed the real Prince Harry then the remarkable Town Council got the real Santa. Yep, there was never anything artificial in Wootton Bassett and nor was the ambience that evening.

I used to thoroughly enjoy policing this event, a chance to really feel part of the community, enjoy the hot soup, and even have my future read by Mystic Ruth. Although if I am honest, I lost a fiver from her words of wisdom, as she tipped Newcastle to win the cup that year and we got knocked out in the first match.

It was a brilliant evening with the retailers creating a wonderful atmosphere, getting into the Christmas mood and dressing in costumes from the Dickens era. As children lined up outside Santa's grotto the townsfolk congregated up by the building on stilts, the Old Town Hall, for the guest to have the honour of switching on the Christmas tree lights.

The honour was bestowed on a local man, the renowned explorer David Hempleman-Adams; the first person in history to reach the Geographic and Magnetic North and South Poles.

With a countdown from ten, which everyone excitedly joined in, the hands of Mr Hempleman-Adams pressed the switch that sent a huge surge of electricity instantaneously lighting up a thousand light bulbs in the trees. It was done with Bassett precision! And the crowd responded with a massive cheer as our guest shouted out 'Merry Christmas everyone.'

It was an evening where the purity of Bassett shone, full of happiness and goodwill to all mankind. If only David Hempleman-Adams could have spread that goodwill when he transcended the North and South hemispheres, the world might have been a better place.

Sadly, the next man to transcend the two hemispheres in our town's High Street was not a local lad, but one who was born in Wellington, New Zealand, who had signed up to serve in one of the world's finest front line fighting units.

Private John 'Jack' Howard, the 23-year-old 'Kiwi' warrior, proudly wore the maroon beret of an airborne soldier serving with 3rd Battalion, The Parachute Regiment.

On 14 December, his family gathered at the terminal at RAF Lyneham as he was brought to UK soil beginning the long journey home to Wellington's Cathedral of St Paul, New Zealand, to bid him a final farewell.

That journey took him along the 46 miles and when St Bartholomew's Church tolled its bell, hundreds stood in respect. His family may have been surrounded by a town of strangers, but they were definitely comforted by the presence of heartfelt sincerity and warmth. The Wiltshire hospitality was offered to the visitors from Wellington understanding the huge sacrifice that had been made.

As this New Zealand warrior made his way back to his country, the RAF station down the road were also on their way home. After a very challenging year their duties were done and they deserved the respite to celebrate Christmas with their families.

Obviously those serving in Afghanistan were not awarded that luxury and the conflict continued. Sadly, that also required a contingency plan in the event of further bad news being received. If I am honest I was tired, emotionally drained, like all the others who were directly involved in Operation Pabbay and decided though I had no intention of going away, I would relax at home with my family.

In the event of further bad news a network of information would be shared with the personalities on call. Four days into Christmas leave, and the shortest day in the year, was to be the longest day for the latest family to have that awful news delivered to their front door. Operation Minimise had just been activated 3,500 miles away.

CHAPTER 30

Joint Casualties Communication Centre, known to us as J treble C, were receiving the information through to task another notification officer to break the news to a family four days before Christmas morning.

Corporal Steven Thomas Dunn was deployed to Afghanistan on 19 September 2010 as part of 216 (Parachute) Signal Squadron. This Squadron work in support of 16 Air Assault Brigade, 2nd Battalion the Parachute Regiment Battle Group (2 PARA).

Corporal Dunn was based at Patrol Base 2 in the Nahr-e-Saraj district of Helmand Province. On 21 December 2010, he was working with 2 PARA Patrols Platoon on a deliberate operation to interdict insurgents in the Bowri desert. He was travelling in a Jackal vehicle which hit an improvised explosive device which killed him.

The date was set for the repatriation of Corporal Dunn as the 30 December and, knowing on this occasion there would be no briefing the day before, I decided to take the opportunity to read the many tributes on the internet.

I knew nothing of the soldier but found I was engrossed in what I read, maybe it was that I could relate to so many things that were written:

'Steven was a loving husband to Cheryl, son to Vicky, and doting dad to Emily. He has left a huge hole in the lives of those he has left behind including his brothers Christopher and Michael. He will also be sorely missed by Kevin, an important person in his life and all his aunts, uncles, cousins and many friends.'

I paused as I read, I would periodically would drift off into my own thoughts; it always seemed the loss of a life was felt with an even deeper sadness around this time of year. Perhaps it was our subconscious thinking, as most of us are sat at home with our own families. A wife, a mother and a daughter, along with two brothers and other family members now distraught, devastated, and I felt almost guilty as I looked at the presents around my own family Christmas tree.

I thought for Vicky 'Merry Christmas mam' a simple message from her oldest son never to be heard again. His wife, widowed before the ink was dry on the wedding certificate and I thought of a poor child I did not know. Emily, Steven's six-year-old daughter, I wondered how a family break the news to a child that her own hero, her dad, has been killed.

I did not even wish to imagine the heartache this caused, seeing the distress of such an innocent child. She should have been having sleepless nights through the excitement of Santa coming but instead those nights would be full of her breaking her little heart for her dad. Although no one can ever console such pain in a child at such a tender age, I could see that Emily would be able to tell the whole world how proud she is of him, because from what I read, your dad, was one 'stand out' soldier. Four tours in combat in the frontline, Iraq and three tours in Afghanistan an outstanding paratrooper.

To be a paratrooper, wearing their wings and the prestigious maroon beret is something you earn. Yep Emily, your dad must have been extremely fit and rugged as you do not get the honour to wear that beret without drive, determination and dedication.

As I continued reading the many amazing tributes spoken about this man I could understand why his family were so proud of him. You could not fail to pick up on his outstanding personality; he certainly was not a grey man, he was noticed that's for sure.

'A devilish Geordie sense of humour with a spark in his eye,' one of his commanders had written; well it looks like he was a character as well as being a top soldier.

The more I read about this husband, father, son and brother, the more I could relate to him and realised how we valued similar things in life, obviously the family, the daughter and the 'Toon'. Out of all the tributes this particular one caught my eye: Major Mike Shervington, Chief of Staff 2nd Battalion the Parachute Regiment Battle Group, said:

> 'Corporal Dunn epitomised all that is best in our soldiers and all that is best about Newcastle and the North East. Especially friendly, suitably aggressive and absolutely loyal, Corporal Dunn was itching to leave the confines of the Patrol Base, get out on patrol and help others. His only yellow (never red) card – anything that clashed with him watching his beloved Newcastle United. I will really miss our chats about football, families and past escapades. Whilst little comfort, the small crumb of solace is the memory that he loved his job, and he loved being an integral member of the 2 PARA Battle group; I often joked that there was more blue than white in his 216 Signals Drop Zone flash. (Meaning more para than signaller.) All our thoughts are with his family, his new bride Cheryl and his young daughter Emily. Words like "you won't be forgotten" have tended to sound a little hollow in recent years but nothing could be further from the truth now.'

Incredible words spoken with passion from one man about another he obviously respected. I also read in *The Sun* newspaper a day or so before the repatriation that the loss of Corporal Steven Dunn had been mentioned in an article in the sports section. It was written by a man who anyone with black and white eyes worshipped. Written by the man himself, Alan Shearer, he referred to Steven Dunn: 'being the true Geordie hero.' For those who do not understand the passion people like Steven, like me, like thousands of others have for that man and that football club, you will not understand. For those who do, those words are massive, and bring comfort.

When I went down to RAF Lyneham the day before the actual repatriation, Station Warrant Officer Nick Dale was putting his watchful eye over the rehearsal preparations. He was offering advice to the bearer party in achieving the military precision required for the duties they would perform the following day. It was then, during the breaks, I got chatting with Sergeant Major Paul Robertson, who introduced himself to me as 'Robbo' and the lads from 216 Signals. We chatted about their mate 'Dunny'. I could almost relate to the conversation as I had read so much through the tributes.

I never met any of the people who paid those tributes, but I did meet some of the soldiers who your dad served with, Emily, when they came to RAF Lyneham to carry their friend, your hero, home.

Their many tributes as they in turn spoke of 'Dunny' reinforced the words I had read. They referred to him as a legend and one thing was very noticeable, Robbo and the men from 216 Signals were genuinely honoured to be chosen to carry your dad on their shoulders.

Whilst the bearer party were going through their drills with Robbo, I received news that a further loss of life had occurred the day before.

No name had been released yet and obviously no date fixed for his return, all that would happen in slow time. However, just as the previous years since we had been involved in the repatriations, before a new year commenced a soldier was waiting to come home. My mind wandered in deep thought; yet another family that would soon be standing where I was now, inside a marquee that had witnessed so much grief. I came out of my trance just as these six warriors were finishing their drills. They huddled around Robbo for his debrief after the final rehearsal. The news was good; he was confident of his men's understanding of the commitment that lay ahead. They were focused, they were ready and, as he stood them down, we all went our separate ways to meet up the following morning.

Thursday 30 December was a cold, chilly, but dry morning as I carried out my normal ritual on repatriation days. As I made my way up the High Street I stopped briefly at the war memorial just as the two Royal British Legion members arrived at the flagpole. The two men lowered the Union flag all the way down then raised it to the half-mast position, in respect for Corporal Steven Dunn who would be honoured that day.

After booking on duty at an empty Police Station I jumped into my patrol car and made my way down to RAF Lyneham. We had our brief with Albins Undertakers who were polishing their fleet of cars.

Robbo and his bearer party were, as expected, switched on, focused with a job to do. We chatted over coffee although the Sergeant Major's eyes were on his airborne soldiers who were polishing their kit. Red light, green light, they were good to go, both physically and emotionally; it's a harrowing task to carry one of your own.

The family had left the Hilton hotel which was my cue to go. A few minutes later I was parked up on the lay-by on Chippenham Road. With the roar of those four massive engines this huge bird once again floated with grace and dignity through the air, dipping his starboard wing to honour Corporal Steven Dunn who was in his care. I watched the plane land on the runway then the same calls as always are made. Thames Valley Police confirmed they were ready and Blondie with his own band of brothers were travelling up from South Dorset.

My next stop was to call in at the Cross Keys for a cuppa and greet anyone who may have travelled down from my native north east. Three lads wearing black and white scarves were outside the pub; they had gone to school with Steven at St Joseph's Catholic School. Having set off in the early hours they were keen to get a pint and a bite to eat, something I assured them that Kirsty could provide with her usual sincere hospitality.

While the military ceremony was taking place inside RAF Lyneham the many standard bearers, bikers and members of the Royal British Legion, started to congregate in the warmth of the Cross Keys.

It was cold and many who sought the warmth joined those inside the pub; amongst the many were Jon and Marina Jenkinson; Steven was their nephew. A lovely couple who like most people who travelled for such a harrowing day were slightly out of their comfort zone, so I put their minds at ease. A few words here and questions answered; I assured them the family were being well looked after.

My call to leave was received and I informed Jon I would let him know when his family were on the way so he could be there for them.

True to my word, I saw the family leaving RAF Lyneham as we formed up with the outriders and police escort vehicles waiting for the cortège, and quickly give Jon the heads up. His distraught family were in need of a huge cuddle. Jon and Marina were there to offer Vicky and her sons some comfort, being a friendly face amongst strangers.

The High Street was bustling with activity as more family and friends offered their condolences. For the final time this year, the Wiltshire town welcomed those who travelled from afar into their care.

Then traffic stops, the bell tolls, and the silence creates a sombre setting as the conductor pages along the road. The Legion salute, the standards are lowered and the family weep as Corporal Steven Dunn is at rest where they stand. The sobbing is awful as always and the conductor shows compassion before he has to leave. No words are spoken, with the subtle tipping of his hat the soldier is led away.

As we escorted Corporal Steven Dunn that day I honestly felt as if I was escorting one of my own. It was truly fitting that when we left Bassett fluttering in the air I saw the Black and White football scarf that had been tied to his hearse when the respects were shown. Emily your dad was really honoured not just in Wootton Bassett but the full 46 mile route. After handing the cortège over to the Thames Valley Police I returned back to the Police Station and booked off duty.

I quite enjoyed the tranquil walk along the High Street on my way home. It was one of those moments when I preferred my own company, to reflect and distance myself a little from the deep sadness I saw on each occasion. I paused at the war memorial, as I always did, to read the cards and crosses that had been laid. Such personal messages that were written from the bottom of broken hearts. 2010 was an awful year with so much heartache and humbling scenes that this small, yet beautifully structured, monument had seen.

It was dark, it was cold, as one would expect this time of year, but across the road was a glow of warmth and I felt a longing to enter. That glow was providing comfort and support to people from my home town and as I walked over to the Cross Keys I did not feel I was intruding, but showing respect to a lad from the 'Toon'. I had only just entered when a port was thrust into my hand. To 'Dunny' was the salute Robbo gave; the first of many that were drunk that evening. Then he introduced me to his friend's family. This is what made each occasion unique, it was the people who had lost someone very special. That day was for Steven Dunn, a lad I never knew, but would have been honoured to stand next to in the Gallowgate End of St James' Park.

Cross Keys is where we remained until they had to make that long journey back home after an emotional day. It was a day when the people from the banks of the river Tyne sadly left their footprints in the High Street of Wootton Bassett.

Though, if I am not mistaken, a few stayed longer, including Steven's brother and a couple of friends. They made the long trek home the next day probably with a thick head and memories of an extraordinary day, filled with so many mixed emotions.

Those who were hurting almost as if they had lost their own brother were the bearer party who carried Corporal Steven Dunn off that C17 aircraft that day.

Sergeant Major Paul Robertson had heard that I was writing this book and he wished for his words to be read. I am truly honoured to include them in this chapter as his own fitting tribute to a man who was more than a friend:

'I remember the call vividly, I was at home with my wife Hayley when the phone rang on 21 December 2010:

"Sergeant Major one of our soldiers has been killed in Action." I felt numb. "Who I asked?"

"Come over to Headquarters and you will be informed."

As I walked the short distance I couldn't stop thinking about all my comrades who had deployed on Op HERRICK 13. Who was it was the question running through my head?

When I opened the door to the HQ building I was met by the Welfare Officer Capt Jordan. "Robbo please take a seat." Then I was briefed that it was Corporal Steven Dunn. My heart skipped a beat, Dunny was in my Troop when he was a young lad, I was his Corporal, Sergeant, Staff Sergeant and now his Sergeant Major – this had to be a mistake! I had watched Dunny grow up and knew him inside out.

After the briefing I rang all the soldiers from our bearer party; we had been preparing prior to going on Christmas leave just in case the worst was to happen. Unfortunately it was all too real and we now had to bring our friend back from Afghanistan draped in his country's Union flag.

I couldn't sleep for days thinking of Cheryl, Steven's wife, and his daughter and his mother, a lovely lady named Vicky.

During our practice sessions, to ensure that we were in good order to receive our friend from Afghanistan, we went to Newcastle and Gateshead to complete a reconnaissance of the local areas and the church and crematorium.

Vicky, Steven's mother, could not have been more hospitable, she would make us all dinner and her home-made soup was excellent. The pain she was feeling could not be measured, but she continued to hold it together and look after all the soldiers who were given the huge task of repatriating Steven and then completing his funeral.

My heart went out to her and her partner Kevin and the boys. I continued to comfort them by insisting that we had the best troops to complete the tasks, as their hero Steven deserved. One thing I did notice whilst we spent a few days in the north east was the community spirit; everyone knew who we were and why we were in their area. Everyone had lovely words to share about Steven and the people could not do enough for us; free food, free hospitality, you name it, they would provide it.

The repatriation was completed on a cold winter's day in Lyneham. I remember the troops preparing for days before, to ensure that we could carry our fallen brother with the dignity and panache that he deserved.

The local bobby, PC Jarra Brown, was a massive help to us all, you could tell he felt for Dunny. I am sure he related a lot to Dunny due to them both being from the North East. Being ex-forces, Jarra fitted in well with the troops and gave me good advice on many occasions. I could not have asked for a better team, they made my job simple due to their diligence and love for Corporal Steven Dunn.

The hardest part was when we marched onto the C-17 Globemaster plane, a huge beast of a plane and there behind the curtains lay Corporal Steven Dunn; draped in our country's Union flag. I halted the bearer party on each side of our hero and inwards turned them, I briefed the men up that we had two minutes to say what we wanted to say to Corporal Dunn. This hit me very hard; there I was the bearer party Commander and I was hit with a tidal wave of emotion at the sight of Dunny lying there. After two minutes, we had a pep talk and pulled ourselves together for what was to be an honour to carry our friend out of the plane, from a foreign land and onto our home soil.

The days leading up to the funeral in the North East were an extremely busy time; in the Army we like to practise and rehearse constantly. This was the least Dunny deserved and the bearer party completed many hours of planning and preparation to ensure the funeral was seamless from an Army perspective.

I remember going to the local funeral directors in Colchester 'John Smiths'. I walked in wearing my uniform and informed him of the tragedy; he already knew and said he was happy to assist us in our preparation.

Mr Smith himself, allowed us to utilise his pristine very old Rolls Royce hearse, a coffin and trestles for five days. This kind gesture allowed our team to prepare fantastically for what we were about to conduct. We turned Bravo Troop garage into a mock Church and practised and practised our drills until it became habit.

The bearer party consisted of Jerry, Buz, Rus, Jim, John, Trev, Kev, Woody and I. All of us knew Dunny personally therefore the challenges were immense. Although there was a lot of pressure on the team, they did a wonderful job and this was echoed when Cheryl and Vicky continued to inform us that they were very proud of what we had done. Although we were just doing our duty, we had lost a brother, a comrade, another airborne soldier, one of us, it was the very least we could do. I would also like to mention Captain Paul Jordan who was the Welfare Officer, he was a very professional man who put everything into ensuring that Corporal Dunn's family were looked after and supported.

Thankfully Corporal Dunn's funeral with full military honours was completed as professionally as we could have wished. I remember vividly the men who were still in Afghanistan and who had carried Dunny onto the C-17 for his flight home, leaving us messages of support and encouragement.

That chapter in our lives will never be forgotten, the pain, but mostly the pride at having being chosen and also knowing that so many people came together to ensure that our friend, the British soldier, who gave his life for our country's interest, was given the most fitting send off.

My heart goes out to Steven's daughter, wife and mother whose pain will never disappear. Steven was no ordinary soldier, he was an airborne soldier who was loved by many.'

After reading these words, those who have not served will begin to understand when I refer to 'band of brothers'. Those powerful personal words that were written by a Sergeant Major about a man, who was more than just one of his soldiers, a man who really had lost a brother.

I wish to dedicate this final paragraph of this chapter to a child who was worshipped by her father. Emily you were young and so very innocent at the time and protected from the grief when your hero died. Those childhood memories when you played in the park and so many others, keep them in your heart. When you get older and understand, walk through Saltwell Park, 'The Garden of Reflection', tell them of your dad, an 'Airborne Soldier' Corporal Steven Dunn, who came from Geordie land.

CHAPTER 31

With the start of any new year there is quite often a feeling of excitement; future projects, plans and things to look forward to. I am sure amongst the many stationed at RAF Lyneham they too were equally looking forward to the new challenges that lay in store on their return from Christmas leave.

One subject the majority had on their mind, was a project that dominated their thoughts – 'Future Brize' – was something they all knew about, but had an honest belief it would never happen. In their minds or maybe their hopes, dismissing it as not practical, too expensive and far more other words to describe something they did not want to know. Like most things that are bad news perhaps if you ignore it, it might go away. They tried that and it didn't, because as soon as they returned from leave it was staring them right in the eyes. Future Brize was the topic of conversation and, as much as many people were dragging their heels to avoid it, it was going to happen. I think for the first time on their return the harsh reality of that happening was there for all to see.

In layman's terms Future Brize was the closing down of RAF Lyneham, all the Squadrons and units within the station which of course included their pride and joy, the C130 Hercules aircraft. Lock, stock and barrel they were going to move to Oxfordshire and become part of RAF Brize Norton

That move had to be completed by December 2012 and, although that might have seemed a long way off in January 2011, when you move a whole station to merge in with another, the logistics were nothing short of massive. It also meant the moving of Operation Pabbay back to its original home RAF Brize Norton; this was to happen by September 2011. There was to be a vast amount of reconstruction and development some 30 miles up the road in Oxfordshire. One of the priorities that had been approved was to build a purpose built 'Repatriation Centre'. With that planning taking place at Brize Norton, here at Lyneham we had a more pending date to focus on, with the repatriation of a man described in the tabloid headlines of one national newspaper: 'The hero of Christmas.'

'A Soldier arranged Christmas Day dinner and a visit from Santa for his men and even had time to defuse a bomb. Three days later, a huge Taliban blast took his life. He was determined that, even in Afghanistan, Christmas Day should be special for the troops serving alongside him. Not only did Warrant Officer, Class 2, Charlie Wood help prepare Christmas dinner for 150 of his men in Helmand; aware that they would be missing their families 3,500 miles away in

Britain, the 34-year-old explosives expert arranged an appearance by Santa.'

Whist many of us at home had eaten too much and were sleeping it off or were watching the *Wizard of Oz* on the box, the day for this man ended with him co-ordinating the clearance of a 44lb bomb – proving both the words of his wife Heather describing her husband as having a 'Heart of Gold' and his commanding officers saying: 'He always strived to lead from the front.'

Warrant Officer Charlie Wood, 34, had volunteered for the dangerous role of an advanced search adviser with 23 Pioneer Regiment, The Royal Logistic Corps. Three days after making Christmas a little special for his men, this hugely respected soldier was dead.

He was leading the clearance of a route through the Khushdal Kalay area of the Helmand River Valley in southern Afghanistan when he was killed in an explosion.

The morning of Thursday 6 January, the day of his repatriation, I received a call from one of my colleagues who had come across a group of military personnel quite early in Wootton Bassett. They had travelled down in plenty of time to be present when their friend flew home.

He relayed my message to them that the flight had been slightly delayed, but if they came down to the Lyneham Neighbourhood Police point, I could take them to a viewing area where they could see their friend return home.

Perhaps I should have asked how many of them there were before I offered my hospitality, as half an hour later a fleet of cars pulled up outside our police door. A building, which I mentioned previously, was a converted three bedroomed property.

Cars full of military personnel all in various uniforms, best dress and others in normal duty rig had travelled from different locations, all having served with the Warrant Officer who was flying home.

Being a good host I invited them in out of that horrible drizzle, the kind when you get soaked before you know you're wet, and offered them a cuppa hoping they would decline; to my horror they replied yes. The wife was the caterer in my family so thinking on my feet I pointed to the kitchen, help yourself, which they did; they were very considerate they even made me one! These people were just some of many that had turned up at this police point and, as Kirsty had done at the Cross Keys in showing her hospitality, it was only right we should do the same, although with somewhat limited supplies.

A mixture of rank, Majors and Senior NCOs with their cuppas held tightly warming themselves up as much as refreshing their lips, stood transfixed as I gave them as much information as I could. Most had seen coverage on the many previous television broadcasts when the news channels were covering the ceremony through Bassett. Although the impact, as they would later find out, when stood on the High Street is even more humbling and emotional than these 20 men and women could ever envisage.

Once I briefed them on the format of the operation the stories of Warrant Officer Charlie Wood began. As they spoke their eyes could not disguise the hurt they all felt. Yes these people were hurting in exactly the same way as those non-military personnel, yep, civilians. Repatriations were definitely a leveller for emotions. Just because they wore medals or had carried guns they were struggling, grief had no respect for them as they bear the loss of a very good friend.

The words they spoke were nothing short of sheer admiration for a very special man, displaying the overwhelming affection and respect they each had for Charles as they referred to him.

While we chatted, I received information that the flight was 30 minutes away and on this occasion after the honourable flypast, the aircraft would land coming in from an easterly direction, as opposed to the northerly runway.

With that information I invited the group to follow me up the back lanes of Goatacre where I knew they would get an unobstructed view of their friend coming home. We could see the terminal roof from where we stood and I pointed in the general direction of the approach the aircraft would make in performing its ritual.

We stood, we watched and we waited, in total silence. Then we heard the unmistakable sound of those four engines holding this huge aircraft in the sky some 200ft high, heading in our direction. The military group stood just as the families did, mesmerised as this image was getting bigger by the second; floating, more than flying towards them, simply hanging in the sky which is why many referred to it as an 'Angel' bringing their loved one home.

I knew from my own experience what to expect. These battle-hardened soldiers huddled together and wept as one. For the first time since hearing the tragic news they had something tangible, confirming what they already knew.

Then the starboard wing salutes with a dip; those who had a personal fight to not cry broke down and crumbled just like those on 'Civvy Street'. That honourable gesture in recognition of the man that this beast of an aircraft was carrying, had symbolically underlined it was their friend that was in its care. If Steven Dunn, in the words of Alan Shearer, was Newcastle's 'true Geordie hero' then Warrant Officer Charlie Henry Wood was most certainly Middlesbrough's. Those representing the British Army who I stood amidst would certainly vouch for that.

The aircraft flew directly over our heads then climbed to make its approach before landing and each slight movement as it flew to that position had 20 heads following its every move. We lost sight of it as it made its touchdown then came back into view as it taxied to its holding position. The engines were cut and numbness was felt where we stood, though many felt comfort hiding under their umbrellas. The group that I chaperoned started to make their way back to their vehicles each taking one final look over their shoulders; trying to come to terms with the emotional scene they had just observed.

My hosting duties completed, I escorted them back to the Cross Keys up in Bassett where they were welcomed by the town with hospitality from a very appreciative community.

There they would remain, sharing stories with people who travelled down from the north east town of Middlesbrough.

The repatriation ceremony, as always, was immaculately done and following on from that the Teesside hero was moved to the Chapel of Rest. How long we waited? No one cared, as this was the private moment that was never rushed, such was the importance of the Chapel of Rest. When the time was ready for the family to take the first steps out from the sacred building they were supported by each other and their Visiting Officer.

As was the tradition they made their way to Bassett, where so many were waiting to try and ease their pain, by sharing their grief.

When the very proud family stepped from the mini bus there were literally hundreds of people, some from their home town, but the majority total strangers. They all had one thing in common, to honour one man Warrant Officer Charlie Wood the first fatality to return in 2011.

With them were also the military personnel who earlier stood with me at the end of the runway when their friend came home. Once again at the sound of the Tenor Bell they had difficulty controlling their emotions. Yep, these scenes were certainly more powerful than those portrayed on the TV at home.

Some days later I received a letter from one of those present, Major Claire Masters of the Royal Logistic Corps.

She wrote from the heart and I hope she does not mind me sharing some of her words:

'Charles was more than our colleague and fellow soldier, he was our friend. To be able to see his flight come home and for us all to be together was something that we will never forget and will help us come to terms with his huge loss.'

Claire also invited me to Sandhurst to share the hospitality of all those who travelled to Wiltshire that day and promised me one hell of a hangover the following morning. I never did get the chance to accept that offer, but who knows one day Claire, I would be honoured to raise a glass in memory of your friend.

CHAPTER 32

Sadly we did not get much chance to reflect as one of those eighty per cent calls on my mobile had us preparing for Op Pabbay again. This was how life for us was over those years; as one family left another was contemplating the journey but on this occasion from further afield. Once again we were planning for the return of another hero this time a man who was described as a 'Gentle Giant'.

Private Joseva Saqanagonedau Vatubua, 24, was killed in Helmand Province on New Year's Day in an explosion. The soldier, originally from Fiji, was in the Argyll and Sutherland Highlanders, 5th Battalion, The Royal Regiment of Scotland. As one can imagine with the mixture of ingredients from Fiji and Scotland he came home to the United Kingdom with a huge amount of honour. That pride was obvious to see, when those two nations stood as one, alongside the residents of this wonderful market town. The ceremony was immaculate, the respects were shown and hearts were broken on a day so many will never forget as we escorted Joseva home.

I read an article in one of the tabloids that two weeks later his wife, family, relatives and friends converged at the Commonwealth War Cemetery in Fiji to pay their last respects to Private Joseva Saqanagonedau Vatubua. It showed the mutual respect for our commonwealth soldiers who also served the Crown. A bearer party from the Argyll and Sutherland Highlanders was present to afford Private Vatubua a full military burial with honours.

His Company Sergeant, Major Scott Clark, and other members of the party, who were there as representatives of their regiment, presented Mrs Vatubua with the Battalion's Wreath, Private Vatubua's medals, his headdress and white belt to the mournful sound of bagpipes.

As the Fijian family were grieving in their homeland, another family in Bradford, West Yorkshire were soon to be distraught, as they heard the shattering news delivered by the notification officers. Private Martin Bell, of 2nd Battalion, The Parachute Regiment, died after he disobeyed a direct order so he could give aid to a wounded friend on 25 January. The soldier was south of Nahr-e-Saraj in Helmand Province when he was struck by an IED. He had been rushing to help the second of two of his friends injured by separate devices that day. Nine days later the Paratrooper was flown into RAF Lyneham in Wiltshire, where, after the military ceremony and private service in the Chapel of Rest, we led the cortège through Wootton Bassett.

When you drive through the High Street and it is a singleton repatriation you tend to see the faces of the grieving more clearly, when it's a multiple loss of life you see a mass of people. It was the former when I drove through on this occasion. I saw the faces of the poor family breaking their hearts. Inconsolable was a word used previously and it really was just that; a mother gripping onto her flowers as she stared down the road through us and to the hearse. The hearse slowly being paged bringing her son home; the raw grief of this conflict is unashamedly displayed once again.

As I try to focus on getting to the end of the High Street I see a 'Maroon Blanket' a mass of the Paras, serving and ex, proudly wearing their berets honouring their own brother. These are scenes that never fail to have an impact; grief is not something that sits comfortably no matter how many times it is seen.

Respects shown, salutes raised and flowers laid, another day of so many mixed emotions but amongst the sadness was so much pride. They would take one last look down the road as the cortège drifted out of sight. As they comforted each other some would break off and were only too willing to fill the journalists' notepads with their tributes in memory of this Yorkshire lad.

Just as I always read the tributes of the fallen before we escorted them home, the following day I would read the heartfelt quotes from those breaking their hearts on the High Street as I drove by. Such as those from his friend Private Stephen Mann:

'Professionally he was an outstanding soldier, very switched on and very dedicated. He was disobeying an order not to go to a casualty and provide aid, but he did so anyway and in doing so he paid with his life – but that was Martin all over – he would never just sit there and watch one of his friends suffer if he thought he could do something about it. I don't think there are many people that could see their friend in pieces and just obey an order to stay put when they think they could get to their friend and help them.'

As Bassett said goodbye to Yorkshire we were hearing confirmation that the bikers were coming back. Although that was planned for April and excitedly anticipated – well it was by me – we were focused on what was happening in February. Sadly that focus was in the form of more bad news as a further seven soldiers who had been killed or died in tragic circumstances: Ranger David Dalzell, 1st Battalion The Royal Irish Regiment. Sergeant Major, Colin Beckett, 3rd Battalion, The Parachute Regiment. Private Conrad Lewis, 4th Battalion, The Parachute Regiment. Private Lewis Hendry 3rd Battalion The Parachute Regiment. Private, Robert Wood, Royal Logistic Corps, 17 Port and Maritime Regiment. L/Corporal Kyle Cleet Marshall, 2nd Battalion, The Parachute Regiment and Private Dean Hutchinson Royal Logistic Corps, Theatre Logistic Group. No matter how each one died as each cortège came through the town, be it a single loss of life or multiple, the respects never dwindled and as had previously taken place for almost four years now, hundreds lined the route. In the wind, sleet or snow the legion, bikers and the public stood with our Armed Forces, not just at Bassett but the full 46 mile route right to the 'final turn'.

CHAPTER 33

For each loss of life there were reviews, inquests and scientific discussions on so many issues; one of those raised was one of their principal enemies – the IED.

The IED – Improvised Explosive Device – was one of the biggest challenges that front line troops had to deal with whilst on patrol, be it on foot or on track. It was the weapon that caused so much devastation to our Armed Forces.

The term Improvised Explosive Device comes from the British Army in the 1970s, after the Provisional Irish Republican Army used bombs made from agricultural fertilizer and semtex to make highly effective booby-trap devices or remote-controlled bombs. An IED is a bomb fabricated in an improvised manner incorporating destructive, lethal, noxious, pyrotechnic or incendiary chemicals and designed to destroy or incapacitate personnel or vehicles. In some cases, IEDs are used to distract, disrupt or delay an opposing force, facilitating another type of attack. IEDs may incorporate military or commercially sourced explosives, and often combine both types, or they may otherwise be made with homemade explosives.

An IED has five components: a switch (activator), an initiator (fuse), container (body), charge (explosive) and a power source (battery). An IED designed for use against armoured targets such as personnel carriers or tanks will be designed for armour penetration. By using either a shaped charge or an explosively formed penetrator, IEDs are extremely diverse in design and may contain many types of initiators, detonators, penetrators and explosive loads.

Anti-personnel IEDs are triggered by various methods, including remote control, infra-red or magnetic triggers, pressure-sensitive bars or trip wires. In some cases, multiple IEDs are wired together in a daisy-chain, to attack a convoy of vehicles spread out along a roadway.

Yes, the IED was an extremely dangerous weapon; an awful component of this conflict with only one purpose to inflict devastation and to kill. The environment of intensive heat, the dust and fall of the land, made the searching for the IED hazardous to the extreme for the front line troops on foot or in a vehicle.

This exemplifies the bravery of anyone on point searching for a clear route, attempting to make it safe for colleagues to follow and why the skills of the 'Explosive Search Dog and his Handler' were so valued by every person in the combat zone.

L/Corporal Liam Tasker had transferred to the Royal Army Veterinary Corps in 2007, and was assigned to the 1st Military Working Dog Regiment. In September 2010, Theo was assigned to L/Corporal Tasker some two weeks prior to deployment, after the first two dogs assigned to him didn't work out. The two of them were described as inseparable, a relationship of love respect and something very important in this role: trust between man and dog looking out for each other.

This was not a dog owner throwing a ball for his dog to fetch, they were looking for a hidden enemy that caused so much devastation. In the Army, years ago, I recall the recruiting posters that said something along the lines 'Join the British Army, be a soldier, be the best.'

L/Corporal Liam Tasker and Theo were quite simply the best. They had as a team undoubtedly saved countless lives with their skills and bravery by searching and locating devices.

In fact, by the time that Liam's tour was almost completed, Theo the springer spaniel had broken all records for his finds of explosives and weapons, which resulted in this outstanding dog having his tour extended for a further month.

Liam was forced to contemplate flying home without his dog, but that was in the future. For the time being the best team in the British Army were focused on the task in hand. There was no shortage of work for this hard working unit of two as Liam's tour drew to an end.

On Tuesday 1 March 2011, the inseparable team, as their commander had referred to them, were out on the front line with the 1st Irish Guards in the Nahri Saraj District in Helmand Province when they came under attack. During the contact L/Corporal Tasker suffered fatal injuries in the firefight and was killed in the battle with the Taliban. Operation Minimise was activated, a signal would be on its way to J treble C, and a notification officer would take that devastating message to a family that their son was dead.

While that information and procedure was being actioned, Theo was recovered to base. Once he was back in relevant safety something extraordinarily happened, that science could not explain.

Theo, that little springer spaniel, died. Those in the K9 world may have their own conclusions as to why and a post mortem was inconclusive. But who would doubt the words spoken by Liam's parents in an interview they gave, that quite simply said, 'Theo died of a broken heart' a few hours after his beloved master had been killed.

Theo was cremated in Afghanistan and plans were made to present the ashes to the next of kin on the same flight home, which his master L/Corporal Liam Tasker would be repatriated on.

That honourable flypast took place on Thursday 10 March 2011, and when the C17 Globemaster dipped its starboard wing tip he did so in honour of L/Corporal Tasker and of Theo the springer spaniel, when they were flown home. Following the repatriation ceremony and the Chapel of Rest private service, the family made their way towards the exit gates escorted up to Bassett by the RAF Police. Inside RAF Lyneham, while the family would be met at the war memorial, Albins Funeral Directors were gracefully carrying L/Corporal Tasker from the Chapel of Rest into their highly polished hearse. A few minutes later we received the message the cortège was moving towards where we always waited. From the Chapel of Rest to the station exit gates is a distance of around 500 metres, on this particular occasion I think it took them about five minutes to get to where we were. The reason for this unusually slow pace was that on either side of the road inside the base were RAF Police dog handlers. They stood to attention in their best kit and medals with their immaculately turned out dogs. Each saluted with personal recognition as the cortège was slowed to walking pace.

It was precise, it was personal. Many from the RAF Police knew Liam when they had bonded on courses or indeed during operations on the same front line. Almost at walking pace the cortège came into my view and as it did we activated our blue lights. 'Bronze this is Mike Delta 2185 we have the cortège we are leaving RAF Lyneham now' was my brief radio transmission.

The RAF Police peeled off and I took the lead with the cortège held tightly in my care. Slowly, methodically, we left the base, knowing the outriders had cleared our entrance onto the busy main road.

One final salute at RAF Lyneham main gate from the old boys, one Royal Navy the other RAF, showing mutual respect for this young Army man about a third of their average age.

We made our way through the village of Lyneham where the community had come out 15 minutes earlier on hearing the bell tolling from St Michael's Church. Steadily, we made progress witnessing once again the scenes of humbling respects; cars approaching the cortège from our front activating their hazard lights and stopping their cars. Some would even get out and bow their heads as they all knew who we were escorting because so much was reported in the press. A young Scottish soldier inside his hearse slept and although many felt the presence of Theo, his courageous spaniel dog aptly by his side, it was in spirit as this was not the case.

Over Skew Bridges one final radio message: 'Bronze we are entering the built up area' as we enter Bassett.

The Tenor Bell of St Bartholomew's Church tolls, our arrival is announced as we stop outside the sacred gates. The outriders and I along with the J treble C vehicle slowly make our way through the sterile area. Royal British Legion standards brace in the carry to our right; on the left was the broken hearted family.

However, on this sad occasion there was something quite unique and something I had never seen before, a guard of honour from those who understood the love and trust of a much valued companion.

Police officers in best kit and medals gleaming bright, each stood to attention while their dogs sat up straight at their sides. So many officers from different forces had travelled down to show respect. They were lined on both sides of the street, from

Wales, Plymouth, Cheshire, the MDP from various stations in the country, and I must mention the prison officer who joined them in immaculate attire from Reading, are just a few examples.

Some may even have had a previous career in the Armed Forces, I do not know, but all these dog handlers both inside RAF Lyneham and on the High Street had one thing in common. The utmost respect and recognition with the knowledge of just how dangerous a job Liam and Theo were employed to do. Many from the Ministry of Defence Police (MDP) had actually known Liam from mutual courses and had so much respect for a man they really knew.

The conductor gracefully paged through this fitting tribute of a dog and handler guard of honour; as Liam passed each officer would raise his or her arm into the salute. The standards were lowered and the Legion saluted as Maurice Baker the Parade Marshal shouted his one word of command and the Scottish hero was brought to rest. It was an eerie silence, provoked by the sounding of the Tenor Bell, but once the young man was at rest, adjacent to where his family waited, the sound of that raw grief was released and difficult to contain.

With Liam once again back in our care, our journey would again flow but on this occasion with hundreds of dogs on the streets held tightly on the leash as their owners bowed their heads. It was another day so many will not forget when so much honour was bestowed to 'the inseparable pair' in life and sadly now in death.

The tributes and honours did not finish there. On 6 April 2011, the mother of Liam, Jane Duffy, was presented with her son's campaign medal at St Georges Barracks, Rutland. In recognition of her son's bravery L/Corporal Liam Tasker was mentioned in dispatches and therefore his decoration of a single silver oak leaf would be sewn diagonally on to his campaign medal ribbon.

I saw an interview by Mrs Jane Duffy on the TV when she was proudly speaking about her son:

'He was not enthusiastic about returning home without his beloved Theo. Although he understood the reasons why and he was planning to complete the paperwork for Theo to be properly recognised for his endeavour, bravery and skills.'

Well, Mrs Duffy, maybe just maybe your proud son had some influence as sometime later in October 2012 Liam had from above completed that report to put his beloved Theo up for recognition. Theo was bestowed the PDSA Dickin Medal posthumously at London's Wellington Barracks, in the company of the family and friends of his master Lance Corporal Tasker. It is the highest award any animal can receive in recognition of conspicuous gallantry or devotion to duty while serving in military conflict.

The award was accepted by Sergeant Matthew Jones and search dog Grace. The citation read:

> 'Theo was deployed by Lance Corporal Tasker as part of the Royal Army Veterinary Corps's 1st Military Working Dog Regiment during conflict in Afghanistan in 2010 and 2011. Their role was to provide search and clearance support, uncovering hidden weapons, improvised explosive devices (IEDs) and bomb-making equipment. During his time in Afghanistan Theo made fourteen confirmed operational finds, the most any search dog in Afghanistan has found to date.'

Rest in peace, Theo and Liam, your duty is done. For your family I hope that amongst the sadness and hurt some small comfort can be taken that so many people, who you did not know, cared with genuine compassion the day they both came home.

CHAPTER 34

The day before Liam came back that deadly weapon, the IED, had claimed another life when Lance Corporal Stephen McKee, from 1st Battalion the Royal Irish Regiment, was killed on 9 March 2011. During an operation to disrupt insurgent activity in the northern Dashte area of Nad-e Ali district his vehicle struck an improvised explosive device.

In Westminster on 16 March 2011, the speaker introduced Prime Minister Mr David Cameron to address parliament during question time. The Prime Minister offered his condolences to the family of Lance Corporal McKee and following that message it was officially announced:

> 'From September, military repatriations will no longer pass through the town of Wootton Bassett. I know the whole House will wish to join me in paying tribute to the people of Wootton Bassett. Their deeply moving and dignified demonstrations of respect and mourning have shown the deep bond between the public and our Armed Forces. It is more than 100 years since the title "Royal" was conferred on a town. I can today confirm that Her Majesty the Queen has agreed to confer the title "Royal" on the town of Wootton Bassett as an enduring symbol of the nation's admiration and gratitude to the people of that town. The town will become Royal Wootton Bassett later this year, in a move that I believe will be welcomed right across our country.'

It was quite a surprise to hear those words spoken by the Prime Minster and the media were present in the town straight afterwards seeking a reaction.

If I am honest, at the time it felt a little strange. Of course the town was proud to have so much honour bestowed upon it. Although when asked the question how I felt about the honour, it was a difficult one to answer. With pride it could easily be construed that you were glorifying in such tragic circumstances. Therefore it was easier, when asked to comment by Helen Callaghan of ITN, for me to decline.

The following day on 17 March I found the same feeling in the High Street when lots of journalists and reporters were asking the same question; the response I witnessed was one of humility.

This enhanced the sincerity and integrity of this wonderful community even more. They were more concerned in offering compassion, warmth and sympathy to the latest visitors who brought their broken hearts with them that day.

It was a day when Irish eyes were not smiling when L/Corporal Stephen McKee returned home. There was so much emotion in the High Street as so many relations had flown back on the same flight. This fallen Irish soldier had strong family connections within the regiment, with two brothers, a cousin and his father-in-law all serving in the First Battalion, and with another brother serving in the Second Battalion.

Yes, that was a day when many faces were seen drained by sadness, almost numb in bringing their loved one home to this close knit family.

I read that at L/Corporal Stephen McKee's funeral at the end of the month, he was buried beside his baby daughter, Keeley, who died after only two days of life, just a year ago almost to the day.

Words of deepest condolences from this policeman seem so inadequate for that poor lady, a wife and mother, for the tragic pain she had suffered. Although, despondently, that is all I could offer and also to the others we were soon to know.

CHAPTER 35

I mentioned earlier about some families I had met whose husbands were serving out in Afghanistan marking off 'a days to do chart'; something like a child with an advent calendar at Christmas. Well, equally as excited as a child is for that day to arrive, then the same could be said for a wife when her 'days to do chart' were almost complete. That day circled was the day marked for the safe return of her husband.

The charts that the wives from the 1st Battalion Irish Guards had on their walls at home had crossed off the months, then the weeks, and they were on the final few days when tragedy struck.

Major Matthew James Collins and Lance Sergeant Mark Terence Burgan, both from the 1st Battalion Irish Guards, were killed in Afghanistan on Wednesday 23 March 2011. They were killed just six days before they were due to fly home. Major Matthew Collins, 38, and Lance Sergeant Mark Burgan, 28, lost their lives when the vehicle they were travelling in was caught in a blast from an improvised explosive device. The two men had been returning to base from an operation aimed at disrupting insurgent groups in the Nahr-e Saraj district of Helmand Province, when the explosion occurred.

The date, 30 March 2011, was not on the 'days to do chart', because they should have all been home, safe and sound by then, but for two families that date will be one they will never forget. It was no wonder there were hundreds on the High Street in recognition of these honourable men described as the 'epitome' of their regiment. When two wives should have been at home with their husband's arms wrapped around them in hugs, happiness and rejoicing in their safe return, instead they found themselves being comforted by family members and friends stricken in grief.

The way in which grief is expressed is never the same; on this sad day there were two completely contrasting groups of people. One a large contingent travelling down from Merseyside; vocal and unashamedly showing their grief for their fallen hero, Lance Sergeant Mark Burgan. The other family were a much smaller group; quiet and equally distraught in the loss of their loved one Major Matthew Collins. There was no right or wrong way to grieve, grief has many emotions and this particular day showed two distinct differences.

The family and friends of Mark lined the streets, many dressed in dark suits, red ties and jackets and yellow ribbons pinned to their lapels at the request of L/Sergeant Burgan's family. They also attached the word 'Burgo' and photographs of the soldier to themselves, with 'A true gentleman who will never be forgotten Mark Burgan our Kirkby hero RIP' written underneath.

The close-knit community from Merseyside hugged each other before they placed a Liverpool FC scarf and yellow roses on the hearse that they surrounded.

The mourners from Somerset quietly placed their flowers onto the roof of the hearse that carried a man they equally loved, then stepped back and withdrew in their sorrow.

As the cortège moved on, one mourner shouted, 'Thank you Wootton Bassett, thank you,' and no doubt broke his heart and cried as others applauded by his side.

I will never forget those two families who were steeped in sadness; just showing their pain in different ways, watching the cortège drift out of their sight as we slowly continued on our journey to Oxford.

When I returned to Bassett I had one final thing to do as I wanted to offer my condolences to the family of Major Matthew Collins.

My Brother Pete had mentioned that Chris Collins, one of the three older brothers of Matthew, was a friend of his. They had both served with the Royal Engineer EOD Squadrons and, on leaving the Army, now worked alongside each other in Plymouth with Devon and Cornwall Constabulary. Pete told me Chris was a top lad in both his careers and asked me if I would keep an eye out for him.

I found Chris with his family sitting together in the Angel Pub on the High Street; they were sombre, almost numb, exhausted and emotionally drained. I introduced myself and said that I had no intention to intrude, but wanted to offer my sincere condolences on behalf of my brother and myself.

He kindly offered me a drink, but I declined and made good my escape from this deep sadness. It really was awful seeing so much pain in good people and something I never got used to. As I walked home that evening I read a text from my brother which he had forwarded on from a message he had just received from Chris Collins.

I can't recall the message verbatim, but it went something like this: 'Pete, gutted mate, an awful day, but the people were so kind. Unbelievable, your brother as busy as they are, has even called in to offer his condolences; awesome.'

You sometimes do not know if you are doing right or wrong, but just taking the time to locate Chris and then receiving the text, gave me the reassurance that on this occasion I did what was right.

Although what was far more important to me was that his family knew that amongst the many hundreds more, Chris knew the 'brothers Brown' did care.

CHAPTER 36

What started off as a card game on line would in time see the winning hand raise thousands of pounds for charity, as Julia Stevenson and Anne Cole chatted away while playing Facebook poker. They were soon to find out that besides cards they both had a mutual interest in bikes and raising funds for charities. During those card games they shared their thoughts and ideas about raising funds whilst they chatted away on this social media website.

Then one day they met at a 'Thunder Rally' and it was love at first sight. Two blondes, each looking at the other wondering if they needed to have a DNA test because they looked so alike. Yes, the similarity of the two had many of us baffled at times. It was one of those friendships that they knew instantly they were fated to meet. With mutual respect for each other, they focused on their two loves – not their families who they loved dearly, but the bikes and charities. Military charities to be precise and you only had to be in their company to hear the passion in their voices and see it in their eyes.

Julia was proud of her involvement in the 'Afghan Heroes Bike Ride' in 2010 and chatted many times with Anne about that marvellous day when well over a £100,000 pounds was raised. It was initially planned as a one-off event, but she was giving serious consideration to doing something similar again the following year. Anne could not help but be impressed and offered her support should Julia decide to progress with the idea that at the moment was just spinning around in her head.

When Anne slipped in that she had previous skills as a qualified secretary and had been employed as a PA, Julia thought of the potential there could be with her newfound friend to help with the administration such a big project would require.

Life immediately changed for Anne when she answered in the affirmative to Julia's question 'Would you write an important letter for me to the Marquis of Bath?' It was in relation to a bike meet in Calne. Julia read the letter and knew from her own experience of being involved in so many other events, that Anne's skills, with her enthusiasm, could only be an asset. At that moment it was almost as if Anne had just signed a contract with Julia to become pillion and rider; two bikers one goal, to raise monies for military charities. 'The Ride of Respect' was officially born.

With success and lessons learned from the 'Afghan Heroes Charity Bike Ride' conversations between the two blondes in leathers were now focused on organising a similar event. It would be a huge challenge to replicate, especially one which was full of emotion and passion whilst at the same time raising funds for charity. However, as they played their card game on line, raising the stakes in poker, they had decided they were going to try.

The location was a no brainer, if you were raising funds for a military charity then there was only one place where the countries heart was – Wootton Bassett. So that was easily doable, Hullavington to Bassett, a route through the country roads of rural Wiltshire. Over the first hand of poker they had a location and route. During the next hand they considered when and decided for the same reasons as previously, these two mothers had no hesitation in recognising the importance of that special day.

A pause in the game with a quick look at the calendar, 'Mothering Sunday' 3 April 2011, was going to be the date.

They say that two's company and three's a crowd, well they disproved that theory as they had one more partner to invite into their organising team – Mr Nick Gale.

Nick Gale is the Managing Director of a company called 'Nick Gale Customs' from Wembley, London. A well known name in the customs motorcycle world, having won many trophies worldwide. Nick came on board the team to help with publishing details about the 'Ride of Respect'. Due to the character of the man he ended up doing a lot more than he agreed when he first signed up.

The meetings started with the proposals between the newly-formed Ride of Respect Team, Wootton Bassett Town Council, Local Authorities, Police, Highways and the MoD to organise the event. The value of experience can never be undervalued and between all those involved in these meetings it was vast. It was not long before the event was approved. Promoting the event? Well as they say, if it's not broken don't fix it, so Facebook was used again and the word was out the bikers were coming back.

One slight tweak was a restriction on numbers; not that they were not wanted, it was just a more comfortable figure to work with, to assist in making the event run more smoothly. All those involved in the 2010 event would agree it was an amazing event, but at times we did get away with it on a wing and a prayer.

The number agreed would be 10,000 bikers and there was one extra ingredient Julia and Anne wanted to incorporate. They wanted it to be even more personal and wanted to invite people to participate who had been directly affected by this awful conflict, including dignitaries of Wootton Bassett. So invites were made to those directly connected, be they an injured soldier, a wife, mother, father or bereaved child. Yes, they understood that widow is the correct terminology for a bereaved wife, but for those hurting they were very much a wife of a very precious man who was still such a huge part in their lives.

The applicants were processed and amongst them were six who were present because of their direct impact with this conflict. Those were the family and a great friend of Royal Marine Adam Brown who was killed in August 2010.

After what seemed a thousand meetings, daily telephone conversations between Julia, Anne and Nick, the Mother's Day weekend arrived. On the policing side we were, once again, inundated with offers from police forces from far and wide. My mate Rich

Bond said his Sergeant Steve Thomson had changed all their duties as it was an event he made sure his team from Devonport in Plymouth would be attending. Steve, being a keen biker, saw it more as a weekend away as he did the previous year. He was really looking forward to the occasion, along with many others whose applications to attend had been confirmed. Sergeant Martin Alvis was the second to volunteer to police the event, but that was mainly because he enjoyed the free breakfast that RAF Lyneham gave us before last year's event and would provide it again this day. No seriously though, Martin was a good bloke who was always keen to be involved in anything that was taking place in his neighbourhood sector; another man who very much cared about his community.

So once again policing the event was not a problem and those officers coming from out of the immediate area were accommodated at RAF Lyneham. Julia and Anne set up their headquarters on the Friday afternoon in a hotel in Calne. On their arrival, the buzz of excitement was rising when they found the accommodation bursting at the seams with leather-clad bikers.

Saturday morning, the two blondes with many others following, made the ten-mile journey from their hotel up along the A3102. Each biker slowed as they passed the gates of RAF Lyneham, recognising where so many dead had been escorted home. A slight tweak of the throttle, they snaked through the village on their way to the magnet that drew thousands that weekend – Wootton Bassett.

To formally commence the weekend's events the organisers had invited the bikers to attend a brief ceremony to lay a wreath on behalf of the 'Ride of Respect' on the war memorial. On duty were PCSOs Jim Wale, Andy Singfield, PC Nick Spargo and myself, waiting without trepidation with the public as the bikers were welcomed back. It was a hugely respectable occasion and once again Bassett was getting into the spirit of the occasion, having decorated the streets with bunting and flags fluttering in the Wiltshire sunshine. Julia, Anne and Nick with so much attention to detail in organising this event, somehow even managed to book the glorious sun to shine on their parade.

A simple ceremony took place at three pm, where hundreds stood in silent tribute to the fallen. A few words were spoken and the three organisers Julia, Anne and Nick stepped forward to lay the floral wreath. Placing it amongst those tributes and crosses that had been laid a few days earlier where many witnessed the deep sadness and respects shown for Major Matthew Collins and Lance Sergeant Mark Burgan. Once again the war memorial bore witness to some of those big ruffty tuffty bikers getting caught up in the emotions as they tried to disguise the tears that had spontaneously formed in their eyes.

Yes, this little town, with what had taken place over the last four years, did have an impact on those coming to visit.

Throughout the day there continued to be a hive of activity, bikers coming, cameras clicking, whilst up at Hullavington old runway, the final preparations were being completed for the main event. Groups of bikers were meeting up all over the place and the breweries were doing well to keep them supplied, enhancing the excitement which was building up for the following morning. No incidents, no nonsense, just thousands of bikers sharing stories and pride in taking part in this charity ride to recognise the fallen, their family and the town. I always found it difficult to sleep the night before these events as I too got caught up in the excitement. Many participating probably did right in having a few refreshments to help them get their heads down before the big event. Those who slept, well done to you! Those who didn't were up before the cocks crowed. One of those getting up before the sun was Anne; she was up and about and arrived at Hullavington around 6am. Early yes, but understandably so, due to her responsibilities in organising the event and why not be a little excited, possibly even nervous, as this was the first 'Ride of Respect'.

It was a fresh spring morning, misty and even a little ice had formed on the country roads, which a biker had managed to just about manoeuvre round and maintain his credibility as he stayed in his seat. Eerily quiet really, a huge sleeping runway were Anne's observations that morning being the first to arrive. Nick soon followed, equally excited, making his way to the reception tent to begin briefing his marshals.

Red and Steve of 'Biker FM' radio speakers squelched with the feedback as they tested their mikes prior to broadcasting the event live. The high pitched squeal startled a few birds that were on the grass as Hullavington was slowly wiping the sleep out of its eyes.

The wonderful smell of crispy bacon was drifting from the griddles as the caterers prepared in readiness for the bikers who thrived on good wholesome food.

Anne stood alone looking around taking in the practicalities of what had started during a hand of poker and now resembled a land of cones as hundreds, all in rows, ran the length of the runway.

It was almost surreal, a special moment in time. The mist was still hovering over the grass wet with dew when she heard it, a sound only a biker recognised. In the distance the faint rumbling, similar to thunder and the hairs on the back of her neck rose as her heart thumped with anticipation. The mist started lifting almost like a curtain being raised at a theatre, and then she saw them as they made their entrance, dozens and dozens of bikers heading towards where she stood.

She stood proud and unashamedly, another ruffty tuffty biker who has discovered one of those spontaneous moments in life that fill the eyes with tears. The dozens grew into hundreds and at one stage she could not see the end of the line as the bikers made their way to the registration point.

The sound of the engines would periodically roar when the bikers, in their own moment of spontaneous reaction to their own emotions, opened the throttle to let her know they had arrived.

Biker FM was pumping up frenzy, mixing the sounds of thunder from the bikes with their selection of music. Those tunes were heard along with their words as they spread the incredible atmosphere via the airwaves as thousands of bikers were heading their way.

'Angel Up Front', a biker's band with guitars and voice, sang their hearts out like never before as the exhilaration was felt by each and every person on that runway in expectation of what lay ahead.

While all this activity was taking place, up the road in Bassett we were ready on our points, as were the marshals and police along the route.

The public were making their way with their picnic hampers and chairs to their preferred viewing point while those in town were starting to line the streets. Just like the public along the route, Wootton Bassett eagerly waited for the opportunity to welcome the bikers back.

By eight forty-five the excitement on the runway reached another level when the words they all were waiting for were blasted out of the FM Radio Speakers, 'Bikers are you ready?'

Those first to set off, suitably refreshed with hot bacon butties and mugs of tea, made their way to the start line to mount their beasts. This was the buzz they had signed up for and the eagerness to start their engines was something they deeply felt. Perched, eager and keen, they were surrounded by everyone on the runway who wanted to see the first pulse of the '2011 Ride of Respect' roar away.

Twelve miles away, those in the High Street heard the St Bartholomew's Church bell strike announcing it was the hour of nine; at that precise moment Nick Gale signalled for the first pulse to move off.

The roar was deafening, but to each biker it was Mozart at his best, as they slowly made their way following the two police outriders out in the front, blue lights flashing who were just as proud to be involved. One thousand bikers were now making their way around the perimeter road of the old air base, wishing to once again show their appreciation to a community which had not forgotten. With two pulses already gone the VIP guests were next.

With pride and honour, the two poker card players took poll position, Julia on her Harley and Anne, pillion on a trike. Mary Champion, the town's Mayor, was one of the invited guests to ride as pillion on the back of a bike. Normally a rider of horses, a bike was literally another animal. When she mounted her friend's motorbike she did so with nervous apprehension, despite having been assured she was safe.

As Anne and Julie led their pulse, Anne describes her journey:

'By the time we had reached the town, my arms were aching from waving to people who were stood on the roadside, the older ones in wheelchairs and people sitting in camping chairs. I remember as we rode into Malmesbury there was a group with a couple of young children and a dog. The dog was wearing a coat which had written on it 'Thank You Bikers, We Salute You'. That started the tears which flowed from my eyes for most of the journey.

In the town I just couldn't believe how many people had turned out to wave; children leaning from the pavements wanting to high-five all the bikers, many of whom were more than happy to comply. I saw Mary, the Mayor, she had the widest grin, she too was overwhelmed by the huge respect her town had for us as we had for them, and she was still grinning from ear to ear as I left her to return back to Hullavington.'

Mary had a famous brother, Bob Champion, who rode Aldaniti on the Aintree Racecourse that April day in 1981. Their victory is one of the most memorable and emotional moments ever to be recorded in the Grand National. Some 30 years later Bob could be equally as proud of his sister as she had similar emotions; leading 10,000 bikers through her honourable town in remembrance of those who had fallen.

When Anne returned to the runway her phone rang 'Happy Mother's Day Mum' from her son. With a sense of sadness she cried when she thought of the many mothers who would not hear those words again. Her son, who was only up the road at Cirencester, had phoned and told her that since five that morning all he could hear was motorbike after motorbike travelling down to her event. He ended the call by telling his mother how proud he was of her, which created another flood of tears, but this time not of sadness but of pride.

While the next pulse was preparing to start I bumped into a lady in the High Street with her dog and a group of people. During a conversation with her I learnt that they had travelled to watch members of her family who were taking part in the event, yet as she talked she looked concerned and I asked her why.

She told me her daughter's husband had been killed in Afghanistan and this was the first time they had returned to Wootton Bassett. It had rekindled some very sad times.

'What was his name?' I asked.

'Adam Brown, a Royal Marine,' she proudly replied.

I couldn't help but notice the surprised look on all their faces as I recalled that day in August some eight months ago. 'A Royal Marine from Yateley,' I said. Yes, I remembered it well, and mentioned placing the scroll of honour in the hearse; John held Luisa and Susie as they huddled closer to hear my every word.

'Were you the policeman?' she asked.

'Indeed, I was.'

She told me how much that gesture had meant to them all, as that scroll had remained with Adam on his journey home. Today, Amy was pillion on her uncle's bike and Susie, like any mum, was worried how she would cope especially when she recognised the place that held memories from the worst time of her life.

As you may recall Amy had been in the town twice before; to support her husband as his friend and colleague 'Darbs' was repatriated and who could forget when her own world was destroyed.

I could understand Susie's worries, while her daughter was making final preparations at Hullavington. She was one of six courageously riding in the memory of her husband Royal Marine Adam Brown. Amy was pillion on her uncle Mike Crankshaw's bike. Adam's parents, Rob and Jenny, were also present on their bike, but amongst the group pride of place went to a very special machine – a yellow Triumph Daytona.

Those honoured to ride that Triumph Daytona were Ed a great mate of Adam and still serving Royal Marine and his pillion passenger Laura. The bike belonged to her brother Adam, who she fondly called her 'Big Brown Bear', which made the event even more poignant to the family.

There were seven in this group even though only six registered, as the presence of Adam was with them all and, like his mother Jenny said, 'Adam would have loved it.' Their love for him shone, as it always will, and on the front of each bike his photograph was proudly displayed. They all knew this was going to be one hugely emotional ride.

It wasn't long after they set off that the impact of this memorable day started to kick in as they saw the warmth, compassion and flag-waving support bestowed upon them. The pride, mixed with deep sadness as to why they were involved in this event was ever present in their minds. Each pillion rider held even tighter to their man in front as the tears flowed from their eyes. With grit and determination they continued on their way wrapped up with so many emotions on such a humbling day. Their wheels spun steadily along, eating up the 12 mile route as they elegantly made their way towards Wootton Bassett.

As painful as it was, they, like many others on this ride still grieving, truly wanted to thank the town that stood still when Adam was brought back home.

'Minutes five we are away,' blared the two escort outriders in our earpiece prompting Inspector Chris Martin, our new Sector Inspector, to give the order to clear the streets. Owen Collier, the Bassett town crier standing immaculately in full regalia with two others from neighbouring towns were close to me. With a brief word in their ear the three flamboyant characters started ringing their bells as they walked down the High Street.

In the broadest of Wiltshire accents the three then cried out loud 'Oyez! Oyez! Oyez! Step back off the road and let the bikers ride.' And the hundreds of people moved away to the side.

John and Susie were already in position underneath the 'Old Town Hall', the building on stilts, looking down the road for three important bikes that were significant to them.

Wave after wave they came both sides of the road heading in our direction – hundreds, two a breast – the emotions were high, the high-fives complied, then suddenly a bike veered to our kerbside.

Mike Crankshaw, who had Amy as pillion, had spoken to her through the intercom that he had sighted her mum and dad and slowed right down. At the same time Susie saw the three bikes approaching and stepped into the road to make sure they were seen. As they got closer to Susie, Amy leaned over in an effort to seek that loving hug from a mother when it was truly needed. And this was one of those occasions when it was desperately needed; the emotions from the previous two visits surfaced when seeing the building on stilts. Amy leant right over, reaching out for her mother's love.

The shift in balance suddenly caused the bike to fall to one side. Mike, with determination, willpower and sheer grit, placed his foot against the kerb to hold it upright while he waited for help.

Without realising what was going on I was stunned by what was taking place and I jumped out as others did to help Mike from grounding his bike. Amy was holding onto her mother for dear life.

The ride was stopped briefly as we righted the bike and looked up to see Mike re-adjusting his position on his machine. Somehow Amy had also stayed on her seat and with a last kiss from her mum, they started to pull away.

A rev of the engine, the clutch released, they were mobile again and on their way. Then crash! Their heads turned to see that 'Adam's Hoofing Hut', a collection box, had decided to stay. Smashing on impact, loose coins were flying around everywhere. The collection box that had been strapped to the back of their bike had come lose as the cable ties snapped in the previous commotion.

The ride was briefly stopped while the coins were picked up and handed to John, Amy's dad. Mike had pushed his bike off the road while Susie and Luisa comforted Amy. Once composed, the blonde little hero from Yateley got back on as pillion, while her uncle once again rode away. They came to Bassett to say their thanks; they were not going back without finishing that task.

The rest of the group Ed, Laura, Jenny and Rob had not seen the incident and had continued through the town to complete their own thanks for respecting their son, friend and brother, with so much honour. The group all met up again at the Churchill Pub on the outskirts of the town and subsequently phoned me to join them. Jenny, following the repatriation of her son, had written me a letter. On hearing I was on duty she wanted to meet the policeman who had placed the scroll of honour in Adam's hearse.

So I did just that, I popped down for a brief chat to meet the family who I had kept my distance from the last time we met. It never fails to impress me the bravery of those whose pain you could clearly see in their eyes, yet they were so grateful and just wanted to say thank you for the little comfort we gave. They also briefly explained that the collection box was a miniature replica of a very special beach hut.

Jenny explained: 'One of Adam's dreams was to own a beach hut at Mudeford near Christchurch where he spent many a childhood holiday. In Adam's own words it is a very special place.' As a family they had just started a fundraising campaign to purchase a beach hut so that they could fulfil his dream. I was mesmerised by Jenny's passion and focus when she explained: 'It will be an extraordinary memorial for an exceptional man.' A fitting charity is what they had created to raise funds to purchase a special place which would be used by the Royal Marine family, in need, to escape, relax and reflect. 'Adam's Hoofing Hut' had made its first public appearance and indeed was not shy in stopping the thousands of bikes in the High Street to announce his arrival.

I knew at that moment we would become lifelong friends this family and I, as I put my own tenner in the slightly damaged hut. I hugged them all, saying my goodbyes, to resume my duties as the ride continued throughout the day.

It was indeed another great event and ticked all the boxes the organisers wanted to achieve. A town was thanked, the fallen remembered, the Armed Forces supported and another £150,000 in the coffers towards military charities.

At the end of the day the two blonde angels sat exhausted back at their hotel in Calne, where they both reflected.

A day once again full of emotion for those standing on the roadside, but probably more so for the bikers, as they had indeed achieved the challenge of lightning striking twice, in thanking the town of Wootton Bassett.

Proud in that they had done exactly what they had intended, they picked up the cards to play poker once again, as they started talking about the next charity ride. They did organise more rides and even to this day if you look on line and type 'Ride of Respect' you will probably find their latest event being promoted. Yep, those bikers can stand proud in the many funds they have raised for charities close to their hearts and minds.

In fact 'Adam's Hoofing Hut' was one of those charities they donated to, and some two years later out of the blue, I received this message.

Jenny Brown was the name in the Facebook box that flashed up. 'Jarra we've done it.' The message was brief and I knew immediately what she meant. I logged onto that special Facebook page. Never have I felt for such a wonderful mother and her family, as I read: 'Adam's Hoofing Hut would like to make an announcement: today 24 April 2013 we have amazing news!!! We are now the proud owners of "Adam's

Hoofing Hut". We can't thank each and every person enough for the amazing effort that everyone has given to make this possible. None of which could have been done without everyone's love and support for Adam.'

We chatted a little longer then said our goodbyes. I thought to myself that night, well done guys you did him proud, £150,000 pounds raised for such fitting a memorial for their fallen hero, Adam Brown.

One of many mentioned in this book that deserve, no demand, not to be forgotten, after they paid the ultimate sacrifice in serving the Crown.

CHAPTER 37

Later in April we, the police, accepted our invitation to attend the BBC documentary created by Henry Singer 'Wootton Bassett: *The Town That Remembers*.'

This was the premier showing to an audience who had all been involved in the production of the hour-long documentary presented in the lecture theatre of Wootton Bassett School. There was an air of apprehension and indeed nervousness with many who had given interviews in the safety of their homes or other appropriate locations. I'll be honest I was also apprehensive as I had been interviewed for one and half hours and could not recall any of what I had said.

Andy Singfield, Coxy and I made our way just around the corner from the Police Station to the school; as I parked the car I saw two ladies making their way chatting between themselves. I asked them were they going to the premier showing, explaining that we were unsure which floor the theatre was on. They said they were and confirmed that they had also been interviewed for the documentary. I followed up by asking them in what role they been interviewed in relation to the documentary. To my utter disbelief the word 'role' was totally inappropriate, as this lady deserved far more respect. 'My son was killed in Afghanistan,' was the lady's reply; I wanted the earth to swallow me up. I offered my deepest condolences and asked what his name was. Jason Mackie was Mrs Lee Mackie's reply.

For me each of the fallen were never a statistic and I was able to reply instantly: 'A Royal Marine who came home in 2009' which caused her eyes to open with surprise. 'Do you remember my son coming home?' she asked. I did, and I offered her my arm to escort her to the premier. During that short walk I told her so much of what I had witnessed along that 46 mile route; so many recognised her son as they stood and saluted. The more I told her, the tighter she held my arm, while I walked her to her seat and gave her one last hug. We were all seated and after the introduction by Henry Singer we sat back to watch the documentary they had worked so hard on.

There were mixed reviews, with some being disappointed that they had not been included, but the team had done so much research it was not possible to include every bit of detail. As for me, well I did feel sorry for the editor having to listen to me for over an hour and half, but I was delighted with the three minutes of my interview that was included. Not for my ego, but for allowing me to make a small point: that the respects shown went a lot further than just Wootton Bassett. More importantly, the reaction I saw from Lee Mackie that her son was mentioned, gave me no hesitation to offer my congratulations to Henry Singer and his team for their efforts in what they had produced.

The documentary we watched coincided with the fourth anniversary since we brought home the first two soldiers. What I had not realised was that in those four years this was the only month we never had a repatriation. However, sadly that did not mean British Forces did not sustain a fatality, as once again the news channels were scrolling along our screens – the latest fatality in Afghanistan was the second female in this conflict to have died.

Captain Lisa Jade Head was a British Army officer. She was the first female bomb disposal officer ever to be killed on operations. She died on 19 April 2011 at the age of 29, having sustained serious injuries while on active service in Afghanistan. At the time of her death, Captain Head was the first female officer and the second British servicewoman to die in Afghanistan since 2001, after Sarah Bryant. She was deployed to Afghanistan on 27 March 2011. As a bomb disposal specialist, Lisa had achieved the 'High Threat IED Operators' status indicating great expertise. She was mortally injured in Nahr-e-Saraj in Helmand Province on 18 April 2011, 22 days after arriving in Afghanistan for her second tour of duty.

Whilst attempting to disable a cluster of improvised explosive devices, Captain Lisa Head had already disabled one device, but was then hit when a second device in the chain went off. She was severely wounded, with catastrophic injures, caused by the impact at close quarters to the explosion. She was evacuated by helicopter to Camp Bastion and then flown back to Queen Elizabeth Hospital in Birmingham where she died there the following day.

Her funeral was held on 6 May 2011 at Huddersfield Parish Church. A guard of honour from her regiment lined the steps of the Church at the funeral procession and the bearer party carried her coffin into the Church. More than 1,000 people attended the funeral, including family, friends, military personnel and residents of Huddersfield. It was so fitting that so many military funerals were being attended up and down the country, as the people of our nation recognised the ultimate sacrifice so many of our Armed Forces had made.

This was not always the case; if you recall the words of Ken Scott when their comrades were killed in battle, they dug a shallow grave, said a few words, and made a makeshift cross.

The policy of Her Majesty's Government was that service personnel who died overseas should be buried close to where they fell. In fact, it was not until the late 1960s when the repatriation of bodies was introduced to allow a privately funded funeral in the UK. Up to that date, funeral arrangements for a deceased serviceman overseas would have been a matter for the formation concerned and burial would have taken place locally with no relatives present.

Now, if a serviceman or servicewoman dies overseas, the remains may be repatriated and buried in a cemetery chosen by the family at the expense of the military. However, the next of kin are still (in non-operational theatres given the choice of local burial or repatriation, and if they choose local burial, they may be transported to attend the funeral at public expense. Repatriation of British service personnel is carried out from many countries, not just operational theatres, by the Service Personnel and Veterans Agency's Joint Casualty and Compassionate Centre (J treble C). Some operational areas have been going on for decades and, unless directly connected, many British tourists may have been on one particular island relaxing on the beautiful beaches of say Ayia Napa, oblivious that some 40 miles away soldiers patrolled on an operation mission. It was far more relaxed than in Afghanistan, nevertheless it was classed as an operational tour. These soldiers serve on a six-month tour of duty with the United Nations peacekeeping force and are responsible for maintaining the integrity of the buffer zone that runs between the Greek and Turkish Cypriots.

On Tuesday 3 May 2011, Warrant Officer Class 2 Graham Bean, serving with the 73 Engineer Regiment Volunteers with the United Nations peacekeeping force in Cyprus, died of natural causes. Ten days later the 54-year-old soldier was flown into RAF Lyneham and after a private ceremony for his family, we escorted his coffin through Wootton Bassett. As had been shown for each and every one of our servicemen and women, if they returned from Iraq, Afghanistan, Bahrain, or in this case Cyprus, the town of Wootton Bassett paid its respects.

WO2 Bean joined the Territorial Army in May 1975 and served on operations in Bosnia and Iraq prior to being deployed to Cyprus. Sir, your duty was done and, quite rightly, you were brought home with respect. Although on this occasion you were not escorted along the 46 mile route. The facilities at the John Radcliffe hospital were not required and, out of the view of prying eyes, the casket was transferred to a private ambulance for the journey to his home town.

That was a different route for us and another one that was being reviewed was the one from RAF Brize Norton to Oxford. This was due to construction of the new purpose-built Repatriation Centre having a target date of the first day of September 2011 set for completion. There were two significant changes from what was handed to RAF Lyneham four years earlier; the construction of the Chapel of Rest and the other, a phenomenon that had grown called the 'Great British Public'. Once they had become involved in showing their respects to the fallen, there was now no intention of letting it go.

Although for RAF Brize Norton that was not directly their problem it was one for Carterton Town Council to review. That town has a small Neighbourhood Policing Team and they were very keen to learn lessons from the experience we had gained over the years; circumstances had changed significantly since March 2007. We started with something small that grew into something rather big, they were getting 'Big' from the start; a phenomenon that had grown legs and was focusing on moving to their town.

CHAPTER 38

Inspector Graham Dix and Sergeant Mags Turner from Thames Valley Police had made contact requesting to shadow the policing operation if there should be another fatality. Sadly 'if' was a word I had given up all hope of saying a long time ago; to be honest these last few years had taught me to forget *if* and focus on *when*.

And sadly, as predicted, if became when, as the Ministry of Defence announced that Marine Nigel Dean Mead from Lima Company, 42 Commando Royal Marines, Combined Force Nad 'Ali (North), was killed in Afghanistan on Sunday 15 May 2011. The repatriation was planned for four days later emphasising to the local policing team and those in Carterton, just how little time we had to prepare. Sergeant Mags Turner made plans with her Inspector to make her way to our small market town, some 30 miles away.

On the morning of Thursday 19 May, Inspector Graham Dix and Sergeant Mags Turner of Thames Valley Police made their way to Wootton Bassett Police Station intending to obtain as much of an insight as possible in relation to the repatriations and therefore assist with their future planning.

As they began their one-hour journey from Carterton, the Automatic Number Plate Recognition (ANPR) cameras on the Severn Bridge were registering a high volume of vehicles with the same post code. They were all heading eastbound on the M4 motorway and all had the registered keeper with an address in Carmarthen.

Graham and Mags were briefed by Inspector Chris Martin on their arrival and were given an overall view on how the policing operation was split in phases.

1. The reassurance searching before the event.
2. The policing within the town centre
3. The police escort of the cortège.

Straight away that third phase was taken out of their remit of concern, as it was already in the hands of Mark Ponting and Rob Langton from their own force Roads Policing Unit (RPU) at Abingdon. They would continue that duty from RAF Brize Norton to John Radcliffe hospital in Oxford.

Notebooks and pencils at the ready, the two officers started to record their observations; September would soon come around.

Around lunchtime that day we received a call from a landlord asking if we could make our way to his pub in Bassett as there were a lot of people asking about details regarding the repatriation. Those vehicles the ANPR camera had captured on the Severn Bridge had arrived in Wootton Bassett and had taken safe haven on friendly ground; the first pub on the right as they entered the town was the Prince of Wales.

Those grieving extended family and friends were seeking advice on their friend who was homeward bound. Of course I saw the surprise in their eyes when I approached them, but soon felt their warmth as my condolences were offered. I explained that as they were early then they may wish to see their hero return and I directed them to that lay-by overlooking the runway.

The route was a simple one, go straight into Lyneham five miles down the road, turn right at the roundabout and drive down Chippenham Road, a further 800 metres where I would be standing in that lay-by on the left.

As I walked out to go I saw many texting words and messages to family and friends as my words were relayed around.

I returned to Bassett Police Station as I was requested to do, to host our visiting colleagues from 30 miles away. The plan was to brief them with as much information as they wished to collate. Our next stop was inside RAF Lyneham to meet the personalities they were soon to be in liaison with.

Introductions were made to Albin Funeral Directors team and the two Army officers from J treble C. Questions were asked by Graham and Mags and pleasantries exchanged as the role of each personality was explained. The importance of communication between us all was such a vital ingredient in the smooth running of this complex operation.

With the clock fast approaching the hour, the C17 Globemaster would soon be making its final approach so we made our escape. Next, on the learning curve was the lay-by. I explained this was a viewing area where friends of the fallen would congregate. On this occasion I explained there would be a few people there who I had met earlier in town and it was an opportunity to brief them as to the proceedings that would unfold throughout the day. Those few from Wales I had met earlier had obviously spread the word as when we arrived there was hardly any space to park. There must have been nearer 40 people present, far more than the original ten I had met, who had made that short five-mile journey to be present when the flight would bring home their Carmarthen, Prince of Wales.

I encouraged them to gather around and offered my sincere condolences before I gave my brief.

With 15 minutes to the fly-past I explained what to expect: 'The aircraft would approach from the north over Wootton Bassett, fly just to our right at a low altitude and go out of sight. As the aircraft left our vision it would hang in the sky and dip his starboard wing to acknowledge their friend's family who would be waiting to watch the honour shown to their son.'

I told them not to worry for their next of kin because the care and support bestowed upon each was a priority that no one could fault.

I continued with my brief:

'Once the fly-past is complete the aircraft will then climb in altitude and make a turn to the right; it will circle around for its final approach and head in our direction slightly to our side. As its wheels touch down on that runway just 100 metres to our right, stand together, do not rush off, as the grief can be painful and it will take time to adjust. Once you are all composed enough to drive, we will stop traffic on this road so you can go as one back to Wootton Bassett to wait for your man. The Cross Keys will support some of your needs and from there we can keep you updated on the proceedings.'

As time was getting close I gave them my last words of advice: 'Take comfort from each other that you are here for your friend, but the sadness you now feel may well turn to utter grief.'

I then told them to gaze north and I pointed my hand in the direction I wanted them to look. Over in the distance there was just a black dot to the right. I saw their heads turn and told them: 'That is the C17 Globemaster preparing for its approach, I will now step back in respect so you can honour your loved one as they bring him home.'

Graham, Mags and I slipped into the background, as we also watched the approach of the aircraft. Those from Carmarthen and the police officers in my presence were about to enter unfamiliar terrain. As for me, I had given that brief so many times before I knew the raw grief that was soon to follow. Those proud people from Wales all lined up as one stretching the length of this hard standing running 30 metres parallel to the road. Their eyes were fixed on that black dot which was getting bigger as it came closer, eventually to fly over Wootton Bassett town.

When the aircraft was about one mile away I noticed many in the group pull out flags of their Welsh Nation waving them frantically up in the sky.

Two equal horizontal stripes, white above green, and a large red dragon passant each on a stick continued to wave as the pilot tweaked his controls slightly to the port to square his approach to fly in front of the terminal building.

There it was, about 800 metres away, that beautiful majestic aircraft hanging in the air. One mother previously referred to it as the 'Angel of a Flight' when it brought her son home; I wonder how many thought the same.

As the aircraft flew out of sight maybe their minds drifted to try and imagine what their family and friends were about to see; the starboard wing dipped in honour for the young Marine from Wales. I know I was certainly thinking of that poor family seeing their son home.

Then, with the roar of the four turbofan engines to climb up into the sky, their eyes watch this huge bird circle around. It heads south, then west and back northward bound. When it is far enough away the pilot manoeuvres his aircraft to head back in our direction to line up for his final approach to land.

Those people from Wales who came to honour Nigel Dean Mead or, more appropriately, 'Deano' to his friends, will never forget the sight of him coming home as this aircraft made its way back to land. They once again raised their flags up high, as the plane got bigger and was heading directly for them, you could not mistake that raw cry. The rawness was awful, it truly was, and even with the best intentions to fly their flags high they started to crumble like a pack of cards. The flags stopped waving as shock seemed to take over; maybe this was the moment when they accepted that their friend really was dead.

One young man stood out with one thing on his agenda, he had vowed to have a drink ready for his friend. This proud man from Wales was fighting back his emotions and his determination won the fight. He walked from the crowd just to his right in the direction of the huge plane coming into land. There he remained, standing tall and proud as he raised a glass with a drink for a special friend. The Globemaster was 50 metres away to his right when he placed the drink on the grass bank shouting out loud, 'Deano you're home now mate, your drink's here on the side.' He stepped back all alone, watching the aircraft wheels touch the ground and then he lost his fight; his heart was broken, he broke down and cried like a child.

The C17 Globemaster tore down the strip and out of sight and those hurting held each other really tight. It really was harder sobbing when you try to fight the pain, it was so much easier just to let the tears flow.

It was at times like this that there was no escape; you feel as though you really are intruding as so many weep. I don't know what emotions Graham and Mags were experiencing, but I was having difficulty once again in winning my own little battle and not letting my tears flow. I sometimes wonder if it is wrong to cry for a man you never knew, but one thing I can tell anyone who reads this book, there is a significant difference between sadness and grief. What I felt was sorrow; theirs was far deeper.

I stood back, head bowed to hide the sadness in my eyes. I thought then, as I do today, the community of Carmarthen you did your local hero proud, and like you all I will never forget the day Deano came home. It took a good time before that heartache started to subside or in reality put back on hold, as there were to be more tears later that I knew would be released. Once they were composed and fit to drive, they got into their cars for that short journey up the road.

We waved them out back onto the road so they could make their way back to Bassett. There they could share their experiences with each other over a cup of tea or something a little stronger.

For me, it was quite a relief to be committed to traffic control, as the fleet of cars drove out of the lay-by one by one. It also gave me sufficient time to brush myself down. What would my two colleagues from Thames Valley Police think if they saw me dabbing my eyes?

The three of us were now left alone and Mags made some more notes, although the experience of standing in that lay-by was something I don't think either of my colleagues expected. I never asked, but I wonder what ran through their heads before we set off for Bassett; all I can say it was very quiet in my car.

Next on the agenda for my colleagues from Carterton was the Op Entourage brief.

The briefing room was packed with all our resources and again the two from Thames Valley looked amazed seeing so many in attendance. They were even more surprised when they realised how many were from the MDP who, as you know, travelled on each occasion from various stations to support the Wiltshire Police.

Yes, with this Operation we could all stand tall. The time and the commitment was never a chore once you had been to Bassett; we all got caught up in doing something right and many volunteered their assistance when the news broke that another soldier was returning home.

Honestly, poor Graham Hurst, who created each Op Entourage order, had so many volunteers – specials would take time off work, put on their uniform, and come in from home; local officers and PCSOs would stay on duty long after it was time to knock off or change their shift, while the MDP set off two or three hours earlier to make sure they were up in time for the brief.

Graham's biggest challenge was telling them 'no' they were not required, as resources were at overflow. The dogs with specialist skills came from counties to assist: Cheshire, Devon and Cornwall, MDP and even the Prison service to name a few. There was no budget or concerns of overtime, this was one Operation which we all felt proud to be involved in. Britain at its best: the public, the military, emergency services, all with mutual respect would stand shoulder to shoulder as each of our fallen made that sad return home. When the Operation Entourage briefing was complete I took my passengers into the High Street where hundreds were now congregating.

The standard bearers were making their way mixing with the bikers and Royal British Legion where they all shared the time of day. Maurice Baker had spotted the visitors from Wales carrying their standards and was briefing them on the simplicity of his parade.

I answered all the questions asked while Mags continued to scribble away observations in her police notebook. Whilst we stood by the war memorial I explained what would take place when the cortège came into town. The simplicity of the ceremony was not missed on them nor was it difficult to co-ordinate, but the results – dignity, respect and honour – were the recipe that Carterton would desire.

While all our phases were explained during the time Mags and Graham were with me, behind the wire five miles away the repatriation of Royal Marine Nigel Dean Mead, from 42 Commando Royal Marines, was well under way.

I answered their final questions while we were mixing with the crowd. Many from

Carmarthen came up to shake us by our hands, a simple gesture but one that sent a message of thanks that we genuinely did care.

My phone rang, it was from Graham Cook of Albins the undertakers whose number I told Mags to underline in her book as for me they were always my best informant in relation to this operation, so you never got caught out.

The message was simple and easily understood: 'Jarra the family are in the Chapel of Rest' which meant for me 'time for phase three' and to say my goodbyes.

I made my way back to RAF Lyneham and met up with the escort group, there we remained for some time before Graham phoned to say the family were on their way.

A few minutes later they were escorted out by the RAF Police. Like so many others I'd seen before from this awful experience, their faces were ashen from grief. Although, if there was any small comfort to have for them that day, there were many familiar faces waiting in Bassett to share their sorrow and pain.

When the message from the cortège informed us they were heading our way, I replied and gave advice for the conductor to be prepared; Carmarthen had relocated to Wootton Bassett to show their respects.

The tolling of the Tenor Bell once again announced we had arrived. Neil Gamble the conductor bows his head, before paging down the street. He knows that he was walking into a scene that would need a huge amount of composure; a challenge that he and his colleagues always met. Those Welsh flags were flying high as the 'Royal' was halted at the war memorial. Their Prince of Wales, a Royal Marine, or Deano to his friends remained there for some time as each wanted to show their respects to an exceptional young man.

There were so many tributes paid, with so many humbling words, he was obviously a very special lad as was shown by his brothers in 42 Commando. Without doubt I had seen evidence of that all day, but maybe as we escorted him out of town we could reflect on what two of his friends said. One from Carmarthen, a lad I had met earlier in the day, the other a Marine from his Commando, who both shared his loss in a similar way.

Tom Boodeny said:

'You were my best friend for thirteen fantastic years, always there when I needed help or just someone to talk to. You were the one person in the whole world that I could trust; I could tell you anything and you would keep it a secret like a best friend should. You were not just a good mate of mine, you were befriended by everyone that you met. You were an entertainer, a peacemaker and fantastic company to be around at all times. I know it's hard to lose a member of your family, but Dean, losing a friend like you is just as painful for me. It was a great privilege for me to know that I was your pal.'

CHAPTER THIRTY-EIGHT

Marine Chris Stanton said:

'My very best mate in the Corps, he was a young man with an enormous personality. He was dedicated and hard-working and took a huge amount of pride in everything he did. I have so many memories of Deano which I will cherish forever, from the times in America or snowboarding in France. I was privileged enough to have him attend my 21st birthday where he became the life and soul and everyone grew to love him. He was a lad you could not fail to get along with. Always cracking funnies and making sure everyone else was smiling. There was no challenge too hard, and he aspired to be the best by looking to join Recce Troop as a sniper. He was a man who would not back down if he believed someone was wrong, and he would always be the first to volunteer, as that was who he was; he was always looking out for others. An extremely generous giver; he will be remembered by us for his taste in music, obscene fashion ideas and the fact he was unbeatable in Call of Duty. I will never forget hearing Deano whistling 'The Wurzels' when he thought nobody was listening. Above all, I remember him for being my best mate. The lad who could make me laugh no matter what mood I was in. Nothing was too much hassle, he loved his friends and he loved his job. Dean 'Deano' Mead, you will never be forgotten.'

With tributes like that 'we will remember him.' Rest in Peace Nigel Dean Mead Carmarthen's 'Royal' Prince of Wales; your duty is done.

CHAPTER 39

One week later the St Bartholomew bell tolled as yet another heartbroken wife approached her husband's hearse to pay her solitary tribute. She was the wife of Colour Serjeant Kevin Fortuna, 36, from A Company, 1st Battalion The Rifles. Sometimes the sheer silence has even more impact as it did on this occasion, rippling through the crowd. Grief has so many faces that no two ceremonies were ever the same. It almost felt like an intrusion to be present on the High Street as the wife of Serjeant Kevin Fortuna, Nia, widowed only four days earlier, wept placing her hand against the glass; pausing and whispering a few final words to her husband. Then he was gone, escorted away full of honour and to receive a lot more along those 46 miles of respect on this very sombre, quiet day.

Over the four years I had been involved in this operation, some days took their toll; the deep sadness we had seen so very often did at times have a massive impact in so many ways. The biggest impact, and one that crept up on you, were the emotions stored so deep within your brain.

Although I started my time in Lyneham as a stand-alone 'Beat officer' from the MDP supported by resources near and far, I was glad when in 2008 my position was reviewed. The support I received from Sergeant Mark Venning and above him, Chief Inspector Phil Lowe, was immeasurable. Both men were people you could turn to, bosses in every sense of the word, and both of whom I would look upon as friends; when I asked, I was always given. The support never dwindled from the resources they had at their disposal.

Mark was often seen in Bassett High Street, a presence you could not miss as he was a man from the land of the giants about 6ft 5 tall standing above the crowd. He was the perfect boss and without his support I probably would have crumbled many times. He attended most repatriations after becoming my boss and his observations were spot on; aware if I needed to clear off and find myself. I had learnt before that the world still turns while I am away, but it's a macho image thing that makes you stay even though your mind is asking for a break.

I would often feel guilty when I took leave, but how can one say 'Boss I'm shattered' when you see so much grief, somehow it felt wrong to run away. It was good he could read the signs, recognising that sometimes I was struggling through and needed a break. Although I think my wife Karen would have a word in his ear and say, 'Mark, Jarra's tired.' One of the factors that eased the guilt when I had a bit of leave was that Mark flew the flag so high, in fact I often got the impression when I came back he had difficulty to let it go.

So yes, I did have a bolthole where I was fortunate to be able to have my own R&R and clear off abroad. Although, if I am honest, I could not switch off and always had one eye on things back home.

My location of escape was a sleepy hollow in a property in North Cyprus where I would often start the day with a walk over the mountains or along the coast and go for a swim in the sea. Without fail on my return home I would always call into the internet café to log on and focus on the news back home. Maybe many were correct in saying that I cared too much. I am who I am, and I certainly would never change my beliefs or stop doing what I perceived to be right.

When I logged on line I would always go straight to the Sky News website and feel absolutely gutted when I saw that our country had announced another fatality. Then, browsing the net, I would read on the MoD page the words that always seemed so bland: 'A soldier had been killed the family informed' and this used to intensify my guilt.

During my own R&R, while I was away, I saw that message displayed five times more. It was always the worst news and I would genuinely feel a deep sadness, almost a pain, in the knowledge that another family's life had been torn apart.

Then some 24 hours later the fallen, their names scrolled on the screen:

Lieutenant Oliver Augustin 42 Commando Royal Marines
Marine Samuel Alexander MC 42 Commando Royal Marines
Corporal Michael Pike, Royal Regiment of Scotland, 4th Battalion
Rifleman Martin Lamb, 1st Battalion The Rifles, A company Reconnaissance Patrol
L Corporal Martin Gill 42 Commando Royal Marines

I knew what the timings would be by logging onto the Wootton Bassett Town Council website and would nip down to a local pub that I knew had Sky television.

When I watched the live broadcast even from afar, the respects and dignity shown on the screen were ones I knew only too well. With no one around I found myself standing and raising my glass in honour of those who were brought home.

Yes, even so far away I found as I watched the screen from 2,000 miles or more, it was difficult to distance myself from that deep sadness. The news would finish, I would return to my seat, glad I was alone as my mind was in the High Street of Wootton Bassett. I would ponder deep in thought, proud of what respects I had seen evolve over the last four years, knowing how the loss of one of our own were truly recognised.

I am really sorry to the families who may open this book to see their loved ones name and feel disappointed their stories are not told. I hope they do not feel anger, but where would my integrity be if I told an untruth about a day I never saw.

From the images I had seen on the television, your loved one was recognised in exactly the same way as so many others, with true honour, dignity and respect.

I knew this for certain and it was confirmed when I read the repatriation reports that Blondie and his band of brothers from the Royal Marines Association had created. All along that 46 miles, hundreds more stood to honour each of those who had fallen.

I realised something else on this holiday for the first time, while I was watching the scenes on the news I knew it was time for me to let go.

I really needed the break away to allow me to sort myself out as I had witnessed 51 months of heartbreak and there was no doubt it had certainly taken its toll.

I never sat down to think what the impact my sadness had on my wife over the years, but she was always there to pick up my pieces. Karen also knew that for me this Operation was almost finished and soon her husband would be back.

It does, even now, seem wrong to open up and share how I felt, as for so many others the devastation could never be undone. To lose a loved one and many so young is far too difficult for me to comprehend. As I finished my beer and walked back home to my wife who was relaxing in our garden, I thought thank God I have her by my side, because without her I would have struggled and have had no place to hide. She shouted over as I walked through the gate. She was relaxed, reading a book and asked if I enjoyed my walk; I looked a bit flat. She was kind, reassuring without probing; she knew that I would have watched the repatriation on the news and on my return would ask if I wanted to talk. I always declined, what could I say? She was on holiday, so why spoil her stay with my sorrow. The easiest answer was, 'No I am fine' and keep my feelings locked inside.

So that's exactly what we did. Karen enjoyed the rest of her holiday but my head was focused on going back on the beat. Although I had learnt a great lesson on this vacation, it was time to move on and when we returned home there was only another ten weeks to go.

CHAPTER 40

I had only been back a couple of days when the phone rang to inform us two more British Soldiers were dead. My goodness, I shook my head, when will this madness ever end. We were advised to plan for the following week; Thursday being the favoured day. Graham Hurst typed away details for his request of support from the MDP and Wiltshire officers for Op Entourage No. 164. Before he even sent the e-mail out he knew he would get more resources than he requested.

Over the weekend the news was there for all to see as that awful scrolling message was seen once again. Another British Soldier has been killed in Afghanistan, which now made it three.

There I sat at home feeling desperately sad for a family we did not know. They would be on the High Street next week when their loved one returned home.

I got up out of my seat and took the dog out for a walk; sometimes it was nice just to be alone and clear my head. With so much sadness it was nice to stroll through the park throwing the ball for Tia, who would excitedly bring it back panting.

Isn't it strange that the simplest of things in life like walking the dog can be so therapeutic to the brain.

When Monday morning came, the confirmation was made that even though three soldiers would return, only two would be repatriated at RAF Lyneham and be escorted from the station by road.

The third soldier would be flown out to another base for military honours to be performed away from intrusive eyes; we all knew the significance of that.

Wednesday soon came around and the preparations for the ceremony had begun under the watchful eye of three warrant officers. Two of them were Regimental Sergeant Majors (RSM) one a Mercian the other Royal Electrical Mechanical Engineer, and Station Warrant Officer Nick Dale. As you know I always popped down to watch the bearer party carry out their training while I waited for the pre-Op Pabbay brief. However, on this occasion I had one of my colleagues shadowing me. Kerrie McGlinchey, a police sergeant from the MDP, was present to observe the procedures in relation to this operation. The Ministry of Defence Police had officers on detached duties mentoring the Afghanistan Police. Superintendent Joe Elder had reviewed their force policy and created a contingency plan in the event that one of his officers were killed and required to be repatriated home. Kerrie had a secondary duty; she would be involved as a family liaison officer should tragic circumstances occur, something similar to the role of the military Visiting Officer. She was therefore very keen to learn as much information as possible, and this was a role where the best way to learn was from the knowledge and experience of those who knew. With notebook and pen at the ready she eagerly questioned the three warrant officers. They answered in great detail; the information was vast as she scribbled away recording everything about the bearer party.

How the bearer parties were chosen, what was expected of them before they had arrived at RAF Lyneham and their preparations to conduct the drills required. A bearer party of six, plus two reserves and one driver (the senior non-commissioned officer in command of the party) would be the standard number and all members of the bearer party must be over 18 years old. In exceptional circumstances this can be raised to eight plus two and one driver. This is required when the deceased is repatriated in an outsized coffin or the overall weight of the coffin is over 170kg. Advice will be given via the morticians from Albin International in theatre who will have the necessary detail concerning the weight of the coffin they will be carrying. The bearer party must be correctly sized at the shoulder and should be free of any pre-existing injuries.

The coffins average 140kg. The heaviest has been closer to 200kg and bearer parties should be able to handle these weights. It was strongly recommended that bearer party selection is based on their ability to do the job rather than their relationship to the deceased. All too often, good friends find the whole process far harder than those who were unknown to the deceased. This detracts from the solemnity of the occasion.

This was the information Kerrie sought to take back to her force headquarters and she was to get more as another very important member of the Op Pabbay team would soon make his presence known. However, before his arrival it was time for the bearer party training to stop, and they made their way for a well earned coffee in the back of the departure lounge. With me never shy to accept a coffee and biscuits, we joined them. We had only just sat down when Major Marcus Elliot-Square entered the room. Marcus was a Major in the Grenadier Guards and specialised in ceremonial parades; a proud and very focused man who paid great attention to detail. Kerrie was very impressed in his style, his panache and even made a passing comment in referring to him as that 'quite dishy Major'.

I said what about me? She replied, 'Oh Jarra, you are just you.' I guess dishy I am not; I finished my coffee. To get my own back on Kerrie I told her to get her notebook and pen back out as she was about to receive a lot more information.

Marcus stood up and introduced himself. His statue and presence immediately gained every person's attention and respect, as he spoke we all listened and Kerrie took in every word.

He would normally turn up around this time after Mr Dale had spent a couple of hours moulding the bearer party into something he could tweak, honing them to achieve the high standards he encouraged.

To achieve that goal he emphasised the four 'P's' – Preparation, Position, Posture,

Perception – as these were his ingredients on achieving that gold standard. There was so much attention to detail and he explained to the bearer party the importance of each of the P's. It was a short, sharp presentation to give the bearer party an understanding before they went out to rehearse again. But his strength of character came out in the way he spoke; his words would motivate these two bearer parties to be focused and get it right:

'On the day of the ceremony, the station is completely closed down for a two hour window. The only things that will be moving will be the C-17, the hearse, and you on parade. It is a unique atmosphere and very intense and intimate.
It will be difficult to replicate some of the elements of the actual parade during the training process. One of these elements will be the march on to the back of the C-17 aircraft. The interior is closed off by a large curtain to stop anyone from seeing in. You will be marching up the ramp when this is drawn back revealing the open expanse of the aircraft, with a Union flag draped coffin resting on some trestles. This is the moment when the whole event becomes real.

We are asking you to move a heavy, unwieldy object over a relatively long distance in a dignified and professional manner. You will have to perform some currently unfamiliar drill movements under some physical strain whilst looking calm and dignified.

You need to invest time in getting your position correct on the coffin. This will take place out of sight on the back of the aircraft.

The family's perception of you as the bearer party will be formed by the way that you treat the most precious thing in the world to them. Their son, husband, boyfriend, brother and your comrade.

During the final stages of the ceremony you will find yourselves in very close proximity to the families of the deceased, as well as your Regimental representatives. To that end, when you get to the back of the hearse and start manoeuvring the coffin into the back of the vehicle, utmost care must be taken to ensure that the coffin is treated with dignity and respect. You must treat the coffin as if it is made of the finest crystal. The slightest knock or jolt will shatter it into pieces. Any knocks or bumps will be amplified in the very quiet conditions.

To succeed you must ensure that you take your time, listen to the words of command and complete your movements in as dignified and controlled manner as possible whilst at the same time avoiding any external shows of emotion. As I said before the family's perception of you will be based on how you treat their loved one.

I now want you to finish off your coffee; work with me and Mr Dale through the training when we return outside, and let's get it right, for your comrade.'

As the men of all ranks stood up to go outside there was a purpose in their stride in the knowledge of what they were about to embark on in achieving the four 'P's and achieving that gold standard for a colleague who deserved the best.

Kerrie made a further comment, 'Inspirational words those Jarra.'

'Indeed they were,' I replied, and that is why, with the attention to detail that each of our fallen were carried home, they received so much honour.

As for us, we made our way for the pre-Op Pabbay briefing, but just before we got out of sight we both turned around for one last look as the Last Post sounded. Those that had heard the voice of Marcus had absorbed every single word he said. The box may have been empty to us, but to them it was that crystal he mentioned and there was no doubting they would get it right.

We walked away from the terminal building. Kerrie was impressed she had made that clear, but prayed she would never be back as this was one duty she would never want to perform.

Just as the attention to detail was seen at the rehearsals, so it was evident in the pre-Op brief; four years on everyone was still just as focused. Although on this occasion, prior to the C17 flight arriving at the set hour, there would be a Chinook Helicopter coming in with one specific operation – to take the special services soldier home to his own repatriation ceremony. Timings and details all confirmed it was now time to say goodbye to Kerrie.

As for me, I returned to the terminal building for another ritual that kind of just happened when the bearer party training had finished. I would drop the two men from Albin Funeral Directors to their digs. A couple of hours later we would all meet up for a pint and a bite to eat and share a pleasant evening.

The following day we all knew the score and carried out our own respective routines as per the orders the previous night. At the precise hour I saw the Chinook Helicopter fly into land.

Then again, as per the timings stated at the Op Pabbay brief, the C17 Globemaster flew in low and slow over RAF Lyneham. Corporal Lloyd Newell, the Parachute Regiment, Craftsman Andrew Found, Royal Electrical and Mechanical Engineers and Private Gareth Bellingham, from 3rd Battalion, The Mercian Regiment were the three soldiers returned that day. After the customary honour of the deft dip of the starboard wing, the aircraft rose in the skies and circled around to make its approach to land.

I patrolled my way around the perimeter external fence to confirm no cameras were spying. My brief was clear that some sights were not to be seen by the public eye for security reasons.

Once the Globemaster had landed, the aircraft manoeuvred into a position where the Chinook was waiting to carry its special passenger home. With those words used once again 'military precision' Corporal Lloyd Newell was carried from one aircraft to another and secured in the Chinook. The twin-engine tandem rotor blades started to turn and the aircraft flew into the distance to a destination the public did not need to know.

When the time had arrived, the C17 Globemaster taxied around to where the chocks were ready to secure the aircraft into position.

It will be not be a surprise to know that after you have read how much attention to detail was shown, that the ceremony for Craftsman Andrew Found, and Private Gareth Bellingham, was completed with immaculate military precision.

It was once again a day that saw the town weep as two heartbroken families were shown so much respect, but sadly could not take their pain away. The High Street was full of emotion when so many people from Yorkshire and Staffordshire came to Wiltshire on an extraordinary day, full of sorrow. Yet, despite their deep sadness, we can only hope they gained a little comfort from the sincerity those who honoured their loved ones showed at the repatriation ceremony and all along the 46 mile route.

CHAPTER 41

One week later, a sadness that surprised so many, including myself, was to take place as a county waved goodbye to a friendship that will never die. Something happened that so many could not believe when it was first announced many years ago and would have thousands looking up into the sky to wave their goodbyes to four 'Migrating Birds' who would never come home. When the press release was made, the date was announced and a different sadness started to hit home.

'The Mighty Hercules' Farewell to Wiltshire – Last flight from RAF Lyneham Friday 1st July 2011 on Route to RAF Brize Norton.'

The letters were bold in the evening's local papers as I sat down to read.

'On Friday, 1st July 2011, the last of RAF Lyneham's Hercules fleet of aircraft will say a final farewell to the County of Wiltshire before their official handover to the Station Commander of RAF Brize Norton. The intention is to have the last of the aircraft transferring to RAF Brize Norton flown at low level, in stream formation to say a final goodbye to the people of Wiltshire. Departing RAF Lyneham at approximately 1030 hours, it is envisaged that the aircraft will follow a route that will start out by flying over Avebury, Calne, Devizes, Warminster, Melksham, Trowbridge, Colerne, Lyneham, Wootton Bassett, Malmesbury, Tetbury and the Blunsdon area of Swindon, before the final leg of the journey to RAF Brize Norton.'

The 1st of July will mark the end of a remarkable era not only for the RAF but for the people of the County of Wiltshire that have supported RAF Lyneham so well over the years. RAF Lyneham's Station Commander, Group Captain John Gladston said:

'This is our last opportunity to say thank you and pay tribute to the people of Wiltshire for all the support they have given to the station over the past 70 years. It is with a heavy heart that I bid farewell to the Hercules Force, a sentiment which I know echoes throughout the Wiltshire community. The Hercules Force will now take a piece of our unique and proud history to RAF Brize Norton where I know they will be most welcome and I am in no doubt that it will flourish and continue to build on our proud heritage for many years to come.'

So with the statement confirming the dates of this sad occasion, preparations were once again being made to make sure that with all the attention of the media and the public focused on this event, it would get the military precision it deserved. The rehearsals began and this was another ceremony that called out for just one man to orchestrate, someone who had Royal Air Force engraved within him like a stick of rock. Station Warrant Officer, Nick Dale, epitomised the honour and glory in serving the Royal Air Force for more than 33 years and was as proud as any man I ever knew.

On the day of the parade, well, let me try and set the scene as I watched down from the balcony of the terminal building.

Four work horses of the skies, each representing their flying squadrons – 24, 30, 47 and 70 – were in a line facing away from the terminal building. The Hercules aircraft on the left had the rear ramp lowered, from that a guard of honour funnelled out immaculately turned out in their best uniforms, medals and rifles. The pilots and crew were on board their respective aircraft in a position out of view with their engines switched off. In front of the terminal building each of the Squadrons departing RAF Lyneham, including the Army Royal Logistic Corps, 47 Air Dispatch Squadron were standing in four man sections. An officer carrying their standard, two members of the Squadron carrying firearms either side, and at the rear a Senior NCO. They stood in a line in front of the terminal building facing outwards towards the four aircraft, which were about 80 metres away.

Hundreds watched the parade unfold under the words of command from Station Warrant Officer Nick Dale. A melody of tunes including *Mist Covered Mountains* and *Highland Cathedral* were played by Flight Lieutenant Ryan Kerr RAF on his bagpipes.

When the words spoken by the Padre had concluded, it was time to say their goodbyes, and the order to slow march was given. Flight Lieutenant Ryan Kerr on his bagpipes, playing *Auld Lang Syne,* stepped out slowly leading the five RAF Lyneham Squadrons Standard Parties to the departing flight.

The guard of honour formed a funnel approach to the rear ramp of the aircraft that was to convey their precious standards to their new home. They stood to attention; firearms presented in the General Salute. SWO Nick Dale was just to their front, his arm raised in salute as each of the Squadron Standard Parties entered up the ramp and onto the aircraft. They went out of sight and then were secured in position, ready to make this final flight. Once all the Squadron Standards were secure on the plane the guard of honour that funnelled them in shouldered their arms and marched onto the same aircraft.

Flight Lieutenant Kerr then followed the guard of honour, his bagpipe music faded as he disappeared and took his seat, leaving a parade ground empty except for one man. Absolute silence all around, then with his unique swagger he marched forward, then wheeled to the right; no better person could have been more honoured to execute this one final act. Station Warrant Officer Nick Dale RAF Regiment; RAF engraved in him, through to the core, came to an immaculate halt facing the terminal building.

This was a moment he was not going to rush; he paused, he looked all around, the huge sign 'WELCOME TO RAF LYNEHAM' is what he would have seen, yet he fully understood, this was no welcome, this really was *goodbye*.

The smartest man I ever saw; his parade stick under his left arm, his sword by his side, medals strung across his chest and another he knew nothing about was on its way, as he was about to be bestowed with the MBE. When he raised his arm in the salute, we could feel his sadness; like the youngest child leaving home, reluctant, but told he had to go.

I looked to my left and to my right. The man had done it again, saying goodbye in his own personal way, had provoked emotions on all those standing by my side.

His salute is brought down, a brisk about turn, he then marched with that immaculate gait onto his waiting aircraft. The ramp closed, the propellers turned, and the chocks removed, the four migrating birds started to move away from their nest never to return.

One by one the aircraft followed the C130 Hercules that Group Captain John Gladston (Gladis) was to Captain that day. Each taxied past the terminal building, the cockpit windows opened and hands were seen to wave, one even flew the Wiltshire Flag. The waves were sent back with the same warmth and sadness in this simple gesture of 'au revoir'.

The four aircraft taxied out of sight then a short stop before getting to the runway allowing a few passengers to jump on board to experience this final farewell flight.

Everyone at Lyneham was caught up in the emotion, I even got Inspector Chris Martin a seat. I chuckled to myself as I knew that low level flying can be bumpy at times.

Hundreds who wished to witness this historic moment had clamoured for a better view. I was another who was not going to miss out as I made my way to watch the four aircraft take off. Then they were gone; not a dry eye in sight, you certainly stirred the emotions Mr Dale before they even left the ground.

Up and up they climbed to the altitude required, then flew off eastbound to circumnavigate Wiltshire to say their goodbyes from the clear blue skies. Once I saw them leave, I made my way back up to Bassett where crowds were gathering in their hundreds. With my contacts in the Air Traffic Control tower giving me updates as to when this majestic sight would fly over the High Street, I stood by the war memorial with the Town Clerk, Johnathan Bourne, Michelle Temple and all the staff from the council offices; there was an air of excitement as we all waited.

I spoke to Michelle and Johnathan suggesting that I believed we should close the road, because when these aircraft flew over it seemed unfitting for the crowd to be hidden by buildings. Of course there are proper procedures to request road closures, but sometimes spontaneous actions were required to reflect the mood. I grabbed the ear of the Town Crier, Owen Collier. The number of times I asked him to assist us, I think we should have sworn him in as a 'Special' for these occasions. PC Nick Spargo and PC Jamie Ball were both on duty with me in the High Street and between us all we were ready to let the town's folk show their emotions, without having to worry about traffic on the road.

Air Traffic control flashed on my mobile; the four migrating birds were on their way for the very last time; that was all we needed to activate our contingency plans. Nick stopped traffic by the Iceland shop as Jamie raised his right hand on the junction of Station Road. 'Oyez! Oyez! Oyez!' Owen Collier the Wiltshire man in his customary regalia cried: 'Step out into the road and show your pride as we say goodbye to our friends in the sky.'

From either side of the street they poured onto the road and looked south up into the skies in the direction of Lyneham. There was an excitement of knowing a historical moment was about to take place as those present were looking for that first glimpse of a special friend they had seen for the last 40 years or so.

We heard the drone; they must be close. Suddenly they came into view; four beautiful aircraft in stream formation as they flew so low. They only came into sight as they cleared the Wiltshire golf course one mile away. The excitement was frenzy, as the public waved frantically. The sight must have been awesome from where Gladis sat in his captain's seat and as the Hercules flew over our heads it really hit home hard – they really had left home!

It surprised many that day as the tears formed in so many eyes; it was another day the war memorial saw sadness but in a different way. Then Owen the town crier rang his bell as he performed his duties once again and cleared the public off the streets.

It lasted for maybe five minutes that historic moment in time, but for those who were there that day, it was a memory they would remember for a very long time. After the crowd dispersed, a quick hug from Michelle and a shake of the hand from Johnathan, I said with an innocent smile, 'Best not tell the inspector about the road closure.' I knew we were safe as he was on the flight, though I wonder now what his thoughts were as he looked down below and saw that his main street had been closed without a Superintendent's authority.

As I drove up to RAF Brize Norton it slipped my mind to let him know what we had done. Although when I picked him up from his little jolly in the sky, he was a little whiter than I had last seen him, he seemed more focused on not being sick. It was, as I thought, a turbulent flight, but one which, like all those on board, he would always remember. It was a sad day, but one that was planned and if you have to say goodbye then do it in style and there could be no doubting that's what they had achieved, on the ground and in the skies when those migrating birds flew away.

CHAPTER 42

On Monday Morning I nipped down to an eerily quiet RAF Lyneham absent of the fleet of Hercules, which was really strange even though expected but it was still very bizarre. I called into the RAF Base to see Nick Dale to congratulate him on the emotional parade he had orchestrated. I walked in, shook his hand, and he said, 'It's been emotional' one of his one liners he would often use, but on this occasion, on the day of that parade it most certainly was.

Together we walked across the corridor into the station media office. We started to browse through the local papers and view the articles that had been written in relation to the migrating birds. Whilst flicking through the papers we both looked up at the TV Screen that was fitted on his office wall, it was always on the News Channels. To our disbelief we were hearing astonishing breaking news on a story that had just flashed up.

Sky News was reporting that a British soldier was missing in Afghanistan. The reporter was stating that the circumstances of his disappearance were unknown at that time and it was believed he may have been in search of some equipment. Whatever the reason there was confusion as another reported he may have even gone for a swim.

Incomprehensible, was the only word I could think of as I tried to absorb the words spoken on the news channel. Throughout the day this was the main news story; troops and all resources were reported to be looking for the missing soldier.

Later that day the breaking news, sadly, was not good and the reporter was saying that the missing soldier had been found dead.

After the normal 24 hours grace, the young soldier's details were released by the MoD.

'A British soldier who was found dead on 4th July, after going missing in southern Afghanistan, has been named as Highlander Scott McLaren of 4th Battalion, The Royal Regiment of Scotland.'

Eight days later on Tuesday 12 July, the 20-year-old Scotsman was repatriated with full military honours.

The ceremony, as always, was immaculate and as was the tradition, hundreds turned up in Bassett to show their respects and deepest sympathy for this young soldier. A soldier whose death, or more so the circumstances leading to it, were shrouded in mystery. After the family had completed their time in the Chapel of Rest they joined other friends and family in the small market town, awaiting their son's arrival at the war memorial.

When Spencer the conductor on duty paged the hearse through the High Street that day, there was a sombre silence. So many were confused as to why this young lad had left the safety of his base in the early hours of that morning.

The inquest at some time in the future would give a verdict as to the cause of death. Maybe because I am a policeman, I could not help wondering why someone would walk alone in hostile territory with so much danger surrounding him. However, what I thought was irrelevant, it was what the family felt that was important and I don't believe there was a person on the streets that day whose thoughts were not with them.

'Scott was a beloved son to James and Ann and brother to Kirsty, James and Ross. His family and friends, Grandmother Evelyn, Uncle Graham, Aunty Heather and close friend Michael will miss him dreadfully.'

Four years on since Scott was killed I read a lot more while writing this book and found out that the Military Police carried out a full investigation into the incident. From the limited information on the internet and reports in the papers the cause of death was conclusive. However, the mystery surrounding the reason why Scott left the checkpoint at 2.19am carrying his weapon, day sack and wearing his full body armour remains a mystery.

CCTV shown at the inquest last captured Highlander McLaren at 2.29am walking away from the base all alone; he was discovered missing an hour later by colleagues preparing to go out on patrol.

The question is simple; the answer is difficult. A three letter word may not be answered or one day it will. 'Why?' I doubt it will give even some small comfort with so many questions still unanswered. But along the 46 mile route we escorted your son that day, not only in Wootton Bassett were the people out to show respect when your Highlander, Scott McLaren came home.

Rest in Peace young Scotsman, I hope one day your family find out the reason why.

CHAPTER 43

I have spoken many times throughout this book about the huge respects shown from the gates of RAF Lyneham to the John Radcliffe Hospital entrance and sometimes beyond. On each occasion members of the Royal Marines Association, who were amongst the first to line the 46 mile route, would compile a report producing tangible evidence of the respects that were shown, from the vigil points they would parade.

I would like to share this information to show that when I have mentioned the words 'respects were shown' there is no doubt in your mind that I mean, overwhelmingly so.

Those humbling scenes had brought once again pride back in our nation for the Armed Forces, some of us had sadly forgotten. When I drove along the route these are the images I used to see.

Outside the gates at RAF Lyneham always stood two men displaying their previous service, one Royal Navy the other RAF, the first people to salute us on our way. A 100 metres further up the road the people of Lyneham would congregate as the St Michael's Tenor Bell would toll.

Those from Bradenstoke would hear the bell and make their way up to the roundabout that takes the A3102 in the direction of Wootton Bassett.

The staff from the petrol station would always be present and bow their heads as we made our way, next would be Eddy Shah and his wife Jennifer, a model and actress who was in the original Bond movie *Casino Royale*. Eddie would push Jennifer in her wheelchair from the Wiltshire Golf hotel and again both would bow their heads in sorrow.

Then we would enter Wootton Bassett, the town that will always remain special for awakening a country into showing respects to our fallen.

After we left those emotional scenes we would flow past static traffic on our right, where many stood with bowed heads outside their cars. Kids leaving school would stop in their tracks, their skylarking stopped as they left the Academy on their way home.

The rolling barrier did its job and the sterile bubble awaited our arrival as we entered the void in traffic on the fast road. Along the M4 we would cruise; there were always people on each bridge and one particular lady would catch my eye as she was always present with her golden retriever standing by her side. Further down, on our left, the Highways Agency patrol would stand outside their vehicles just off the hard shoulder with their heads bowed.

On the approach to the White Hart roundabout the residents from the local estate would stand next to the tallest postman I had ever seen standing to attention next to his post office van.

I will let the Royal Marines Association tell you the rest from their repatriation report you are about to read. These people travelled for hours to get to their own parade point, not only too Wootton Bassett but to vigil points all along the route, just read the list of Standards that are mentioned below.

The report is sincere, no spin from a politician or a journalist with a romantic eye; it was written with passion from a 'band of brothers' who for no other reason than they thought it was the right thing to do.

For any person who reads this book who lost that very special person please take some comfort knowing that from November 2008, their records show, they were also there that day your own loved one came home.

Yes, without doubt, when I refer to the word 'humbling', the scenes we the police escort group saw really were humbling as the country recognised the loss of Corporal Palin and L/Corporal Watkins this day.

REPATRIATION REPORT
Thursday 21st July, 2011

From operations in Afghanistan, the repatriation of:

Lance Corporal Paul Watkins (24), 9/12th Royal Lancers (Prince of Wales)
L/Corporal Watkins was fatally wounded by small arms fire while providing covering fire from his Jackal armoured vehicle for a foot patrol in an area west of Gereshk, Helmand Province, on 16th July, 2011.

Corporal Mark Anthony Palin (32), 1st Battalion, The Rifles
Corporal Palin died as a result of an explosion from an IED while operating in the Nahr-e Saraj District of Helmand Province on 18th July, 2011.

Service veterans and members of the public turned out in the following 'stations of vigil' to pay their respects to the fallen as the cortège made its way on the 46 mile route from the point of arrival at RAF Lyneham to the John Radcliffe Hospital at Oxford.

Royal Wootton Bassett - Town Centre (1640)

This report from Duncan Wostenholm, Royal Marines Association (RMA)
There were about 50 military personnel in uniform attending this repatriation and joined the veterans wearing berets and medals and 47 members of the Royal British Legion Motorcycle Branch, supporting the families and friends of the repatriated soldiers.

24 standards were paraded, including: Royal British Legion - Swindon, Abertillery, Devizes, Merthyr Tydfil, Gloucester City, Brockworth & Winchcombe, Newnham, Beckford & Ashton-under-Lyme. Associations: 43rd Wessex Division, The Rifles (Dorset and Somerset), The Dorsetshire Regiment (Gillingham and Bath), Aden Veterans, Royal Observer Corps, Canal Zone Veterans, The Parachute Regiment (Swindon), Royal Navy (Swindon), RAF (Corsham), The Royal Berkshire Regiment (Windsor), The Royal Regiment of Wales (Newport) and The Wiltshire Guards Association.

Gable Cross Police Station – On the A420 just east of the junction with the A419 (1655)

This report from Pat Bristow, RMA
There were four Association standards paraded; Royal Marines (Reading), Royal Signals (Reading), Royal Engineers (Swindon) and the RAF Lyneham Old Boys.
Ten veterans attended, along with 20 members the public and 80 police officers.

At the Road Bridge - B4000 over the A420 between Shrivenham and High worth (1705)

Report by Derrick Jeans, RAF Association
By the B4000 Bridge over the A420, District Councillor Elaine Ware and nine others stood to pay their respects to the cortège as it passed by at walking pace. Traffic pulled over into the lay-by opposite and the occupants stood by their cars. Oncoming traffic drew to a halt as the cortège approached.

United Kingdom Defence Academy - at the Watchfield Roundabout on the A420, adjacent to the UKDA (1710)

Report by Jim Hawkins, RMA
There were eight Royal Marines veterans from RMA Poole and Guildford, accompanied by some wives. The standards of RMA Poole and Guildford were paraded. Other veterans included Air Commodore Marcus Witherow, RAF Regt., Major Peter Hasting, RM and their wives Mary and Diana respectively, and Lieutenant MacKarness, Coldstream Guards. Uniformed officers from the Defence Academy included Majors Pawlowski and Baz Melia of The Rifles, Major Eyre Brook of The 9/12th Royal Lancers, Majors Richards and Prideaux of The Queens Royal Lancers, Majors Catton, Pennefather, Titericks, Allen, Pritchard, Waldemayer and Carson, of The Royal Marines, Captain Nick Gasson, Royal Navy, Chief Officer Chris Locke of the Royal Fleet Auxiliary and Major Claire Heighington, RMP. There were also some 15 Academy civilian staff and members of the public in attendance. The salute to the cortège was led by Major Eyre Brook, 9/12th Royal Lancers and ordered by WO1 (ATO) Scott Johnstone, Royal Logistics Corps.

CHAPTER FORTY-THREE

Many thanks to PCs Page and Pennington, MoD Police, for their traffic control.

Folly Hill Lay-by - east of Faringdon on the A420, just north of the A417 junction (1715)

This report by Joy Blake, RBL

The Folly Hill lay-by was well attended once again, with 68 people attending, to await the arrival of the cortège, which passed us by at 5.15pm, with the rain more or less holding off. More people also attended the Fernham Road junction as they normally do. Many regular stalwarts attended, but we had a number of new faces. One of these was a motor bike rider on his way home from work, told me his father, was the standard bearer of the Islip Royal British Legion and would be attending at Oxford. His attendance with us, together with his workmate and other people stopping off on the main road, was much appreciated.

Among the usual veterans wearing berets and medals, together with townspeople from Faringdon and many surrounding villages and towns, we had attending the Mayor of Faringdon, Dr. Mike Wise, the Chairman of the Vale of The White Horse District Council, Mrs. Alison Thomson, Mrs. Wendy Simpson of the Wantage Neighbourhood Support Group and the community police assisting with traffic control and telephone contacts. The standards paraded were the Union flag, Royal British Legion Faringdon, Bampton, Highworth, Shrivenham, Wantage, and the Royal Navy Veterans Association of Wantage.

John Radcliffe Hospital, Oxford – near Anthony Padua Parish Church, Headley Way (1805)

This report from John Walker, former RDG

We here at the Final Turn stood true and firm to honour these two soldiers.
There were 10 Royal British Legion standards paraded: Bicester & Launton, Bloxham, Chalgrove, Headington, Henley, Kidlington, Kidlington Womens Section, Marston and Wheatley. Association standards included The Coldstream Guards, Guards Division (Newbury), RAF Police, Royal Marines (Bicester), Royal Navy & Royal Marines (Oxon), The Royal Tank Regiment (Oxon) and The Banner of The Royal Dragoon Guards.
Deputy Lord Lieutenant of Oxford Rod Walker, Lord Mayor Councillor Elise Benjamin, Chairman Oxfordshire County Council Councillor Patrick Greene, Colonel (Rtd) BAC Duncan MBE., Royal Tank Regiment.

There were 54 veterans wearing berets and medals and 35 others from all three services. Thames Valley Police was out in force doing their normal duties and also standing alongside us on parade, under Chief Inspector C. Agger.

There were also Graham Cloudcroft (Chaplain to the Thames Valley Police), Mary and John from the Church (John having half-masted the Union flag), and John Jones of the St Johns Ambulance. Two RBL Bikers, Tony and D. Dickinson joined us, Martyn being elsewhere on duty. The Oxford public was out in force, not only here at the Final Turn, with their huge Union flags and the Ulster flag, but also from the Oxford ring road into Marston and all the way up the hill to us.

Many thanks to Harry Mennie (former Para) for helping me put these lists together; also to the wives and partners of the veterans for their help in organising tea and coffee. We thank also Father Aldo for the use of the church facilities, not only for the wash area but also for the use of the large car park. The parade marshal was J. Lewendon (former RA).

G. Whelan was away on other duties.

The weather was kind, with late sun and 15°C. The cortège passed us by at 1805hrs.

Their Courage and Sacrifice Will Not Be Forgotten
They will not be forgotten

Complied by PH (Duty Scribe)
On behalf of the Royal Marines Association

These reports started after November 2008 and continued long after the repatriations returned to RAF Brize Norton. They were recorded and archived by the Royal Marines Association. Just like Ken Scott with his album, those who compiled these reports did so for nostalgia and in time people could see just how much respect was shown.

CHAPTER 44

With one month to go before the repatriation operation returned to Oxfordshire, RAF Brize Norton was all but prepared, although in Carterton there was a lot of attention being focused on them and pressure was mounting for them to get it right. I was just glad I was not involved, as some media were provoking agitation, having possibly forgotten the devastation, the true meaning that the loss of a life meant to a family. What happened at that location might be written in another book by a different author.

One thing I will share is that it was decided in preparation of RAF Brize Norton taking over full responsibility that a full rehearsal would be carried out on the last three Thursdays of August. This would also include the respects that were being planned in Carterton, which were fully choreographed, as opposed to the spontaneous respects shown at Bassett.

While they were planning, we were praying that there would be no more, but as we all know now, our sadness was not complete, our duty was not done, as Op Minimise was activated twice more.

On 5 August, Marine James Wright, 22, from Juliet Company, 42 Commando Royal Marines, died in Camp Bastion after he was wounded by a grenade. The following week after his death the 'spirited and passionate' Marine, as quoted by his Commanding Officer, was flown back to RAF Lyneham.

After the repatriation ceremony and private time in the Chapel of Rest was completed, the young Marine's family were driven up to Wootton Bassett where hundreds were waiting to show their respects.

We had been briefed the day before that the young Marine's partner, Shelley Robertson, was expecting the couple's first child. She stood at the war memorial holding a single red rose all solemn and dignified. Amongst the group of close knit family and friends were the Marine's parents, Sallie and David Wright. After the respects had been shown the emotions took over as devastation and numbness followed while James was paged away from them.

The tributes from his family and Marines say it all: 'He was a hero who would be solely missed.' They had our deepest respect and sympathy which, as you now know, would continue for the rest of the route.

I received a lovely letter from the parents of James some time later; the words were private and very moving. It was hard to believe that with their world crumbled, they still found the time to say, 'Thank you for looking after our Son.'

I heard through the grapevine, later that year a baby was born making her grand entrance into the world; all 6lbs and 15.5ozs of her on 3 December 2011. The baby was the daughter of James Wright and Shelley Robertson.

I read in a local paper that Shelly said, 'She and James had decided on the name Lily Marie if their baby was a girl, just before he was deployed to Afghanistan. We wanted to have the middle name as Marie because that's my middle name; we both liked the name Lily and James liked the flower.'

Well Lily Marie from what I read about your dad he was a real Great British hero, an outstanding 'Bootneck' with a wicked sense of humour. May you, like so many other children who also lost their fathers, stand proud each and every one of you as you tell them about your very special dad.

Yet sadly on the same day as Marine James Wright was returned to RAF Lyneham an IED exploded causing devastating injuries and another fatality.

Lieutenant Daniel Clack, of 1st Battalion, The Rifles, was killed while leading a ten-man patrol into the village of Dactran. They were to speak to the local nationals and discuss a shura due to take place the next day. Approximately 150 metres from the front gate his patrol was struck by an improvised explosive device, killing him and injuring five others.

Lance Corporal Hayley Teresa Ridgeway, Royal Army Medical Corps, was one of those soldiers on the patrol injured in the incident. Whilst receiving treatment for her own serious injuries the man she had tried to save with all her skills, including bringing him back to life four times, had died on the aircraft flying him to hospital.

I, like many millions of others at a later date, saw the trauma on her face when she recited that incident on national television. She spoke in detail of the heroic efforts the patrol carried out trying to save 'The Boss'. However, as she and the other soldiers injured in that same incident lay in hospital in Camp Bastion, J treble C was activating their next of kin informing.

We, the police, received notification after we completed the escort of Marine James Wright and with the final three rehearsals taking place up at RAF Brize Norton being on a Thursday, the chances that it would conflict with this Operation Pabbay were a possibility. It would have no impact on the military, but it would on Thames Valley Police, as their resources were required for both. This was quite easy to rectify, I would escort the full route with a Wiltshire Roads Policing Unit at the rear. Rob Langton would provide outriders from his force from Gablecross to the John Radcliffe hospital.

When it was established that the repatriation would take place on Thursday 18 August, our contingency plan for the escort was confirmed.

Although we did not know for sure that this would be the very last repatriation with this timescale it seemed very likely it would be. Our perception was in fact correct; we all know now it was indeed to be the final Operation Pabbay at RAF Lyneham.

There were two personalities who wanted to share the final journey with us; Station

Warrant Officer Nick Dale and Graham Hurst. Mr Nick Dale had been present over 100 times on the sacred ceremonial ground during his tenure while Mr Graham Hurst had created 168 Operation Entourage Orders for the police. We were honoured to have both men join us in our final escort and to allow them to take in the sincerity of those showing their respect along the 46 mile route.

With the normal rehearsals and the pre-Op Pabbay brief completed the day before, so another ritual developed; I dropped the two Albin men Nick and Charlie off at their accommodation. The Wiltshire hotel Golf and Country Club is where they stayed and I would always join them later that same evening. For us this evening would be the last supper we would share.

The following morning I took my steady walk up the High Street on my way to the Police Station and stood in silence as the two Royal British Legion men lowered the Union flag, then hoisted it back to half-mast. Once I booked on for duty I drove down to Lyneham and met up with the funeral team in the hangar at the rear of the terminal building for a coffee. They were carrying out their normal pre-ceremonial duties including polishing their fleet of vehicles. They are brilliant blokes, these Albin lads, dedicated to the cause; the finest team I have ever seen and their standards were so high. They even decided my car was not gleaming enough for their liking and buffed it up which was a rare treat for me.

It was strange really as these people that I had got to know so well since April 2007, suddenly, after today were no longer going to be in my life. It was a genuine friendship of mutual respect between a copper and his undertaker mates. I think that's when I suddenly realised I was letting go of something that had just grown out of all expectations. If I am to be honest, I was in conflict with what I mentioned ten weeks earlier and I was not sure I wanted to let go.

However, I knew I had to. It was only just then that the reality had hit home, when you realise you really did mean *goodbye*. I also promised Karen that the weekend after the operation was concluded we would be on a flight out to our place in the sun; tickets I knew she had already booked.

RAF Lyneham was quite a strange place to be these days with all the flying Squadrons now based at RAF Brize Norton and in less than two weeks' time the runway would be closed. So much change in such a short time. I drifted in thought and then I got focused on my routine just as I had so many times before, but everything seemed different today.

When I watched the C17 Globemaster, that awesome sight with the deft dip of the starboard wing flying so low to honour Lieutenant Daniel Clack, then circle around for the final approach, it was for the very last time. I went up to Bassett for the police briefing then made my way back into town waiting for the call that the family were inside the Chapel of Rest. I called into the Cross Keys and spoke to many extended family and friends, to inform them what would take place and sat quietly with my cup of tea, soaking up this scene which I had seen so many times before.

My call came and I made my way to pick up Station Warrant Officer Nick Dale, who confirmed whilst getting into my patrol car that the ceremony had gone extremely well.

The family were leaving the sacred building with one last look over their shoulder; they commenced a journey to a town five miles away which had been witness to some extraordinary scenes.

The faces are different, the pain is the same; we stand up straight to show our respect; as the family are escorted off the base. A High Street who mourned, who shed a river of tears, was ready to offer condolences and support one final time.

The family have gone, the outriders are perched at the ready at the exit of the main gate. St Michael's Church is informed and their bell tolls to signify that the cortège will soon be leaving. However, before we roll I have one brief call to make: 'Blondie it's time to get your brothers on parade.' His response as always, 'We are ready and waiting.'

I see the cortège head in my direction and I activate my lights. 'Bronze, Mike Delta 2185 the cortège is leaving Lyneham now,' was my brief message which I had transmitted God knows how many times.

The outriders and rear police patrol car activate their blue lights, the cortège is ours and we are on our way for the 168th and, significantly, the last time we leave the gates of dear old RAF Lyneham. The Royal Air Force station that did the fallen proud with a repatriation team that truly did care.

Everything seems to be going in slow motion as we exit the main gate. I reduce our speed even more as we approach the two men I mentioned before. One Royal Naval the other RAF who throw up their salute as a mark of respect, although it almost felt like they were saying goodbye.

To the sound of St Michael's Bell, the village community stand along the road; salutes are raised and heads are bowed as they witness another chapter in history coming to an end. The good folk of Bradenstoke stand on their side of the roundabout while those working in the garage across the road do exactly the same. The traffic is stopped, we will not be rushed, this was a journey of dignity and mutual respect which has been taken for the last four and half years.

Up the A3102 road from Lyneham to Bassett; on our right as always were Eddie and Jennifer who both bow their heads. The police commentary continuously flowed, advising Bronze Commander Inspector Chris Martin we were at The Wiltshire, which was his cue for the High Street to be closed.

Next is Skew Bridges and the radio message is clear; Bronze confirmed we were good to continue our journey into the town which was soon to be recognised, deservedly so, with Royal status.

Up the hill past the infant school, children even at such a tender age know what is happening. Their mothers most certainly do, as they hold their child's hand tightly as sorrow is felt in knowing that another mother has lost her son. St Bartholomew's Church bell begins to toll, as it announces another hero is in our tow. There was no mistaking the solemn mood which that sound created, enhancing the sadness in the air. Although today I stopped for a brief moment to ponder; maybe amongst the many present some would also have difficulty in letting their spontaneous ceremony go.

The conductor prepares to page up the High Street whilst we, the police escort, drift up the road to our designated position where we stand and wait. Neil Gamble, the conductor, starts to page towards the war memorial that has been witness to so much grief. Maurice Baker the Parade Marshall who stands out in front shouts his one word of command 'up'. A simple word that created so much honour; those wearing headdress raise their arms in the salute, whilst each of the standards are lowered one by one as the hearse makes its approach.

The ceremony is carried out with so much dignity and grace as Lieutenant Daniel John Clack, of 1st Battalion, The Rifles, comes to rest at the war memorial. This may well have been the 345th Great British hero to be shown respect, but at that precise moment our thoughts are with only one. With the most humbling dignity I think I ever saw, a young lady dressed in black walks alone to the hearse. Two thousand eyes are mesmerised and see a pain that none of us could describe as this lady placed a single rose on the vehicle's roof. That personal moment was created with so much love for a man she had lost. Although known as 'The Boss' by those Swift and Bold, to Amy Tinley he was more valued than that, he was her fiancé Daniel Clack.

For that moment even the birds do not sing, the only noise is the sound of the toll of the Tenor Bell as we all felt we were intruding by just being present. Some moments were private; this certainly felt like one of those moments. The world has stopped spinning and the ambience was enhanced with so much love and honour for the Army Lieutenant. No words are spoken and with as much dignity as she approached the hearse, the young lady moves back to the safe haven with her own mechanism of support. Then each member of the family and close friends step forward one by one for their own personal moment to stand before their man. Some laid flowers, others placed a hand on the glass, whilst others stood with a bowed head and said their own private words.

Neil Gamble the conductor knows it is time and checks if it is safe to move the hero on. With a look down either side of the cortège, he confirms all is clear. He turns to his right, he looks at the war memorial, then a pause – a final salute in the raising of his hat. It is a ritual he has performed so many times, but I wonder what runs through his head knowing he will not be back.

If he did pause for thought no one would ever have known, as he always showed so much dignity and respect. With a slow turn on his heels he starts to page the cortège to where we wait. Those same eyes that watched Amy lay her precious rose were now focused on the rear of the hearse as it prepared to drift away. The standards and Royal British Legion, although not in the salute, remain in position. The Mayor, the Town Crier and the people of Wootton Bassett, without intruding, offer their sincere condolences to the family and their friends. The bikers proudly displaying their badges and insignia from their previous military career stand next to the many present who honourably still serve.

It was an emotional affair for so many reasons. Although we knew this was the end of something that had started with so few it made so many proud to be British. Neil by this time had paged down the High Street; our right arms were raised in the salute. When I saluted Lieutenant Daniel Clack, I had the feeling I was also saluting the town, in a way, my own thank you for doing something I believed was right.

We set off again slightly slower than normal; one last look in my rear view mirror and I knew I would never see the like again. To my right were the butchers in traditional attire, a few doors further down stood the Town Council, Johnathan Bourne and his team, bowing their heads as they always did, with sympathy and sincerity.

After leaving the town we entered our sterile bubble eastward bound on the 'B' carriageway of the M4. We cruised as we always did at 50mph. I looked above and there was the lady with her golden retriever, a bow of her head and I also knew I would never see her again.

Four vehicles from the Highways Agency parked on the raised hard standing off the hard shoulder; a bow of their heads then we were gone. Coming off the M4, junction 15, the outriders have stopped those on the roundabout as we float past and make our way along the A419. Off the slip road that leads to the White Hart roundabout we slow right down, there is the postman by his van. As a mark of respect he is ridged to attention, there is no doubting this man had served. He stood out to the front with many behind him from the nearby estate.

Gablecross is next and Wiltshire police outriders will peel off as Thames Valley Police take over the lead, but before we arrive there are so many present that the senior police officer has stopped the traffic. They all stood to attention, a mixture of many uniforms who all served the emergency services – Paramedics, Police and Fire Service – were in a line and the veterans who wore berets raised their arms in the salute. Whilst in the salute we slow and the exchange of outriders is done with almost military precision, and then we meticulously continue on our route with Thames Valley Police at our front.

The next vigil point is the Road Bridge a few miles up the A420. The weather is not pleasant but these people who showed respect did so because they care. A little drizzle was no hardship when those they honoured had served their country with their life. And there they were, in their masses, as we drove underneath the bridge where they stood. Looking to our right a lay-by is full of cars; people who knew we were coming had no hesitation in standing out in the rain.

Blondie and his band of brothers who had been protecting their wives with umbrellas from the rain, quickly fold them down on sighting the outriders and briskly come to attention. All present and correct on parade at Watchfield roundabout, the Royal Marines Association stand proudly with those still serving from the Defence Academy. We all but stop for their final salute and why not, they had travelled for hours to stand out in the rain. I saw Blondie standing proud with his right arm in the salute and I raised mine back in his honour; with the slight nod of his head I know he had noticed my personal message to him.

The Folly Hill lay-by was full along with 'Bamboo Charlie' a pet name that Stephanie, a Major with J treble C, called him after his Union flag standard was lowered by a bamboo shaft. It was a nickname he was soon to be proud of when I later told him that it was created out of respect. His standard lowered and 70 others stood in the unrelenting rain where they raised their arms in the salute or bowed their heads in honouring the young Lieutenant.

There was one vigil point left, the 'Final Turn', which is just before we enter the hospital so this would be included in the route from RAF Brize Norton.

The outriders in these awful weather conditions did a sterling job keeping us floating, literally, in the heavy rain as we enter the built-up area off the A40. Yet still they stood waiting for us and the scenes at the 'Final Turn' were equally as humbling as they were at Wootton Bassett. There were so many standards that lined either side of the street as we formed up for our final respects.

There were hundreds of people present, a mixture that represented all of our society and amongst them many who proudly wore their berets.

The cortège was really tight with the two outriders side by side to my front. In the gloomy light our blue lights flashed even brighter; those who were waiting knew we escorted someone very precious.

Methodically we made our way with grace towards where the many veterans and dignitaries had joined the public near Anthony Padua Parish Church on Headley Way, Oxford. This for us was a moment that was not going to be swift but it was bold, it was to be done with compassion, sincerity and the utmost respect.

Each of the standards were lowered as we approached, then the next and the one after that. It continued as we made our way; it was precise, it was orchestrated and it was done with pride. Those congregating then all came to attention and saluted as we drifted past them into the grounds of the John Radcliffe hospital.

This was a day I will never forget for so many reasons: sadness at another valued person gone and yet with chest-swelling pride in seeing so many extraordinary scenes along those 46 miles.

While Albin Funeral Directors carried out their duties, we stood around chatting when one of the Thames Valley outriders approached me to shake my hand. I was taken aback, but very humbled that he felt the need to do so. We chatted for a while and I told him how it all started when on that March day in 2007 I had just witnessed the repatriation rehearsal.

Recalling the day Barry Albin-Dyer and Rob Rowntree asked if the police could assist them by getting them to the M4, my reply was filled with emotion. If I can refresh your memory: 'Sir after watching that ceremony I will get you to the moon.'

Maybe in the spirit of the words I used, and the recognition shown to our fallen during those escorts, we did just that, we did get them to the moon. A simple gesture that resulted in so much honour and respect to our nation's heroes.

Our simple gesture was to escort the cortège up the road for eight miles to the M4 motorway, the rest you now know.

The Thames Valley Police outrider and I shook hands and I wished him good luck and seriously hoped that the operation that his sergeants were rehearsing up at RAF Brize Norton would be one that is never required. When we left the hospital grounds I honestly felt my duties were done and, like everyone else that day, I was immensely proud to have been involved in enhancing the dignity and respect along with honour to the 345 fallen we escorted home. Our duties were completed but for Thames Valley Police they would continue to escort the fallen until the conflict was over.

CHAPTER 45

Planning and preparation had been completed after months, if not longer, in both RAF Brize Norton and the town of Carterton, as the day was fast approaching for the transferring of Operation Pabbay to Oxfordshire. Everything was ready, the rehearsals finished, and inside the RAF station the purpose built 'Repatriation Centre' incorporating the Chapel of Rest was completed. Carterton had constructed a purpose built memorial garden where they would carry on the customary traditions that had spontaneously been created at Wootton Bassett war memorial.

Johnathan Bourne, the Town Clerk of Wootton Bassett Council, liaised with dignitaries to consider an appropriate way to conclude this historical moment of his town. Once his proposal was approved these were the headlines of the Wootton Bassett Town Council, press release:

> 'A special Sunset Ceremony will mark the end of repatriations through Wootton Bassett's High Street on Wednesday 31st August 2011.
>
> The ceremony will reflect the simple and dignified manner of repatriations and will involve the lowering of the Union flag as the sun sets, the same flag that will have flown at half-mast for the last fallen serviceman to be repatriated into RAF Lyneham.
>
> Starting at 8.00 pm, it will be led by the Mayor of Wootton Bassett, Councillor Paul Heaphy and The Reverend Canon Thomas Woodhouse, Chaplain of the Wootton Bassett branch of the Royal British Legion.
>
> The moving words of The Exhortation will be recited before the flag is blessed and the ceremony brought to a close.
>
> The flag will be transported to Oxfordshire the following day to be presented as a symbolic gesture from the people of Wootton Bassett to the people of Carterton who, sadly, may see fallen service personnel repatriated into RAF Brize Norton.
>
> Everyone is welcome to attend the Sunset Ceremony, which will be a final gathering of the town to remember those who have lost their lives, in Iraq and Afghanistan and to reflect upon the passing of a profoundly significant era for the people of Wootton Bassett.'

With the excellent relationship between the town and RAF Lyneham, the ingredients for success in creating the appropriate ceremony were there, especially with one man who was perfect for such occasions.

Station Warrant Officer, Nick Dale, had offered his assistance and was present in his advisory capacity on the night of the rehearsal, along with the main players who would be carrying out certain responsibilities. The ceremony would take place off the road on the hard standing between the war memorial and the old town hall, the building on stilts, where a small dais would be erected.

Johnathan and Nick started to place those with particular roles into their positions for this relaxed dress rehearsal. The musician was placed just in front of the shops in line with the flag pole; this is where the band would be located on the night. The Royal British Legion standards would be placed in a line from the band to the dais therefore creating a backdrop to the ceremony. This evening the one standard bearer present adopted his position. We, the police, were to be in a line across from the standard bearers, with the dais to our left and the war memorial to our right, therefore creating a clearing for the ceremony to take place.

A further two Royal British Legion members were positioned either side of the flag pole, their role was to lower the Union flag, fold it and then hand it to their Chairman, Ted Sharpe. Ted would salute as he stood with them when the Union flag was lowered. Mr Dale gave these three men guidance and refreshed their memory on the drills they were to perform. This was possibly the most sacred part of the ceremony, the lowering of this precious gift to Carterton, where it was emphasised for them to cherish it as it was held in their hands.

On the dais would stand the Mayor of Wootton Bassett, and The Reverend Canon Thomas Woodhouse; from this position the service would be conducted where speeches and prayers would be given. Johnathan Bourne was like a director of arts as he talked us through the itinerary of the ceremony. As he pointed in the direction of St Bartholomew's Church announcing:

'It would start as all repatriations did with the tolling of the Church Tenor Bell, followed by words spoken by the Mayor of Wootton Bassett and a Prayer by the Reverend Canon.'

Sunset, also known as the 'Retreat Call', is a bugle call played in the United Kingdom and British Commonwealth countries to signal the end of the official military day. What more fitting music could be played as the Union flag was lowered, salutes raised and standards dipped. As the last bar of *Sunset* was concluded the salutes would come down but the standards would remain lowered, whilst the Union flag would be handed to the Royal British Legion Chairman in a triangular fold. A time of reflection would then commence with a two-minute silence. The Exhortation would be recited by Maurice Baker, President of the local Royal British Legion. The Reverend Canon would then introduce the National Anthem. The Union flag would then be presented to the Reverend Canon Thomas Woodhouse on the dais.

Once that was completed the standard bearers would raise their emblem into the carry. Closing words by the Mayor of Wootton Bassett and one final prayer from the Reverend Canon would conclude the brief ceremony, and then gracefully they make their exit to place the Union flag on the altar of St Bartholomew's Church. A blessing would take place followed by a candlelight vigil overnight. Meanwhile, Maurice Baker, known locally on occasions like this as the 'parade marshal' would dismiss the standard bearers and they would march off.'

Simple, everyone understood their role: where they were to stand, do what they had to do. So they did a walk through, not quite with the same military precision but just a very simple dignified gesture to conclude some of the most humbling and respectful days in this little market town's history.

Everyone left that night knowing what was expected on the evening of the planned ceremony.

Sadly, on Tuesday 30 August, the Ministry of Defence announced the day before the Sunset ceremony that another member of the British Forces had been killed in Afghanistan. This awful news meant that those in Oxfordshire would have one more week before that C17 Globemaster would be arriving with this latest fallen hero.

The previous week I had been invited up to Carterton by Sergeant Mags Turner and her colleague Sergeant Nicole James, to shadow them whilst watching the final rehearsal. My biggest observation was that I could not understand why a memorial garden had been constructed in Carterton, when Brize Norton Village, which was the first built up area after the cortège left the newly constructed 'Britannia' gate at the RAF station, had all the amenities required.

This village seemed to be the perfect location particularly as the Brize Norton war memorial was in the grounds of St Britius Church. There seemed to be much debate amongst the local community and I imagine there was a lot of pressure from many people to get it right. Another observation was that Carterton had marshalls to coordinate their ceremony, so in effect the local Neighbourhood Policing Team was on the periphery, on stand-by if required.

However, from what I had seen and heard both RAF Brize Norton and Carterton were indeed ready to continue with the same professionalism and compassion as the country had witnessed over the last 53 months in Wiltshire.

I sincerely wished them well, not for any other reason than that the fallen deserved to be recognised with honour, dignity and respect. What happened in Wootton Bassett was the past, this was the future. Although for a bereaved, grieving family, sadly it was the present and they were the most important people to consider as they would make their way there next week.

Carterton Council also knew that the country's media would be keenly focusing on them to make sure they got it right, in particular in the vicinity of the memorial garden which was still under wraps.

If I am honest, it saddened me a little when I heard people say things such as it's not going to be like Bassett or it's not going to be like it was at RAF Lyneham. No it wasn't and nor should it try to be; that was then, this is now, it was not a competition, it was about respect. Such comments weren't needed especially on the eve of the operation being transferred to Oxfordshire.

Wednesday 31 August 2011 and the Sunset Ceremony is for me another date I will never forget; walking down from the Police Station to the High Street in my best kit and medals. Around 7.30pm we followed Coxy and Mark Levitt, two of our former Inspectors, who both had their footprints engraved in the policing of Operation Entourage. It was quite an overwhelming feeling as we walked through the crowd; people wanted to shake our hands, it really was quite a humbling experience. When we finally managed to get to where we would stand it was slightly manic due to the volume of people present. With a little bit of persuasion, we helped the Town Council clear the many people who, without knowing, were standing on the small ceremonial area. Once they recognised this they moved to an area where they could watch the ceremony that Johnathan Bourne, Station Warrant Officer Nick Dale and members of the Royal British Legion had orchestrated.

With thousands present and the eyes of the nation sat at home watching live coverage on Sky News and BBC 24 News channels, a little bit of pressure was on Johnathan. After all, it was his desire that there should be a fitting end to the huge amount of respect that had been shown over the years, although he had possibly not calculated just how much interest it would create. In this town with the X factor appeal, it did not surprise us. The Mayor of Wootton Bassett, Councillor Paul Heaphy and The Reverend Canon Thomas Woodhouse took their positions on the dais as we looked at our watches and waited.

Dong!!! Dong!!! Dong!!! Dong!!! The unmistakable sound that always announced our arrival was on this occasion announcing the beginning of the end. The silence rippled through the thousands, just as it always did, when they heard the tolling of the Tenor Bell of St Bartholomew's Church. The sombre ambience it created was not missed by those present. At exactly 8pm Paul Heaphy made his opening speech to welcome thousands in the street, and millions more on the screens, to his little market town.

The ceremony unfolded as per the script; words were spoken, prayers were said, the band played. Then the tears flowed with the lowering of the Union flag to the sound of *Sunset;* it was beautifully orchestrated due to its simplicity. Standards were dipped as those who saluted did so proudly.

As the last bar of *Sunset* was concluded, the salutes came down but the standards remained lowered. It was just at this point there was a slight glitch in the proceedings amongst the 81 standards – yes, 81 – from all over the country came that night. Some were unsure exactly when to raise their standards back to the carry. For a few seconds it looked like some sort of Mexican wave as standards were raised then quickly lowered once again.

'No! Lower them back down,' in hushed voices were the words I could hear.

That was the difference between military precision and this wonderful town, just doing what they thought was the right thing to do. Everything they did was just to try their very best, almost with an innocence which for me made everything special, because it was done with so much sincerity.

Once the standards were in the correct position, all dipped, the ceremony continued. The Union flag was folded and handed to the Chairman of the Royal British legion. The two-minute silence followed; an opportunity to reflect on our own private thoughts. Mine, well I saw myself at the top end of the High Street watching the conductor paging the fallen towards where the grieving family stood and, yes, I could feel the emotions trying to be released.

The silence was brought to an end with the 'Exhortation' being recited by Maurice Baker; though this time in his role as President of his branch of the Royal British Legion:

'They shall grow not old; as we that are left grow old; age shall not weary them, nor the years condemn. At the going down of the sun and in the morning; we will remember them.'

The thousands replied and in doing so never have I heard four words spoken with so much sincerity: 'We will; remember them.'

The Reverend Canon then invited the band to sound the National Anthem as the community stood proud and sang with their allegiance to the Crown.

On completion of the final bar the standards this time were raised collectively into the carry.

The sacred Union flag was then carried to the dais almost like a newborn baby in the hands of the Royal British Legion Chairman, Ted Sharpe, which he presented to the Reverend Canon Thomas Woodhouse.

A few more words said, a final Prayer as the two men charged with the safety of this sacred gift from Bassett to Carterton, made their way to the alter in St Bartholomew's Church where it was blessed and remained overnight with a candlelit vigil.

The thousands remained where they stood and were deep in thought as the sombre music played. It was a beautiful service, simple, yet perfect, and as I looked around many unashamedly shed tears.

To announce the ceremony was concluded, Maurice Baker assumed his other role in the Royal British Legion – the 'parade marshal'. He first commanded the standard bearers to attention with his final words 'Standard Bearers Dismissed'. Their response was military precision as they all turned to the right, paused, marched three paces and then fell out.

The crowd applauded, then a voice, one from one of the thousands in the street, shouted out, 'Three cheers for Wootton Bassett... hip hip hooray,' and the war memorial witnessed a roar three times over, along with further tears to end this hugely emotional evening.

A few of us went for a few pints after those humbling scenes as guests of Mr Dale in his sergeant's mess at RAF Lyneham, which was the perfect end to the evening out of sight of the public and media.

Before leaving I wanted to do one final thing, to congratulate one very special man who epitomised all that is good in a person. Always behind the scenes, never seeking attention, always calm, the rock of the Town Council, whose surname should have been humility. There he was, just to the side when so many others were giving TV interviews. I grabbed his hand and held it tight and said, 'Johnathan Bourne, you did your town proud; it was an honour to have worked with you these last four years.' With him as always was his trusty lieutenant Michelle Temple who heard what I said; so with a kiss on her cheek I left the scene as I knew she would soon be in a flood of tears. Yep, I was ready for those beers in the sergeant's mess.

I enjoyed those couple of beers, they went down well, but I did not stay late as it was another long day and with another to follow in the morning, so I made my way home.

You know when you walk into a room and something is not right, well that is exactly how it felt when I got home. When I walked through the front door I found my wife Karen upset as she explained she had received a call from one of her best friends in Plymouth, Gillian Paull. Gillian was heartbroken; Joanne Weston, who was almost a surrogate daughter to her from a friendship that blossomed through employment, was the latest wife to feel the desolation from that dreaded knock on the door. Joanne was the wife of Sergeant Barry Weston, 42 Commando Royal Marines, who had been killed the eve before the Sunset ceremony. We knew Jo when she was employed by Gillian in Plymouth Pannier Market; the same location my wife had her café. Jo would have been about 17 then, and every morning she would come into the café for her doorstep toast and cuppa before she started work. She was always a character, full of mischief and fun, just a really lovely girl. That young girl grew up and got married to her soul mate who just happened to be an outstanding Royal Marine; and when their three daughters Jasmine, Poppy and Rose came along the family was complete.

I slumped down in my chair as Karen broke the news to me. I was absolutely gutted;

totally devastated beyond words that Jo's husband, who I did not know, had been killed and gutted that her three daughters would never see their father again.

That night I hardly slept after such an emotional day; a feeling of pride wiped out instantly on hearing this awful news, which was replaced with a feeling of guilt that we would not be able to support her on that most harrowing day that lay ahead.

CHAPTER 46

The following morning I was very subdued and I had to go to Carterton as part of the Wootton Bassett contingent which included: The Mayor, Town Council, members of the Royal British Legion, Police both local and the MDP including my Divisional Commander; so I could not opt out. The event was organised to hand over the Union flag as a symbol to transfer the respects and support for our nation's fallen from one community to another.

This ceremony was the complete opposite of what we had witnessed the previous evening, from simplicity with a few appropriate words from the Mayor and the Church. Carterton had the Prime Minister, Mr David Cameron, and numerous dignitaries who all appeared very keen to make their presence known in front of the mass of News Channels covering the event live.

As each speaker was replaced with another I do not think I heard one word, as my eyes were focused across the road where a vast amount of cameras, TV and paparazzi were perched like vultures on a purpose-built platform.

All I was thinking of was that this time next week, a friend of mine would be standing there distraught and prayed someone would be present to protect her.

I'm sure that the ceremonial handing over of the sacred gift, the Wootton Bassett Union flag, went the way the organisers wanted it to, but honestly I was just lost in my own thoughts feeling concern for a friend and her three girls.

We came to Carterton and with the symbolic handing over of the Union flag the town's spontaneous duties were done.

I had a few weeks holiday owing to unwind, relax and, more importantly, let go of the extraordinary happenings that had grown over these recent years. I was not kidding myself that after three weeks break that everything would once again be normal; four and a half years of deep sadness had to have an impact. As you have read I am not ashamed to share mine and this book is testament to how I still feel some years on, but, yes, it was to be a new beginning for us all.

Wootton Bassett would also be starting a new chapter in its own history. However, there was one final official ceremony and one of recognition from the highest level – Her Majesty Queen Elizabeth II.

Sunday 16 October 2011 would be the date the letters patent would be bestowed upon the town of Wootton Bassett. Perhaps that was the perfect opportunity for the community to move on.

CHAPTER 47

I t was always going to be a challenge for some to move forward and leave so much sadness behind. Never forgetting, but Wootton Bassett had to move on in its efforts to find out what normal was and in doing so, not feeling guilty to learn how to smile. So when an idea was presented to the Council of uniting many parts of the community together and raising smiles, there was no hesitation to listen to a proposal even though it initially may have seemed a little bizarre.

The project, or at this stage, the idea was from a lady who in her own way wanted to send thanks to a town close to her heart.

Tracey Rogers, along with many guests, had been invited to 10 Downing Street to celebrate 90 years of the Royal British Legion in June 2011.

On this day her thoughts were not of her own loss as she stood together with her stepmum, sister, sister-in law Brenda and her niece Alix in the presence of so many inspirational people. Those present included soldiers who were living with the devastating injuries that had forever changed their lives; widows and children of soldiers killed in action who had experienced the same emotions as her family when her brother Captain Mark Hale was repatriated through Wootton Bassett.

With a couple of glasses of wine her mind drifted on that journey home. If she had spoken openly about what was spinning in her head, her family would of thought she had lost it and certified her as mad.

Tracey had decided to set up a project whereby the people and community of Wootton Bassett could work together by releasing a record to raise funds which would provide support for bereaved families and injured soldiers.

Some people in life talk about it, others walk the talk; there was no doubting which pack of cards this lady had come from, and at times she felt someone above was driving her on.

I had read so many tributes about her amazing brother, whose repatriation I vividly remembered. That day in August 2009 was another day of much sadness yet a huge amount of respect shown by so many for the three heroes who returned home. Captain Mark Hale, Rifleman Daniel Wild also of 2nd Battalion, The Rifles and Lance Bombardier Matthew Hatton of 40th Regiment Royal Artillery, were returned with full military honours. So many people lined the streets that day and personally knew her brother Captain Mark Hale. When they spoke they did as if talking of a legend, he certainly was an icon in many of their eyes.

So when Tracey mentions she felt his presence from above driving her on, I feel the comfort and belief this gave her as she explains to me how this project came about:

'Initial contact was made with Mayor Paul Heaphy; the idea was to make a record and music video that captured the essence of this vibrant, community-spirited town. A way of moving on from the sad period of the repatriations, showing the world a different side of the town – the one the people of Wootton Bassett knew and also to raise some money for military charities.' At this point Tracey had considered a few options for the song although one really stood out, it was the Green Day hit *Wake Me Up When September Ends*. The reason for this was because it dealt with the death of the lead singer's father.

Tracey continued: 'It's about remembering someone and it references September, which is quite fitting in the light of the fact there were no more repatriations through Wootton Bassett from that month.'

So they had a song; next the location. With passion in her eyes, her words were clear and were said with so much emotion for so many personal reasons.

'The High Street would be the inspiration for the video, it had legendary representation; it had to be the backdrop.'

Tracey next approached Mark Kenna of Dream Base Studios in Wootton Bassett. Mark immediately committed his time, energy and expertise in bringing the story she wanted to tell to life. This was then further supported by dozens of amazing local people who drove the project forward through many difficulties over the coming weeks ... and this was the story they created together as Tracey later explained to the Mayor and the rest of the Wootton Bassett Town Councillors as she shared her vision with them:

'The male singer is holding a gerbera which represents his brother who has been repatriated through the town.

As he walks down the street, more and more people join him, support him, show him love and respect, the people of Bassett do this in their own unique way; they want to show him that life will still be colourful and full of fun.'

Tracey explains the importance of the route he walks:

'The singer is walking along the High Street although the opposite way to the way the cortège would go, as it was symbolic of a new start and turning things around.'

She continues with the script:

'This swell of love grows as he travels along the street, as he passes the war memorial. However, there is a tinge of sadness and remembering, just for a moment as the music slows.'

She had in mind a veteran soldier to stand adjacent to the war memorial who stood there on so many previous occasions. For this clip she had personally approached the perfect man to carry the ambience with pride and compassion, Ken Scott and this was why:

'Not only was he an old soldier but he did something remarkable which had touched her personally. Ken had taken the trouble to save all the love tokens that families had left at the war memorial during the repatriations. He couldn't bear to see them damaged or thrown away, so he had saved them all, in his own book of remembrance. Stood at the war memorial just to his side would be his lady friend who would be proudly holding this treasured album, close to her heart.

The final part of the video shows the family in the café, the parents, the widow, the child, the brother and the missing soldier given his place at the table. They are quietly getting on with their lives, never forgetting but beginning to smile again. The camera will then focus back out to the street where the people of Bassett have gone; they want to show their respect to the family by receding into the background quickly and not claiming any glory or wanting to impose themselves – so typical of Wootton Bassett.'

There was one other small challenge that Tracey had set herself and the rest of the wonderful team, as if this one was not enough to ponder. The project had to be completed by the end of September to coincide with the end of the repatriations and before the 'Royal' decree. After being spellbound with so much enthusiasm on hearing those words, the decision was simple and the Council gave their blessing. The project was called 'Wootton Bassett Rocks' where over 800 people were involved, including over 150 local people who were seen to be singing their hearts out on their own charity single.

It was simply brilliant, seeing so many people singing in the street who had so often wept but who had now learnt to smile, and while they smiled monies were being raised. Yep, Bassett was a community that certainly deserved the Queen's recognition that was soon to be bestowed upon it.

It really was a fabulous project maintaining that great community spirit. The beautiful florist lady, who had supplied so much comfort with flowers to so many grieving families over the years, was to be the catalyst to commence the start of the video. And so the story starts with that gesture, when she handed on this occasion a gerbera to the lead vocalist.

Then the video continues to perfection as per the script that of course had been tweaked by so many people in the production team, all motivated to getting it just right. A milkman on his delivery round, skate boarders whizz across in front of the singers as they walk down the street, pillow fighters engage in battle while a hockey match is in full flow on the other side of the road outside the chemist.

The Police and Ambulance service are on standby but not for public order in case the pillow fight gets out of hand, but to join in the chorus of this wonderful song as they cruise down either side of the singing group.

I am sure I saw Sergeant Martin Alvis singing his head off as he drove the police car with blue flashing lights; I told you earlier he was a top community man. With the same steady pace, the group gets bigger as they walk singing down the road. The Mayor joins in, he's not missing out and brings his family along, as they smile with all who are around.

Dancers, actors, singers and musicians, the junior town crier, sports and youth groups, Brownies, Girl Guides, Scouts and all waving at their friends as they walk by, then, like the others, fall in behind. Just like the Pied Piper in that famous German town they all sing with wide smiles across their faces.

The Royal British Legion bikers start up the engines of their huge bikes and take the lead through the streets. A band of men and women who, along with the standard bearers, wore their military insignia with so much pride. Yes, everyone played their part in this video, as they did for those humbling years. The bikers peel off as the singing group has grown from big to huge; most are from this generation who only know of the recent conflicts of Iraq and Afghanistan.

After you have read the script you now know why Ken Scott is at the war memorial. Proudly dressed in his formal battle dress uniform, the one he was issued with when he was about the age of those youngsters singing with a smile. I wondered as I saw him standing alongside his lady friend if his thoughts were similar to mine. How time has moved on, but between each generation a pride in our nation still runs strong.

The sporting side of Bassett is represented by the Rugby, Hockey and Martial Arts Clubs as the song continues along the street. The Fire Brigade form a guard of honour by the building on stilts, across the road up from the Summerfield store the local female choir sing the last verse.

The beautiful song starts to fade away just like the entourage of a community that followed; they know it is time to drift back and leave the vocalist to be alone. One step, two step, or even a few more, he reaches the 'Town Hall Tea Rooms' and enters through the door to the strumming of the electric guitar. He sits down at the table to join his family, the ones who are left behind and places the gerbera flower at the place setting of that symbolic empty seat. Then he looks out of the window in reflection of what had just taken place; but the streets are bare. Everyone has gone, only emptiness and a tinge of sadness lingers all around. This epitomises the people of Bassett; to give the family space having shown them so much respect.

I paused for thought when I watched the video for the first time, for me it had a massive impact when I saw a place setting empty at that table with a family sat around. I wondered if the empty seat was to reflect that a family had one special person missing, having been honoured to share the script I now find my observations were correct. I had said that Bassett had learnt once again to be normal and smile, well, if that's normal I can hear you say.

So did they complete the project in time? Of course they did. On 18 September 2011 it was finished and amazingly it was done in one take. If you look on the internet you will find 'Wootton Bassett Rocks'. How can you not watch it after reading this. If you open your mind and take in the story it tells it is sheer brilliance and outrageously unique, behind the fun, the laughter, the singing and the dancing was a message I now fully understand. The smiles and pride should still be worn by the 800 people who were involved in the so many sides of producing something so brilliant. In doing so funds were raised to help those inflicted from that conflict that many of us still find difficulty to understand.

From this amazing lady's mind came that production, or certainly the story she wanted to tell, so it seems only fitting for her to say a few personal words:

'I wanted to do something meaningful that involved as many people as possible from this wonderful community to remember my brother and other fallen heroes. To mark the end of an era of repatriations through Royal Wootton Bassett and also to raise much needed funds for military charities that focus on supporting bereaved families and also help and support wounded servicemen and women.'

I seriously think in doing that production, Tracey Rogers, Mark Kenna and your 800 friends, you did your brother and the other heroes proud!

CHAPTER 48

On a day of glorious sunshine there was an atmosphere in the town that was difficult to describe, one that I myself only understood on New Year's Eve, later that year. It was a historical date: Sunday 16 October 2011, seven months since the Prime Minister announced the great honour Her Majesty Queen Elizabeth II had authorised. The day had arrived when the Letters Patent were to be bestowed upon Wootton Bassett.

How is one meant to react when such a huge honour is bestowed upon them? What is the appropriate way to show gratitude for such prestige? Still in the back of their minds the townsfolk of Wootton Bassett only needed to close their eyes and they could see the hundreds of people who showed raw grief on this very High Street.

Yes, of course the community were proud, but it was getting the right balance. I think that's why not many people spoke to the media because quite simply they did not know the best way to answer the simple question: 'How do you feel being known as Royal Wootton Bassett?'

Just as in May when asked that same question, humility remained.

It was to be the final time the streets of Wootton Bassett were lined in relation to those humbling years I have now spoken of in this book. On this occasion it was to welcome HRH the Princess Royal for a very special ceremony.

It is only the third town in Britain to have such an honour bestowed on it, and the first for over 100 years. The town has a new flag with a golden lion, a symbol of royalty dating back to medieval times; new road signs and a new cake 'The Bassett Crown'. The Mayor of Wootton Basset, Paul Heaphy, said that the new motto for the town would be: 'We honour those who serve.'

To mark the occasion, shops and businesses on the High Street decorated their buildings with Union flags and the street was swept and made ready for the ceremony in the afternoon. Prime Minister David Cameron attended with his new Defence Secretary Philip Hammond and Sir Peter Wall, Chief of the General Staff.

With attention on military precision everything was orchestrated, this time under the watchful eye of Garrison Sergeant Major Bill Mott, the most senior non-commissioned soldier in the British Army. He is responsible for all ceremonial events in London, from providing guards of honour to orchestrating major occasions such as state visits, the State Opening of Parliament and the Queen's Birthday Parade. On this day he was in Wootton Bassett and personally measured the 355 paces from where the parade stepped off to the exact position HRH the Princess Royal would take the salute. Each of those 355 steps was in recognition of each of the fallen who had been repatriated through the town and nearby RAF Lyneham; including the ten killed when the Hercules aircraft was shot down in 2005. The Wootton Bassett March was specially written for the town by Major Curtis RM, but not for this event. It was written for an event in Portsmouth, but needless to say on a day such as this, it was the most appropriate music for the Band of the Royal Marines to play. British Legion members, the town band and the town crier, Owen Collier, all had a part in the proceedings, as did an RAF C17 Globemaster which once again dipped its wing, but this time in recognition of Royal Wootton Bassett. I sat just to the left of the dais and absorbed every word as the Mayor invited Her Royal Highness to speak.

'Mr Mayor, my Lord Lieutenant, distinguished guests, ladies and gentleman. I was delighted when the Queen asked me to present Letters Patent to Wootton Bassett.

Over the years I have enjoyed a close association with the town; officially opening the Police Station, the new secondary school and the CCTV suite in the Town Council Offices.

As many of you will know, I am the honorary Air Commodore to RAF Lyneham. Wootton Bassett has long shown its support for the service personnel based at Lyneham, and over the years the station personnel have talked fondly about the warmth of this community and the close links that they have enjoyed with the people of the town.

In January 2005, the crew of an RAF Hercules, from 47 Squadron, was lost in Iraq. I attended the repatriation ceremony at RAF Lyneham and was touched to learn of the hundreds of people that lined the High Street here in Wootton Bassett to pay their respects as the hearses passed through.

The local newspaper recorded: "That hundreds gathered along the route, bitterly cold winds no reason not to pay respect to those who gave their lives for freedom. Some bowed their heads, some crossed themselves, some stood to attention and others just stared in shocked disbelief as people paid their last respects in their own way."

The people of Wootton Bassett paid their respects in their own way, and they have continued to do so in the years that have followed. But without intention, you have also paid respect on behalf of the nation whose gratitude you have earned.

The award of Letters Patent is rarely bestowed and Wootton Bassett becomes only the third town in history to be recognised in this way, and the first in over 100 years.

Seldom does a community come together in the way Wootton Bassett has around repatriations. I would like to take a moment to pay tribute to the community, not only to its Civic Leaders, successive Mayors and Officers of the Royal British Legion, but also the Church leaders who have led the liturgy of repatriation, Police Officers who have given up their rest days to help the community pay its respects, young people who have been represented at repatriations, shopkeepers who step out to pay respects and the publicans like those at the Cross Keys who offer refreshments to the grieving families.

This is a community of depth, rich in tradition and secure in its sense of values.

Throughout this time the community has never lost sight of its simple and dignified aim of paying respect and in so doing, you have also respected the democratic freedoms we have in this country and for which the Armed Forces have fought so hard to protect.

The nation is proud of you and what you have done will never be forgotten.

On behalf of the Queen, I am delighted to present Letters Patent to the town of Wootton Bassett.'

The words spoken by HRH Princess Royal were powerful, sincere and the people of Wootton Bassett were proud to accept their royal recognition. But never far from everyone's mind was the fact that the privilege of Royal status was because of the high price paid by our Armed Forces.

It was a strange event as many people, although proud, quite simply did not understand the protocol of how one should react during the ceremony. It was a huge event to organise with much advice coming from many sources; it was a marvellous acknowledgment to Royal Wootton Bassett.

I remember the brief chat I had with the Prime Minister David Cameron and he was another I just politely reminded, in response to him telling me how proud he was of Carterton, that it was not a competition. Respects should be shown but there is no need for fabrication, people will come because for them it is the right thing to be done and there can be no other reason. Speaking to Her Royal Highness the Princess Royal shortly after the Prime Minister moved along, the compassion and sincerity in her voice was there for all to recognise and the genuine admiration held for the Wiltshire market town.

CHAPTER 49

Even with Royal status, to the locals this small market town will always just be Bassett as it was long before they were known throughout the land. They had an unassuming Town Council, a group of people who had an interest beyond local politics and a genuine empathy for their community in an effort to do their best.

In the Council Chambers there was a dedication to community issues. Of course they would not always agree; there would be debate in the appropriate manner. No egos, no scoring points, just one ambition – to do their best – to improve the quality of life in a market town which had not lost traditional, old fashioned values. Values which society was in danger of forgetting due to the speed and pace of modern life.

They first showed their true compassion, a sight never before seen, when, following the loss of a loved one, this wonderful community united as one. Without even knowing it they did something that caused a curiosity in the nation's eye by showing respect with compassion for their brothers just five miles down the road. The darkest hour in that quaint village's history, when Lyneham saw so much sorrow, was, as the records show, when on 30 January 2005, RAF Lyneham lost one of its aircraft RAF C-130K XV179, taking ten on board to their graves.

When those ten fallen were repatriated home and later escorted to GWH (Great Western Hospital) it set the foundation as to how the town, led by its Council, would stand along that unknown High Street and show their utmost respect.

Yes, in 2005 the people of Bassett did not hide and were there to support their neighbours in their grief. No one anticipated then the significance of that humane compassion that would in time be seen again and again plagued with further grief. Each Mayor, who was proud to wear the regalia and pendant of their own little town, did so without trepidation, but with integrity, sincerity and an honest belief in leading a Council that always tried to do things for the best.

Percy Miles, who held office when the first repatriations passed through the High Street in April 2007, stood at the war memorial wearing two hats or maybe even three. Percy, an ex-Sergeant Major, and at the time the youngest in the British Army, wore his medals presented to him during his career along with the Mayor's chains proudly around his neck. Behind all that decoration was a Wiltshire man who genuinely did care as he stood to show respects with everyone else who was there.

As each Mayor took the post they followed the example that had been set, each with their own personality and, as years progressed, found themselves often in the limelight of the nation's press.

From Percy Miles taking the first salute in his last month in office, the respects he had started were continued throughout Mayor Audrey Wannell's 12-month tenure. Air Chief Marshall Sir Clive Loader presented a parchment scroll to Mayor Mike Leighfield at the appreciation parade in 2008. A wonderful speech was given by Mayor Steve Bucknell as the town was recognised for its humility in honouring the nation's fallen at the Millies awards in December 2009. Then, in April 2011, Mayor Mary Champion was flying the Bassett flag high as a pillion rider welcoming the bikers back. Six months later Mayor Paul Heaphy was deeply honoured to accept the 'Letters Patent' from Her Majesty the Queen as he stood before everyone on national television dressed in his ceremonial regalia and gown.

No egoistic status was sought or wanted as they held that position in office, in their tenure they stood with the true feeling of representing their market town.

There were many events that the Town Council were invited to over those years as the country fell in love with a community that quite simply cared. The list of those invites and engagements are far too many to mention, but to give you a flavour they were no strangers to dignitaries in high places.

They were invited to 10 Downing Street to discuss the appropriate recognition for Wootton Bassett, which is how the Letters Patent became a symbol to reflect on the town as a whole and not individuals. They were invited to many military events, for example, the Defence Academy just up the road at Shrivenham, the Royal Navy in Portsmouth and even NATO in Brussels as the name of this community spread across the globe. There was even a visit to the Races in York, where a horse was named after the town. Mary the Champion of the horse riding world, took Melanie Nicholls from the Council office to receive another award on behalf of Wootton Bassett. I have found one fact that keeps on repeating itself throughout this book, there are no egos floating, but a team ethos of working together, a friendship forming and transcending the community of a very special place. From the Church with the Reverend Canon Thomas Woodhouse, the Mayors and Council of the town, the Police and of course RAF Lyneham working in harmony to honour the fallen, they became a community who become so loved by a nation for showing so much respect. Behind the scenes so much went on to get things right, people who by working together had formed a very special bond. Away from public exposure from the interest of inquisitive eyes, a team of people worked together far beyond their normal job description and just because they knew what they were doing was right.

No event was ever signed off without crossing their fingertips as they dotted the I's crossed the T's, answering the phone a thousand times to give a simple instruction or advice after the words they had typed went on public display.

My, were they a proud bunch. You had to take a step back sometimes and pinch yourself and acknowledge with the greatest of respect that these were a small market town's administrators, employed for the everyday support of a town's Council, not the nation's events planners. Yet during their time in this very special office, there would be no surprise to hear them in dialogue with Whitehall's top brass, Clarence House, Buckingham Palace and the Prime Minister in Downing Street.

Yes, for them, answering the phone was never to be the same; on the other end of the phone be it from Royals or Politicians, Military or Public the response was always the same; no one could mistake their Wiltshire charm. So who were the team I am so proud to name? Johnathan Bourne the Town Clerk with Michelle Temple, Kalpesh Patel, Avril Reeves, Lyn Reynolds, Susan Gavin, Melanie Nicholls, Emily Maiden and on the CCTV in the early days was Mike Tupman, then Dai Williams, who I served with in the Police.

So many times a letter or e-mail would add to Johnathan's workload and he would probably sit shaking his head wondering how to take on this latest challenge. A true gent was this man; never giving the impression of being under stress, always in control and deflecting pressure off his team. Respected across the county, further afield and more. Yet, with the latest challenge he held in his hand he would speak to his trusty lieutenants and brief them with a plan.

I could just imagine Michelle's reaction, bursting into laughter on hearing the latest Bassett challenge. The opposite of Johnathan, where he was quiet Michelle was the tornado who would light up the room and create a passion to shout 'Come on guys let's go.' What a wonderful inspiration to have in any team.

Kalpesh was the accountant who looked after the pounds shillings and pence but always a man who would get involved in assisting the girls in the front office. And, oh my goodness, those ladies in that front office, no matter what time of day they would always stop what they were doing to show that Wiltshire welcome of hospitality and sincerity as you walked in through the front door. Those were the faces many saw when they walked in off the street; always a welcome smile, not because it was the best impression to give but because it was natural to them all.

Dai Williams was the CCTV manager, another man who fell in love with the town having now retired. Before he hung his uniform up, he was often seen on repatriation days with his dog carrying out the security searches with the police. They were the perfect team and maybe it was by fate that they all came together at the right time, to complement each other in getting things done.

On each sad occasion when we escorted the fallen through, they would line up outside their office next to the butchers. Two groups of people, those from the Council offices and the butchers in time-honoured regalia reassured me that this was a really traditional town. As I lead the cortège past their doors I would raise my right hand in their direction as a form of a salute; their eyes could not disguise that genuine deep sadness just before they bowed their heads. I was proud to know those who were employed by the Bassett Council then. I'm even prouder now to call them

Royal Wootton Bassett as that honour was truly fitting to recognise this wonderful Wiltshire market town.

The words I have written can only scratch the surface of appreciation but what better a man than The Reverend Canon Thomas Woodhouse who always spoke with passion about this wonderful town to share a few more. Just as he did when he gave a speech to honour the community:

'*We honour those who serve*: I have used the words of the town's new motto – we honour those who serve – to cast a light onto the selfless actions of men and women thousands of miles away from Wiltshire, actions that have defined the last four years in Wootton Bassett. The town council have chosen their motto very carefully, believing that it reflects a desire to honour all who serve, across every discipline of service. Wootton Bassett or Royal Wootton Bassett as it is now styled has been my home for six and half years. It is impossible to have imagined in 2005 what lay before us, back then we used to tell people we live in Wootton Bassett, a town near Swindon, now we have dropped Swindon!

The events that took place in, through and over Wootton Bassett between April 2007 and August 2011 did not change the world! However, by their activity the townsfolk showed that change is possible when communities stand together – in our case – in silence with one single purpose. When together we honour those who serve!

The story of Wootton Bassett is long – in keeping with the histories of most Wiltshire market towns. We know what it means to offer hospitality to strangers. Indeed towns like Wootton Bassett and Chippenham owe much to the passing trade of generations: it was just that for the months of Repatriation our guests were honoured in a very particular way.

The Armed Forces across Wiltshire have long been a valued part of the county's life and in particular for Wootton Bassett, our relationship with RAF Lyneham is important. Until flying ceased from the airbase, generations of people had looked with excitement upwards to see what was going to land.

This excitement was tempered from April 2007 by a solemn gravity, as people anticipated the Liturgy of Repatriation. The sight of the police escort and the hearse with the coffin draped with the Union flag was always sombre and always poignant as it moved down the High Street.

This was initially an interruption in the normal bustling activity of everyday life which you expect in a market town. People always stopped what they were doing, looked, and responded in their own way. However, the cumulative memory of these events adds to the effect on everyone who witnesses.

The great thing for us in Wootton Bassett is that we were not left as individuals trying inadequately to make sense of it; we approached it as a community. Numbers attending at the roadside increased and media coverage meant that an informal, almost ad hoc gathering gained a momentum of its own.

At their heart, however, the gatherings, the Liturgy of Repatriation, remained a response of the community of Wootton Bassett. People who were strangers became friends and, on occasion, found themselves offering support and encouragement, building up community without ever realising they were doing so.

There was great sadness at the loss of young lives in their prime, and concern for grieving families. But the townsfolk gathered, honoured the dead, showed concern and friendship for the families and friends of the dead, and returned to their everyday tasks until called on again to stand and 'honour those who serve.'

And as you all know they did honour all those who served and the impact of that was not lost when you read the letter received by the Town Council from an unknown soldier. As you read these sombre words, no one can miss the huge amount of pain and sadness he is feeling from the conflict that he has fought. Who wrote these words? We may never know, but they are in here so his message can be passed on.

Dear Sir / Madam,
I am writing this letter to thank you, your staff and all the residents for all the help and support you have given me, my friends and their families during what has been a very difficult time for all.

The attached poem was written by me in early 2011 and I have wanted to send it to you for a long time but lacked the courage to see it through. The reason I wrote this poem was because in 2010 I returned home from my third tour of Afghanistan. As I left many of my friends from my previous unit went out for what was their first tour and for some it turned out to be their last.

In July 2010 my best friend was shot in the neck and left with life changing injuries. Between July and Remembrance Day 2010 I visited your town three times and watched three friends being driven down the High Street; this had a profound effect on me and I was ill for some time.

I have just spent the week before Christmas with my best friend and he is well and truly on the road to recovery and so am I. I am about to prepare to go on my fourth and final tour of Afghanistan as I am coming to the end of my military career as an Infantier after 22 years' service. I wanted to send this off whilst I had the time, as you can imagine I'm going to be very busy over the coming weeks getting ready to go away.

I hope you like it and I hope it shows what a difference you made to me during those days. You are a special town filled with special people and fully deserve to be recognised for all your amazing support.

Thank you Royal Wootton Bassett.

Regards,

A grateful Soldier

Then when I read the poem I thought, is it fate that this has to be the title of my book, a symbol of mutual respect of a soldier to Wootton Bassett and those who lined the 46 miles route.

46 MILES

If I should fall in that far foreign land,
With my blood sweat and tears soaked up in the sand.
I shall not fear or fall with regret,
The 46 miles will never forget.
I won't lay to rest or just drift away,
46 miles will have something to say.
I have one last task, one more mission to be done,
46 miles before the going down of the sun.

As we step off, uncertain if it's our last,
I think of my friends that have already passed
I remember the silence as Wootton Bassett stood still,
Shoulder to shoulder the High Street would fill.
Curiously as I stood, I felt so at ease,
Surrounded by strangers outside the Cross Keys.
I have one last task, one more mission to be done,
46 miles before the going down of the sun.

From Tarmac to Motorway its 46 miles in all,
Police stand over me, keeping me safe standing tall.
They lead the way and watch over my kin,
For this I thank with all I have been.
The young and old fill 46 miles together,
Flags and banners, salutes in all weather.
I have one last task, one more mission to be done,
46 miles before the going down of the sun.

This is how we go to these far foreign lands,
Where our blood, sweat and tears are soaked up in the sand.
Wootton Bassett did welcome us home,
Standing side by side our families were shown.
We have done our best and given our all,
The nation remembers 46 miles stands tall.
I have one last task one more mission to be done,
Thank you Royal Wootton Bassett from a nation's grateful son.

You have to pause and absorb those words; it feels wrong to just move on, or maybe like me you read both the letter and the poem again. I reflected on what I had just read for even though he has no fear, the trauma is clear and I pray that one day his pain will be gone.

CHAPTER 50

S tation Warrant Officer Nick Dale and Major Marcus Elliot-Square call it
military precision; Wootton Bassett called it honour, dignity and respect. When
you mention F.A. Albin & Sons Funeral Directors, add to that list of words,
compassion, sincerity and professionalism at its best.

Barry Albin-Dyer OBE, JP, DL is the owner and Chairman of F.A. Albin & Sons, the
World renowned Funeral Director and Undertakers with whom he has been for over
45 years, since he was 13! He's the author of several books and one day he might even
write another in relation to the repatriations and the humbling scenes that his team
saw far too often.

I heard Barry speak once on a TV interview of what unfolded before his eyes; how
the small market town just grew from just a few into something he never thought he
would witness in his lifetime:

> 'From the very early days in April 2007 when people would come out of their
> homes or out from the shops to show respect, and at the war memorial, a small
> group stood who wished to salute. That few grew into larger numbers and when
> requests were made for the cortège to be slowed down the conductors paged
> and paused at the war memorial for those desires to be established.'

But for the funeral team who I got to know well over the years, their duties started
well before the repatriation.

From the first sounding of Op Minimise the call would be for the undertaker to stand
by and fly out into the combat zone, on an RAF aircraft to bring the fallen home. Lee
Cook, one of the team, shared one of those experiences with me which for me shows the
dedication of the company. He was out in downtown Baghdad having arrived as a soldier
had been killed. While he was out in theatre a further incident occurred with another
loss of life. It was suggested that he should go out with the armed convoy of vehicles to
recover the fallen soldier. When he was given his brief, it suddenly made Deptford seem
a much safer place to go out alone in the middle of the night. Body armour and helmet
replaced his top hat and tails as his heart beat faster than when he worked out in the
gym. He was strapped in tightly in the armoured truck; the engines roared and with a
thrust he jumped forward as they moved into hostile terrain. To his left and right the
soldiers were armed to the hilt for his protection as his nerves set in. I think it is fair to
say he was slightly out of his comfort zone; who would not feel concerned, but to his
credit he went with those armed troops and brought the soldier home.

As a team they did so much more than page so many heroes with their immaculate gait through Wootton Bassett High Street. But when they did I often wondered what went through the minds of the Albin Funeral Team, in particular the conductors and the hearse drivers throughout that emotional day. This was not like any other funeral due to the rawness of grief displayed, initially at the repatriation ceremony when the conductor would be separated from that heartbroken family by just a few feet.

From there they moved the loved ones coffin into the Chapel of Rest, out of sight of invading eyes, which they did with awesome dignity and respect. Everything in slow motion with almost military precision, the coffin would flow on their shoulders in preparation of the family needing that time alone. After that private service the family would make their way to Bassett to be comforted by some they did and didn't know.

Then the undertakers would carry this precious fallen soldier and feed his coffin into the hearse. Once secured, the cortège would join the police and we would escort them up the road.

At St Bartholomew's Church I often felt we left the conductor on his own, the only reassurance that he was not alone was the tolling of the Tenor Bell in his ear. Yet on each occasion they paged with an immaculate gait, slowly towards an emotion that many lesser men with that responsibility may fear.

Hundreds, sometimes thousands, would line those streets and this lonely man would be exposed to it all, be it in Bassett or on the TV screen. One loss of composure would destroy the dignity, honour and ambience he and the Tenor Bell created, which is why the attention to detail made them so professional and respected.

With professionalism, compassion, sincerity, the lot, this band of brothers never let anyone down; with panache and so much grace they brought the fallen home.

Tens, twenties and sometimes many more would be grieving around each hearse, dealing with a rawness they had never felt before, but the drivers remained focused on what their responsibilities entailed. I do not know how they dealt with their own composure and defusing after each repatriation.

The story of F.A. Albin & Sons Funeral Directors in this chapter of their own history is really a book within a book. I hope that I have been able to express the utmost respect in words that I have for them, from all those humbling scenes we shared together over those 53 months.

I found a documentary about them scrolling the internet that portrays all the words I use and so many more, they were chosen for a six series documentary called *Don't Drop the Coffin*. Although the series does not cover any of the repatriations it portrays the personalities that looked after those who paid the ultimate sacrifice.

If you view the series you can see and hear in the interviews the sincerity, the compassion, the general empathy of the team that was charged with caring for the fallen. I can't encourage anyone strongly enough to view a clip from that TV series. Episode 4 presents all the ingredients that demonstrate the old fashioned true family values of this awe-inspiring company. Just before Christmas they hold their own remembrance service in their memorial garden each and every year, a service one day I would be honoured to attend.

I viewed the series with pride in knowing all the team, not just those who came to Bassett, but the administration behind the scenes. I saw what happened behind the scenes from a visit to their hub in Bermondsey, South London. I attended with a group of police officers who, for their duties, wished to understand the role of the undertakers in returning the fallen home. It really is a family who cared from top to bottom; generations of understanding the closeness of each and every one, checking the welfare at the start of each day whilst they sat around the breakfast table for the most important meal of the day.

It was during that meal that their duties would be shared, without asking they knew each other's mannerisms and could see if one was struggling, as deep sadness is something that is difficult to avoid no matter how professional one would like to be. Visiting them on their home ground just reinstates the dedication, sincerity and compassion they showed each and every one of our country's fallen. I got to know these people well, with mutual respect, and they had an ambience that was most welcome from a generation I thought had disappeared with the years.

For anyone who lost a loved one I cannot reassure you enough how proficient and skilled this dedicated team of 52 were. I really hope the words I have written will give anyone reading this tribute comfort in knowing the level of care that was administered when returning each precious loved one home.

Maybe one day you may find yourself in the vicinity of their premises in Culling Road, Bermondsey. Give them a call or pay them a visit and see their memorial garden or the Albin Museum which was opened by HRH Princess Anne in December 2009. If you do that you will see their sincerity when you speak to them and gain further comfort in their genuine compassion.

I say this without any trepidation because believe you me F. A. Albin & Sons Funeral Directors were proficient in their duty of care.

CHAPTER 51

Before I close there are a couple more chapters that I would like to share as, on a personal note, I had one further engagement to complete, in fact two, one I was totally oblivious of until the end of the year. The first was an invite I received to stand with the guard of honour around the Cenotaph on Remembrance Sunday, 13 November 2011. With uniform, best bib and tucker all packed, I arrived in the hotel for the formal brief on the Saturday night. The first thing on the agenda was the timings for the following day which took me by surprise when they mentioned breakfast was at 5am and drill an hour later. Although surprised at what time we were starting, this was an occasion that I would have swam the Thames to be on parade, as some things are special and this one certainly was for me.

Four am was soon upon us and to be honest on such occasions I did not value sleep; I was too caught up with the honour of standing on parade. Two hours later, with breakfast finished, we were transported to the Foreign and Commonwealth Office quadrangle to refresh our basic marching skills. Guardsmen, we were not, but pride got us to the start line so we could all march in step and halt. A last sip of coffee and we had just enough time to ease springs, as standing on parade for two hours in the cold could be a challenge. The time had come when we were all lined up to march on, two contingents, members of the emergency services were finally called to attention. The words 'Quick March' were heard and the mass bands did the rest. Never had I felt so proud to serve the Crown and we even kept in step. We marched directly across to the far side of the road; I am in the rear rank, the one adjacent to the hundreds in the crowd. Unbelievable but true, I hear a voice shout out my name as we march. I turn my head and my old Inspector, Graham Jewell, makes his presence known. Some time later he kindly sent me the images he had taken for my own personal nostalgia. We come to our halt and form up into our allocated positions. The contingents of Royal Navy, Royal Marines and Royal Air Force are on the far side of the road; the British Army is to our right, with the Cenotaph directly in front of where I stood.

Once in position we stood at ease, waiting for the orders to brace and stand straight; as we waited the bands in the centre of the road up to our left played military music that I had heard so many times before.

I see Garrison Sergeant Major Bill Mott marching up and down Whitehall, saluting every time he makes a pass of the Cenotaph. The last time I met him was in our little High Street, exactly four weeks ago; I am tempted to say hello, but thought best not as he might lock me up for talking on his parade.

It was an amazing experience to stand on a parade with so much history around.

I had done my research and I knew when we heard a certain British patriotic song that we would be under way. Until that time, I just took in the atmosphere of that sombre setting.

Then suddenly the unmistakable sound as the massed bands commenced the opening of *Rule, Britannia!* originating from the poem by James Thomson and set to music by Thomas Arne in 1740. Could they possibly have known or imagined the impact that they had created, particularly on days and settings like this. I had watched the Remembrance Day Service several times before on the BBC but being present especially as part of the guard of honour was a very proud moment and one that I will always treasure. Those watching the Remembrance Sunday Service on the BBC at home would see what was unfolding before my eyes, but what they were next to view on their screens, those of us on the parade could not see.

The impact of that interview being shown was equally captivating but for different reasons, as a nation viewed the trauma of a man being interviewed who had lost his son. Royal Marine Paul Warren from Charlie Company, 40 Commando Royal Marines, was killed in Afghanistan on Monday 21 June 2010. The interview began. The words of a broken man were exposed to all. The hurt, the sadness, and yet his overwhelming pride was witnessed by millions as Cliff Warren spoke about his son:

'He was like any other boy full of mischief, full of fun and I can never see him now as I speak, without that smile. A smile that even when he needed to be told off, I just smiled back at him. Even from as young as eight he knew what he wanted; he just wanted one thing, to be a British soldier. That time came around and if Paul wanted to do things he only knew one way, he was going to join the best and he enlisted in the Royal Marines. Getting his Green Beret was outstanding. The 22 June 2007 our family saw the smartest man that ever walked this earth pass out for duty. God, was I one proud dad, just like his mam, brothers, grandad and grandma. I'm sure it was the same for every family present; those lads were immaculate on parade. But, if you pass out fit for duty there was only one place calling and we dreaded the thought; then suddenly he is out there. He flew out on his first tour of Afghanistan in September 2008. He returned in March 2009 and the homecoming was like all the best days in my life coming at once: proud, delighted and the biggest feeling of all, sheer relief. I thought well, he's done that, got it out of his system, let him do something else, see some of the things they advertise in the Marines. But Paul was who he was, as much as we feared, he decided he wanted to go back to Afghanistan and he went back out there with 40 Commando. It was Father's Day, then the phone rings and hearing Paul was, well how do you explain in words, the simple word is relief; he was safe. I love all my sons but all parents will tell you when one is in a place of danger those you worry about for obvious reasons are always on your mind. The cards and messages I had received from Paul's brothers Neil and Richard were equally valued as we are a close family. When those same simple words were said by Paul later that day then emotions get involved, as they did when I heard in my ear Happy Father's Day Dad.'

Happiness though with a cloud always hovering, reminding Cliff where his youngest son was. Although, yes, that night they went to bed with the comfort of Paul's voice still in their ears. The camera zooms in and no words were spoken as Cliff sits for that brief moment very deep in thought. Cliff describes how he and his wife Lynn were sitting on the settee from where they can see into the street. He then continues: 'I saw a man with a black robe on, that's strange,' and as Cliff speaks his face goes white as he once again sees that image in his memory and tells the viewer that the gentleman is a priest.

'I had to stand up and go to the window,' he tells the interviewer who had taken Cliff back to that exact moment he can never blank out. The viewers are transfixed reliving this awful moment with a man they do not know, listening to every word he speaks. Cliff fights to keep his composure as he tries to tell of an experience that is so raw: 'I had automatically realised but did not know why; I was saying to myself, No! and repeating it, No! No! No! inside my head. And as I did, two Marines got out of the vehicle and followed the man in black.'

Everyone watching this poor man could not have done so without seeing his grief. He tried, but stuttered, then tried again, attempting to spit from his mouth the most painful words, which would not come out: 'I knew Paul had been killed.'

Cliff's words are spoken with excruciating pain as the country falls in sorrow. What a brave man wanting so much to tell millions how much he loved Paul, trying to keep his dignity as this father spoke with a heart that had been ripped out. Trying so desperately hard to tell the country how his little smiling lad grew into a Royal Marine and was killed in a war while so very young. The footage of a tortured man fades away then returns to show Cliff standing in a cemetery overlooking Paul's headstone, gripping his wife Lynn's hand tightly.

The camera zooms in on the Headstone.

Paul Warren
Marine P064885K
Royal Marines
21 June 2010. Age 23

Below the inscription, is the Royal Marine Globe and Laurel Corps Badge in the centre of the cross. Cliff, wearing the Elizabeth Cross on his lapel, once again starts to speak: 'I feel close to Paul when I am here stood at his grave, I really do feel him with me.' Then Cliff shakes his head, 'He wouldn't like it you know, the attention, the flowers on his grave. He liked to be the grey man, the low profile, keep under the radar.' That distant look in Cliff's eyes; he can see his son as he speaks, 'Yep, that was Paul.'

The interview continues but has now returned back to his front room and the producer captures a poignant personal moment. Cliff is on a sofa with Paul's Green Beret placed by his side with his hand caressing it, as if stroking his son's head. There is a pause while Cliff composes himself with so much dignity and refers to his son's beret: 'When I hold this I feel I have part of Paul with me.' The camera zooms in. There is so much pain in Cliff's eyes; then the image slowly fades away and as it does it was not hard to imagine a father and son together on that same settee.

Those who watched that interview must have felt compassion and sympathy on seeing the devastation of a father who has lost his precious son. And if they did, they would also understand that 'Remembrance Day' was not just one Sunday a year to those who lost loved ones, each and every day is a day to remember.

The BBC reporter brought his viewers back to where I was stood as the Royal Party made their way to begin the Remembrance Service and we were brought to attention. The Royal Horse Artillery then fired the gun to commence the two-minute silence. Never had I been so deep in thought through the two-minute silence. My eyes were looking in the direction of that huge Cenotaph monument in Whitehall, but my mind was elsewhere. My memory was showing a movie that replayed the raw grief that we witnessed in that little market town High Street 168 times. I saw in my mind 345 coffins draped in our Union flag; families not in silence but breaking their hearts, an image I could not get out of my head.

That was the true cost of conflict, no matter what spin is put on it to justify a politician's rationale of why our country had upped arms to fight another war. Although I will remain true to my word that this story will not go into that debate. The ceremony, the march past, was of course a proud one and for some two hours I stood watching the pomp, the swagger of thousands who had served Her Majesty's Crown. After we marched off the parade, we were halted in the quadrangle of the Foreign and Commonwealth Offices and dismissed to return back home.

I got changed in this vast room within the building and I had a two-minute chat with Sir Hugh Orde, our contingent commander for the parade that day. As I left, I shook hands, thanking him for the honour of being present on this Remembrance Sunday parade.

I threw my bag on my back and walked along Whitehall with one last look at the Cenotaph still deep in thought as I made my way up the road. Pubs and cafés along the street were bursting with hundreds of people wearing their demob suits. Berets and medals proudly worn and why not, I thought, they had done their time. In different circumstances I would have joined in, but maybe the movie that had earlier played in my mind, meant for me today was just not the right moment.

Four hours later I was in my home laid on the sofa with Karen for another debrief and realised just how deeply the four years of sadness had penetrated my brain.

CHAPTER 52

When I stared to write this story I was unsure where it should end as I have released so much sadness in writing this book. In a conversation with a friend she mentioned something I was previously unaware of, and it is for that reason I wish to close this final chapter of my manuscript in what I hope is an appropriate way.

When Wootton Bassett received Royal recognition with the Letters Patent and was to be called Royal Wootton Bassett, I mentioned that people were unsure how to react with the honour bestowed upon them.

I also mentioned that later the same year, on New Year's Eve, I found myself equally confused and it was then as the announcement was made that I truly understood how people felt back in October during that ceremony.

If you remember they were reluctant to answer the question. How do you feel being bestowed this honour? Immense pride, even embarrassed, and most certainly confused. What is the correct way to react? They were conscious of possibly coming across insensitive, but perhaps there was no need to say anything at all as it had all been said before.

When I was asked in an interview by Katie Stallard on Sky News a day or so before the Sunset Ceremony how did I feel having been involved?

I replied then: 'If what we have done over the last four and a half years or so has given the families some small comfort that we care, then in that case I'd be immensely proud to have been involved in something that's enhanced the dignity, the honour and the respect of the fallen.'

On New Year's Eve 2011 that was my answer again and it will be the answer I will always give. Prior to the day of the investiture, Jenny Brown who by now was a real family friend, made contact. When she did I was once again humbled by the words she said to me, which eased the slight embarrassment I had genuinely felt. During our conversation, I asked her permission for one small gesture I wished to make and to that she gave her consent.

On Friday 2 March 2012 at Windsor Castle, I stood before Her Majesty Queen Elizabeth II. When The Queen spoke of the pride in seeing what the community of Royal Wootton Bassett did during those years, she continued, that I should be equally as proud in the honour bestowed upon me.

I thanked her, by saying, 'Your Majesty, Mam, of course we are immensely proud in what we did, but for me and for many others who were involved, it is not about us.' I brought her attention to a blue wristband I wore: 'It is about the fallen like the name on this wrist band, Royal Marine Adam Brown, who deserves never to be forgotten.'

'Absolutely,' was the Monarch's reply as she shook my hand that displayed the blue band; my time to bow and move away.

What I had not known at that time was the name on the wristband had also met Her Majesty The Queen almost 20 years earlier.

When I told Jenny about the conversation I had had with her Majesty, she told me that when Adam was age seven he presented the Queen with a 'posy of flowers'. It was in 1992 at South Railway Jetty in Portsmouth Dockyard prior to Royal Yacht *Britannia* departing with the Queen and Duke for their Western Isles cruise. It is for that reason that this short story is included as memories are so very important in what must have been a wonderful treasured moment for a mother seeing her little boy that day.

It is for those memories of our fallen that I have written this book after my duties were done. In doing so my biggest hope is that it may give some small comfort for those left behind. That you know your loved one is not forgotten and with sincerity and compassion, I vow to thee, I genuinely did care.

PAGES OF REMEMBRANCE

They shall grow not old, as we that are left grow old:

Age shall not weary them, nor the years condemn.

At the going down of the sun and in the morning

We will remember them.

BRITISH FATALITIES IN IRAQ

I t is with very deep regret that the Ministry of Defence has confirmed the following fatalities suffered during Operation TELIC.

A total of 179 British Armed Forces personnel or MOD civilians have died serving on Operation TELIC since the start of the campaign in March 2003.

Of these, 136 were killed as a result of hostile action.

Forty-three are known to have died either as a result of illness, non-combat injuries or accidents, or have not yet officially been assigned a cause of death pending the outcome of an investigation. The balance of these figures may change as inquests are concluded. The following list of the fallen is in chronological order.

Private Ryan Wrathall, 1st Battalion The Princess of Wales's Royal Regiment, age 21

Corporal Lee Churcher, 20th Armoured Brigade, aged 32

Lance Corporal David Kenneth Wilson, 9 Regiment Army Air Corps, aged 27

Sergeant Duane 'Baz' Barwood, 903 Expeditionary Air Wing, Royal Air Force, aged 41

Guardsman Stephen Ferguson, 1st Battalion Scots Guards, aged 31

Corporal Lee Fitzsimmons, Royal Marines, aged 26

Lance Corporal Sarah Holmes, 29 Postal Courier and Movement Regiment, aged 26

Sergeant Mark Stansfield, 32 Close Support Squadron, UK Logistic Battalion, aged 32

Sergeant Eddie Collins, the Parachute Regiment, aged 33

Lance Sergeant Chris Casey, 1st Battalion, Irish Guards, aged 27

Lance Corporal Kirk Redpath, 1st Battalion, Irish Guards, aged 22

Leading Aircraftman Martin Beard, No 1 Squadron Royal Air Force Regiment, aged 20

Private Craig Barber, 2nd Battalion The Royal Welsh, aged 20

Corporal Steve Edwards, 2nd Royal Tank Regiment, aged 35

Lance Corporal Timothy Darren Flowers, The Corps of Royal Electrical Mechanical Engineers aged 25

Snr Aircraftman Matthew Caulwell, No 1 Squadron Royal Air Force Regiment, aged 22

Snr Aircraftman Christopher Dunsmore, Royal Auxiliary Air Force Regiment, 504 Squadron, aged 29

Snr Aircraftman Peter McFerran, No 1 Squadron Royal Air Force Regiment, aged 24

Corporal Christopher Read, of 158 Provost Company, 3rd Regiment Royal Military Police, aged 22

Lance Corporal Ryan Francis, 2nd Battalion The Royal Welsh, aged 23

Rifleman Edward Vakabua, 4th Battalion The Rifles, aged 23

Corporal Paul Joszko, 2nd Battalion The Royal Welsh (The Royal Regiment of Wales), aged 28

Private Scott Kennedy, Black Watch, 3rd Battalion The Royal Regiment of Scotland, aged 20

Private James Kerr, Black Watch, 3rd Battalion The Royal Regiment of Scotland, aged 20

Corporal John Rigby, 4th Battalion The Rifles, aged 24

Major Paul Harding, 4th Battalion The Rifles, aged 48

Lance Corporal James Cartwright, Badger Squadron, 2nd Royal Tank Regiment, aged 21

Corporal Rodney Wilson, 4th Battalion The Rifles, aged 30

Corporal Jeremy Brookes, 4th Battalion the Rifles, aged 28

Private Kevin Thompson, Royal Logistic Corps, aged 21

Major Nick Bateson, Royal Corps of Royal Signals, aged 49

Rifleman Paul Donnachie, 2nd Battalion The Rifles, aged 18

Kingsman Alan Joseph Jones, 2nd Battalion The Duke of Lancaster's Regiment, aged 20

Corporal Ben Leaning, The Queen's Royal Lancers, aged 24

Trooper Kristen Turton, The Queen's Royal Lancers, aged 27

Colour Sergeant M L Powell, The Parachute Regiment, aged 37

Sergeant Mark J McLaren, Royal Air Force, aged 27

Second Lieutenant Joanna Yorke Dyer, Intelligence Corps, attached to The Duke of Lancaster's Regiment, 2nd Battalion, aged 24

Corporal Kris O'Neill, Royal Army Medical Corps, aged 27

Private Eleanor Dlugosz, Royal Army Medical Corps, aged 19

Kingsman Adam James Smith, 2nd Battalion The Duke of Lancaster's Regiment, aged 19

Rifleman Aaron Lincoln, of the 2nd Battalion, The Rifles, aged 18

Kingsman Danny Wilson, 2nd Battalion, The Duke of Lancaster's Regiment, aged 28

Private Johnathon Dany Wysoczan, First Battalion The Staffordshire Regiment, aged 21

Rifleman Daniel Lee Coffey, Second Battalion The Rifles, aged 21

Private Luke Daniel Simpson, 1st Battalion, The Yorkshire Regiment, aged 21

Second Lieutenant Jonathan Carlos Bracho-Cooke, 2nd Battalion The Duke of Lancaster's Regiment, aged 24

Private Michael Tench, 2nd Battalion The Light Infantry, aged 18

Kingsman Alex Green, 2nd Battalion The Duke of Lancaster's Regiment, aged 21

Sergeant Wayne Rees, The Queen's Royal Lancers, aged 36

Sergeant Graham Hesketh, 2nd Battalion The Duke of Lancaster's Regiment, aged 35

Sergeant Jonathan Hollingsworth, the Parachute Regiment, aged 35

Warrant Officer Class 2 Lee Hopkins, Royal Corps of Signals, aged 35

Staff Sergeant Sharron Elliott, Intelligence Corps, aged 34

Corporal Ben Nowak, 45 Commando Royal Marines, aged 27

Marine Jason Hylton, 539 Assault Squadron Royal Marines, aged 33

Kingsman Jamie Hancock, 2nd Battalion, The Duke of Lancaster's Regiment, aged 19

Lieutenant Tom Tanswell, 58 (Eyre's) Battery, 12 Regt Royal Artillery, aged 27

Lance Corporal Dennis Brady, Royal Army Medical Corps, aged 37

Gunner Lee Thornton, 58 (Eyre's) Battery, 12 Regiment Royal Artillery, aged 22

Gunner Samuela Vanua, 58 (Eyre's) Battery, 12 Regiment Royal Artillery

Gunner Stephen Robert Wright, 58 (Eyre's) Battery, 12 Regiment Royal Artillery, aged 20

Corporal Matthew Cornish, 1st Battalion The Light Infantry, aged 29

Corporal John Johnston Cosby, 1st Battalion The Devonshire and Dorset Light Infantry, aged 28

Lieutenant Tom Mildinhall, Queen's Dragoon Guards, aged 26

Lance Corporal Paul Farrelly, Queen's Dragoon Guards, aged 27

Private Joseva Lewaicei, 2nd Battalion, The Royal Anglian Regiment, aged 25

Private Adam Morris, 2nd Battalion, The Royal Anglian Regiment, aged 19

Wing Commander John Coxen, RAF, aged 46

Lieutenant Commander Darren Chapman, 847 Naval Air Squadron, Fleet Air Arm, aged 40

Captain David Dobson, Army Air Corps, aged 27

Flight Lieutenant Sarah-Jayne Mulvihill, RAF aged 32

Marine Paul Collins, 847 Naval Air Squadron, aged 21

Lieutenant Richard Palmer, the Royal Scots Dragoon Guards, aged 27

Captain Richard Holmes, 2nd Battalion, The Parachute Regiment, aged 28

Private Lee Ellis, 2nd Battalion, The Parachute Regiment, aged 23

Trooper Carl Smith, 9th/12th Royal Lancers (Prince of Wales's), aged 23

Corporal Gordon Alexander Pritchard, Royal Scots Dragoon Guards, aged 31

Lance Corporal Allan Douglas, Highlanders (Seaforth, Gordons and Camerons), aged 22

Sergeant John Jones, 1st Battalion The Royal Regiment of Fusiliers, aged 31

Sergeant Chris Hickey, 1st Battalion the Coldstream Guards, aged 30

Captain Ken Masters, Royal Military Police, aged 40

Major Matthew Bacon, Intelligence Corps, aged 34

Fusilier Donal Anthony Meade, Royal Regiment of Fusiliers, aged 20

Fusilier Stephen Robert Manning, Royal Regiment of Fusiliers, aged 22

Second Lieutenant Richard Shearer, 1st Battalion Staffordshire Regiment, aged 26

Private Leon Spicer, 1st Battalion Staffordshire Regiment, aged 26

Private Phillip Hewett, 1st Battalion Staffordshire Regiment, aged 21

Signaller Paul William Didsbury, 21st Signal Regiment (Air Support), aged 18

Lance Corporal Alan Brackenbury, The King's Royal Hussars, aged 21

Guardsman Anthony John Wakefield, 1st Battalion The Coldstream Guards, aged 24

Private Mark Dobson, Tyne-Tees Regiment, aged 41

Squadron Leader Patrick Marshall, Headquarters Strike Command, aged 39

Flight Lieutenant David Stead, 47 Squadron, RAF Lyneham, aged 35

Flight Lieutenant Andrew Smith, 47 Squadron, RAF Lyneham, aged 25

Flight Lieutenant Paul Pardoel, 47 Squadron, RAF Lyneham, aged 35

Master Air Engineer Gary Nicholson, 47 Squadron, RAF Lyneham, aged 42

Chief Technician Richard Brown, RAF Lyneham, aged 40

Flight Sergeant Mark Gibson, 47 Squadron, RAF Lyneham, aged 34

Sergeant Robert O'Connor, RAF Lyneham, aged 38

Corporal David Williams, RAF Lyneham, aged 37

Acting Lance Corporal Steven Jones, Royal Signals, aged 25

Sergeant Paul Connolly, Royal Electrical & Mechanical Engineers, aged 33

Acting Chief Petty Officer Simon Roger Owen, HMS Chatham, aged 38

Private Pita Tukutukuwaqa, The Black Watch, aged 27

Sergeant Stuart Robert Tennant Gray, 1st Battalion The Black Watch, aged 31

Private Paul Lowe, 1st Battalion The Black Watch, aged 19

Private Scott McArdle, 1st Battalion The Black Watch, aged 22

Staff Sergeant Denise Michelle Rose, Royal Military Police, aged 34

Private Kevin McHale, The Black Watch, aged 27

Corporal Marc Taylor, Royal Electrical & Mechanical Engineers, aged 27

Gunner David Lawrence, Royal Artillery, aged 25

Fusilier Stephen Jones, The Royal Welch Fusiliers, aged 22

Lance Corporal Paul Thomas, The Light Infantry, aged 29

Private Marc Ferns, The Black Watch, aged 21

Private Lee O'Callaghan, Princess of Wales' Royal Regiment, aged 20

Private Christopher Rayment, Princess of Wales' Royal Regiment, aged 22

Flight Lieutenant Kristian Gover, 33 Squadron RAF, aged 30

Fusilier Gordon Gentle, Royal Highland Fusiliers, aged 19

Corporal Richard Ivell, Royal Electrical & Mechanical Engineers, aged 29

Sapper Robert Thomson, 35 Engineer Regiment, Royal Engineers, aged 22

Rifleman Vincent Windsor, Royal Green Jackets, aged 23

Lance Corporal Andrew Craw, Argyll & Sutherland Highlanders, aged 21

Major James Stenner, Welsh Guards, aged 30

Sergeant Norman Patterson, Cheshire Regiment, aged 28

Private Ryan Lloyd Thomas, The Royal Regiment of Wales (24th/41st Foot), age 18

Corporal Ian Plank, Royal Marines, age 31

Sergeant John Nightingale, Royal Logistic Corps, age 32

Fusilier Russell Beeston, 1st Battalion King's Own Scottish Borderers, age 26

Major Matthew Titchener, 150 Provost Company, aged 32

Company Sergeant Major Colin Wall, 150 Provost Company, aged 34

Corporal Dewi Pritchard, 116 Provost Company, aged 35

Captain David "Dai" Martyn Jones, Queen's Lancashire Regiment, aged 29

Private Jason Smith, 52nd Lowland Regiment, aged 32

Captain James Linton, 40 Field Regiment, Royal Artillery, aged 43

Sergeant Simon Hamilton-Jewell, Royal Military Police, aged 41

Corporal Russell Aston, Royal Military Police, aged 30

Corporal Paul Long, Royal Military Police, aged 24

Corporal Simon Miller, Royal Military Police, aged 21

Lance Corporal Benjamin Hyde, Royal Military Police, aged 23

Lance Corporal Thomas Keys, Royal Military Police, aged 20

Mr Leonard Harvey, Ministry of Defence Fire Service, aged 55

Corporal David Shepherd, Royal Air Force Police, aged 34

Gunner Duncan Pritchard, 16 Squadron RAF Regiment, aged 22

Private Andrew Kelly, 3rd Battalion, The Parachute Regiment, aged 18

Lance Corporal James McCue, Royal Electrical and Mechanical Engineers, 7 Air Assault Battalion, aged 27

Fusilier Kelan Turrington, Royal Regiment of Fusiliers, aged 18

Lance Corporal Ian Malone, 1st Battalion, Irish Guards, aged 28

Piper Christopher Muzvuru, 1st Battalion, Irish Guards, aged 21

Lieutenant Alexander Tweedie, Household Cavalry Regiment, aged 25

Lance Corporal Karl Shearer, Household Cavalry Regiment, aged 24

Staff Sergeant Chris Muir, Army School of Ammunition, Royal Logistic Corps, aged 32

Lance Corporal Shaun Brierley, 212 Signal Squadron, 1 (UK) Armoured Division HQ & Signal Regiment, aged 28

Major Steve Ballard, 3 Commando Brigade, Royal Marines, aged 33

Marine Christopher Maddison, 9 Assault Squadron Royal Marines, aged 24

Lance Corporal of Horse Matty Hull, Household Cavalry Regiment, aged 25

Corporal Stephen Allbutt, The Queen's Royal Lancers, aged 35

Trooper David Clarke, The Queen's Royal Lancers, aged 19

Lance Corporal Barry Stephen, 1st Battalion The Black Watch, aged 31

Sergeant Steven Roberts, 2nd Royal Tank Regiment, aged 33

Sapper Luke Allsopp, 33 Engineer Regiment (EOD), aged 24

Staff Sergeant Simon Cullingworth, 33 Engineer Regiment (EOD), aged 36

Flight Lieutenant Kevin Barry Main, 9 Squadron, RAF Marham aged 35

Flight Lieutenant David Rhys Williams, 9 Squadron, RAF Marham aged 37

Lieutenant Philip D Green, RN, 849 Squadron, RNAS Culdrose, aged 30

Lieutenant Antony King, RN, 849 Squadron, RNAS Culdrose, aged 35

Lieutenant Marc Lawrence, RN, 849 Squadron, RNAS Culdrose, aged 26

Lieutenant Philip West, RN, 849 Squadron, RNAS Culdrose, aged 32

Lieutenant James Williams, RN, 849 Squadron, RNAS Culdrose, aged 28

Lieutenant Andrew Wilson, RN, 849 Squadron, RNAS Culdrose, aged 36

Major Jason Ward, Royal Marines, UK Landing Force Command Support Group, aged 34

Captain Philip Stuart Guy, Royal Marines, aged 29

Warrant Officer Second Class Mark Stratford, Royal Marines, aged 39

Colour Sergeant John Cecil, Royal Marines, UK Landing Force Command Support Group, aged 35

Sergeant Les Hehir, 29 Commando Regiment Royal Artillery, aged 34

Lance Bombardier Llywelyn Evans, 29 Commando Regiment Royal Artillery, aged 24

Operator Mechanic (Communications) Second Class Ian Seymour, RN, 148 Commando Battery Royal Artillery, aged 29 years

Marine Sholto Hedenskog, Royal Marines, aged 26

BRITISH FATALITIES IN AFGHANISTAN

It is with very deep regret that the Ministry of Defence has confirmed the following fatalities suffered during operations in Afghanistan.

As at 26 April 2014, a total of 453 British forces personnel or MOD civilians have died while serving in Afghanistan since the start of operations in October 2001.

Of these, 404 were killed as a result of hostile action. Forty-nine are known to have died either as a result of illness, non-combat injuries or accidents, or have not yet officially been assigned a cause of death pending the outcome of an investigation. The balance of these figures may change as inquests are concluded.

Captain Thomas Clarke, Army Air Corps, aged 30

Flight Lieutenant Rakesh Chauhan, Royal Air Force, aged 29

Warrant Officer Class 2 Spencer Faulkner, Army Air Corps, aged 38

Corporal James Walters, Army Air Corps, aged 36

Lance Corporal Oliver Thomas, Intelligence Corps, aged 26

Sapper Adam Moralee, Royal Engineers, aged 23

Captain Richard Holloway, Royal Engineers, age 29

Warrant Officer Class 2 Ian Fisher, 3rd Battalion. The Mercian Regiment aged 42

Lance Corporal James Brynin, The Intelligence Corps, aged 22

Corporal William Thomas Savage, Royal Highland Fusiliers, 2nd Battalion The Royal Regiment of Scotland, aged 30

Fusilier Samuel Flint, Royal Highland Fusiliers, 2nd Battalion The Royal Regiment of Scotland, aged 21

Private Robert Murray Hetherington, 51st Highland, 7th Battalion The Royal Regiment of Scotland, aged 25

Lance Corporal Jamie Webb, 1st Battalion The Mercian Regiment, aged 24

Kingsman David Robert Shaw, 1st Battalion The Duke of Lancaster's Regiment, aged 23

Sapper Richard Reginald Walker, 28 Engineer Regiment aged 23

Captain Walter Barrie, Royal Scots Borderers, 1st Battalion The Royal Regiment of Scotland, aged 41

Lieutenant Edward Drummond-Baxter, 1st Battalion The Royal Gurkha Rifles, aged 29

Lance Corporal Siddhanta Kunwar, 1st Battalion The Royal Gurkha Rifles, aged 28

Corporal David O'Connor, 40 Commando Royal Marines, aged 27

Corporal Channing Day, 3 Medical Regiment, aged 25

Captain Carl Manley, Royal Marines, aged 41

Captain James Anthony Townley, Corps of Royal Engineers, aged 29

Sergeant Jonathan Eric Kups, Royal Electrical and Mechanical Engineers, aged 38

Sergeant Gareth Thursby, 3rd Battalion, The Yorkshire Regiment, aged 29

Private Thomas Wroe, 3rd Battalion, The Yorkshire Regiment, aged 18

Lance Corporal Duane Groom, 1st Battalion Grenadier Guards, aged 32

Sergeant Lee Paul Davidson, The Light Dragoons, aged 32

Guardsman Karl Whittle, 1st Battalion Grenadier Guards, aged 22

Guardsman Jamie Shadrake, 1st Battalion Grenadier Guards, aged 20

Lance Corporal Matthew David Smith, Corps of Royal Engineers, aged 26

Lieutenant Andrew Robert Chesterman, 3rd Battalion The Rifles, aged 26

Warrant Officer Class 2 Leonard Perran Thomas, Royal Corps of Signals, aged 44

Guardsman Craig Andrew Roderick, 1st Battalion Welsh Guards, aged 22

Guardsman Apete Saunikalou Ratumaiyale Tuisovurua, 1st Battalion Welsh Guards, aged 28

Corporal Alex Guy, 1st Battalion The Royal Anglian Regiment, aged 37

Lance Corporal James Ashworth, 1st Battalion Grenadier Guards, aged 23

Private Gregg Thomas Stone, 3rd Battalion The Yorkshire Regiment, aged 20

Corporal Michael John Thacker, 1st Battalion The Royal Welsh, aged 27

Captain Stephen James Healey, 1st Battalion The Royal Welsh, aged 29

Corporal Brent John McCarthy, Royal Air Force, aged 25 from Priorslee

Lance Corporal Lee Thomas Davies, 1st Battalion Welsh Guards, aged 27

Corporal Andrew Steven Roberts, 23 Pioneer Regiment, The Royal Logistic Corps, aged 32

Private Ratu Manasa Silibaravi, 23 Pioneer Regiment, The Royal Logistic Corps, aged 32

Guardsman Michael Roland, 1st Battalion Grenadier Guards, aged 22

Sapper Connor Ray, 33 Engineer Regiment (Explosive Ordnance Disposal), aged 21

Corporal Jack Leslie Stanley, from The Queen's Royal Hussars, aged 26

Sergeant Luke Taylor, of the Royal Marines, aged 33

Lance Corporal Michael Foley, of the Adjutant General's Corps (Staff and Personnel Support), aged 25

Captain Rupert William Michael Bowers, 2nd Battalion The Mercian Regiment, aged 24

Sergeant Nigel Coupe, 1st Battalion The Duke of Lancaster's Regiment, aged 33

Corporal Jake Hartley, 3rd Battalion The Yorkshire Regiment, 20

Private Anthony Frampton, 3rd Battalion The Yorkshire Regiment, 20

Private Christopher Kershaw, 3rd Battalion The Yorkshire Regiment, 19

Private Daniel Wade, 3rd Battalion The Yorkshire Regiment, 20

Private Daniel Wilford, 3rd Battalion The Yorkshire Regiment, 21

Senior Aircraftman Ryan Tomlin, 2 Squadron RAF Regiment, aged 21

Lance Corporal Gajbahadur Gurung, Royal Gurkha Rifles, aged 26

Signaller Ian Gerard Sartorius-Jones, 20th Armoured Brigade Headquarters and Signal Squadron (200), aged 21

Rifleman Sachin Limbu, 1st Battalion The Royal Gurkha Rifles, aged 23

Private John King, 1st Battalion The Yorkshire Regiment, aged 19

Squadron Leader Anthony Downing, Royal Air Force, aged 34

Captain Tom Jennings, Royal Marines, aged 29

Sapper Elijah Bond, from 35 Engineer Regiment, Royal Engineers, aged 24

Rifleman Sheldon Lee Jordan Steel, 5th Battalion The Rifles, aged 20

Private Thomas Christopher Lake, 1st Battalion The Princess of Wales's Royal Regiment, aged 29

Lieutenant David Boyce, 1st The Queen's Dragoon Guards, aged 25

Lance Corporal Richard Scanlon, 1st The Queen's Dragoon Guards, aged 31

Lance Corporal Peter Eustace, 2nd Battalion The Rifles, aged 25

Private Matthew Thornton, 4th Battalion The Yorkshire Regiment, aged 28

Private Matthew James Sean Haseldin, 2nd Battalion The Mercian Regiment, aged 21

Rifleman Vijay Rai, 2nd Battalion The Royal Gurkha Rifles, aged 21

Marine David Fairbrother, Kilo Company, 42 Commando Royal Marines aged 24

Lance Corporal Jonathan James McKinlay, 1st Battalion The Rifles, aged 33

Sergeant Barry John Weston, Kilo Company, 42 Commando Royal Marines, aged 40

Lieutenant Daniel John Clack, 1st Battalion The Rifles, aged 24

Marine James Robert Wright, 42 Commando Royal Marines, aged 22

Corporal Mark Anthony Palin, 1st Battalion The Rifles, aged 32

Lance Corporal Paul Watkins, from 9th/12th Royal Lancers (Prince of Wales's), aged 24

Highlander Scott McLaren, The Highlanders, 4th Battalion The Royal Regiment of Scotland, aged 20

Private Gareth Leslie William Bellingham, 3rd Battalion The Mercian Regiment (Staffords), aged 22

Corporal Lloyd Newell, The Parachute Regiment

Craftsman Andrew Found, Royal Electrical and Mechanical Engineers, aged 27

Rifleman Martin Jon Lamb, 1st Battalion The Rifles, aged 27

Lance Corporal Martin Joseph Gill, 42 Commando Royal Marines, aged 22

Corporal Michael John Pike, The Highlanders, 4th Battalion The Royal Regiment of Scotland, aged 26

Lieutenant Oliver Richard Augustin, Juliet Company, 42 Commando Royal Marines, aged 23

Marine Samuel Giles William Alexander MC, Juliet Company, 42 Commando Royal Marines, aged 28

Colour Serjeant Kevin Charles Fortuna, A Company, 1st Battalion The Rifles, aged 36

Marine Nigel Dean Mead, 42 Commando Royal Marines, aged 19

Captain Lisa Jade Head, 11 EOD Regiment RLC, aged 29

Colour Sergeant Alan Cameron, 1st Battalion Scots Guards, aged 42

Major Matthew James Collins, 1st Battalion Irish Guards, aged 38

Lance Sergeant Mark Terence Burgan, 1st Battalion Irish Guards, aged 28

Private Daniel Steven Prior, 2nd Battalion The Parachute Regiment, aged 27

Lance Corporal Stephen McKee, 1st Battalion The Royal Irish Regiment, aged 27

Lance Corporal Liam Richard Tasker, Royal Army Veterinary Corps, aged 26

Private Robert Wood, 17 Port and Maritime Regiment Royal Logistic Corps, aged 28

Private Dean Hutchinson, 9 Regiment The Royal Logistic Corps, aged 23

Lance Corporal Kyle Cleet Marshall, 2nd Battalion The Parachute Regiment, aged 23

Private Lewis Hendry, 3rd Battalion The Parachute Regiment, aged 20

Private Conrad Lewis, 4th Battalion The Parachute Regiment, aged 22

Warrant Officer Class 2 (Company Sergeant Major) Colin Beckett, 3rd Battalion The Parachute Regiment, aged 36

Ranger David Dalzell, 1st Battalion, The Royal Irish Regiment, aged 20

Private Martin Simon George Bell, 2nd Battalion The Parachute Regiment, aged 24

Private Joseva Saqanagonedau Vatubua, 5th Battalion The Royal Regiment of Scotland, aged 24

Warrant Officer Class 2 Charles Henry Wood, 23 Pioneer Regiment Royal Logistic Corps, serving with the Counter-Improvised Explosive Device Task Force, aged 34

Corporal Steven Thomas Dunn, 216 (Parachute) Signal Squadron, attached to 2nd Battalion the Parachute Regiment Battlegroup, aged 27

Private John Howard, 3rd Battalion The Parachute Regiment, aged 23

Guardsman Christopher Davies, 1st Battalion Irish Guards, aged 22

Ranger Aaron McCormick, 1st Battalion The Royal Irish Regiment, aged 22

Senior Aircraftman Scott 'Scotty' Hughes, 1 Squadron Royal Air Force Regiment, aged 20

Sapper William Bernard Blanchard, 101 (City of London) Engineer Regiment (Explosive Ordnance Disposal), aged 39

Corporal David Barnsdale, 33 Engineer Regiment, aged 24

Sergeant Peter Anthony Rayner, 2nd Battalion The Duke of Lancaster's Regiment, aged 34

Rifleman Suraj Gurung, 1st Battalion The Royal Gurkha Rifles, aged 22

Corporal Matthew Thomas, Royal Electrical and Mechanical Engineers aged 24

Sergeant Andrew James Jones, Royal Engineers, aged 35

Trooper Andrew Martin Howarth, The Queen's Royal Lancers, aged 20

Kingsman Darren Deady, 2nd Battalion The Duke of Lancaster's Regiment, aged 22

Lance Corporal Joseph McFarlane Pool, The Royal Scots Borderers, 1st Battalion The Royal Regiment of Scotland, aged 26

Captain Andrew Griffiths, 2nd Battalion The Duke of Lancaster's Regiment, aged 25

Lance Corporal Jordan Dean Bancroft, 1st Battalion The Duke of Lancaster's Regiment, aged 25

Sapper Ishwor Gurung, 69 Gurkha Field Squadron, 21 Engineer Regiment, aged 21

Sapper Darren Foster, 21 Engineer Regiment, aged 20

Rifleman Remand Kulung, 1st Battalion The Mercian Regiment (Cheshire), aged 27

Lieutenant John Charles Sanderson, 1st Battalion The Mercian Regiment (Cheshire), aged 29

Marine Adam Brown, 40 Commando Royal Marines, aged 25

Lance Sergeant Dale Alanzo McCallum, 1st Battalion Scots Guards, aged 31

Sapper Mark Antony Smith, 36 Engineer Regiment, aged 26

Corporal Matthew James Stenton, The Royal Dragoon Guards, aged 23

Lance Corporal Stephen Daniel Monkhouse, 1st Battalion Scots Guards, aged 28

Staff Sergeant Brett George Linley, The Royal Logistic Corps, aged 29

Sergeant David Thomas Monkhouse, The Royal Dragoon Guards, aged 35

Marine Jonathan David Thomas Crookes, 40 Commando Royal Marines, aged 26

Senior Aircraftman Kinikki "Griff" Griffiths, 1 Squadron RAF Regiment, aged 20

Marine Matthew Harrison, 40 Commando Royal Marines, aged 23

Major James Joshua Bowman, 1st Battalion The Royal Gurkha Rifles, aged 34

Lieutenant Neal Turkington, 1st Battalion The Royal Gurkha Rifles, aged 26

Corporal Arjun Purja Pun, 1st Battalion The Royal Gurkha Rifles, aged 33

Marine David Charles Hart, 40 Commando Royal Marines, aged 23

Bombardier Samuel Joseph Robinson, 5th Regiment Royal Artillery, aged 31

Private Thomas Sephton, 1st Battalion The Mercian Regiment, aged 20

Trooper James Anthony Leverett, Royal Dragoon Guards, aged 20

Corporal Seth Stephens, Royal Marines, aged 42

Corporal Jamie Kirkpatrick, 101 Engineer Regiment (Explosive Ordnance Disposal), aged 32

Bombardier Stephen Raymond Gilbert, 4th Regiment Royal Artillery, aged 36

Colour Sergeant Martyn Horton, 1st Battalion The Mercian Regiment, aged 34

Lance Corporal David Ramsden, 1st Battalion The Yorkshire Regiment, aged 26

Private Douglas Halliday, 1st Battalion The Mercian Regiment, aged 20

Private Alex Isaac, 1st Battalion The Mercian Regiment, aged 20

Sergeant Steven William Darbyshire, 40 Commando Royal Marines, aged 35

Lance Corporal Michael Taylor, Charlie Company, 40 Commando Royal Marines, aged 30

Marine Paul Warren, 40 Commando Royal Marines, aged 23

Marine Richard Hollington, 40 Commando Royal Marines, aged 23

Trooper Ashley Smith, Royal Dragoon Guards, aged 21

Corporal Taniela Tolevu Rogoiruwai, 1st Battalion The Duke of Lancaster's Regiment aged 32

Kingsman Ponipate Tagitaginimoce, 1st Battalion The Duke of Lancaster's Regiment, aged 29

Marine Steven James Birdsall, 40 Commando Royal Marines, aged 20

Lance Corporal Andrew Breeze, B (Malta) Company, 1st Battalion The Mercian Regiment (Cheshire), aged 31

Private Jonathan Monk, 2nd Battalion The Princess of Wales's Royal Regiment, aged 25

Lance Bombardier Mark Chandler, 3rd Regiment Royal Horse Artillery, aged 32

Corporal Terry Webster, 1st Battalion The Mercian Regiment (Cheshire), aged 24

Lance Corporal Alan Cochran, 1st Battalion The Mercian Regiment (Cheshire), aged 23

Marine Anthony Dean Hotine, 40 Commando Royal Marines, aged 21

Marine Scott Gregory Taylor, 40 Commando Royal Marines, aged 21

Gunner Zak Cusack, 4th Regiment Royal Artillery, aged 20

Corporal Stephen Curley, 40 Commando Royal Marines, aged 26

Corporal Stephen Walker, 40 Commando Royal Marines, aged 42

Corporal Christopher Lewis Harrison, 40 Commando Royal Marines, aged 26

Sapper Daryn Roy, 21 Engineer Regiment, aged 28

Lance Corporal Barry Buxton, 21 Engineer Regiment, aged 27

Corporal Harvey Holmes, 1st Battalion The Mercian Regiment, aged 22

Fusilier Jonathan Burgess, 1st Battalion The Royal Welsh, aged 20

Rifleman Mark Turner, 3rd Battalion The Rifles, aged 21

Guardsman Michael Sweeney, 1st Battalion Coldstream Guards, aged 19

Rifleman Daniel Holkham, 3rd Battalion The Rifles, aged 19

Lance Corporal of Horse Jonathan Woodgate, Household Cavalry Regiment, aged 26

Serjeant Steven Campbell, 3rd Battalion The Rifles, aged 30

Lance Corporal Scott Hardy, 1st Battalion The Royal Anglian Regiment, aged 26

Private James Grigg, 1st Battalion The Royal Anglian Regiment, aged 20

Captain Martin Driver, 1st Battalion The Royal Anglian Regiment, aged 31

Corporal Stephen Thompson, 1st Battalion The Rifles, aged 31

Lance Corporal Tom Keogh, 4th Battalion The Rifles, aged 24

Rifleman Liam Maughan, 3rd Battalion The Rifles, aged 18

Rifleman Jonathon Allott, 3rd Battalion the Rifles, aged 19

Corporal Richard Green, 3rd Battalion The Rifles, aged 23

Rifleman Carlo Apolis, 4th Battalion The Rifles, aged 28

Sergeant Paul Fox, 28 Engineer Regiment, aged 34

Rifleman Martin Kinggett, 4th Battalion The Rifles, aged 19

Senior Aircraftman Luke Southgate, II Squadron Royal Air Force Regiment, aged 20

Lance Sergeant David 'Davey' Walker, 1st Battalion Scots Guards, aged 36

Lieutenant Douglas Dalzell, 1st Battalion Coldstream Guards, aged 27

Sapper Guy Mellors, 36 Engineer Regiment, aged 20

Rifleman Mark Marshall, 6th Battalion The Rifles, aged 29

Kingsman Sean Dawson, 2nd Battalion The Duke of Lancaster's Regiment, aged 19

Lance Sergeant Dave Greenhalgh, 1st Battalion Grenadier Guards, aged 25

Lance Corporal Darren Hicks, 1st Battalion Coldstream Guards, aged 29

Warrant Officer Class 2 David Markland, 36 Engineer Regiment, aged 36

Corporal John Moore, The Royal Scots Borderers, 1st Battalion The Royal Regiment of Scotland, aged 22

Private Sean McDonald, The Royal Scots Borderers, 1st Battalion The Royal Regiment of Scotland, aged 26

Corporal Liam Riley, 3rd Battalion The Yorkshire Regiment, aged 21

Lance Corporal Graham Shaw, 3rd Battalion The Yorkshire Regiment, aged 27

Lance Corporal Daniel Cooper, 3rd Battalion The Rifles, aged 22

Rifleman Peter Aldridge, 4th Battalion The Rifles, aged 19

Corporal Lee Brownson, 3rd Battalion The Rifles, aged 30

Rifleman Luke Farmer, 3rd Battalion The Rifles, aged 19

Captain Daniel Read, 11 Explosive Ordnance Disposal Regiment, Royal Logistic Corps, aged 31

Private Robert Hayes, 1st Battalion The Royal Anglian Regiment, aged 19

Sapper David Watson, 33 Engineer Regiment (Explosive Ordnance Disposal) aged 23

Rifleman Aidan Howell, 3rd Battalion The Rifles, aged 19

Lance Corporal Tommy Brown, The Parachute Regiment, aged 25

Lance Corporal Christopher Roney, A Company, 3rd Battalion The Rifles, aged 23

Lance Corporal Michael David Pritchard, 4th Regiment, Royal Military Police, aged 22

Corporal Simon Hornby, 2nd Battalion The Duke of Lancaster's Regiment, aged 29

Lance Corporal David Leslie Kirkness, 3rd Battalion The Rifles, aged 24

Rifleman James Stephen Brown, 3rd Battalion The Rifles, aged 18

Lance Corporal Adam Drane, 1st Battalion The Royal Anglian Regiment, aged 23

Acting Sergeant John Paxton Amer, 1st Battalion Coldstream Guards, aged 30

Sergeant Robert David Loughran-Dickson, 4th Regiment Royal Military Police, aged 33

Corporal Loren Owen Christopher Marlton-Thomas, 33 Engineer Regiment (EOD), aged 28

Rifleman Andrew Ian Fentiman, 7th Battalion The Rifles, aged 23

Rifleman Samuel John Bassett, 4th Battalion The Rifles, aged 20

Rifleman Philip Allen, 2nd Battalion The Rifles, aged 20

Serjeant Phillip Scott, 3rd Battalion The Rifles, aged 30

Corporal Steven Boote, Royal Military Police, aged 22

Corporal Nicholas Webster-Smith, Royal Military Police, aged 24

Warrant Officer Class 1 Darren Chant, 1st Battalion The Grenadier Guards, aged 40

Sergeant Matthew Telford, 1st Battalion The Grenadier Guards, aged 37

Guardsman James Major, 1st Battalion The Grenadier Guards, aged 18

Staff Sergeant Olaf Sean George Schmid, 11 Explosive Ordnance Disposal Regiment, Royal Logistic Corps, aged 30

Corporal Thomas 'Tam' Mason, The Black Watch, 3rd Battalion The Royal Regiment of Scotland, aged 27

Corporal James Oakland, Royal Military Police, aged 26

Lance Corporal James Hill, 1st Battalion Coldstream Guards, aged 23

Guardsman Jamie Janes, 1st Battalion Grenadier Guards, aged 20

Acting Corporal Marcin Wojtak, 34 Squadron RAF Regiment, aged 24

Private James Prosser, 2nd Battalion The Royal Welsh, aged 21

Acting Sergeant Michael Lockett MC, 2nd Battalion The Mercian Regiment, aged 29

Acting Serjeant Stuart McGrath, 2nd Battalion The Rifles, aged 28

Trooper Brett Hall, 2nd Royal Tank Regiment, aged 21

Kingsman Jason Dunn-Bridgeman, 2nd Battalion The Duke of Lancaster's Regiment, aged 20

Corporal John Harrison, The Parachute Regiment from East Kilbride, aged 29

Private Gavin Elliott, 2nd Battalion The Mercian Regiment, aged 19

Lance Corporal Richard Brandon, Royal Electrical and Mechanical Engineers, aged 24

Sergeant Stuart 'Gus' Millar, The Black Watch, 3rd Battalion The Royal Regiment of Scotland, aged 40

Private Kevin Elliott, The Black Watch, 3rd Battalion The Royal Regiment of Scotland, aged 24

Sergeant Lee Andrew Houltram, Royal Marines aged 33

Fusilier Shaun Bush, 2nd Battalion The Royal Regiment of Fusiliers, aged 24

Serjeant Paul McAleese, 2nd Battalion The Rifles, aged 29

Private Johnathon Young, 3rd Battalion The Yorkshire Regiment (Duke of Wellington's), aged 18

Lance Corporal James Fullarton, 2nd Battalion The Royal Regiment of Fusiliers, aged 25

Fusilier Simon Annis, 2nd Battalion The Royal Regiment of Fusiliers, aged 22

Fusilier Louis Carter, 2nd Battalion The Royal Regiment of Fusiliers, aged 18

Private Richard Hunt, 2nd Battalion The Royal Welsh, aged 21

Sergeant Simon Valentine, 2nd Battalion The Royal Regiment of Fusiliers, aged 29

Captain Mark Hale, 2nd Battalion The Rifles, aged 42

Lance Bombardier Matthew Hatton, 40th Regiment Royal Artillery (The Lowland Gunners), aged 23

Rifleman Daniel Wild, 2nd Battalion The Rifles, aged 19

Private Jason George Williams, 2nd Battalion The Mercian Regiment, aged 23

Corporal Kevin Mulligan, The Parachute Regiment, aged 26

Lance Corporal Dale Thomas Hopkins, The Parachute Regiment, aged 23

Private Kyle Adams, The Parachute Regiment, aged 21

Craftsman Anthony Lombardi, Royal Electrical and Mechanical Engineers, aged 21

Warrant Officer Class 2 Sean Upton, 5th Regiment Royal Artillery, aged 35

Trooper Phillip Lawrence, Light Dragoons, aged 22

Bombardier Craig Hopson, 40th Regiment Royal Artillery (The Lowland Gunners), aged 24

Guardsman Christopher King, 1st Battalion Coldstream Guards, aged 20

Captain Daniel Shepherd, 11 Explosive Ordnance Disposal Regiment, The Royal Logistic Corps, aged 28

Corporal Joseph Etchells, 2nd Battalion The Royal Regiment of Fusiliers, aged 22

Rifleman Aminiasi Toge, 2nd Battalion The Rifles, aged 26

Corporal Jonathan Horne, 2nd Battalion The Rifles, aged 28

Rifleman William Aldridge, 2nd Battalion The Rifles, aged 18

Rifleman James Backhouse, 2nd Battalion The Rifles, aged 18

Rifleman Joe Murphy, 2nd Battalion The Rifles, aged 18

Rifleman Daniel Simpson, 2nd Battalion The Rifles, aged 20

Corporal Lee Scott, 2nd Royal Tank Regiment, aged 26

Rifleman Daniel Hume, 4th Battalion The Rifles aged 22

Private John Brackpool, 1st Battalion Welsh Guards, aged 27

Trooper Christopher Whiteside, The Light Dragoons, aged 20

Captain Ben Babington-Browne, 22 Engineer Regiment, Royal Engineers, aged 27

Lance Corporal Dane Elson, 1st Battalion Welsh Guards, aged 22

Lance Corporal David Dennis, The Light Dragoons, aged 29

Private Robert Laws, 2nd Battalion the Mercian Regiment, aged 18

Lieutenant Colonel Rupert Thorneloe MBE, Commanding Officer, 1st Battalion Welsh Guards, aged 39

Trooper Joshua Hammond, 2nd Royal Tank Regiment, aged 18

Major Sean Birchall, 1st Battalion Welsh Guards, aged 33

Lieutenant Paul Mervis, 2nd Battalion The Rifles, aged 27

Private Robert McLaren, The Black Watch, 3rd Battalion The Royal Regiment of Scotland, aged 20

Rifleman Cyrus Thatcher, 2nd Battalion The Rifles, aged 19

Lance Corporal Nigel Moffett, The Light Dragoons, aged 28

Corporal Stephen Bolger, The Parachute Regiment, aged 30

Lance Corporal Kieron Hill, 2nd Battalion The Mercian Regiment (Worcesters and Foresters), aged 20

Lance Corporal Robert Martin Richards, Armoured Support Group Royal Marines, aged 24

Sapper Jordan Rossi, 25 Field Squadron, 38 Engineer Regiment, aged 22

Fusilier Petero "Pat" Suesue, 2nd Battalion The Royal Regiment of Fusiliers, aged 28

Marine Jason Mackie, Armoured Support Group Royal Marines, aged 21

Lieutenant Mark Evison, 1st Battalion Welsh Guards, aged 26

Sergeant Ben Ross, 173 Provost Company, 3rd Regiment, Royal Military Police, aged 34

Corporal Kumar Pun, The 1st Battalion The Royal Gurkha Rifles, aged 31

Rifleman Adrian Sheldon, 2nd Battalion The Rifles, aged 25

Sergeant Sean Binnie, The Black Watch, 3rd Battalion The Royal Regiment of Scotland, aged 22

Lance Sergeant Tobie Fasfous, 1st Battalion Welsh Guards, aged 29

Corporal Dean Thomas John, Royal Electrical and Mechanical Engineers, 1st The Queen's Dragoon Guards, aged 25

Corporal Graeme Stiff, Royal Electrical and Mechanical Engineers, 1st The Queen's Dragoon Guards, aged 24

Lance Corporal Christopher Harkett, 2nd Battalion The Royal Welsh, aged 22

Marine Michael 'Mick' Laski, 45 Commando Royal Marines, aged 21

Corporal Tom Gaden, 1st Battalion The Rifles, aged 24

Lance Corporal Paul Upton, 1st Battalion The Rifles, aged 31

Rifleman Jamie Gunn, 1st Battalion The Rifles, aged 21

Lance Corporal Stephen 'Schnoz' Kingscott, 1st Battalion The Rifles, aged 22

Marine Darren 'Daz' Smith, 45 Commando Royal Marines, aged 27

Corporal Daniel 'Danny' Nield, 1st Battalion The Rifles, aged 31

Acting Corporal Richard 'Robbo' Robinson, 1st Battalion The Rifles, aged 21

Captain Tom Sawyer, 29 Commando Regiment Royal Artillery, aged 26

Corporal Danny Winter, 45 Commando Royal Marines, aged 28

Marine Travis Mackin, Communications Squadron, United Kingdom Landing Force Command Support Group, aged 22

Serjeant Christopher John Reed, 6th Battalion The Rifles, aged 25

Corporal Liam Elms RM, 45 Commando Royal Marines, aged 26

Lance Corporal Benjamin Whatley, 42 Commando Royal Marines, aged 20

Corporal Robert Deering, Commando Logistic Regiment Royal Marines aged 33

Rifleman Stuart Nash, 1st Battalion The Rifles, aged 21

Lieutenant Aaron Lewis, 29 Commando Regiment Royal Artillery, aged 26

Marine Damian Davies, Commando Logistics Regiment Royal Marines aged 27

Sergeant John Manuel, 45 Commando Royal Marines, aged 38

Corporal Marc Birch, 45 Commando Royal Marines, aged 26

Lance Corporal Steven 'Jamie' Fellows, 45 Commando Royal Marines, aged 28

Marine Tony Evans, 42 Commando Royal Marines, aged 20

Marine Georgie Sparks, 42 Commando Royal Marines, aged 19

Marine Alexander Lucas, 45 Commando Royal Marines, aged 24

Colour Sergeant Krishnabahadur Dura, 2nd Battalion The Royal Gurkha Rifles, aged 36

Marine Neil David Dunstan, United Kingdom Landing Force Command Support Group, aged 32

Marine Robert Joseph McKibben, United Kingdom Landing Force Command Support Group, aged 32

Rifleman Yubraj Rai, 2nd Battalion, The Royal Gurkha Rifles, aged 28

Trooper James Munday, D Squadron, the Household Cavalry Regiment, aged 21

Lance Corporal Nicky Mason, 2nd Battalion The Parachute Regiment, aged 26

Private Jason Lee Rawstron, 2nd Battalion, The Parachute Regiment aged 23

Warrant Officer Class 2 Gary 'Gaz' O'Donnell GM, 11 Explosive Ordnance Disposal Regiment Royal Logistic Corps, aged 40

Ranger Justin James Cupples, 1st Battalion The Royal Irish Regiment, aged 29

Corporal Barry Dempsey, The Royal Highland Fusiliers, 2nd Battalion Royal Regiment of Scotland, aged 29

Signaller Wayne Bland, 16 Signal Regiment, aged 21

Private Peter Joe Cowton, 2nd Battalion The Parachute Regiment, aged 25

Sergeant Jonathan Mathews, The Highlanders, 4th Battalion, The Royal Regiment of Scotland, aged 35

Lance Corporal Kenneth Michael Rowe, Royal Army Veterinary Corps, aged 24

Corporal Jason Stuart Barnes, Royal Electrical and Mechanical Engineers, aged 25

Lance Corporal James Johnson, B Company, 5th Battalion The Royal Regiment of Scotland, aged 31

Warrant Officer 2nd Class Dan Shirley, Air Assault Support Regiment, Royal Logistics Corps, aged 32

Warrant Officer 2nd Class Michael Norman Williams, 2nd Battalion The Parachute Regiment, aged 40

Private Joe John Whittaker, 4th Battalion The Parachute Regiment, aged 20

Corporal Sarah Bryant, Intelligence Corps, aged 26

Corporal Sean Robert Reeve, Royal Signals, aged 28

Lance Corporal Richard Larkin, 23 Special Air Service Regiment, aged 39

Trooper Paul Stout, 23 Special Air Service Regiment, aged 31

Lance Corporal James Bateman, 2nd Battalion The Parachute Regiment, aged 29

Private Jeff Doherty, 2nd Battalion The Parachute Regiment, aged 20

Private Nathan Cuthbertson, 2nd Battalion The Parachute Regiment, aged 19

Private Daniel Gamble, 2nd Battalion The Parachute Regiment, aged 22

Private Charles David Murray, 2nd Battalion The Parachute Regiment, aged 19

Marine Dale Gostick, 3 Troop Armoured Support Company, Royal Marines, aged 22

James Thompson, 21 Special Air Service Regiment aged 27

Trooper Ratu Sakeasi Babakobau, Household Cavalry Regiment, aged 29

Trooper Robert Pearson, The Queen's Royal Lancers Regiment, aged 22

Senior Aircraftman Graham Livingstone, Royal Air Force Regiment, aged 23

Senior Aircraftman Gary Thompson, Royal Auxiliary Air Force Regiment, aged 51

Lieutenant John Thornton, 40 Commando Royal Marines, aged 22

Marine David Marsh, 40 Commando Royal Marines, aged 23

Corporal Damian Mulvihill, 40 Commando Royal Marines, aged 32

Corporal Damian Stephen Lawrence, 2nd Battalion The Yorkshire Regiment (Green Howards), aged 25

Corporal Darryl Gardiner, Royal Electrical and Mechanical Engineers, aged 25

Sergeant Lee Johnson, 2nd Battalion The Yorkshire Regiment, aged 33

Trooper Jack Sadler, The Honourable Artillery Company, aged 21

Captain John McDermid, The Royal Highland Fusiliers, 2nd Battalion The Royal Regiment of Scotland, aged 43

Lance Corporal Jake Alderton, 36 Engineer Regiment, aged 22

Major Alexis Roberts, 1st Battalion The Royal Gurkha Rifles, aged 32

Colour Sergeant Phillip Newman, 4th Battalion The Mercian Regiment, aged 36

Private Brian Tunnicliffe, 2nd Battalion The Mercian Regiment (Worcesters and Foresters), aged 33

Corporal Ivano Violino, 36 Engineer Regiment, aged 29

Sergeant Craig Brelsford, 2nd Battalion The Mercian Regiment, aged 25

Private Johan Botha, 2nd Battalion The Mercian Regiment, aged 25

Private Damian Wright, 2nd Battalion The Mercian Regiment

Private Ben Ford, 2nd Battalion The Mercian Regiment, aged 18

Senior Aircraftman Christopher Bridge, C flight, 51 Squadron Royal Air Force Regiment, aged 20d

Private Aaron James McClure, 1st Battalion The Royal Anglian Regiment, aged 19

Private Robert Graham Foster, 1st Battalion The Royal Anglian Regiment, aged 19

Private John Thrumble, 1st Battalion The Royal Anglian Regiment, aged 21

Captain David Hicks, 1st Battalion The Royal Anglian Regiment, aged 26

Private Tony Rawson of 1st Battalion, The Royal Anglian Regiment, aged 27

Lance Corporal Michael Jones, Royal Marines aged 26

Sergeant Barry Keen, 14 Signal Regiment, aged 34

Guardsman David Atherton, 1st Battalion Grenadier Guards aged 25

Lance Corporal Alex Hawkins, 1st Battalion The Royal Anglian Regiment, aged 22

Guardsman Darryl Hickey, 1st Battalion Grenadier Guards aged 27

Sergeant Dave Wilkinson, 19 Regiment Royal Artillery, aged 33

Captain Sean Dolan, 1st Battalion The Worcestershire and Sherwood Foresters, aged 40

Drummer Thomas Wright, 1st Battalion The Worcestershire and Sherwood Foresters, aged 21

Guardsman Neil 'Tony' Downes, 1st Battalion Grenadier Guards, aged 20

Lance Corporal Paul "Sandy" Sandford, 1st Battalion The Worcestershire and Sherwood Foresters, aged 23

Corporal Mike Gilyeat, Royal Military Police, aged 28

Corporal Darren Bonner, 1st Battalion The Royal Anglian Regiment, aged 31

Guardsman Daniel Probyn, 1st Battalion Grenadier Guards, aged 22

Lance Corporal George Russell Davey, 1st Battalion the Royal Anglian Regiment, aged 23

Guardsman Simon Davison, 1st Battalion Grenadier Guards, aged 22

Private Chris Gray, A Company, 1st Battalion The Royal Anglian Regiment, aged 19

WO2 Michael 'Mick' Smith, 29 Commando Regiment Royal Artillery, aged 39

Marine Benjamin Reddy, 42 Commando Royal Marines, aged 22

Lance Bombardier Ross Clark, 29 Commando Regiment Royal Artillery, aged 25

Lance Bombardier Liam McLaughlin, 29 Commando Regiment Royal Artillery, aged 21

Marine Scott Summers, 42 Commando Royal Marines, aged 23

Marine Jonathan Holland, 45 Commando Royal Marines, aged 23

Lance Corporal Mathew Ford, 45 Commando Royal Marines, aged 30

Marine Thomas Curry, 42 Commando Royal Marines, aged 21

Lance Bombardier James Dwyer, Royal Artillery, aged 22

Marine Richard J Watson, 42 Commando Royal Marines, aged 23

Marine Jonathan Wigley, 45 Commando Royal Marines, aged 21

Marine Gary Wright, 45 Commando Royal Marines, aged 22

Lance Corporal Luke McCulloch, 1 Royal Irish Regiment, aged 21

Lance Corporal Paul Muirhead, 1 Royal Irish Regiment, aged 29

Corporal Mark William Wright, 3rd Battalion, The Parachute Regiment, aged 27

Private Craig O'Donnell, The Argyll and Sutherland Highlanders, 5th Battalion the Royal Regiment of Scotland, aged 24

Flight Lieutenant Steven Johnson, 120 Squadron, Royal Air Force Kinloss, aged 38

Flight Lieutenant Leigh Anthony Mitchelmore, 120 Squadron, Royal Air Force Kinloss, aged 28

Flight Lieutenant Gareth Rodney Nicholas, 120 Squadron, Royal Air Force Kinloss, aged 40

Flight Lieutenant Allan James Squires, 120 Squadron, Royal Air Force Kinloss, aged 39

Flight Lieutenant Steven Swarbrick, 120 Squadron, Royal Air Force Kinloss, aged 28

Flight Sergeant Gary Wayne Andrews, 120 Squadron, Royal Air Force Kinloss, aged 48

Flight Sergeant Stephen Beattie, 120 Squadron, Royal Air Force Kinloss, aged 42

Flight Sergeant Gerard Martin Bell, 120 Squadron, Royal Air Force Kinloss, aged 48

Flight Sergeant Adrian Davies, 120 Squadron, Royal Air Force Kinloss, aged 49

Sergeant Benjamin James Knight, 120 Squadron, Royal Air Force Kinloss, aged 25

Sergeant John Joseph Langton, 120 Squadron, Royal Air Force Kinloss, aged 29

Sergeant Gary Paul Quilliam, 120 Squadron Royal Air Force Kinloss, aged 42

Corporal Oliver Simon Dicketts, the Parachute Regiment, aged 27

Marine Joseph David Windall, Royal Marines, aged 22

Ranger Anare Draiva, 1 Royal Irish Regiment, aged 27

Lance Corporal Jonathan Peter Hetherington, 14 Signal Regiment (Electronic Warfare), aged 22

Corporal Bryan James Budd, 3rd Battalion the Parachute Regiment, aged 29

Lance Corporal Sean Tansey, The Life Guards, aged 26

Private Leigh Reeves, Royal Logistic Corps, aged 25

Private Andrew Barrie Cutts, Air Assault Support Regiment, Royal Logistic Corps, aged 19

Captain Alex Eida, Royal Horse Artillery, aged 29

Second Lieutenant Ralph Johnson, Household Cavalry Regiment, aged 24

Lance Corporal Ross Nicholls, Blues and Royals, aged 27

Private Damien Jackson, 3rd Battalion the Parachute Regiment, aged 19

Corporal Peter Thorpe, Royal Signals, aged 27

Lance Corporal Jabron Hashmi, Intelligence Corps, aged 24

Captain David Patton, The Parachute Regiment, aged 38

Sergeant Paul Bartlett, Royal Marines, aged 35

Captain Jim Philippson, 7 Parachute Regiment Royal Horse Artillery, aged 29

Lance Corporal Peter Edward Craddock, 1st Battalion The Royal Gloucestershire, Berkshire and Wiltshire Regiment, aged 31

Corporal Mark Cridge, 7 Signal Regiment, aged 25

Lance Corporal Steven Sherwood, 1st Battalion, The Royal Gloucestershire, Berkshire and Wiltshire Light Infantry, aged 23

Private Jonathan Kitulagoda, The Rifle Volunteers, aged 23

Sergeant Robert Busuttil, Royal Logistic Corps, aged 30

Corporal John Gregory, Royal Logistic Corps, aged 30

Private Darren John George, the Royal Anglian Regiment, aged 23

I would like to finish off by announcing the main charity I will be donating funds towards from the proceeds of my book. There are so many fabulous military-related charities and it is not possible to support each and every valued one. So, with a lot of thought and consideration, I decided to predominantly support just one charity, as it supports so many children from tri-service families. How could I ever forget the impact it had on me, seeing so many children breaking their hearts when we escorted their fathers home. It is a memory that will forever be etched on my mind. I recognise the focus, sincerity and reasons why this charity was formed and that is why Scotty's Little Soldiers is the charity for me.

SCOTTY'S LITTLE SOLDIERS is a charity dedicated to supporting bereaved British Forces' children.

Inspired by the experience of Army widow Nikki Scott, the charity honours husband Corporal Lee Scott's memory – both as a loyal soldier and a loving father – and provides a practical, yet personal, way for the public at large to show their appreciation for those brave individuals who make the ultimate sacrifice in the service of their country.

Nikki and Lee have two children, Kai and Brooke, so Nikki saw first hand the effect the loss of a loved one in these circumstances can have on a child. It was on a family holiday some nine months later that Nikki saw her son Kai, five at the time, laugh and smile for the first time since his Dad's death. She realised that there must be so many more children who had also lost a parent in the British Armed Forces but hadn't had that opportunity to smile again. She decided to set up the charity Scotty's Little Soldiers to do just that, to help their children smile.

The charity provides opportunities for the children to smile again by offering holidays at its Scotty Lodges, gifts at difficult times of the year, special experiences and an amazing Christmas party.

As well as these fun activities the charity also provides access to professional bereavement counselling and a range of grants to help with the children's personal development. These grants can cover the cost of music lessons, swimming clubs, after school activities, driving lessons and even University tuition fees.

The charity now supports hundreds of bereaved British Forces' children across the UK, many of whom are still very young and will rely on the activities offered by Scotty's for years to come.